The Library Screen Scene

The Library Screen Scene

FILM AND MEDIA LITERACY IN SCHOOLS, COLLEGES, AND COMMUNITIES

RENEE HOBBS

LIZ DESLAURIERS

and

PAM STEAGER

OXFORD
UNIVERSITY PRESS

OXFORD
UNIVERSITY PRESS

Oxford University Press is a department of the University of Oxford. It furthers
the University's objective of excellence in research, scholarship, and education
by publishing worldwide. Oxford is a registered trade mark of Oxford University
Press in the UK and certain other countries.

Published in the United States of America by Oxford University Press
198 Madison Avenue, New York, NY 10016, United States of America.

© Renee Hobbs, Liz Deslauriers and Pam Steager 2019

CIP data is on file at the Library of Congress
ISBN 978–0–19–085432–4 (pbk.)
ISBN 978–0–19–085431–7 (hbk.)

9 8 7 6 5 4 3 2 1

Paperback printed by Webcom, Inc., Canada
Hardback printed by Bridgeport National Bindery, Inc., United States of America

Contents

About the Companion Website   vii

1. Introduction   1

Part I   FIVE CORE PRACTICES

2. Viewing   29

3. Creating   67

4. Learning   103

5. Collecting   141

6. Connecting   181

Part II   PAST, PRESENT, AND FUTURE

7. Past   221

8. Present   261

9. Future   291

Acknowledgments   307
Appendix: Copyright, Fair Use, and Licensing Issues   309
Notes   313
Bibliography   333
Index   349

About the Companion Website

We welcome you to explore *The Library Screen Scene* website where you can view many of the short films and videos mentioned in the book. The website also includes a crowdsourced interactive map of many ongoing film and media literacy programs and services offered in school, public, and academic libraries. At the website, users can upload and share examples of film and media literacy programs in school, public, and academic libraries in the United States and around the world. The website is available at www.libraryscreenscene.com.

1

Introduction

Questions Answered in This Chapter
- How has people's use of audiovisual media changed over time?
- Why is film and media literacy important for school, public, and academic libraries?
- How can film and media literacy help advance democratic citizenship?
- Who are the authors and why did they write the book?
- How can the effective use of film and media help libraries to be positive change agents in their communities?
- What different types of readers might find value in this book?
- What are the key ideas of this book?
- How can the emotional power of film be harnessed for learning?
- How can the position of film and media be elevated in the library world?
- What are the different approaches to film and media education pedagogy in libraries?
- Why is film screening and discussion a transformative type of learning experience?
- Why is the job of the media librarian so important?
- How do library leaders support innovation?
- How is the book organized and what can readers expect to learn?

What would happen when rural and urban teens got a chance to experience the power of the spoken word, sitting together in a little public library in rural Rhode Island? When Karen Mueller created a poetry slam film program for the teens in her community library in Foster, Rhode Island, in the spring of 2015, she was building upon the success of an established Friday night library program.

The teen thank-goodness-it's-Friday (TGIF) program had long offered a technology "petting zoo" to provide hands-on experiences to young learners, giving them a chance to "hang out, mess around, and geek out"[1] at the library, using technology tools to which they might otherwise not have access. Teens in this rural community had otherwise few opportunities for peer social interaction.

A Friday night film screening, complete with refreshments, she imagined, could draw teens into the library and expose them to the art of film. Working in collaboration with fellow graduate students enrolled in LSC 597, Library Film Education, a course at the University of Rhode Island, the Foster Public Library hosted a screening of *Louder Than a Bomb*, a documentary by Jon Siskel and Greg Jacobs created in 2010. The documentary explores the journey of four high-school teams who compete in the world's largest youth spoken word poetry slam. As a result of her vigorous marketing efforts and her established relationships with teens, nearly 30 teens and adults attended the Friday evening program in the library.

The film introduces viewers to young adults in Chicago struggling through many challenges who eventually learn to speak out, make noise, and find their voice through writing and spoken word poetry. Karen Mueller and her team had selected this film as a result of consultation with Anisa Raoof from the Providence Children's Film Festival. As Mueller explained it, *Louder Than a Bomb* was selected because it was believed the subject matter would speak to young adults in Foster and perhaps empower them "to find their own voice on subjects that matter in their lives."

Before viewing, participants were given some guiding questions to consider while viewing. The pre-viewing questions included the following:

- Why did the director decide to focus on the teens and teams that he followed in this film and not others?
- Why are the kids in this film doing slam poetry? What do they get out of it?

After viewing, participants responded to open-ended questions designed to promote reflection, sharing responses to these questions:

- Which character spoke to you and why?
- Which moment stood out for you and why?
- Why do you think the director chose the title *Louder Than a Bomb*?

After the film screening, there was a short live performance of spoken word poetry by students in a Providence-based youth program, ZuKrewe, which is a creative incubator for at-risk and beyond-risk young people aged 14–21. The program engages participants in artistic practice, increasing their skills, knowledge, understanding, and appreciation of artistic expression and its power to connect people and influence change.

Mueller could see that rural teens and urban teens shared some common experiences, given the stresses of poverty as well as social and cultural isolation. After the performance, there was a question-and-answer session. Participants were also invited to complete a short survey. Some described the program as "amazing and inspiring" and "powerful," while others saw "good messages from poems" and got the message that "art can be found anywhere." Still others recognized that "slam poetry is not just for nerds." Overwhelmingly, those who attended felt that the combination of film screening and live performance was an unbeatable combination.

As you will see in the pages that follow, when librarians are at their most inventive, they provide transformative learning experiences that inspire, educate, and entertain. Film, media, and community partnerships are key elements of this important work.

Moving Image Media Education

A TIME OF CHANGE

There's no doubt about it: how we use audiovisual media has changed dramatically in the past 10 years. The rise of short-form media is indisputable. Fragmentary and self-contained, short-form media includes segments, trailers, clips, or edited extracts hosted on YouTube, Facebook, or Twitter. Henry Jenkins and his colleagues have termed this type of audiovisual content "spreadable media" because it reaches its target audience through social media.[2] Teens and college students have migrated much of their entertainment use to social media platforms, which according to one scholar "foreground connection, engagement, and interaction as primary features . . . using social media not merely to consume entertainment but also as a vehicle for action, political engagement, and identity formation."[3]

What we watch and how we watch have both been transformed by the rise of the Internet and digital culture. Even when it comes to network television, many of us are watching it online. Consider the popular NBC dramatic series *This Is Us*, an ensemble drama that tells the past and present story of three siblings from Pittsburgh. Nearly half of the revenue earned by the series has come from online advertising.[4] Of course, not every show gets a large online audience. But young adults, in particular, watch differently now. Between 2011 and 2016, traditional TV viewing (i.e., linear TV viewing on set-top boxes, either live or recorded) had fallen by 9 hours per week for viewers aged 18–24, reflecting a 38% drop.[5] According to one study, viewership for movies and television shows declined by 13% globally and by 11% in the United States in just one year.[6]

Naturally, as a result of this reality, educators are changing how they teach with and about film and media. Film historian Dana Polan has documented the history of teaching film in his book, *Scenes of Instruction: The Beginnings of the U.S. Study of Film*. In exploring the earliest examples of film education, Polan shows how the major traditions in teaching film first evolved at the university. Over time, film was first studied as a professional production practice—an industry. Then it was studied as a form of storytelling, a new type of art. Over time, it came to be studied as a sociological phenomenon shaping American culture and values.

Today, it's important that film and media literacy education moves far beyond its specialist origins as a training ground for future professionals. Everyone, everywhere needs a fundamental set of competencies that enable them to enjoy and appreciate moving image media and learn from it. The terms used to describe this work vary, however. Figure 1.1 shows a Google Trends graph that illustrates the frequency of some key terms used between 2004 and 2018, including terms like *film education, media education, visual literacy, media literacy,* and *digital literacy.*

Film education: this term describes the work of educators who explore film as an art, a business, and as part of society and culture.

Media education: this concept refers to the formal academic study of media industries, aesthetics, and representation.

Visual literacy: a multidisciplinary term used by educators and artists with interests in photography, images, and graphic design.

Media literacy: a term used to describe the practice of critically analyzing mass media and creating media messages in a wide variety of forms.

Digital literacy: refers to the many competencies needed for active participation in the use of the Internet and social media.

Depending on your academic background, geographic location, and age, you might also use other terms such as *information literacy, transmedia literacy, new literacies, metaliteracy, multimodal literacy, digital literacy,* or *web literacy.* Scholars have attempted to define and pin these down for decades now, but what's clear is this: How you understand these terms depends on what field or discipline you come from.

We're not overly concerned about hammering down precise definitions because we are writing this book for a multidisciplinary audience; furthermore, we have seen how these terms change and morph over time. For what we're focusing on in this book, we think it's more important to consider the common underlying principles that unite these new literacies. We see these concepts as fundamentally tied to literacy, which we define as *the sharing of meaning in symbolic form.*[7] Some commonalities among the new literacies include the following:

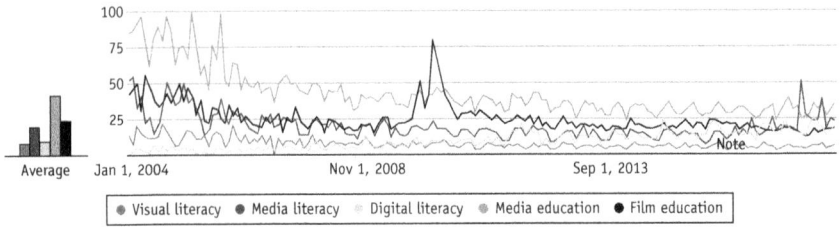

Figure 1.1 Frequency of terms according to Google Trends.

- Sensitivity to the constructed nature of multimedia messages
- Examination of the relationship between a message's content and its form
- Appreciation of the pleasure of the multimedia experience
- Attention to the personal and social dimensions of meaning-making and interpretation
- Awareness of the dialectic between analysis and production ("reading" and "writing")
- Consideration of the economic, political, and cultural context in which media circulate
- Understanding potential impacts and consequences of media on individuals, culture, and society

In this book, we sometimes use terms like *media, film,* and *video* interchangeably, depending on the context of the topic we're examining. We also like the broad term *moving image media,* which was developed by Scottish media educators in the 1990s as a way to refer to film, television, animation, advertising, documentary, and online video.[8] Because Renee developed the term *digital and media literacy,* we use this phrase to represent practices for advancing people's competencies of accessing, analyzing, creating, reflecting, and taking action in creating and consuming media in a wide variety of forms.[9] As we amply illustrate in this book, such work can happen inside and outside of formal learning contexts. For this reason, librarians are key agents of change to bring film education, media education, visual literacy, media literacy, and digital literacy to the schools, colleges, and communities they serve.

FILM AND MEDIA EDUCATION IN LIBRARIES

It's time we admit it: Film and audiovisual media are *texts* that have just as much value as books and print media. The rise of audiovisual media as a central part of cultural life amply demonstrates that the concept of literacy is expanding as new forms of expression and communication continue to be developed and shared. After all, today those symbols increasingly come in visual, digital, audiovisual, and interactive forms.

Most public libraries spend at least 12% of their budgets on DVDs and moving image media in streaming formats. Today, one third of total library circulation consists of audiovisual materials.[10] Film education has a long tradition, having operated in schools, colleges, and universities for over 100 years, since the invention of the medium at the turn of the 20th century. School librarians help educators use film and media for learning purposes. Academic librarians help build film libraries for use in higher education programs. New forms of film distribution and marketing are creating opportunities to develop film collections that reach everyone around the globe.

Beyond the library, YouTube is a major source of both play and learning for millions of people around the world. For children and teens everywhere, film, video, and moving image media are increasingly central to the process of growing up. Viewing occurs on smartphones that most American children receive when they are between the ages of 10 and 12.[11] In most Western societies, children and young people spend more time watching television than they spend in school. As film and video have grown in popularity as a tool for teaching and learning, media literacy educators have emphasized the development of critical thinking about authors and audiences, and the constructed nature of audiovisual media, with its linear structure and its ability to represent reality and evoke strong emotional response.

But today, we're not just media consumers; we're also media creators. As low-cost digital media production tools and technologies have become more available, school librarians have developed programs that enable children and youth to create media as part of the library program, thus standing at the forefront of the media literacy movement in K–12 education. The rise of user-generated content has enabled even the most elderly people to begin to discover the power of digital authorship, developing their creative expression skills and reaching audiences with oral narratives, digital storytelling, and songs. Thus, the very nature of writing and composition is also in a state of transformation as people compose and share new forms of entertainment, information, and propaganda as part of everyday life.

School, public, and academic librarians increasingly recognize the value of being outward-facing community agents of change in offering new programs and services to meet the changing needs of people today. Through partnering with community organizations either with expertise in film and media, or in any field that film and other media explore, librarians are extending the services they offer to meet the 21st-century learning needs of the people in the communities they serve.

LIBRARIES EXPLORE FAKE NEWS

Who could forget the season we first heard the term *fake news*? Educators and librarians found many different ways to address the topic. Emily LeMay, a children's and young adult librarian in the Providence Community Library system, read about the widely-publicized research by Sam Wineburg and his colleagues at Stanford University, which shows that middle-school students cannot tell the difference between advertising and news. In a survey of nearly 8,000 students, 82% of middle schoolers were unable to differentiate between an ad labeled *sponsored content* and a real news story on a website.[12]

This young librarian was up for the challenge of designing a learning experience on fake news. Only a few months earlier, at the Mount Pleasant Library in Providence, LeMay had created Alt-ComicCon, where she introduced kids and teens to people and organizations working creatively in the fields of technology, art, and pop culture. As she wondered about the skills of her library kids, she continued to read and research the emerging brouhaha developing over the problem of fake news. She decided to host an educational event for her teens at the library. She promoted the event by designing a poster and telling teens about the program. She even sent messages to individual teens to remind them of the event via their Instagram accounts. By early March, Emily LeMay had designed and implemented a library program that was attended by 17 teenagers.

The program was among the first formal educational programs she had developed in her 5 years working at the Providence Community Library. She began the program by checking their existing knowledge, asking, "What's media? What's literacy? Why together?" Then they discussed key terms, including *clickbait, echo chambers, propaganda,* and *satire.* Emily used examples from contemporary culture to define these concepts. She explained a bit about the long history of fake news, going back to the Founding Fathers, and identified the constellation of factors that have created a perfect storm: the decline in journalism, echo chambers and the rise of alt-right conspiracy theorists, and the election of a president who lies and spins.

In describing the program, LeMay is quick to acknowledge her bias. "I don't like anything '45' has said or done leading up to or post-election, and that probably comes across in some of my information. However, I did try to present as many facts about the situations surrounding him and as little interpretation as possible." One of the big ideas she tried to express to teens is that "everyone and everything has a point of view, but that the more facts you omit and truths you sugar coat, the further away from a normal point of view you move and the closer to a dangerous agenda you get."[13]

What was the secret to LeMay's success? First, she designed a set of open-ended questions to jump-start discussion and allow kids to participate and take partial ownership of the session. Second, she selected relevant, emotionally resonant examples for teens to discuss, helping them practice critically analyzing fake news. For example, in one part of the session, she showed students an image depicting a CNN interview with President Obama, with the lower-third graphic reading, "Obama: I Won't Leave if Trump is Elected." Figure 1.2 shows an image that appears to come from CNN but is, in reality, a fake. LeMay found this image on her social media feed. Was it true? Kids debated the issue. Then she explained that sometimes it's easy to tell if something has been Photoshopped, but other times it's not. She asked them to look carefully at the image, asking, "Would the President of the United States be speaking live to CNN at 10:28 p.m., if it wasn't an emergency situation? Where's the ticker that's usually scrolling at the bottom of the screen on CNN? Is the banner straight or slanted? Why isn't there a space after the colon and before the quotation mark?"

LeMay noted how important it was to "check your emotions," explaining "if you're feeling angry or smug, you might be getting played." She concluded by explaining

BREAKING NEWS
OBAMA:"I WON'T LEAVE IF TRUMP IS ELECTED"

LIVE
10:28 PM ET

Figure 1.2 Learning to recognize "fake news."

that teens should pick their news sources like they pick their friends. They should be reliable, fair, and not too dramatic, someone who can be trusted.

Emily LeMay felt comfortable designing this program, and she had the support of her director, although she acknowledges that not all librarians would be as courageous to offer a similar program in their communities. In Cleveland, Ohio, one youth services librarian told Renee that he would never offer a fake news program in his community because his own political beliefs were so different from the community in which he worked. He didn't want to do anything that would raise concerns that might shake the perception of the library as a trusted, neutral public space.

Clearly, fake news is a huge issue that does not have an easy solution. It can be challenging to discuss in politically diverse communities. We are grateful that documentarians are beginning to address the topic in films like *Nobody Speak*, a 2017 film by Brian Knappenberger, or the BBC Newsnight's *The Rise of Fake News*. But school, public, and academic librarians are well positioned to provide resources and trainings to help people critically analyze news and information. When people think critically about entertainment content, social media posts, information sources, memes, domain names, pop-up ads, and more, they become more discriminating readers and viewers.

But such work can happen in libraries only when there is an outward-facing librarian who has the motivation and skills to search out and cultivate community partnership. As Alvarez explains, "From providing outreach to local organizations and at events, to partnering with businesses and schools, meaningful relationships are critical to having honest conversations about needs, fears, and aspirations. If librarians want the community to view their public library as a place that provides valuable information and equitable access, community members must feel that the library is their peer, not their patronizer."[14] When librarians attend public gatherings and gather information about their community, they are better able to discern community needs.

Why We Wrote This Book

We love libraries and we love film, video, and media. We wrote this book to better understand how librarians support film and media education in school, public, and academic libraries. We wanted to share our learning with librarians across all venues and with people far outside the library world—especially those in public education, the nonprofit sector, higher education, and the independent film and media community—to appreciate and understand the important work that is now underway in libraries.

Although the American public love their libraries, many members of the general public are just now beginning to understand that libraries are more than book repositories. We have noticed that many elementary and secondary teachers as well as university and college faculty lack a good understanding of how librarians support and enable the practice of film and media literacy.

We are not librarians. In writing this book, we consider ourselves to be bridge builders. Renee teaches graduate courses for educators and librarians, and Pam and Liz have conducted many film and media programs in public libraries. We have a combined fifteen decades as devoted library patrons, and our research process put us in contact with more than 170 librarians and educators from all across the country. In the process of writing this book, we observed film screenings in rural, suburban, and big-city libraries. We visited school librarians and attended conferences and meetings where educators and librarians shared their insights. We met with independent filmmakers, attended film festivals, and participated in a wide variety of screening and discussion events. We read and watched everything we could get our hands on. We discussed what we were learning as we developed the chapters that you hold in your hands.

As nonlibrarians, we offer our perspective on what we have learned with deep humility. We are aware that our outsider status enables us to see with fresh eyes and ask critical questions rooted in our identities as educators, critics, researchers, and activists. Some may see our efforts as reflecting a certain naïveté about the practice of librarianship. It's possible that we missed some very important goals, frameworks, or initiatives that could shed further insight on the many different uses of film and media in libraries. We hope this book has value for you, but we are also aware that the perspective we offer is limited by our own experience.

In this book, we examine and reflect upon the practice of film and media literacy in libraries as we imagine how it might evolve to meet the needs of a new generation. We think of ourselves as critical friends. Indeed, the Critical Friends approach to professional development was developed by the Annenberg Institute for School Reform at Brown University, and it relies on creating occasions for reflection. Generally done face to face, it involves careful description, listening, and feedback, followed by generalizations that synthesize ideas and embody lived experiences. It's a type of pedagogy that is rooted in valuing dialogue and discussion. These elements are embedded in this book.

By describing a variety of practices, listening thoughtfully, and offering questioning feedback, we aim to be encouraging and supportive while providing candid and constructive ideas about the practice of film and media literacy in school, public, and academic libraries. For more than 20 years, Renee's colleagues have indulged her need to include Critical Friends–style dialogue and debriefing at the conclusion of all the professional development programs offered by the Media Education Lab. "Warm" feedback consists of supportive, appreciative statements about the work presented. "Cool" or more distanced feedback offers different ways to think about the work presented or raises particular questions. "Hard" feedback challenges assumptions and engages in wondering about consequences of particular strategies presented.[15]

Through time limits and agreed-upon conversational norms, reflection becomes a profoundly social practice. With feedback like this, we help each other be the best we can be. When done well, the Critical Friends protocol generates insights, promotes a culture of trust and respect, and inspires people to be reflective practitioners. Feedback from disinterested outsiders can often be valuable because it includes a mix of perspectives from those not deeply socialized to status quo realities. As a reader of this book, you are part of our circle of Critical Friends, and we welcome your warm, cool, and critical feedback.

When we first started this journey as authors, we were inspired by the work of library experts Joyce Valenza, a professor at Rutgers University, and David Lankes of the University of South Carolina. Both of these amazing leaders offer a big-picture perspective on "new librarianship," and they remind librarians of their mission to improve society by facilitating knowledge curation and creation in their communities. Like Valenza and Lankes, we believe that librarians and their many allies benefit from opportunities to explore many different arguments, examples, and ideas for fulfilling this mission. Innovative approaches to the use of film and media play a role here as librarians think about themselves as "radical positive change agents in their communities" and everyone learns to appreciate libraries in a new way.[16]

While our primary audience is librarians and educators, if you're reading this book, you might also be a filmmaker or media professional, eager to learn how to engage with communities through a partnership with a public library. You might be a parent or film lover who's interested in advancing public discourse about media. You might be a scholar with research interests in film and media education in libraries. Perhaps you're an activist looking for ways to have meaningful conversations about socially-relevant films with the people in your community.

If you are an elementary or secondary educator, a technology specialist or school leader, or a teacher educator or faculty member teaching at a college or university, you'll see how collaboration between educators and librarians can advance the practice of film and media literacy education. You will learn how film and media literacy is integrated across subject areas and disciplines, and you will develop a deep understanding of the foundational elements of effective teaching with and about moving image media.

You may be a school librarian, an academic librarian, a public librarian, or a faculty member teaching future librarians in a school of library and information studies. You may be enrolled in a graduate program, exploring topics such as Media and Children; Library Services for Children and Youth; Moving Images Programming; Information and Digital Literacies; Media Literacy; Leadership in Educational Technology; or Media, Library, Community, and Culture. You might be interested in research on media literacy and media education, new literacies, and digital literacy. Many academic programs are beginning to support teaching and research that examines how these concepts integrated into learning in and out of school. This topic is a growing area of interest among accredited library graduate programs in the United States.

Perhaps you support the needs of children, youth, and families through work in the nonprofit sector, at a museum, civic or cultural organization, a settlement house, alternative school, or other organization. By reading this book, you will gain practical experience in creating programs working in collaboration with school, public, and academic librarians. You'll learn about the strategies and pedagogical concepts that are essential for program development, marketing, and outreach. Whatever reason has brought you to hold this book in your hands, in the pages that follow, we're determined to demonstrate the value of harnessing the emotional power of the moving image for learning.

Other Key Players
MEDIA LIBRARIANS AND ARCHIVISTS

When librarians themselves think about film and movies, some may focus on the specialized collections of films that are maintained in academic library archives. Film scholars and researchers depend upon access to archival collections that enable them to understand the history of film and specialized film, and media librarians play a role in teaching both students and faculty the research methods for using film archives to access films from the past and create new knowledge. Sometimes this work relies on robust and powerful collaboration, as in New Jersey, where a group of academic and public librarians, working with museums and K–12 education leaders, have created the New Jersey Video Digital Media Repository to preserve and make available hundreds of locally produced video programs created by universities, schools, and cultural organizations from across the state. Through collaboration, media librarians and archivists are working to overcome technical barriers to digitizing and making video available to users.

Although you will learn more about the development of specialized film collections as well as the preservation and archiving of film and digital media in this book, we pay closer attention to the more general instructional and support services that academic librarians provide when they enable access to film and media making to advance the educational mission at colleges and universities around the country. In this book, you'll learn about the many decisions librarians must make when they acquire films and videos in physical or streaming formats. We'll unpack copyright, licensing models, fair use exemptions, and digital rights management issues. In the Appendix, you'll find a brief summary of relevant legal issues related to film and media in libraries.

But most of the focus of this book is on pedagogy: We want to better understand libraries as learning spaces that make film, video, and media resources more powerful and effective across the lifespan. Films and videos are cultural artifacts that have value for entertainment, information, and learning. Academic and public librarians know that streaming media in libraries can support people's lifelong learning. Because people today are more and more likely to access and use audiovisual media through streaming and cloud-based services rather than use physical copies like DVDs, VHS tapes, and film reels, media librarians are leaders in understanding streaming media. Netflix, YouTube, and other streaming media services are easily available to consumers, but dozens of other services also make audiovisual content available to viewers.

But the field is dramatically changing, and so librarians must themselves be lifelong learners to keep abreast of these changes. Fortunately, librarians continually help each other to learn. For example, the Boston Library Consortium maintains a subgroup of librarians who evaluate the landscape of external streaming media providers and recommend the appropriate mix of hosted and cloud-based streaming content and delivery solutions for both commercial and locally produced media.

FILM AND MEDIA REVIEWERS

For film and media literacy to thrive in the library context, providing access to content is a key first step, and it's something that librarians do best. With the overwhelming volume of audiovisual content that is released every month, it takes work to make choices about what to view and what to collect; in this regard, film and media reviewers provide an essential service.

Librarians rely on Kirkus, Booklist, *Choice, Publisher's Weekly, Library Journal,* and *School Library Journal,* and many use reviews from the *New York Times* and *The New Yorker* as well as specialized websites like Common Sense Media. Media librarians rely on *Video Librarian,* published by Randy Pitman and featuring reviews from more than a dozen professional reviewers. Plus, there has been an explosion of user-generated reviews as a result of our increasing use of streaming services on Amazon and Netflix. It takes courage, time, and talent to formulate a response to something you read, view, or use. Professional and amateur reviewers offer a profound service in helping people make wise decisions about media use, and we think more formal attention to their work is needed in both higher education, school, and public library contexts.

Librarians don't just read reviews; they also compose and create reviews, of course. But when we compare the attention that book reviewing gets as compared with the reviewing of film, television, and popular culture, things have not changed much since 1989, when Virgil Blake first noted the short shrift that nonprint media get in the world of collection development. Only a very small fraction of the nonprint content available for purchase was reviewed, as compared with the extensive availability of reviews for print media.

Noticing the extreme disparity in treatment between print and nonprint media, he wondered: "Does the treatment given non-print media in these books provide evidence . . . concerning the existence of a printist elite?" Blake found that the reviews and reviewing of nonprint materials has been in large part neglected in library land. He wrote, "If libraries are to fully enter the multi-media age and provide their patrons with information in all of its diverse packages, these matters have to be addressed."[17]

DISCRIMINATING CONSUMERS AND MEDIA MAKERS IN THE COMMUNITY

Reviews matter to an increasing number of people who are faced with the information age challenge of "too much content." Many parents want information about the best quality books, film, media, and digital resources available for young children. They want to know how to balance TV time with reading and other nonmedia activities. Libraries are where parents seek information about child development, where children attend their first story times, and where guidance about good books is readily available. Today, parents have many questions about the experience of raising children in a broadband wireless household, with cell phones, tablets, and laptops as ubiquitous as televisions in many rooms of the house. School librarians cultivate students' critical thinking about information sources and help learners make good choices about what they watch, see, listen to, and read.[18] Technology classes in libraries help people from all walks of life gain skills in using computers.

Independent filmmakers are another group of key players. They value opportunities that librarians can provide to help them reach public audiences and distribute their work. In the highly competitive and dynamic market economy for audiovisual entertainment, librarians' emphasis on community service is truly a breath of fresh air! Film lovers and those who curate and run film festivals are twin treasures in any community. When librarians and film festival staff coordinate efforts, the results can be impressive. It takes knowledge and skill, of course, but most of all it takes imagination to develop film and media literacy education programs in school, public, and academic libraries.

As we will see in this book, librarians do more than suggest quality films, TV shows, books, podcasts, and other media to their patrons. They also build film collections, curate film festivals, develop professional development programs for educators, offer film discussion groups, offer instruction, and create public programs that explore topics like privacy and security, digital citizenship, and the smart use of social media for entrepreneurship. Through all these practices, they introduce people of all ages to fundamental concepts of digital and media literacy.

A Model for Film and Media Literacy Education in Libraries

Librarians can harness the emotional power of film and media for learning purposes by elevating the position of these resources in the library, using a variety of programs and practices to support lifetime learning.

We want to ensure that film and media education are part of the future of librarianship. By elevating the place of movies and media in the library, it will be necessary to appreciate the many approaches to film and media education in libraries that prepare people for a lifetime of learning. As we reflected on the more than 170 examples of film and media programs we examined in the research we conducted for this book, we created a diagram to capture the diversity of practices that we found in school, public, and academic libraries. As Figure 1.3 shows, at the center of it all is a constellation of competencies: viewing, collecting, creating, learning, and connecting. These competencies can be developed through formal and informal learning activities of all kinds. In this book, you'll learn about the programs, services, and instructional practices that support the development of these competencies in public, school, and academic libraries.

Five major practices drive how film and media education is supported in school, public, and academic libraries. In Part I of the book, we devote a chapter to each of these themes. They include the following:

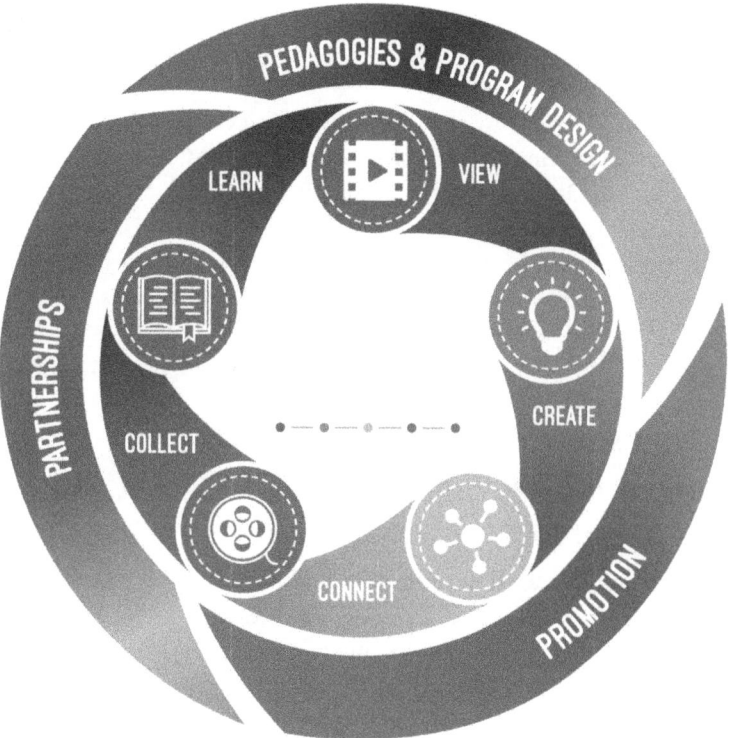

Figure 1.3 Elements of film and media education in the library, school, and community.

Viewing: Film and media screenings and programs that focus on sharing interpretations through discussion help create a sense of community, and special events that feature filmmakers and local experts provide commentary and context that deepen interpretation and promote intellectual curiosity.

Creating: People can inspire, inform, and entertain through a variety of low-tech and high-tech media creation experiences. Whether librarians help people of all ages to create or they themselves create using media, they expand the concept of literacy to advance self-expression, empowerment, and civic engagement.

Learning: Learning to analyze the content and format of audiovisual media takes practice, and this begins with the process of learning to read picture books. Photographs, documentaries, and visual images may seem real, but they need to be interrogated with a critical eye, just as print information sources must be.

Collecting: People make choices about what to view and use, and today, curation can be understood as a literacy practice. Ratings and reviews can be valuable tools to support wise decision making. Librarians make key decisions about what resources to showcase and acquire, and some even develop viewer advisory services to recommend TV shows, movies, video games, and more.

Connecting: Librarians are change agents in their communities. They use the power of moving image media to tell the story of their programs, collections, and services. Through community partnerships, librarians bring the emotional power of film and media to wide and diverse audiences and magnify the opportunity for community dialogue and discussion that advances cultural understanding and the democratic process.

Key Themes in the Library Screen Scene

HARNESSING THE EMOTIONAL POWER OF THE MOVING IMAGE FOR LEARNING

Although films are screened in most libraries, many librarians don't think much about film screenings. For some, film programs just don't seem to have a strong connection to the library mission. In some public libraries, film screenings are an easy-to-implement program that enables librarians to check off a box and count the number of attendees for their end-of-year report.[19] But they can be so much more! In this book, we argue for a fresh approach to film screenings in libraries, one that taps into the powerful emotional pull of film, television, and popular culture.

The emotional power of movies can be harnessed to activate intellectual curiosity and promote learning. Films activate strong emotions of all kinds—we laugh, feel fear, experience suspense, delight, disgust, and every other human emotion. As one scholar points out, "In all of the academic talk about film interpretations, meanings, negotiated readings, comprehension, and so on, what is often forgotten is that for the vast majority of film spectators, movie viewing is first and foremost a pleasurable experience, suffused with affect." The activation of emotion is what motivates us to pay for this experience with money, time, and effort. But, in exchange, we "expect to be fascinated, shocked, titillated, made suspenseful and curious, invited to laugh and cry, and in the end, given pleasure."[20]

For most people, the experience of emotional activation through film viewing leads to intellectual curiosity and spurs an interest in further learning. Librarians can help harness the emotional power of film for learning purposes. After all, emotions are intimately tied to our cognition, inferences, and judgment. Strong feelings make ideas and images seem important and memorable. Sharing viewing experiences can contribute to the formation and maintenance of shared cultural values. As we will see in the chapters that follow, although this kind of learning can be sometimes scary and unpredictable, it can also be transformative.

What makes film so effective in activating people's emotions? While still in graduate school, Renee explored the work of Hugo Munsterberg, who wrote the first scholarly study of film at Harvard University in 1916. In *The Photoplay: A Psychological Study*, he noticed that film is constructed in ways that mirror human consciousness. For example, the device of the close-up visually represents the process of paying attention, when we focus our energies on a part and ignore the larger scene. Fast editing visually represents the state of agitation we experience when stress activates our perceptual senses and everything is a jumble of action and sensation. Because film mimics natural aspects of human consciousness, it can be easily understood by everyone, even people who have never experienced it. As a young scholar, Renee and her colleagues conducted research to explore how various film editing techniques are interpreted in narrative stories. She found that a variety of film editing conventions were easily understood by a group of Pokot tribespeople in Northwest Kenya who had no previous exposure to film or television.[21] This powerful quality of moving image media to reach wide audiences makes it a universal language of sorts, accessible to people from all walks of life.

The universality of film and media is a treasure that needs to be more fully appreciated. Carl Platinga asserts that we "experience movies with our bodies, as we sway with the action, erupt in laughter, or feel that knot of suspense in our stomach."[22] Movies activate the head, heart, hands, and spirit. We all learn from movies and television, even though we might not be fully aware of it.

Learning from popular culture is a case in point. Television shows have been shown to have meaningful educational value on matters of public health. During the 1990s, the episodic TV series *ER* was at its height of popularity. This long-running medical drama was created by novelist and doctor Michael Crichton and featured an ensemble cast. To explore the impact of the show on people's knowledge of public health and health policy, the Kaiser Family Foundation conducted national random-sample telephone surveys of regular viewers. One episode, aired on April 10, 1997, features a patient who has been the victim of a date rape and who requests information about what she can do to prevent pregnancy. In the story, there is a very brief mention of the use of birth control pills for emergency contraception. Viewers' awareness of emergency contraception increased 17% in the week after the episode aired. In another episode, a nurse sees a teenage patient who is diagnosed with cervical cancer. The nurse explains that the cancer could be related to the sexually transmitted disease HPV.

Researchers found that the proportion of viewers who said they had heard of HPV nearly doubled in the week after the episode aired, from 24% to 47% of regular viewers. Compared to surveys conducted before the broadcast was aired, three times as many people could correctly define HPV and were aware of its link to cervical cancer. More than 50% of participants said that they talked with family and friends about the health issues that were addressed on the show, and a third said that they had gotten information from *ER* that helped them make choices about their own or their family's health care.

People get inspired by watching television to seek information about health topics. Researchers found that about 20% said that they had been inspired to seek out other information sources to find additional information about a health issue because of something they saw on *ER*. In a survey of physicians conducted by the Kaiser Family Foundation in 2001, 20% of doctors said patients want to talk about specific diseases or treatments they learned about on entertainment shows like *ER*. Watching a TV show can promote public health.

Movies and TV shows also cultivate intellectual curiosity about history, technology, politics, science, the arts, philosophy, and other topics. Librarians at the reference desk sometimes recognize these patterns. Many librarians have noticed the influence of Oprah's book list, and they see how topics and issues in the news and current events inspire patrons to want to learn more. When Moya Mason, a librarian, asked more than 150 librarians how TV and radio have helped them to answer reference queries, she found that two thirds have had experiences where their awareness of media and popular culture aided their work. One third were adamant that television and radio play no role in anything related to reference services, however. Most did recognize that patron queries are sometimes inspired by what they hear on the radio or watch on TV. A few even described how their familiarity with advertising was useful in helping them to answer patron queries. One librarian said, "Knowing what our patrons are listening [to] and watching can only help us do our jobs better." She described her experience watching a PBS program and a week later, several patrons came asking about books by the author featured in the TV program. She said, "One patron couldn't remember any details about her name or the book title. Fortunately, I remembered it and had actually requested the new title already for the library."[23]

Sometimes an interest in television and movies even helps expand our reading choices. Matt Grant describes how he was never much of a fan of horror until he started watching the TV series *Stranger Things*, written and directed by Matt and Ross Duffer. Set in a small Midwest town in the 1980s, this investigative drama has sci-fi and pop culture elements and features young outcast kids who face the unseen forces of evil. As he was drawn into the TV series, he saw the trailer for *It*, the horror film directed by Andy Muschietti, based on the 1986 novel of the same name by Stephen King. His interest in reading the Stephen King book was stimulated. He writes, "I wonder what other great stories and books I've missed out on in my life because I've refused to open myself up to the idea that, while there might be many things I don't like about the genre, there might be many things I do like, too."[24]

Movies also help us become more aware and more sympathetic toward people who are different from us. To understand a narrative story, we must sympathize or empathize with fictional characters. This process of identification is intensified through film editing conventions, where we are invited to take the point of view of the character, to walk in his or her shoes, so to speak. Music, lighting, costume, and setting are all carefully structured to intensify the feelings of being embodied in and with the character. How we think about the characters in a film is influenced by how we feel about them.

In our opinion, the tight connections between viewing, thinking, feeling, and action should be better exploited by educators as well as school, public, and academic librarians to support learning and civic engagement. We must recognize the centrality of viewing experiences, emotions, and the senses as they support lifelong learning.

One of the reasons why school, public, and academic libraries are shifting their emphasis from collections toward programs is an awareness that learning is stimulated through experiences that activate social interaction and produce states of feeling. More and more, we crave social interaction in community contexts. A library is not and should not be merely a book repository because learning isn't merely a matter of getting access to content and information. It is through shared forms of experience that people learn best.

ELEVATING MOVIES AND MEDIA IN THE LIBRARY

Who knows how many times it's been repeated in the library world that the book is always better? In this book, we argue that movies and media can no longer be treated as the stepchildren of the library world. They need to become siblings, treated as books are, as equal members of the library family. Film and media resources need to be a cornerstone of the library experience, not an ancillary concern. Right now, this is not yet a reality. For example, in certain parts of library land, books are perceived as having such integrity that making a film adaptation is regarded as a form of abuse. At some libraries, checking out too many films will cause librarians to give you the side eye of disdain, disgust, or even pity. We think such perspectives, while occasionally amusing, are outdated and potentially dangerous. With a plethora of innovative programs, services, and pedagogies, school, academic, and public libraries can encourage community engagement and deeper learning.

But film has never been a high priority for the library community. Just type the words "film," "television," "movies," or "popular culture" into a database for library and information professionals and notice what little comes up. Peruse the literature of the field and see how infrequently these forms are mentioned. Go to a library website and see what appears on the home page. How many clicks does it take to access information about the film collection?

Audiovisual media is still undervalued by many in the library community. But librarians shouldn't feel guilty that film, media, and popular culture have been given short shrift. The 20th century was defined by specialization; books were at the heart of libraries for a very long time. Indeed, the rise of film studies, media studies, and cultural studies all developed in parallel to the development of the field of library and information studies, each with their own specialist discourses. Although librarianship as a discipline has centered on books in the past, now the Internet and the rise of digital culture are disrupting that norm and enabling librarianship to be more truly a more transdiciplinary profession.

Many librarians (and educators) have conflicted attitudes about film, television, and popular culture, and this contributes to the way that movies and media are handled in libraries, schools, and other educational settings. As we will see in Chapter 2, film and television have had a problematic reputation among members of the educational establishment for a very long time. Plenty of evidence from scholarly research conducted over the past 100 years suggests that we should be concerned about the ways in which film and television influence children and youth. Exposure to media does affect the development of children's attention spans and may cultivate stereotypes that contribute to racism, sexism, and homophobia. Many of the general public have been fearful of the negative impact of media. Each generation, it seems, gets a dose of fear about the potential risks and dangers to new forms of media. Certainly, the power of film to influence emotions, attitudes and behavior has contributed to the perception that movies, television shows, and YouTube videos are risky, problematic forms of expression.

Yet movies, television, and videos can be empowering and have positive effects on people's behavior, attitudes, and values. When Renee was in high school, the show *Happy Days* was at its zenith of popularity, and she remembers an episode that first shook her faith in the common wisdom, still prevalent today, that television is bad for children. The TV show, set in the 1950s, featured Richie Cunningham (played by Ron Howard) and his good pal Fonzie (played by Henry Winkler) as a slick, leather-clad high school dropout with a high moral code. In one episode, Richie complained that he didn't have a date to the homecoming dance. Fonzie's solution was to recommend a trip to a local library. In this episode, Fonzie obtained a library card and checked out his very first book. The series creator, Gary Marshall, claimed that requests for library cards among children aged 9 to 14 increased by more than 500% in the days following the airing of the episode.[25] The news was widely reported in the news media of the time. Imagine! The Fonz was a positive influence on American kids!

But where did this statistic come from? In attempting to fact-check the matter, no documentation could be found from the American Library Association (ALA). The ALA itself notes that they were unable to verify that any library organization or publication had reported such a claim. In fact, at that time, only a few states tracked the number of library cards held by patrons. They write, "There is no report in ALA's American Libraries or in any other library press periodical telling of a surge in signups in the months following the episode."[26] In attempting to fact-check this urban myth, Snopes researchers suspected that the statistic may have been generated by the show's marketing team as they began to take on more serious themes in the

Figure 1.4 "Fonzie gets his library card" still resonates in library land.

later seasons of the long-running show and wanted to demonstrate the positive influence of the show.[27] As Figure 1.4 shows, some librarians still promote the outdated and inaccurate myth. Promoting the library by perpetuating urban legends does not align with the library mission.

The rise of social media and the increasing convergence between media forms and genres suggests a new path forward for the 21st century. As librarians are able to embrace movies, television, music, podcasts and popular culture alongside their love of books and graphic novels, they build bridges that help to reach unserved and underserved community members.

LIBRARY STRATEGIES FOR FILM AND MEDIA EDUCATION PROGRAMS

In this book, we illustrate, celebrate, and critique the wide variety of ways that film and media are a part of libraries in schools, colleges, and communities. To discover the many practices that characterize film and media literacy, we designed, developed, and implemented programs and learning activities ourselves, working collaboratively with librarians. In the pages that follow, we show how important it is to cross borders to expand thinking and generate new ideas about how to exploit the full potential of film and media in libraries. By challenging accepted norms, we also deepened our respect for the value of many different approaches to film and media in school, public, and academic library contexts.

For example, many children's librarians are not keen on big-media empires like Disney. Some feel that by peddling princess stereotypes along with merchandising, Disney has become an inescapable part of American childhood. Would you expect to hear anything about the Disney empire at a library? Whatever your attitude is toward the House of Mouse, Disney's influence on the children's media landscape cannot be ignored. Renee and Pam took on the good, the bad, the fans, and the critics during their workshop entitled "Deconstructing Disney" during the 2018 Providence Children's Film Festival.

The event was held at the Athenaeum, a historic library in Providence, Rhode Island. Twenty-five participants (who ranged in age from 7 to 77) engaged in a critical discussion about character archetypes, stereotypes, tropes, the eras of Disney in historical context, and changes (dare we say progress?) over time in the values Disney films portray and instill. Renee and Pam confronted Disney's empire-like control over popular media while also appreciating the emotional power of those Disney movies we grow up with.

Voices of all ages contributed to the discussion, including parents and their children. Most impressively, the youngest among the group held their own in discussing what aspects of Disney movies they liked, even while acknowledging Disney's downsides. A boy around 10 years old explained, "It's not something to be afraid of. It's something to enjoy." A girl no older than 7 grappled with the merchandising and money-making goals of Disney verses what the mega media maker can accomplish as it starts to diversify the stories and characters portrayed in feature films like *Moana, Coco* and *Black Panther*. Yes, the old films had problematic gender and racial stereotypes. But what mattered most to her was that better films were being made now, and that was a good thing.

Disney movies are low-hanging fruit for bringing people together for dialogue and discussion in libraries because Disney does have that attention-getting power that is often an instant draw for patrons of all ages. There's nothing wrong with taking advantage of that appeal. Disney movies are deeply woven into popular culture, and it makes sense to view and discuss them at any age. We only suggest sprinkling in some critical thinking and constructive discussion along with that magical Disney fairy dust.

While some librarians may be appalled by a screening and discussion of a Disney film, some librarians celebrate it. For a little over a year, in 2014, media editor Stephanie Klose at *Library Journal Reviews* hosted a series called Pop Culture Advisory. Katie LaMantia and Emily Vinci of the Schaumburg Township District Library in Schaumburg, Illinois, offered a workshop, "Using Popular Culture to

Create Great Library Programs." They aimed to reach younger people in the 20s and 30s by recognizing and celebrating pop culture, fandom, and nostalgia.

Librarians with an interest in film and media can have a transformative impact on the communities they serve. At the Princeton Public Library in New Jersey, the impetus to create an environmental film festival began with a group of patrons, including a student who was head of the environmental club at the local high school along with youth services librarian Susan Conlon. An English major at Rutgers, and a long-term employee at Princeton Public Library, Conlon always held a deep interest in movies. Her love of visual arts and visual storytelling was deeply connected to print media, both fiction and nonfiction. Conlon finds both narrative and documentary films interesting as they portray life stories and offer a distinct point of view. She notes that documentaries and librarianship have a lot in common—as she puts it, "they both involve researching, having a point of view and being the voice."[28]

It takes creativity to create a film festival in a public library, and it takes tenacity to sustain them. Conlon started the Princeton Student Film & Video Festival (PCF&VF) in the summer of 2003 to, in the words of their mission statement, "encourage and support the work of youth filmmakers (ages 14–25) in a range of genres and styles, with the opportunity and a venue for the filmmakers to show their work to a broad audience." Conlon adds it provided "a chance for adults to really see what young adults are thinking." It has also proven worthwhile in various ways for many of the student filmmakers who participated. For some, it has led to careers in film; for others, the opportunity to experience an audience reacting to their work and getting feedback beyond that which they receive online or to connect with other young filmmakers has been reward enough. The renamed Princeton Student Film Festival is now an annual library tradition and has gained an international reputation. They screened over 200 student films in its first decade and have expanded from one night of screenings to three, receiving about 150 submissions each year.

LEADERSHIP ADVANCES FILM AND MEDIA LITERACY IN LIBRARIES

What inspires librarians and faculty to provide opportunities for students to view, critically analyze, and create media? Sometimes it's a matter of simply noticing carefully what's happening in the present. As Associate Dean for Learning and Research Services at the University of Miami Libraries, Kelly Miller sees students reading or writing—but they're not just dealing with words. They are reading numbers and infographics and images on pages and screens. They are watching short videos. They are writing in spiral notebooks, on laptops, and expressing themselves via sharing social media. Today's students are multimodal learners.

Faculty, students, and librarians are co-constructing the competencies needed to analyze and create media through project-based learning. For example, at UCLA, students are active in developing the Community Collections, which are collections curated by students in collaboration with librarians and faculty advisers. Undergraduate students assist with the curation of popular fiction, cookbooks, and zines. How do such projects get started? By noticing carefully what's happening in the present. When the 2012 Los Angeles Zine Fest launched in downtown Los Angeles, it helped create something of a "zine renaissance" in Southern California.

Zines are popular among writing instructors because these low-budget, self-published works of prose, poetry, art, and nonfiction engage student creativity and self-expression and connect to a unique cultural tradition stretching back across the 20th century. Student interest groups at UCLA began to form around that time, and the Library was responsive to the community's needs for a zine collection. Involving students in curating zines was a natural process.

As faculty learned about the launch of the zine collection at the library, some writing instructors decided to create assignments that involve zine making. UCLA librarian Julia Glassman started her outreach to writing teachers because she wanted to add students' self-published zines to the library's collection. By developing a relationship with an instructor who taught upper-division thematic writing courses, Glassman was able to provide zines from the collection to support students who were assigned to create them. Glassman visited the class to talk about zine culture and show the students samples from the collection. She helped students with the zine production process and then made copies for each student—plus one for the collection.[29] When student media work is included in library collections, it can be a transformative experience for the entire community.

This kind of academic librarianship occurs when library leaders truly value being responsive to the present needs of the community, using frank and candid conversations with faculty, students, staff, and other stakeholders to discover fundamental values. When librarians focus on supporting teaching and learning, it can transform how students experience the academic library. Academic librarians at UCLA aim to:

- Position the student and learning at the center of all work.
- Build community around the practice of teaching and learning.
- Stay true to the educational mission of the university.
- Inspire questions by cultivating the imagination.
- Model peer-to-peer learning.
- Make visible and celebrate learning, both its results and processes.
- Gather, interpret, and share evidence of student learning.[30]

What You Can Expect From This Book

Here's what lies ahead. In Part I, you'll learn about the five elements of film and media education in school, public, and academic libraries. In Chapter 2, entitled "Viewing," we examine the power of film and media viewing and discussion to deepen people's appreciation for the art of the film. In Chapter 3, entitled "Creating," we show how creating media in libraries can advance literacy competencies, build collaboration skills, and advance democratic community empowerment. In Chapter 4, entitled "Learning," we share the essential pedagogical practices we observed in school, academic, and public libraries. In Chapter 5, entitled "Collecting," we look at how people select and access film and media. In Chapter 6, entitled "Connecting," we examine how film and media education is developed through community partnerships and how film can be used to connect generations, cultures, communities, issues, and ideas.

In Part II, we'll provide deeper context in Chapter 7, entitled "Past," where we uncover the history of film and media education in libraries. In Chapter 8, entitled "Present," we focus on the forms of professional development that enable librarians to advance their knowledge and skills about film and digital media. In Chapter 9, entitled "Future," we contextualize film and media education in libraries in relation to larger trends in culture and society.

Today, school, public, and academic libraries are becoming community hubs for digital and media literacy education. Although aspects of the digital divide persist, as John Palfrey writes, "individuals' access to our shared culture is not dictated by however much money they have."[31] Libraries are not only places where people get information, but they are places where we satisfy our recreational and cultural needs. As the Internet brings us more and more choices of content at our fingertips, what people are longing for is a sense of connection. As we will see in the pages that follow, film viewing and discussion along with media making are experiences rooted in valuing and sharing lived experience in ways that deepen and cultivate our humanity.

Part I

FIVE CORE PRACTICES

2

Viewing

Questions Answered in This Chapter
- Is it true that the book is always better than the movie?
- How can reading children's picture books support visual and media literacy?
- How are film screenings tailored to community interests?
- What are the best practices of a library film screening?
- What does it take to build a robust film program in a public library?
- How are such programs staffed, marketed, and managed?
- What is the value of partnerships between libraries and public broadcasters?
- Why are filmmaker–author visits important for learners?
- How can digital media use in storytime promote learning?
- How have cellphones and social media changed the way we view?
- How are digital citizenship norms best learned?
- How do media messages shape our understanding of the world?
- What are some risks and potential harms of viewing?
- How can popular culture be addressed in a university library?
- Why is the emotional power of film important for developing relationships?

It was a film club, and students were talking about whether texting can save lives. One student named Nicole said, "I used to think that maybe phones and Internet were ruining connections with other people, but I now have a different understanding. I think that phones really help people talk to others and become more confident and get help. There are, of course, downsides to phones and stuff, but this video made it clear that phones really help people out."

Another student, Oscar, agreed, explaining, "When seeing the title, I assumed this would be bashing on how phones are ruining the newest generation." Often, he explained, films about teen texting rely on "cliché stuff," but he was pleasantly surprised to see it was about something more positive. He noted, "It's a big problem for many people, and I really do like the idea of people getting help from others all while being anonymous. To be anonymous really does allow for more people to be comfortable talking about personal things."

You might be surprised to learn that this film club was virtual, and students from all over the country were participating in it. This online film discussion program was developed by Katherine Schulten of The Learning Network, the education program of *The New York Times*. Learners had watched a 6-minute short film, *Can Texting Save Lives?* produced in December 2017. The film featured the work of Crisis Text Line, a suicide prevention organization that is revolutionizing the practice of crisis intervention. Crisis Text Line trains, coaches, and supervises 3,700 virtual volunteers who provide high-quality counseling over a digital platform, exchanging more than 56 million messages with a wide range of clients who use the service.[1]

The film features one of the virtual counselors, Ronni Higger, a young woman who works as a crisis counselor from a hospital bed where she is receiving treatment for a rare form of cancer. In the film, we see the emotional and psychological benefits that occur to the volunteer counselor as a result of being able to provide meaningful support to someone who is struggling with thoughts of suicide or self-harm. In general, a client interacts with a volunteer by exchanging 40 to 60 messages over 45 minutes. After building rapport, the volunteer helps the client explore support systems and identify a goal. They engage in collaborative problem solving and wrap up the conversation by sharing resources. Through interviews with the staff of the organization, we learn that with the power of data science, algorithms help to flag users who are most at risk for suicide. At the end of every crisis interaction conducted through text messaging, users are invited to rate their level of satisfaction, and an overwhelming majority rate it as highly valuable.

It was such a different perspective on the topic of text messaging. Many students who participated in this film discussion commented on how the film offered a real counterpoint to the typically negative coverage of texting, which often focuses on problems like texting and driving or cell phone addiction. Over the course of 10 days, 43 students participated in The New York Times Learning Network's film discussion. Some read a news story that offered additional details about the organization. Some used a double-entry journal while watching the film, making notes of any powerful quotes, moments, or images, and then commenting on those elements to gain awareness of how the filmmaker structures the emotional response of the viewer through careful choices of image, language, and sound.

The creators of Film Club use short documentary films "to challenge assumptions and offer new perspectives," telling stories that often remain hidden. New films are released every 2 weeks so there's always a fresh conversational opportunity. In England, where film viewing and discussion clubs are well supported by government and industry, educators, librarians, parents, and community leaders appreciate the powerful ways in which dialogue about films can activate thinking, emotion, and learning in and out of the classroom. In British film clubs, media literacy skills are learned through discussion of moving image texts along with media production experiences. In practice, film clubs consist of three elements: discussing and analyzing film clips as if they were printed texts; using films as stimuli for imaginative, personal, and functional pieces of writing; and creating a class moving image text by storyboarding, filming, or animating and then editing a short film. British novelist and film educator Sabrina Broadbent writes, "In an education system so shackled to print and the written word, perhaps it is not surprising that 81% of children say they enjoy coming to school more because of their film club."[2]

What's the point of all this viewing? For many, viewing is the first step into entering the world of imagination and possibility. It's a thrill ride of feeling and ideas. Filmmaker David Lynch said, "The cinema is really built for the big screen and big sound, so that a person can go into another world and have an experience."[3] Film viewing is an emotionally stimulating and meaningful experience where people get to learn about themselves and the world around them through stories that activate the head, heart, and spirit. The social act of sharing responses to audiovisual media builds reflective and critical competencies needed for life in an image-saturated society.

In this chapter, we explain why film programming is essential for librarians. We reflect on the library adage that the book is always better and unpack the complex love-hate relationship that librarians have about viewing, including concerns about language development, attention, stereotypes, self-esteem, and violence. We'll discover why film screenings and discussions are a vital element of library programming and appreciate the power of moving image media to facilitate intellectual curiosity. We learn how the dynamic practice of actively reading a children's picture book supports literacy practices that support lifelong learning. We'll consider the potential of popular culture discussions in the context of academic library programs. Of course, we offer practical advice on the key elements that make for a successful screening program in a public, school, or academic library.

Viewing Matters
THE NECESSITY OF FILM PROGRAMMING IN LIBRARIES

Let's go see a movie! The mere notion can conjure excitement and anticipation as one looks forward to a treat of pure entertainment. No one says you have to go to a big box movie theater either. Libraries that offer a vibrant selection of current, popular, and less well-known but quality films find they can draw patrons who may also view films at smaller independent theaters, drive-ins, film festivals, and pop-up movie screenings in public spaces.

Film is a powerful art form: it can promote engagement, cultivate character strengths, and help initiate dialogue that may advance people's personal growth and development. It's important to rethink what it means to show a movie in the library. A first step toward doing so is to work out a shared language for discussing film programs in the library. If you say you're going to "show" or "play" a movie, meaning you just turn it on at the scheduled time and let it run through to the credits, that's typically going to align with a passive experience for everyone involved. When you have people coming out to watch a film in a library, there's an opportunity to make it a more interactive experience than patrons would get at home or in a movie theater. When educators and librarians use video in a classroom, they have a clear educational purpose that they communicate before the screening begins. Afterward, there is some kind of activity that aims to get participants to reflect on the meaning-making process.

It's worth reflecting why people might be choosing to see a movie in a public library. More than likely, it's not just because they want to see the selected movie for free, although that's part of it, of course. Think about the culture of moviegoing, the sensory experience of a bustling lobby, the visceral experience of it all. For patrons coming out to a library to see a film, it is also about the social and interactive experience that comes with a public shared experience. Librarians who merely "press play and walk away" miss out on the opportunity to engage with patrons who, just by showing up, signal their willingness to be open to something more.

In trying to present a unifying and coherent conceptualization of film and media programming, we must have an understanding of its importance. Some librarians perhaps see film programming as a more passive activity. But when done well, library film programming can even act as a mechanism for community transformation, encouraging connections, exposing injustices, altering opinions, and calling attention to problems and solutions, much like literature does.

IS THE BOOK ALWAYS BETTER?

We've noticed that there is a deeply embedded value among many in the library profession that "the book is always better than the movie." Among some, it's a mantra; other librarians sometimes feel twinges of guilt about expressing it. Mark Flowers, a young adult librarian in Vallejo, California, has wondered about this old library trope. He compiled a list of over 150 movies that he believes are better or equal to their literary source, noting that filmmakers all over the world "have a penchant for making great art out of relatively minor, or even trashy, material." In his view, the belief that the book is always better does an incredible disservice to filmmakers and viewers alike. Even worse, says Flowers, is that the mantra has the potential to belittle people for preferring one particular art form to another. Ultimately, this point of view backfires "on the cultural 'guardians' (teachers, parents, and librarians) who make the claim, when audiences realize they are wrong."[4] But Figure 2.1, which displays some of the hundreds of digital images that claim "the book is always better," shows how widespread this particular cultural meme has become.

Librarians may or may not agree with this claim. But one group of librarians with especially ambivalent (and often negative) attitudes toward film and television tends to be children's librarians. They generally have some good reasons for their views. Children's librarians support child development through library collections

Figure 2.1 Google images on "The book is always better" perpetuate outdated, inaccurate ideas.

and programs and routinely invent new ways to integrate play and learning. With approximately 16,000 public library branches and bookmobiles in the United States, many staff are trained specifically to serve young children and their families. They have considerable expertise in recommending and selecting books that promote a love of reading. But children's librarians generally have less knowledge about films and media than they do about books. Some are familiar with popular mass media, including those ubiquitous Disney movies or the many film adaptations of children's literature, but they may be less familiar with the YouTube celebrities that children love, the family TV shows they watch regularly, and the apps or video games they enjoy.

We have observed that some children's librarians even actively or passively display resentment toward those parents who seem to stock up on a pile of DVDs every time they come to the library but barely touch the picture books or children's magazines. Based on research on the influence of media on child development, this is perhaps a well-justified stance. Certainly, the deep-seated concerns about the potential risks and harms of television, film, video, and popular culture contribute to the development of polarizing attitudes about books as superior to film and digital media.

However, this kind of either/or thinking perpetuates the idea that books are seen as distinct from—indeed, often times in competition with—other forms of media. And the idea of a competition between print and nonprint media is a very problematic idea indeed. As librarian Kiera Parrott wrote on the ALSC Blog, "Technology is not the enemy. It is tempting to operate as if supporting literacy is a zero-sum game in which the players are technology versus books. But it is not a simple dichotomy."[5]

While some children's librarians are experimenting with new forms of technology in their public programming by using apps in storytime, many still lack knowledge about and comfort with nonprint and digital media resources that are now a fundamental component of children's lives. In short, many librarians are still not taking full advantage of all that digital media and popular culture have to offer. Rather than urging librarians to jump on the bandwagon for every form of nonprint media that comes along, we think it is important to encourage librarians—and those who use their services—to think critically about the nature, purpose, and value of film and digital media. This, in turn, will help them empower patrons to thoughtfully access, analyze, and create media in a variety of ways.

LEARNING TO READ PICTURES

One big reason for their focus on the idea that "books are better" is that children's librarians treasure the children's picture book, that remarkable genre which has entranced generations of children and inspired them to love reading.

You might not have thought of it this way, but learning to read pictures is a viewing skill, one that reading specialists and scholars are still trying to understand. And because pictures are everywhere—they are in children's books, of course, but they are present in the daily environment, wherever we go—we use pictures as a major source of information and entertainment all across the lifespan, not just in childhood.

The idea that reading pictures is central to the process of learning to read alphabetic symbols has been a foundational part of literacy education for nearly 100 years.[6] Novice readers benefit from explicit instruction in reading pictorial elements, which supports comprehension. Unfortunately, many well-meaning people treat images in children's picture books as illustration that merely decorates the page. In 1986, David Considine, a professor at Appalachian State University, wrote an article in *School Library Journal* about the importance of using children's picture books as a means to teach visual literacy.[7] In it, he reports on how adults scaffold the practice of learning to "read" by inviting conversation about the story and the pictures of a children's book.

As Considine explains, reading a picture book requires active interpretation of the illustrations and images. For example, when reading Gail Haley's picture book, *The Green Man*, comprehension of the narrative is aided with prompts like these:

- **Visual Information:** What do you see?
- **Sound:** What kinds of noises might be in Claude's village?
- **Emotion:** What feeling is he experiencing now?
- **Inference:** Why did he want to leave?
- **Prediction:** What do you think might happen next?

Illustrators and authors work carefully to construct pages that convey meaning, using a wide variety of strategies. Considine points out four of the most frequently used techniques and calls them the 4 Ps of reading picture books: Posture, Point of view, Props, and Position. For example, he notes that artists' depiction of posture—which includes body language and facial expressions—offers children rich, intuitive clues about emotion, mood, and feeling. To understand point of view, children can look at how close or how far away the images appear to be from the reader. Children's authors use props to offer information about the lifestyle of the character as well as provide clues about the story's time period and setting. And the position of the character within the frame of the page can indicate something about how important they are or their role in the story.

Scholars of the children's picture book have described the many clever ways children's authors and illustrators have designed the relationship between text and images. For example, sometimes the words and images are symmetrical and redundant, while in other cases, the pictures expand upon or enhance the visual narrative. Sometimes the pictures serve as a counterpoint or even offer a contradiction to the verbal narrative.[8] When these patterns are noticed and commented upon, children develop a heightened awareness of how images and words work together in complex ways to convey meaning.

Now it must be obvious why we define literacy as the sharing of meaning through symbols. Writers (and illustrators and filmmakers) construct meaning as they shape symbols, and readers (and viewers and users) construct meaning as they interpret them.

Writers and readers are thus connected in a chain of meaning-making. One of the best ways that librarians support their identities as lifelong learners is through interaction with children's authors and illustrators. At the 2010 conference of the Association for Library Service to Children, one session, entitled "Drawn to Delight: How Picturebooks Work (and Play) Today," offered a substantive look into the world of picture books. At that session, Brian Selznick, who illustrated *The Invention of Hugo Cabret*, helped demonstrate how picture books help people really "learn to see" when looking at art and life around us.

Learning activities with picture books can actively scaffold and support the development of visual, digital, and media literacy competencies. They shouldn't just be thought of as books for children: Picture books can help develop visual literacy among people of all ages. Renee has had success using wordless books, including *Something's Not Quite Right* by French artist Guy Billout. The book shows a variety of surreal images that depict impossible acts, like a man who is lifting up the edge of the ocean to look for his car keys. David Weisner's *Flotsam* received a Caldecott Medal in 2007, and it features a magical story of a boy who finds a camera washed up on the ocean shore. Both books are quite effective tools for initiating visual literacy dialogue with children, older teens, and even adults.

REPRESENTATION AND STEREOTYPES

Film and video, like books, often make use of stereotypes as a shorthand way to depict characters. In young adult literature, you can find the jock, the cheerleader, and the nerd. Of course, there are complex, nuanced, and unpredictable characters, too. The depiction of people in media messages is an issue of *representation*, and this topic has been at the forefront of media literacy for many years. This term describes a concept in cultural studies and media studies where signs and symbols stand in for reality.

Some use the word representation to mean a depiction of something that is already out there in the world. But at the heart of it, the term calls our attention to the larger fact that media messages are constructed to convey meaning through symbols. Through selection and omission, authors make decisions about how to depict events, ideas, people, and stories. They make choices that influence our feelings and attitudes. Librarians deal with the issue of representation when they consider the cultural diversity in the materials they acquire and choose for collections, story hours, book groups, and more.

Inevitably, we must confront the overwhelming presence of stereotypes in media. As with print materials, finding movies that reflect the diversity and complexity of the world we live in can sometimes be a challenge. For example, one study of 400 films and TV shows released in 2014–2015 showed that 28% of characters with dialogue were from non-White racial/ethnic groups, though such groups are nearly 40% of the US population.[9] As Brooks and Hebert wrote, "Much of what audiences know and care about is based on the images, symbols, and narratives in radio, television, film, music, and other media. Individuals construct their social identities by considering how they come to understand what it means to be male, female, rich or poor, foreigner or native-born, black, white, Asian, Latino, Native American—even rural or urban. Our identities are shaped by commodified texts produced by media for audiences that are increasingly segmented by stereotypes of many kinds. Media, in short, are central to how we represent and understand our various social realities."[10]

Writing this book in the immediate aftermath of the release of *Black Panther*, the 2018 Disney/Marvel superhero film directed by Ryan Coogler, we are reminded of the adage, "If you can see it, you can be it." Widespread acceptance of female leaders, happily married gay couples, and even an African American president occurred, in part, because the public became familiar with these representations in entertainment and popular media culture.

Kids appreciate diverse genres of media just as adults do. For children and youth programming, you might provide access, perhaps for the first time, to a documentary film with children's voices, or to a film shot in their own community, state, or region and have the filmmaker come talk about her or his experience in making the film. You might want to introduce a young audience to basic analysis and evaluation of media messages, including looking at patterns of gender representation. When

Pam developed a library film program in Providence, Rhode Island, at the Fox Point Library, she wanted to incorporate all three elements. Like so many urban areas in the United States, Providence is now a "minority majority" city, with a population that in 2019 included 42% Hispanic or Latino, 16% Black or African American, and 6% Asian.

She started her film program by welcoming children to the library and introducing a short film, *Woven*, a music video shot in Providence and created by local filmmakers Sean Greene and Giancarlo Lavall of a day in the life of a skateboarder. It was obviously exciting for the children in the audience to recognize their own local neighborhoods in the short film. But when one of the college-aged filmmakers made an entrance, riding his skateboard into the room, the children's excitement reached a whole new level. They were thrilled to ask him questions and get his autograph. For most of the children in the room, this was the first time they had ever met a real filmmaker.

Film Screenings in Libraries

TAILORING SCREENINGS TO COMMUNITY INTERESTS

Partnering with community or media organizations can be a powerful strategy when the event is responding to something immediately relevant to the community. PBS has well-developed outreach programs that use media screenings and discussions to engage the public; and school, academic, and public librarians are key allies in these efforts. But sometimes librarians, teachers, and parents recognize their own the need to host screening and discussion events just by keeping their ears to the ground and listening to what kids are talking about.

When Netflix premiered the teen drama series *Thirteen Reasons Why* in 2017 (which was adapted from the book by Jay Asher), there was an immediate firestorm from parents, mental health professionals, teachers, and counselors. The show features a high school student and his friend, Hannah, a girl who committed suicide after suffering a series of demoralizing circumstances brought on by people at the school. A box of cassette tapes recorded by Hannah before her suicide details 13 reasons why she ended her life. The series features suicide, mental illness, sexual assault, rape culture, and bullying.

Youth services librarian Robin Brenner partnered with the school district to host a community round table at the Brookline (MA) Public Library in June 2017. She did not want to screen the show; instead, she wanted to create a space where adults and teens could talk through the issues raised by the series. As Brenner notes, "The power of a piece of pop culture, especially in mass media like television or film, can spark conversations across a community." She invited a middle school guidance counselor, a teacher, a clinical graduate intern and peer leader adviser, and three high school students. Most attendees were adults, including representatives from school groups such as the Brookline Public Schools Wellness Committee and the high school library, as well as parents and interested community members. The event helped build a spirit of solidarity among participants, helping them feel united in their efforts to care for the youth in their community.

Sometimes partnerships enable librarians to reach new audiences. In a joint project with the Latina Women's League and the Alachua County Library in Gainesville, Florida, partners organized a 5-week film festival for Hispanic Heritage Month on Saturday afternoons. At these well-attended sessions, which reached over 100 patrons, the vibe was a little different from a normal film screening. According to Travis Fristoe, who works in the Adult Services Department of the Alachua County Library, "People showed up early and stayed late." He explained that this event was very social and interactive. "People seemed excited and interested in what the films would offer. This event also helped raise awareness of the resources the library is able to offer. A few people were not aware of our foreign language section, for example." In Chapter 6, we'll learn much more about the transformative impact of community partnerships.

Best Practices of Planning a Film Screening

PLANNING AND MARKETING

- Read reviews, view films, write reviews, and create lists.
- Give your film program a catchy, memorable name.
- Use themes to group films together into a series.
- Select at least one box-office film that audiences will want to attend.
- Pair it with thematically linked less-known independent, alternative, or documentary films.
- Place announcements in local newspapers and online communities.
- Use social media marketing to raise awareness.
- Create take-away flyers and post them at entrances and exits.

SET-UP

- Use theater-style seating with a center aisle and place additional chairs against the back wall for latecomers.
- Use a late-model data projector and external speakers for the best sound possible.
- Darken room appropriately.
- Test equipment, lighting, and sound before the event.
- Use closed captioning to enable full access to film content by all viewers.
- Have a sign-up sheet for attendees who wish to provide email for future contact.

Best Practices of Film Screening in Libraries

INTRODUCTIONS AND CONCLUSIONS

- Stand at the door and greet people as they arrive.
- Identify yourself by name and welcome attendees to thank them for participating.
- Announce the name of the film, the director, and the year it was created.
- Offer a brief synopsis of the film with no spoilers.
- If any awards have been given to the film, mention one or two.
- Hold up a flyer and promote upcoming film screenings.
- Ask people to silence their cell phones.
- Announce that people can stay for informal discussion afterward if they like.
- End with a question to focus viewer attention or a short phrase that creates anticipation and links to the theme of the film.
- Sit in the room and watch while you also observe the behavior of viewers at key moments in the film.
- Play the film all the way through the complete credit roll.
- Turn the sound down during the credit roll and remind people about the optional postviewing discussion.
- Stand at the door and thank people for attending.
- Listen to comments and chat about the film as people leave.

DISCUSSION

- Thank people for staying and start them off with a general question to discuss using a pair-share activity to warm people up to the process of sharing.
- Use open-ended questions about characters, conflict, and theme to elicit divergent interpretations.
- Invite people to make connections between the film and their own lives, or to another creative work.
- Provide emotional support (using head nodding, smiling) to acknowledge those who share and comment.
- Look for nonverbal clues (yawning, squirming) to determine when it's time to wrap things up.
- Mention the next film event to encourage people to return for another shared viewing experience.

BUILDING A ROBUST FILM SCREENING PROGRAM

Among the most thought-provoking and robust film programs we have found in a public library is called GlenViewings, the film screening program offered at the

Glenview Public Library, a suburban community north of Chicago. In 2017, more than 6,700 patrons attended a film screening event there. They now host four or five screenings a month, with both a 2:00 p.m. matinee and a 6:30 p.m. evening screening every other Friday, along with a special event once a month on Tuesday evenings.

When communications director Jennifer Black first started work at the library, she described the existing film program as "sleepy." Back then, the film screening programs were held in a dank basement room of the old library. The spirit of these programs was rooted in the spirit of "press play and walk away." Black's love of film drove her to reimagine the program, and over a period of 10 years, she has transformed it into a much-beloved community jewel.

Film screenings cost money, of course. But by investing her time and talent, GlenViewings film screening events now attract 80–120 people per event. For some events, she has had to turn people away because the Community Room seats only 180 people.

When she launched the program, she carefully selected films by reading reviews and screening films. She worked with Swank Motion Pictures for the rights to screen more popular films and worked with Film Movement to select foreign and independent films. In developing the marketing materials to promote the program, she created names for each program (which included two or more films as part of a series). "By grouping movies together, it encourages people to see the whole series," Black explained. As her audience grew, Black decided to add a formal focus on postscreening discussions. As part of this work, she developed a film resource guide to launch the program and help her and her team support the needs of patrons. The resource guide offered an opening description of how the films were linked together by theme, followed by information about the director, budget, and awards received for each film.

Because Black knew that each film would deepen people's emotional connection to the topics and characters presented in the film and inspire their intellectual curiosity, she collaborated with library staff to create a list of books, DVDs, and online resources as well as other films addressing the theme and other films by the directors of films showcased in the library film screening series. For example, in 2012, the GlenViewings fall film series was titled "Going Global." To prepare for launching a discussion-based film series, these film resource guides ensured that Black and the library staff were well prepared to support the postscreening needs of their patrons who were inspired to want to read and view more deeply on the important topic of globalization. She selected three films that explore the impact of immigration, divorce, and the AIDS epidemic on families in Los Angeles, Iran, and South Africa. The films for the "Going Global" series included *A Better Life*, a 2011 drama/romance directed by Chris Weitz; *A Separation*, a 2011 drama/

mystery directed by Asghar Farhadi; and *Life, Above All*, a 2010 drama directed by Oliver Schmitz.

In her film discussion guide, Black explains why she selected these three films for the series:

At the center of each film is a child, innocently tossed into a family struggle with cultural forces. Luis Galindo lives under the fear, shame, and insecurity of his father's illegal status, Termeh is forced to choose between her parents buckling under the pressures of a conservative Islamic society, and Chanda must protect her AIDS-stricken mother from the brutal judgment of their village neighbors. Each action taken by the adults in the three very different stories sets in motion almost unbearable responsibilities and decisions for the children.

This orientation to the three films clearly demonstrates the thoughtfulness behind the selection of the films for the series and, more important, we sense how much is to be gained from film's power to enable us to imaginatively enter the world of another.

Another key feature of this same particular series was the screening of *War Horse*, Steven's Spielberg's Great War film that was scheduled as part of a Veterans Day matinee showing. A salute to the soldiers of the era and a spectacularly visual film, *War Horse* demonstrates the tragic impact of war— touching even a horse called into wartime service. With six 2012 Oscar nominations, including Best Picture, this tale of "loyalty, hope, and tenacity" on November 11 commemorates the end of the "war to end all wars."

Black's resource guide lists works of fiction and nonfiction based on the themes for each film. For the film about immigrants in Los Angeles, she lists fiction, including *Tortilla Curtain* by T. C. Boyle and the nonfiction book *Illegal People* by David Bacon. For the film about the family in Iran, she includes *Saved by Beauty* by Roger Housedon, a book that describes Housden's encounters with the scholars and artists who embody the deep humanistic tradition in Iran. To pair up with *Life Above All*, the librarians selected a work by acclaimed South African writer Zakes Mda entitled *Sometimes There Is a Void: Memoirs of an Outsider.* For the intellectually curious, the film resource guide invited patrons to explore DVDs on tourism in Iran, a selection of stories written about life in South Africa by Nobel Laureate Nadine Gordimer, and more than a dozen other films on the themes of immigration, divorce, and the AIDS crisis. This film resource guide, part of the GlenViewings tradition for 4 years, firmly established the credibility of the library staff as thought leaders in quality film and media selections, demonstrating that they were highly competent to provide patrons with advice on films that extend upon and advance the topics explored in the film series.

GlenViewings Schedule

MONTH OF FEBRUARY 2018

Just drop in; no tickets required. A casual, audience-led discussion follows matinee screenings.

February 2
80S MOVIE NIGHT

5:00 p.m. Join the Teen Advisory Board (TAB) for an 80s movie night featuring the classics *Ferris Bueller's Day Off* and *Sixteen Candles*. Hang with friends, enjoy snacks, and experience life as a teen back in the 80s. Just drop in.

February 15
PASS THE ENVELOPE, PLEASE: A NIGHT AT THE OSCARS

6:30 p.m. Just days before this year's Oscars, long-time *Daily Herald* movie critic Dann Gire and film historian and novelist Raymond Benson offer a fun-filled "star-studded" evening. This dynamic duo will share film clips and quips about the movies and actors nominated this year. A great way to catch up on this year's crop of Oscar nominees. Register by telephone or sign up at the Reader Services Desk.

February 16
STRONGER

At 2:00 p.m and 6:30 p.m. The inspiring real-life story of Jeff Bauman, an ordinary man who captured the hearts of his city and the world to become a symbol of hope after surviving the 2013 Boston Marathon bombing and loss of his legs.

February 23
VICTORIA AND ABDUL

At 2 p.m. and 6:30 p.m. Queen Victoria strikes up an unlikely friendship with a young Indian clerk, Abdul Karim. They form a devoted alliance that her household and inner circle attempt to destroy.

February 25
THE FLORIDA PROJECT

At 1:30 p.m. A precocious 6-year-old and her troubled mother live in the shabby shadows of Disneyworld. A rare glimpse into this struggling, transient population raises sobering questions about modern America.

How did Jennifer Black develop these film programs in the beginning? When she first started creating library film programs, she relied on a friend in the film industry to offer direction and advice. "He helped me at the beginning to find a way to go," she explains as she described how she experimented with classic movies, first-run movies, foreign films, and more. It was a process of trial and error. "We tried a lot of different things," she explained. "When we started, we would get sometimes between 5 and 50 people, but that changed when we moved to a modern new facility in 2010."

The Glenview Public Library Community Room, just steps from the main entrance, offers two large projection screens for both sides of the room and state-of-the-art surround sound. One thing Black insists upon is the use of closed captioning. "It's a little bit controversial, and some people are annoyed by it. But because we have seniors as well as a substantial immigrant Korean community, captioning helps them both. We think it's important because it increases access—and as a library, we are all about that," she explained.

By collaborating with a Chicago-based documentary company, Kartemquin Films, they have been able to host screening events of documentary films where the film director answers questions at the end of the program. Black also collaborates with her library colleagues in other departments. In trying to break down the silos between departments, they have started to collaborate on film screenings for teens. At one event, they hosted a screening of the classic film *The Wizard of Oz* as an audience participation event, where a master of ceremonies led the audience through several participation activities before the film starts, including wand waving and a floor maze designed as a yellow brick road. Participants sang along to their favorite songs, including "Follow the Yellow Brick Road," "Ding Dong the Witch Is Dead," and many others, as the words were projected on the film screen.

CHALLENGE: FILM SCREENINGS WITH NO DISCUSSION

One fine summer day, Renee and a 6-year-old young friend stumbled into a public library to check out a summertime film screening event. Sadly, it was an unmemorable experience. We had learned about the event from a poster at the library that showed an image of the DVD cover, the name of the film, the date, and time. The movie was *Sing*, a 2016 3D computer-animated film directed and written by Garth Jennings. The story, set in a world like ours but inhabited by animals of all shapes, sizes, and personalities, features a singing contest and includes more than 60 songs from artists, including Stevie Wonder and Ariana Grande along with the vocal talents of Matthew McConaughey, Reese Witherspoon, and Seth MacFarlane. The fast-paced plot, variety of adorable characters, and the challenges and conflicts they experience, plus the familiarity of the pop music and references to pop culture, of course, were crowd-pleasing ingredients.

But the library event itself was rooted in the spirit of a phrase well known in the worlds of both library and education, "Just hit play and walk away." This term refers to the relative ease of hosting a film screening in a public library or using video in school to deliver content to learners.[11] We arrived in the all-purpose room of the library, along with about 25 other parents and children aged 6 to 60. The children's librarian had set up the data projector at the front of the room along with some comfy pillows near the front and chairs in rows with a center aisle. There was a table set up with glasses of water and small bags of popcorn. So far, so good.

But the librarian's welcome and introduction to the film were uninformative and disappointing. She did not introduce herself or explain briefly why she selected this film for screening. She did not offer any previewing questions to create an active viewing stance among parents and children. She did not even provide any information about the film, including a mention of its title, director, or the year it was created. The audience was not informed of the running time, and the poster advertising the event inaccurately listed it as a 1-hour program.

Can you imagine a librarian reading a book without mentioning the title or the author? She merely said, "Let's get started now," as she popped in the DVD and navigated the player controls to access the film. Because the librarian had not set up external speakers, the sound quality was tinny and thin coming through the internal speaker of the data projector. Considering that the film was a musical, the lack of external speakers made the viewing experience truly subpar.

Today, because many people have large-screen home theater displays in the home, an old data projector without sufficient light quality or external speakers can significantly erode the quality of the viewing experience, especially when the room is not sufficiently darkened. At the end of the film, as the credits rolled, the librarian returned to the front of the room to promote another upcoming children's event. She said nothing about the film we had just viewed and enjoyed. At the back of the room were crayons and preprinted cartoon worksheet pages with characters from the film. That was it. The event was over. Parents and children filed out of the room. One or two took a worksheet to color at home. There was no interaction whatsoever between participants, even though it seemed like there was an interest among parents and teens in sharing reactions to the film.

As Renee returned back into the hallway, she made eye contact with attendees. She struck up a conversation with some of the children and teens who had attended the screening and who were hanging out, waiting to be picked up. Wanting to talk about the film, she simply asked, "I wonder: who was your favorite character?"

Some among the group of children in the hallway were eager to talk. "I liked Buster," said one Latino girl, about 9 years old. "He worked hard to make the singing contest a success." Another girl described Meena, the timid teenage elephant with an enormous case of stage fright. When asked why she liked the character, she explained, "She's scared to sing to an audience, but she gets over her fear with help from the others."

Renee explained how she liked Gunter, the goofy, spandex-wearing pig who is a terrible singer but supremely enthusiastic about performing. Kids smiled, appreciating the choice. Then one 11-year-old African American boy said, "I liked Johnny the gorilla."

"Why?" Renee asked.

"He's trying to avoid becoming like his dad," the boy said. Everyone laughed. We looked around and nodded at each other. Everyone in the conversation had identified with a different character in the story. And, in this film, there were so many different characters to like. Kids then spontaneously shared details about the favorite songs they liked from the movie; they were proud to be able to tell me how the songs were spin-offs of contemporary pop music they recognized from stars like Taylor Swift, John Legend, and Lady Gaga.

Renee's 10-minute conversation with the kids in the hallway reminded her of the central importance of talking about the media we consume. A big part of the significance of seeing a film in a public setting outside the home is the chance to interact with others and share interpretations. Through discussion, children came to appreciate some of the film's characters in a new way. Without discussion, a sense of community cannot form.

CHALLENGE: MANAGING TIME AND TALENT

It can be difficult to design film programs that create community, given the constraints of time and talent. One of the challenges often cited by librarians when talking about film programs is scheduling. Everyone wants to know: What is the best time for a film program event? Most librarians agree that film events should occur at regular, recurring times during the week or the month. But it takes a process of careful experimentation to find times that work best for potential patrons. For example, a 10 a.m. or 2 p.m. screening may be better for older people, who prefer to get an out-of-the-home adventure during the daytime. For working people, a 6:30 p.m. screening may be ideal. In an academic library, college students may appreciate a midnight screening!

When public librarians talk about film screenings, they sometimes ask: Who staffs these programs? There are a wide range of approaches used in public libraries based on the size of the library and the interests of librarians. In public libraries, sometimes a dedicated Communications and Outreach Librarian is responsible for film programming. Other times, the job of programming a film event falls to the Adult Services librarian.

Although some universities and colleges have active film screening and discussion programs with dedicated staff, others do not. Librarian Laura Jenemann at George Mason University has developed a very helpful guide for faculty who might be interested in hosting a screening event on campus. She clearly sees faculty as full-fledged partners in initiating on-campus screening events. Sometimes those responsible for student services are key partners. For example, at the Albion

College Student Life website, a special section labeled "Movie Viewing" explains the guidelines for securing public performance rights for screening by student organizations, fraternities, and sororities.[12]

Staffing issues are a very real limitation in many libraries. In a robust dialogue on the #ALATT Facebook page, librarians weigh in on staffing strategies for film programs. Because these programs often occur in the evenings, they sometimes present particular staffing challenges. For film screenings that target adults, the film program is sometimes staffed with "low-level" personnel, including pages or reliable volunteers. Some librarians feel comfortable leaving viewers alone in the screening room. In other libraries, union rules prohibit the use of pages, part-timers, circulation staff, and volunteers for any program-related services, and full-time information staff must be present for film events.

Sadly, we have observed that some librarians multitask during movie screenings, by sitting in the back and working on their laptops answering emails or ordering books. Some librarians start the movie, make sure it's playing well and sounds good, and then quietly exit. Perhaps this is required due to busy schedules and the demands of the job, of course. But all of these actions send a clear signal that film viewing is just not a high priority, worthy of full attention.

By contrast, some librarians who have vibrant, well-attended film programs make every effort to attend and interact with patrons, recognizing that film screening events are opportunities for community and relationship development. For example, Jennifer Black makes a point to greet patrons as they enter the Community Room. She watches the film along with patrons to notice how people engage with the content and stands at the exit after the film concludes in order to solicit or overhear feedback. These practices help her develop a real relationship with library patrons, and this informs her decisions about future programming.

PARTNERING WITH PBS ON VIEWING AND DISCUSSION PROGRAMS

Public broadcasting outreach professionals have significant experience in partnering with librarians to promote films and television programs. In 2017, working in collaboration with the American Library Association, WETA and PBS developed programming support opportunities for 50 public libraries who received *The Vietnam War* by Ken Burns and Lynn Novick, which offers a complex interpretation of the war in relation to colonialism, propaganda, leadership, and the changing American cultural landscape. The film aired on PBS in 2017 and reached more than 33 million viewers, making it the second highest Ken Burns film ever.

At the heart of the film are interviews with men and women service members, journalists, civilians, protesters, diplomats, intelligence officers, and prisoners of war, including people from both North and South Vietnam. The study guide for the film notes:

The film does not seek to find a single interpretive lens through which to understand the war. Documentary film as a medium is uniquely suited for presenting a story with divergent perspectives, allowing a range of viewpoints to be placed side by side for audiences to consider and interpret. The film acknowledges and builds its narrative around the enormous complexity of its subject and embraces as an essential part of its story the profound differences and disagreements that tore apart lives and nations.

The American Library Association created a film guide with suggestions for screening and discussion events. The guide notes that people with posttraumatic stress disorder (PTSD) may participate in screenings and programs. It recommends including a caveat noting that the film excerpts and discussions may trigger anxiety or anger, especially for those with PTSD, and suggests that, at the opening of the event, a skilled program facilitator should "acknowledge that the film screening or program might cause intense feelings and anxiety for those that served in or survived the war."[13]

The film guide suggests pairing the documentary with feature films that have addressed the subject of the Vietnam War, including such films as *Birdy*, the 1984 film by Alan Parker that features the power of friendship in relation to the emotional and physical scars that haunted Vietnam veterans upon their return home. However, at the Peoria Public Library, only two people showed up when they screened *Born on the Fourth of July*, the 1990 biopic from director Oliver Stone that recounts the story of Ron Kovic, a gung-ho American patriot who returns from Vietnam paralyzed from the waist down and becomes an antiwar activist. Perhaps it was because they scheduled the program on opening day of deer hunting season, which one librarian noted is "practically a state holiday" in Iowa.[14]

The guide also includes suggestions for exhibitions, music, and art programs in addition to the use of lecturers and panel discussions. As expected from a guide produced by the American Library Association's Public Programs Office, the film guide also suggests an admirably long list of books on the Vietnam War. But missing from the film guide are any suggestions about how to lead a postviewing discussion or specific insights on meeting the needs of immigrant communities.

So librarians who developed film programs for Ken Burns' *The Vietnam War* series experienced some successes and some failures, as is to be expected. When Mandy Carrico was charged with developing a film screening for the Harris County Public Libraries in Houston, she decided to spread the screenings and events out across six of the libraries. (After all, the Houston metropolitan area is larger than the State of Rhode Island!) She and her team were able to find local experts, including Albert Nahas, author of *Warriors Remembered*. All these programs drew tiny but enthusiastic audiences.

Figure 2.2 Two versions of a film poster promoting PBS's *The Vietnam War.*

But Houston librarians learned a lot by developing a program for Vietnamese residents who live near the Parker Williams Branch. As they prepared the program, they intended to use a film clip and host a book discussion. However, librarians learned that the original marketing materials created for the program, shown on the left in Figure 2.2, which featured an image of the film's DVD cover art, activated feelings of loss and sadness. Vietnamese residents told librarians that they were resistant to attend such an event. Also notice how the first version of the poster advertised multiple dates and events. This could be confusing. Responsive to feedback, librarians adjusted the marketing and created a new poster, shown in Figure 2.2. on the right-hand side. They renamed the program "Vietnamese in Houston." The poster promoted a single event. The session included an open-dialogue program that gave people a choice to enjoy Vietnamese food and crafts while listening to local residents telling their immigration stories or viewing the film. With the active support of a Vietnamese-speaking librarian, 58 patrons showed up.[15] In Chapter 8, we'll learn more about research on film screenings in libraries that aim to explore whether or not PBS–library partnerships activate civic engagement.

Connecting Authors and Audiences

THE VALUE OF FILMMAKER/AUTHOR VISITS

Librarians have always treasured author visits, and there is a wealth of "how-to" advice on organizing them. The American Library Association even offers an award to support an author visit, funded by an annual gift from Simon & Schuster

Children's Publishing. Learning about how an author or illustrator creates a book demystifies the creative process. It can strengthen the professional expertise of librarians and teachers, and it can motivate children's interest in reading and writing. When students are able to ask questions to real authors, it transforms their learning from something that just happens at school to the kind of learning that "feels real."

A visit from a filmmaker gives audiences a chance to learn more directly about a filmmaker's motivation. It can also empower people with a sense of possibility in relation to creative works of the imagination. Too often, when film and media are used in the classroom, the author of the film or television program is not identified. In Renee's Digital Authorship course, she likes to use the term *authorship* in a truly multimodal sense, describing the work of photographers, filmmakers, poets, novelists, and graphic designers as authors. The media literacy question "Who is the author?" is intentionally designed to evoke a dual focus on both individual and institutional authorship. Students can learn about individual production roles, including screenwriter, producer, and executive producer, and they can understand how production companies and distribution companies support a film's creation and distribution in a complex and multifaceted marketplace.

When a teacher or librarian introduces a film by saying, "This is by Frontline," "This is from the History Channel," or "I found this on YouTube," she or he is shortchanging a media literacy education opportunity to deepen learners' understanding of individual and institutional authorship. Precise language about authorship helps people think more deeply about concepts like purpose, motivation, and tone.

When Renee and her students developed a partnership with an elementary school in suburban Philadelphia, the school district was deeply committed to integrating technology into the curriculum; computers and interactive white boards were in plentiful supply. Teachers wanted to use film to support children's emotional identification with the people and cultures of the Middle East. Massachusetts-based filmmaker Raouf Zaki created a short independent film titled *Santa Claus in Baghdad*, based on a children's story of the same name by Elsa Marston, which tells the story of a family whose lives are disrupted by the US embargo in 1980. In this story, a young boy believes that Santa Claus is coming to Baghdad when his teacher reads a book about the mythical character and his family awaits a visit from Uncle Omar from the United States.[16]

Grade 3 students watched the film and discussed the moral lessons embedded in the film that focus on the values of family love; appreciation of teachers, books, and learning; and the blessings of a generous spirit. Some classroom teachers read aloud with their students the short story that the film is based on to explore basic concepts in literary adaptation. Teachers also used the film to stimulate writing activities and art projects related to students' feelings and thoughts about the film.[17]

We encouraged teachers to screen the "making of" video that accompanied the feature film, where they learned about the process of recreating the Baghdad book market, which was filmed in a warehouse in Framingham, Massachusetts. Then we helped arrange a classroom visit from the filmmaker, Raouf Zaki, who participated in a question-and-answer session with students. We observed high levels of engagement from students during this activity. Children asked a range of thoughtful questions, offering questions such as the following:

- Why did you make the film?
- What was it like working with child actors?
- How long did it take to make the film?
- How did you decide who would play the different characters?

Many children excitedly came up to the filmmaker after the session and asked for his autograph. Interview data from teachers revealed that they noticed a connection between the children's ability to recognize stereotypes, their careful viewing of the film, and their new knowledge of Middle Eastern culture.[18]

VIRTUAL AUTHOR/FILMMAKER VISITS

Children benefit from the chance to see a filmmaker as a type of author even when the individual is present virtually through recorded or synchronous video. When Kate Spiller worked with Grade 1 students at the Russell Byers Charter School in Philadelphia as part of the Powerful Voices for Kids project, she wanted students to be able to understand and abstract concepts like target audience, purpose, and types of authorship. She showed students a short film created by the African American filmmaker and writer Barry Jenkins, who wrote and directed *Moonlight*, a coming-of-age film about an African American young man, which won the 2016 Academy Award for Best Picture. Spiller asked the children to imagine questions to ask the filmmaker. Using the question formulation technique, the children generated questions for the filmmaker to answer.

In response, Barry Jenkins composed a video to "talk back to the kids." Figure 2.3 shows a screenshot from the video he created. Jenkins answered the questions, one by one, incorporating a musical soundtrack as he addressed each child's question. Jenkins explained how he worked to create a film with friends he went to school with and how writing stories and writing films are very similar processes. He described his work as "independent media," which means he's "making film because he wants to say things." He shows clips from some of the short films he has made, and he describes his target audience as "people who we don't see that much in movies, like me." He explained that when you see what's on TV and realize that it's not showing a topic or issue that's important to you, then you can

Figure 2.3 Filmmaker Barry Jenkins makes a virtual author visit.

make a film so that other people can see it. He explains, "I made movies for people who are underrepresented."[19]

Kate Spiller and Barry Jenkins called this a *call-and-response project*, reflecting the African American tradition of robust interaction between performer and audience, such as that which occurs at public gatherings, religious rituals, and musical performances. As a culminating experience, Spiller videotaped as kids viewed Jenkins's video response and discussed their feelings. After viewing, children asked even more questions.

Most important, the children experienced a profound emotional reaction in feeling heard and listened to. One student said, "I felt surprised that he actually answered the questions in person." Another said, "I felt like I wanted to cry." Another child noted that the music was influencing her feelings, noting, "I felt sad because of the music." One child noted, "He used our names when he answered the questions, and that made me feel happy." As Jenkins explained, you can see "the palpable epiphany of how video, the web, and the act of questioning can open the world when those tools are properly harnessed."[20]

Author visits connect learners to the real-world media production. But merely meeting an author through face-to-face or virtual engagement is not all that students can do to make real-world connections. School librarian Sue Dahlstrom of the Wayne Elementary School in Radnor, Pennsylvania, not only arranged for children to meet popular children's author James Agee, but children also produced their own "remix" responses to his book *The Life of a Retired Kid* to present to him when he visited the school. As a result, they interacted with the author's text more deeply by creating their own work as part of the reading process.

Considering the Needs of Children and Families

DIGITAL MEDIA IN LIBRARY STORYTIME

The paradigm of risk and harm that has dominated the dialogue about media, children, and youth has probably limited the level of innovation in the uses of digital media in both early childhood education and in public library programs. Otherwise, we would expect to see more varied and frequent description of the uses of audiovisual media in these contexts. But there is some important momentum in the field of librarianship in relation to the use of nonprint film and digital media resources for children.

One of the mainstays of library services to children is storytime, where library professionals plan and implement early learning experiences designed to expose families with young children to high-quality content. In storytime, librarians model strategies for engaging young children in literacy-supportive practices. These efforts are often based around parent engagement models like Every Child Ready to Read (ECRR), Mother Goose on the Loose, Prime Time Family Reading Time, and others. Evaluation and curation of children's media have always been essential elements in the children's librarian's job description, along with the planning and implementation of programs for babies, toddlers, and preschoolers, and the adults who love them. With the swiftly changing realities of the digital age, however, that job description is changing and expanding.

Some children's librarians are beginning to incorporate new media into library collections, services, and programs for young children and their families. And some libraries are beginning to use apps or e-books in storytime programming. In these programs, librarians demonstrate and model how particular apps can be used as part of healthy media consumption experiences. Children's librarians may even make recommendations to parents at the reference desk about how to best use media together at home or to share the latest research on the intentional and appropriate use of new media with very young children with child care centers and teachers.[21]

Cen Campbell has been a pioneer in helping children's librarians explore the potential of new media in library programming for children. She founded a professional learning coalition of over 200 children's librarians interested in digital media called Little e-Lit, which is helping children's librarians incorporate new media into library collections, services, and programs for young children and their families. She has enrolled numerous children's librarians into moving away from the "books are better" ideology that has dominated the field for decades.

When a librarian uses an app during library storytime, parents learn that tablets are not just a babysitting device. Such informal parent education can make a big difference to a generation of parents who aren't sure how digital media should be used in the home with young children. Along with her colleague Claudia Haynes, whose Never Shushed blog is a great resource for children's librarians, they've identified how librarians can be *media mentors*. This important initiative has led to the development of a number of promising practices for the use of new media in library collections, services, and programs for young children. When the use of digital devices, apps, and tablets is intentional and appropriate, young children can benefit from the use of new media in storytime.[22]

Children's librarians may be eager to incorporate new media into library collections, service, and programs because they understand that reading on digital devices is a normal reading practice for many families. When mom is reading a newspaper article or Facebook post on her cell phone, children will naturally be curious about what they can read on these devices, too. Librarians help bring the right resources to the right people at the right time, and increasingly, some of those resources are digital, even for the youngest of children.

Since digital picture books are now available as a reading choice for many families, librarians are applying their traditional skill set to new formats of books and other media. For example, Amy Wright at the Garfield County Public Library District in Colorado, created digital felt boards at her library's new media storytime. Children's media researchers are discovering that when it comes to comprehension, "*how* parents talked to their children remained an important element of the book-reading experience while the *type* of book was less important."[23] The physical proximity and orientation between adult and child, the order and timing of the pages read, the tone of voice, and the content of the adult language, including comments and questions, all have an influence on the child's behavior and engagement.

Librarians can see that there is a need for curation and readers' advisory services in the children's digital media marketplace. Carisa Kluver, the editor of DigitalStorytime.com, offers assistance to those trying to make sense of the ever-growing app industry. There are a lot of players in the crowded field of children's apps, and the quality can be uneven. App developers like Toca Boca have developed a track record of success that inspire confidence among parents and children's media professionals. Today, it's more and more likely that apps have been designed with the needs of children in mind. More and more, apps enable children to create media as a natural interconnection between the practices of reading and writing. One of Renee's favorite apps is Shadow Puppet, which enables children as young as age 5 to create their own simple movies by combining video, recorded voice, still photos, titles, music, and more.

To understand the choices available, librarians may read reviews from DigitalStorytime.com, Common Sense Media, and Children's Media Review in making selections for their libraries and offering guidance to parents. Parents benefit from seeing the educational use of apps modeled by librarians and caregivers and appreciate reliable recommendations from trusted sources for high-quality, age-appropriate content.

Because adoption rates for mobile technology are increasing exponentially, even for young children, children's librarians who get stuck in the "print books are better" trap will find themselves less and less able to meet the genuine needs of families in their communities.

Librarians can support the development of people in at-risk communities by intentionally and appropriately using new media in programming for young children. Lisa Guernsey and Michael Levine note that supporting and empowering underresourced and vulnerable families has become an imperative for education leaders nationwide. Although a majority of low-income parents see the library as a valuable resource, only 22% of children's librarians report having digital devices available for programs including demonstration and mentoring, and only 2% report offering programs for nonnative speakers. To move forward, librarians and community leaders need to take stock of the real needs of people in their communities, participate in professional learning programs, invest in physical infrastructure, and create a cycle of continuous improvement.[24]

EDITING OUT OBJECTIONABLE CONTENT FROM MOVIES

What options do parents have if they want to see the latest Hollywood films, but they don't want all the sex, violence, or other objectionable content in the movies they watch? Actually, a number of software services provide clipping or filtering services for home use. For example, Vid Angel, whose motto is "Watch Movies However the BLEEP You Want," is a subscription service that allows users to personally select filters for objectionable content they find on Netflix or other streaming services. When users purchase the content, they obtain the right to apply filters to objectionable content in their home. The company says, "Producers and directors should have the personal freedom to create whatever movies and TV shows they choose. We condemn censorship of their content in the public sphere. But individuals, in the privacy of their homes, should have the personal freedom to watch that content any way they choose."[25]

Another company, Clear Play, is a subscription services that works with streaming movies purchased through Amazon. You can select which types of content to omit, including violence, sex, nudity, and vulgarity. Companies like this benefit from the Family Entertainment and Copyright Act, which legally protects companies who create software to sanitize potentially offensive DVD and video-on-demand content. It's popular among religious conservatives because they can watch television without being exposed to offensive content. The legal language protecting these filtering services says that, for the services these companies provide, (1) the filtering must occur during the viewing; (2) a tangible edited version (a "fixed copy") cannot be created; and (3) the only place the filtered films can be seen is in a private home (i.e., no public performances of the version are permitted).[26]

As you might expect, we have mixed feelings about digital services like this. On the one hand, we value digital tools that can help parents and families make good choices about media content, and we applaud efforts to protect children from potentially harmful content. However, like many of you readers, we find censorship distasteful and find these services somewhat troubling.

What options do educators have when it comes to the objectionable content that can be found in otherwise wonderful and educationally valuable films? Educators and librarians have faced situations where they wanted to bring short segments of a film into the classroom for learning purposes, but they want to omit certain portions, too. Perhaps they want to remove a sexual double entendre in a scene with a lot of dialogue, fearing that might distract students. Maybe they want to remove a fight scene in a film because it was too long or simply not relevant to the learning goal.

Under Section 110(1) of the Copyright Act, an instructor can use any legally acquired copyrighted material in the classroom for face-to-face teaching. Because teachers aim to use classroom time well, showing short portions of a film is recognized as socially responsible. Deciding which portions to show is the responsibility of the educator.

Let us make this perfectly clear: Making a copy of a copyright work (including print, visual, audiovisual, audio, or digital works), editing portions of it, and using it in the classroom is lawful. It always has been. Sometimes the media industry (represented by MPAA and the RIAA and Warner Brothers) tells educators that they don't have the right to copy digital media content because they could rely on DVD playback technologies to fast-forward or skip chapters. They may want you to believe that making a copy of a scene in a movie is inherently unlawful. They may want to exploit fear, uncertainty, and doubt. As Renee explained in her book *Copyright Clarity: How Fair Use Supports Digital Learning*, this was a trick designed to erode fair use. Too many people fall for it, sadly. We know plenty of librarians, technology specialists, and teachers whose understanding of copyright and fair use is shaky, and the fear and doubt they carry around stifle their own potentially creative and effective use of media for learning purposes.[27]

Although fast-forwarding the DVD or skipping through movie chapters may be an appropriate method for some situations, we would not want to set up hierarchies saying it's preferable to or better than creating short video clips. English and film professor Peter DeCherney offered a very powerful demonstration of the pedagogical limitations of fast forwarding and chapter skipping to the Copyright Office. For some learning situations, it's essential to have one or more digital clips that have been copied from the whole film. As a result of the DMCA 1201 exemptions for educators, it is legal to bypass copy protection software to make a copy for educational use.[28] Many media teachers rely on fair use for the ability to curate multiple film clips to show specific portions, or even to show whole films, minus certain scenes.

Some people may object to omitting portions of a film based on their ideas about the moral rights of authors or some other ideas about the integrity of the film as an artwork or best practice in pedagogy. But Section 110(1) of the Copyright Act, in particular, respects educators' judgment on the matter of selecting print, visual, audio, or digital content for learning purposes. Whether you agree or disagree with the teacher's judgment is irrelevant. She has the right to select content to meet the learning needs of her students. Even when she makes a poor pedagogical choice, the law allows for her autonomy. We should be grateful that the law doesn't interpose the wishes of school leaders, filmmakers, politicians, school board members, experts—or even librarians—in this regard.

FOCUS ON SOCIAL MEDIA

There is intense attention and concern around how social media platforms are shaping the next generation. Many parents struggle to find the fabled happy medium between policing their children's screen time and building enough trust to leave teens to their devices. The first line of parental defense is often the limited or monitored use of social media and digital devices. And while instilling an appreciation for time spent disconnected is critical, it can be a disservice to teens' realities to wall off all tech and treat all screen time as equal. The documentary film *Screenagers*, directed by Delaney Ruston in 2016, takes us to the front lines of parenting in a digital age. Ruston made a video to document the decision she must make about when to get her daughter a cell phone.

Not all parents are so troubled by their children's use of digital devices. On the other side of the argument, many who embrace the tech tide, including teens themselves, argue that they know what they're doing and there's no need to worry. And sure, the ever-growing population that can be labeled as digital natives can bring up a YouTube video faster than a speeding bullet or navigate an app with a single swipe, but without structured discussion and education, they wouldn't necessarily understand the impact their interactions online could have on themselves or their peers.

Viewing media is more likely to occur on a cell phone than ever before, for teens and adults alike. That teenagers use and interact through digital means at rates well beyond the generations before them is no secret and no surprise given the myriad ways in which digital media is integrated with everyday tasks and daily life. From homework to social networks, there are roughly a million reasons for teens to keep their digital technology within reach at all times. As for exactly what teenagers are doing online and on which platforms, that changes as steadily as software update prompts. The younger generations gravitate toward the most popular platforms used among their peers, and by the time adults catch on to the trend, teens move on. Honestly, if Grandma has an account, teens are well on their way to finding the next networked frontier.

Digital Bytes

Viewing media sparks people's thinking. Dialogue and conversation can be a highly effective way to advance digital and media literacy competencies. Using a series of online screening and discussion activities that include watching videos and commenting on them, teens can consider a variety of digital and media literacy issues by using the Digital Bytes curriculum developed by Common Sense Media.[29] Some examples of videos featured in the series include:

Copy-Paste Culture: What's the difference between being inspired by others' creative work and copying others' creative ideas? What crosses the line legally? How about ethically?

Micro-Lingo: How has technology changed the way we communicate? Has texting redefined how our brains process information? How has the development of emoticons influenced our emotional ability to connect with others?

Online Tracking: Who is keeping track of what we do online, and why?

Selling Out: How are advertisers and marketers targeting our youth?

The Power of Likes: How does showing our preferences online generate data that companies and individuals can use?

Haters and Trolls: What are the differences among teasing, harassing, cyber-bullying, and trolling online?

Gender and the Media: How is one's perception of oneself shaped by the media?

Instafamous: How has social media changed the concept of "celebrity," and what implication does this have?

Step Forward: What are the advantages of using the Internet to engage people in social causes? What are the limitations?

Disconnected: What does it mean to have a healthy media diet?

DIGITAL CITIZENSHIP

In many communities, school librarians are charged with providing a focus on digital citizenship, which includes competencies required for accessing and using digital resources; digital etiquette and the social norms associated with appropriate behavior and language; legal and ethical norms, including plagiarizing, identity theft, and cyberbullying; and privacy and safety issues associated with data security and platform capitalism.

In some states, groups of educators and librarians have helped to pass legislation designed to expand school and district access to digital citizenship and media literacy.

Renee and Pam collaborated to lobby Rhode Island state legislators to pass legislation to incorporate "Media Literacy" into Rhode Island's Basic Education Plan. The legislation was signed into law on July 19, 2017, by the governor of Rhode Island.

Digital citizenship is about access as it relates to the normative behaviors and knowledge that are needed for responsible participation in digital culture. It seems like the term has been around forever, but really the term emerged only in the early 2000s, according to Mike Ribble. He reminds us that when students started to bring mobile phones into schools, it caused a variety of problems with classroom management. By the middle of the decade, YouTube was capturing the interest of children and teens, and educators began to recognize the need to address the emerging shifts in social norms that were occurring from children's out-of-school uses of media and technology. Although schools created legal-type documents called "acceptable use policies" to control and regulate student behavior, it was clear that such documents were not enough.[30] Learning was needed to help students understand why social norms about technology use are important. So the term was used to describe lessons on legal and socially appropriate uses of the Internet and social media.

For some educators, digital citizenship implies broader ethical, social, and cultural issues, including approaches to rectify the significant inequalities of access to information as well as the uses of digital media for social justice. Many of us who were exploring media and technology in education framed these issues as "the social impacts of technology." When the International Society of Technology in Education included a focus on social issues, they emphasized the value of teachers who understand the social, ethical, legal, and human issues surrounding the use of technology in PK–12 schools and apply those principles in practice. But few curricula in digital citizenship include attention to information inequality, social justice, user rights and responsibilities under platform capitalism, or engaging in civic action through the use of digital texts, tools, and technologies.

Instead, the term *digital citizenship* focuses on protecting children and teens from potentially risky, dangerous, or illegal behavior. As Ohler traces the history of the term in his book *Digital Community, Digital Citizen*, it's obvious that pervasive fears about the Internet anchor and underlie the concept. Digital citizenship curriculum stems from a powerful urge to protect children and young people from potential risks and harms that result from using the Internet. Sonia Livingstone has catalogued those potential risks and harms to include aggression, sexuality, values, and commercial content. As Figure 2.4 shows, risks come from the content that is accessed online, the contact between users, and the user's own conduct or behavior. These three types of risk prove to be useful for learners themselves who are conceptualizing the nature of online safety and social responsibility.

Naturally, teachers and parents are concerned about the unintended consequences of students' engagement with digital media and the Internet. Cyberbullying and sexting concern parents more than copyright violation, but fears about privacy are

	CONTENT	CONTACT	CONDUCT
Role of Child	Viewer-Reader	Participant	Perpetrator or Victim
Aggression	Depictions of violence	Harassment or stalking	Bullying
Sexuality	Pornography	Grooming, sexual talk & abusive behavior	Sexual harassment, sexting
Commercial	Advertising and embedded marketing	Personal data exploitation and misuse	Gambling, copyright infringement
Values	Racist or hateful speech	Ideological persuasion	Creating or using harmful content

Figure 2.4 Potential risks and harms of media use.

Source: Adapted from Livingstone, S., & Haddon, L. (2009). *Kids online: Opportunities and risks for children*. Bristol, UK: Polity Press.

now on the rise as well. Still, digital citizenship curricula in the United States do little to address pornographic content, grooming, or sexual abuse. We believe that digital citizenship curriculum should continue to develop creative ways to have educational dialogue about pornography, a topic that's just beginning to be explored in the context of media literacy education.

According to Maggie Jones, porn is affecting young people's attitudes about sexuality, and it's a topic that adults find difficult to discuss with children and youth. But educators are finding creative ways to open up dialogue about this important (and often taboo) topic.[31] People also need opportunities to understand and evaluate commercial risks like online gambling, advertising and embedded marketing, conspiracy theories, hoaxes and scams, and personal data exploitation for political purposes. Although it will take courage and a spirit of experimentation to discover what works, librarians are well poised to support these information needs by providing innovative educational programs and services.

CULTIVATION EFFECTS

Some children's librarians are concerned about the rise of consumerism as it affects child development. Parents and children request books based on licensed media characters and toys such as Dora, Diego, Barbie, Transformers, and many others. Children's librarian Jill Bickford wonders:

How can libraries promote creativity and imagination through services and collections in a world where popular television characters dominate children's products such as toys, books, clothing, vitamins, packaged foods, and toothbrushes?

She recommends that children's librarians limit the amount of attention given to books that feature characters from films, mass media, and popular culture.[32] Although we appreciate her interest in addressing the problem of consumerism, we see the solution in education, not in limiting access or reducing visibility.

When it comes to consumer culture, media influence our attitudes and behaviors in complicated ways that are still not fully understood. Because human attention is such a valuable commodity, advertising is the primary funding mechanism for radio, television, newspapers, magazines, the Internet, and social media. After all, when you have someone's attention, you can influence her knowledge, attitudes, behaviors, and even her values.

One way to see this clearly is to look carefully and critically at advertising. Everywhere we look, it seems that media messages are telling us, "Buy something to solve your problems." And whether we admit it or not, we live in a drug culture. In 2016, spending on alcohol and tobacco advertising topped $1.7 billion. To put those numbers in perspective, consider that the same year, Kellogg's spent a mere $32 million in advertising Pop Tarts, and Coca-Cola spent only $269 million advertising Coke.[33]

Regardless of your attitudes about sugar and nutrition, drug culture is inescapable on television and in digital media. In 2016, pharmaceutical drug and nutritional supplement advertising through direct-to-consumer pharmaceutical advertising topped $5.6 billion, outstripping the marketing of alcohol by a factor of five. All the while, abuse of prescription drugs has become a serious problem, with more than 60,000 deaths resulting from the misuse of opioid drugs in 2017. In 2014, 15 million people used prescription drugs for nonmedical, recreational purposes, including 15% of high school seniors. These statistics are alarming, but statistics alone won't convince people not to experiment with drugs and alcohol.

Conversations about the values of our culture—especially immediate gratification, pleasure, and escape—are needed. Indeed, it seems ironic that depictions of pleasure may have unintended harmful and potentially devastating consequences on the day-to-day practice of living a good life. Children and young people grow up seeing drugs and alcohol depicted in pleasurable, attractive ways, used by thin, attractive people in the movies and on television. It's unavoidable: There are plenty of "thin ideals" out there—nearly every actor, actress, athlete, musician, or reality show personality is thin. If you have ever found yourself shocked and depressed when visiting a mall, it's probably a media-related effect. Real Americans are much larger and less attractive than the characters we encounter every day in film, television, and social media.

Researchers have investigated how media images differentially affect people. Most readers know someone whose obsession with weight and slimness is undoubtedly influenced by media and celebrity culture, but no one thinks that his own body weight perceptions are influenced by media—this is the so-called *third-person effect*, the tendency to believe that others are more affected by media than oneself. Yet exposure to thin-ideal media contributes to increased body dissatisfaction in adolescent girls. When the thin-ideal standard is internalized, both men and women may face negative outcomes, including lowered self-esteem and increased risk of eating disorders.[34]

Regardless of people's perceived sense of immunity to media influence, hundreds of studies have shown striking consonance between people's attitudes and beliefs and the kinds of media they use. This phenomenon is called the *cultivation effect*. When the Girl Scouts of America conducted a survey of 1,100 girls aged 11–17 across the country to discover their thoughts on reality TV shows, they found that about half considered themselves to be regular viewers. Shows like *America's Next Top Model, The Real Housewives* franchise, or *Keeping up with the Kardashians* influence girls' attitudes about beauty, relationships, and social power. For example, the study found that those who watch more frequently admit that they "spend a lot of time on their appearance," "think that a girl's value is based on how she looks," and "would rather be recognized for their outer beauty than their inner beauty."

To create drama, reality TV shows feature verbal aggression, gossiping, and bullying. A majority of the girls in the Girl Scout study believed the shows "often pit girls against each other to make the shows more exciting," "make people think that fighting is a normal part of a romantic relationship," and "make people think it is okay to treat others badly." When compared to girls who do not watch reality TV, girls who are regular viewers were more likely to believe "gossiping is a normal part of a relationship between girls," "it is in a girl's nature to be catty and competitive with one another," and "find it more difficult to trust other girls." Regular viewers were more likely to believe it was important to be mean or lie to get ahead, indicating "you have to lie to get what you want," "being mean earns you more respect than being nice," and "you have to be mean to others to get what you want." [35]

Cultivation effects refer to the cumulative influence of television messages on audiences over time. Television reality shows offer a skewed and biased portrayal of relationships, and frequent exposure results in the internalization of values, attitudes, beliefs, and perceptions that are consistent with the world as portrayed on TV. Cultivation effects have been documented in numerous studies, demonstrating that heavy cumulative exposure to media messages shapes viewers' concepts of reality, attitudes, and behavior, particularly when, as in the case of children and young adults, they have little direct personal experience.[36]

Today's media includes plenty of content that depicts children's sexuality. In *The Mick*, a 2017 FOX television comedy about a dysfunctional family, children are depicted in a variety of sexualized situations—and the content is being marketed to families as kid-friendly. In some recent episodes, a boy of about 13 plans to have two adult men photograph him naked so that he can falsely accuse his guardian's boy-friend of possessing child pornography. A middle-school-aged boy plans a three-some with a high-school aged girl and his best friend. Two boys are shown in a bathtub together while waiting for the girl to join them. A teenaged boy receives a sext and fantasizes about the girl in the photo—only to discover it is his own sister. Media producers recognize that it's easy to get and hold people's attention by using sexual content.

If there's one phenomenon that's become normative among adolescents when it comes to social media, it's sexting. Broadly defined as sending or receiving sexually explicit content communicated via text messages, photos, smartphones, or social networking sites, sexting has considerable legal, health, and social consequences. In some states, it can be considered a form of child pornography. Public health researchers find that it is associated with sexual risk behaviors, substance use, delin-quency, and depression.[37]

When sexting is paired with bullying and harassment, it can have profound emo-tional and psychological consequences. But some have wondered: Can sexting play a constructive role in adolescent development? Sexting is undoubtedly influenced by the current media and popular culture landscape where depictions of sex and sexuality are increasingly prevalent and sexuality is openly discussed. Celebrities post sexy pictures of themselves to objectify their bodies. Pornography and explicit depictions of sexuality are ever-present on television and in the movies. Nearly four in ten teens have sent a sext and 20% of teens have posted nude or seminude photos or videos online. Among young adults under age 30, the prevalence of sexting jumps to 59%.

But how can we address secretive behaviors that are hard to talk about? Standing on a soapbox and wagging a finger does relatively little. But talking with young people about media's distorting influence on perceptions of one's own body can help. Some researchers have found that media literacy can be a protective factor to address the problem of thin-ideal internalization. For example, research has shown that when people have high levels of critical thinking about media, their level of body satisfac-tion increases.[38] People realize that unrealistic standards are constructed by media makers and that they can be recognized and resisted.

At the Ridgefield (CT) Library, librarians developed a series entitled "Parenting the Selfie Generation: Instilling Resilience" by hosting a panel discussion with members of the local police department, a middle school principal, the district's technology director, a high school student, and Chris Parrot, a therapist who has developed the YourSelf Series, a website and outreach program designed to address adolescent mental and physical health. This panel aimed to give people a balanced perspective on social media usage and recognize the difference between the use and misuse of social media. By facilitating dialogue between teens, parents, and commu-nity leaders, these kinds of programs represent an important form of media educa-tion for the entire community.

Building Communities of Critical Viewers
POPULAR CULTURE IN THE UNIVERSITY LIBRARY

Can students' interest in popular culture be activated to promote learning? At Eastern Kentucky University, the library hosted a series of open discussions over the course of the 2014 spring semester talking about some of the most popular series dominating pop culture. Many academic librarians love pop culture and seek creative ways to apply it to their information literacy mission. As Figure 2.5 shows, the Pop Culture series events centered on familiar and popular movies, books, and TV shows, including discussions about *The Walking Dead, Star Wars, Harry Potter,* and *Game of Thrones.*

Because a large number of the student body includes first-generation college students, many students arrive at college unprepared to analyze texts, read critically,

Figure 2.5 Pop culture in the academic library.

and make inferences. In Kentucky, nearly 75% of elementary and secondary school students qualify for free and reduced lunch, which is an index of socioeconomic class. However, students and teachers there have plentiful access to computers, with more than a 1-to-1 ratio of devices to students as of 2017.[39] Internet access in the home is uneven, however, with 15% of the population without access to broadband.[40]

Librarians had a good rationale for the program. Because freshman students are often required to attend a certain number of campus events each semester, librarians expected this program would be appealing. They advertised the program on Facebook. Heather Beirne, reference and instruction librarian, explained, "We knew that students have a hard time critically engaging with texts that they've only just read. Students often aren't quite ready to read the complex texts they are asked to read when they arrive at college, let alone analyze and evaluate them on a deeper level." If students could engage critically with well-loved, popular, movies, books, or TV shows, perhaps it could remove one part of the burden of having to both learn new content and analyze the form as well.

But the program did not go as planned, and it was a disappointment to the Eastern Kentucky University librarians. They put a lot of work into the process of preparing questions for the discussions. But students were not active participants. According to Beirne, a lot of students merely came to the event for the proof of attendance and "were surprisingly not well-versed enough in the source material (either the books or the movies) to be able to talk confidently or at all about it." For example, Beirne noted, "Many of the discussion questions we had prepared turned out to be unusable, because students could not engage with the content on even the most basic level." When students lack knowledge of the popular culture under examination, they can't activate prior knowledge. Librarians were particularly disappointed with the *Star Wars* session, where there was very low turnout.

According to the librarians, not all sessions were a failure. *The Walking Dead* program was considered a success. A small group of students attended, and there was a lively discussion around the show. According to Beirne, "The students who attended really seemed to enjoy it, and expressed the hope that we would do it again." What made this one event so different? Perhaps it was student familiarity with the *Talking Dead* talk show, launched in 2011 by the AMC network. The live talk show, hosted by Chris Hardwick, airs immediately following the broadcast of new episodes of *The Walking Dead* and *Fear the Walking Dead*. Perhaps the academic discussion came closer to what the librarians had intended because there was already a culture of discussion around the show or because the show was at peak popularity at the time. Beirne reflected, "It's all about choosing things that are truly of the moment as students are more likely to engage with it."

But the librarians were so disappointed with the Pop Culture series that, after the spring of 2014, they chose not to repeat the program. Beirne explains, "Though we mulled it over, we could not come up with a way to repeat it in a way that was more effective. We all felt like we had put in a lot of work without achieving the desired outcomes." We certainly are sympathetic with the frustration of hosting a program that does not meet expectations. But we also wondered about whether and how the librarians' expectations might have contributed to the lack of dialogue and discussion. In reflecting on this program, these questions remain:

- Might a panel discussion format before open discussion help scaffold "how to talk about popular culture" to model appropriate forms of talk for learners?
- Could the screening and discussion of a trailer or short clip from the program have helped to engage students' more active participation?
- Did the design and use of carefully prepared discussion questions interfere with librarians' openness to engage with participants' lived experience as media consumers?
- Would collaboration with communication and media studies faculty (who have considerable experience leading discussions about popular culture) have helped the program to be a success?

It's not always easy—but exploring popular culture in academic libraries is important work. At the University of West Georgia, one academic librarian found a way to engage students in information literacy in her course called Academic Research and the Library by using what she calls "unlikely examples." For example, she screened the first minute of Beyonce's "Single Ladies" music video followed by the first minute of "Mexican Breakfast" video choreographed by Bob Fosse.[41] Students discussed how Beyonce acknowledges Fosse as her inspiration, and they consider whether or not she is plagiarizing. Students then search to locate a variety of information sources on the subject of cultural appropriation in music and dance.

At the web blog In the Library with the Lead Pipe, Anne Helen Petersen asks librarians to help students "dissect, but not destroy, the meaning and pleasure they receive" from celebrity culture and popular media. She suggests placing movie posters of current Hollywood films next to documentaries that historicize and explore celebrity, including the 2011 film directed by Leon Gast about the paparazzi photographer Ron Galella entitled *Smash His Camera*.[42]

Clearly, the place of popular culture in the school, academic, and public library needs more discussion, experimentation, and documentation. As librarians consider their own relationship to it, it will be important to reflect on the unstated assumptions that structure the relationship between pleasure, power, and inquiry.

WHEN PEOPLE FEEL, THEY LEARN

We love film and audiovisual media because of its power in connecting us to the lived experiences and emotions of others. Storytelling has the capacity to enlarge the human spirit. Brendan Stone of the University of Sheffield talks about how people's ordinary lives are rich, complicated resources for knowledge and creativity. They should be mined for the wisdom and creativity that they hold.[43] Coauthor Pam Steager developed her storytelling skills as a health educator in the service of connecting people's feelings to their knowledge and behavior. Her 15 years of writing a column for a local newspaper honed her ability to take a story from her own life or the life of her community and connect it to national and international issues. Her interest in film and media in libraries stems from the recognition that storytelling makes people more receptive to learning.

Talking about film and media stories also helps deepen our social relationships. James Frieden and Debbie Elliott created Teach with Movies more than 30 years ago when they decided to show the 1982 film *Gandhi*, directed by Richard Attenborough, to their young son. As their son asked questions, the family rewatched the film, which led to lots of productive discussion that deepened the emotional connection between parents and children. After watching the 1992 Baz Luhrmann film *Strictly Ballroom*, their son's engagement with the story led him to explore flamenco dancing. It's then they realized that watching films with family discussion was having an important influence on parenting. Teachers, librarians, and parents benefit from access to the more than 450 films described on the Teach with Movies website with suggestions and ideas about how to use film to promote relationships that matter.

Truthfully, books, music, movies, and television shows are sometimes enlightening to the human spirit, and sometimes they are worthless dreck. We are comforted by the insights offered by Gilbert Seldes, nearly 100 years ago, when in his book *The Seven Lively Arts*, he observed that there must be no opposition between the fine arts and the popular arts. At a time when Charlie Chaplin was being derided by intellectuals, Seldes understood the dangers of dismissing, ignoring, or trivializing popular culture through a "genteel tradition" that prevents the just appreciation of its authentic value.[44]

As we have seen in this chapter, the practice of viewing film and media in the world of school, public, and academic libraries include a complex array of issues. We see patrons and learners as active, sympathetic, and responsive to lifelong learning. Because film and media engage the head, heart, and spirit, they can stimulate complex discussion about social, political, moral, and ethical issues. Film and media, when used well, show us that when people feel something, they're ready to learn something.

3

Creating

Questions Answered in This Chapter
- Why do libraries develop media centers and makerspaces?
- How is creating media a part of the K–12 curriculum?
- How do online learning tools support learners in the creation of media?
- How do academic library spaces help students to create media?
- What kind of videos do librarians create?
- Who are BookTubers and why do they create videos?
- What does it take to sustain a community-based media production project?
- What happens when patrons create promotional videos for a library?
- What is learned from creating literary adaptations?
- What makes video book trailers a powerful creative form?
- What does it take to create a teen film festival?
- How can music videos express the deep values of librarianship?

Coding is a little bit like making a movie, Seth explains. Riley thinks coding is fun. Amylee said, "I was really bad at it. It's really hard." Olivia is interested in making a website using coding. Zach likes working with numbers and sees it as a career option. Ilad thought moving the characters around was fun. Other kids don't really care about it, and some even found it a little boring. Ellie hates it.

Students at the Alan B. Shepard Middle School in Deerfield, Illinois, reacted in different ways but generally with enthusiasm when given the opportunity to learn coding through Hour of Code, which has partnered with Disney to develop Wayfinding with Code, a set of specially designed coding activities using the characters of *Moana*, the 2016 Disney film directed by Ron Clements. Launched in 2013, Hour of Code is a nonprofit organization that expands access to computer science and increases participation by women and underrepresented students of color. One-hour introductions to computer science, designed to demystify the process of coding, help inspire interest in coding and programming as part of STEM education.

In a 1-hour session, students learn basic principles of visual object-oriented programming by using a drag-and-drop editor to create simple animations to move characters on a screen. The lesson includes 19 linked short activities, where students receive a verbal and musical "reward" when they produce a correct response. It's fun to help Moana and Maui steer their boat using basic coding commands of sequences and loops. Students learn some principles of the logic of coding while increasing their appreciation of computer science principles and their use in film animation.

When the activity concluded, their computer science teacher, Maria Galanis, invited students to reflect on the learning experience using Flipgrid, an online platform that enables students to contribute 90-second video reflections on their learning. Some kids even completed the Flipgrid assignment on Saturday from their homes. Galanis believes that weekend homework completion suggests much about their high level of interest in the activity.

More and more schools are incorporating coding and programming into the curriculum, usually led by an enthusiastic teacher, librarian, or technology specialist. Faculty, students, and staff are also using social media to develop and deepen their own sense of community connectedness. Through social networking and the use of hashtags to form a virtual community, researchers and activists like us can learn about the fabulous activities at schools all across the country, including the Alan B. Shepard Middle School, as Figure 3.1 shows. There, the school librarian, as well as dozens of classroom teachers, school leaders, and staff, all share examples of learning practices on Twitter using the #engage109 and #engagesms hashtags. From this, we can easily see what a dynamic learning community it is!

Figure 3.1 Coding to learn at the Alan B. Shepherd Middle School.

That's how we learned about Andrea Trudeau, the school librarian for the Alan B. Shepard Middle School, who maintains the Twitter account @Shepard_LC to document the many activities of the Shepard Learning Commons, which includes a corner that is well stocked with art supplies and a charging station for student digital devices. Andrea also hosts Drop Everything and Read, a library program that was launched with the publication of Beverly Cleary's classic book, *Ramona Quimby, Age 8*. During the month of April, in honor of Mrs. Cleary's birthday, there's a 15-minute, free-choice reading activity for the whole school. The school principal and teachers all contributed photos to document the community's in-school reading.

Reflecting her deep appreciation of community partnerships, Andrea also asked the public librarians from the nearby Deerfield Public Library to come to the school. She wanted to make sure that all the middle school students are aware of the many resources available at their community library.

Social media can be used to develop whole-school integration of digital media into the learning environment. The Shepard Learning Commons is a lively place because Andrea live-streams special events in her school library using Periscope, the live digital video-streaming function on Twitter. At one library event, social studies students gathered with representatives from the community to explore the five major religions. Each member of the community described the key elements of their religion in a 3-minute lightning-style talk and then students asked them questions. It was a thought-provoking and riveting experience and the students were deeply engaged in learning. At another event in honor of Veterans Day, the Learning Commons hosted US Army veterans, and students could have a discussion with members of the community. Activities like this model lifelong learning and accelerate innovation in professional learning communities because live streaming and Tweeting about library programs enable new practices to be shared with others who may benefit from learning about them.

School librarians have a mission to empower intellectual curiosity and self-directed learning. Many perform vital curation services for the entire community when they help amplify traditional learning practices through the use of digital and social media. At the heart of this work is helping learners develop meaningful questions and evaluate the quality of information in ways that lead to learning. Some people see spaces like the Alan B. Shepard Learning Commons as radical. What's so radical about this? According to Rutgers University professor Joyce Valenza, "School libraries are the antidote to test-driven, rote-learning cultures" where school is just an endless series of tests, assignments, and assessments. Librarians help embody the value of reading, viewing, and information cultures within the school community. They demonstrate the deep values of service by being responsible, responsive, and kind to students, staff, and faculty alike.

Librarians recognize communication as both the end point—and the beginning point—of the inquiry process.[1] What's the point of creating media? Authorship is a fundamental impulse rooted in the value of telling your own story. When people engage in practices of creating media, they deepen their understanding of the constructed nature of all forms of media. We also find that making media shifts people's identity in certain important ways. As author Mark Hatch puts it, "Since making is fundamental to what it means to be human, you will become a more complete version of you as you make."[2] As people gain confidence in self-expression and recognize the value and power of using communication to address national, cultural, social, and community issues, they take on the role of active citizens in a democratic society.

In this chapter, we will examine the creative media production practices that are at the heart of our use of audiovisual media and digital technologies. We consider the rise of media centers in school, public, and academic libraries. We'll take a look inside school libraries where children are learning how to be media creators and see how academic libraries support the media creation competencies of undergraduate and graduate students, faculty, and staff while helping advance a spirit of community connectedness. We'll meet librarians who create videos and other media for marketing purposes and those who create media to teach information literacy. We'll learn about the challenges of sustaining a community documentary project in a middle school and get to know some BookTubers who are using video to be part of a community of readers. We'll consider the power of creating literary adaptations, book trailers, and youth film festivals in a library context. As we will see in the pages that follow, school, public, and academic librarians are responsible for helping to promote people's creativity, critical thinking, collaboration skills, and their imagination through creating media.

Making Media in the Library

The library has always been a source of inspiration for people who want to make things. Those fortunate enough to experience the library as children learn to stretch their imaginations as they enjoy storytime readings, craft activities, performances, and movies. As teens, their interests become more self-driven, and they may find the library offers them access to things like computers and software that will fuel their imaginations—whether that leads to coding or perhaps beat making, music composition, graphic design, photo editing, or audio and video recording and editing. For those adults who blink and find themselves falling behind with the latest technology, the library holds the door open, offering a hand up for them, too. The library is more than books, and it always has been. The library is a community hub where people can come to learn, create, and explore possibilities.

It sometimes seems like librarians do everything: selecting and purchasing new books, DVDs, and software; evaluating apps; teaching classes; helping students check out books; reshelving books; repairing damaged books; running book fairs and reading programs; weeding the collection; creating bulletin boards and displays; hosting coding and programming workshops; and more. Of course, as is true in life, some do more and some do less. In some schools, librarians manage special programs for parents, make decisions about software for classroom use, and provide lessons in digital citizenship. Most public librarians are familiar with children's literature and are able to help select books that best meet the interests and needs of a particular child. Others support workshops on coding and programming, explore issues of privacy and safety in online environments, and introduce students to good study habits that will last a lifetime. Librarians often have deep knowledge of young adult literature, library databases, and other digital and physical resources. Some academic librarians have highly specialized skills in media production and others actively consult with faculty to support project-based learning across the subject areas.

MAKERSPACES VERSUS MEDIA CENTERS

Grant funding from philanthropies, government, and Silicon Valley has helped many communities to build makerspaces after the Great Recession in 2008, positioning it as a form of workforce development that advances entrepreneurship by democratizing access "to the tools of the next industrial revolution."[3] It seemed then like everyone jumped on the makerspace bandwagon. But librarians and educators also know that a makerspace is more of a mindset than a tool set, according to Casey Shea, a curriculum coordinator at the Sonoma County Office of Education. Many of the most successful makerspaces started with very little equipment. During those years, many people learned that simply dropping a 3D printer into a room does not create a makerspace.[4]

Librarians are well aware of the ways that makerspaces and media centers can support their mission. One of the calls to action of the Future Ready Librarians framework is "Empowering Students as Creators." In a webinar, Diana Rendina, a media specialist at Tampa Preparatory School in Florida, and Traci Chun, a teacher librarian at Skyview High School and Vancouver Public Schools, presented their experience and advice about encouraging creativity. Rendina acknowledges there are varying definitions of what a makerspace is, but she defines it as "a place where students can gather to create, invent, tinker, explore, and discover using a variety of tools and materials."

Still, any definition that would limit what a makerspace can or should be is missing the point. Rendina stresses that it's not about what kind of stuff the space has, but the experience the space provides.[5] As part of the planning process for creating such a space at the school's library, students had the opportunity to weigh in: They wanted a dedicated space. And so the library weeded the collection of outdated, underused materials and found space in a corner of the library to be their makerspace. Funding from a Donors Choose project helped them give the space an update with fresh paint, a whiteboard wall, and a Lego wall where students could play.

Some librarians choose to provide video production experiences as a means for play, learning, and storytelling. Giving students the chance to tell their stories helps learners gain confidence and share what they know with others. Librarians also learn alongside their students in a media center or makerspace, because the informal structure allows for mistakes and discovery, which can often lead to the deepest learning experiences. At the Defiance (Ohio) Public Library, grant funding enabled the library to purchase Go Pro cameras, studio-quality microphones, a Zoom audio recorder, green screen, LED studio lighting, tripods, Adobe Creative Cloud software, and a sewing machine. Children there learned how to write an original story and practiced hand and machine sewing to create costumes.[6] They learned some acting techniques and created storyboards and props. At the final screening, children were excited to see their hard work on the big screen as parents, peers, and librarians watched the final production.

Upon starting a makerspace in her school's library in Vancouver, Washington, teacher librarian Traci Chun quickly realized that just providing the materials wasn't enough. Whereas younger kids may naturally settle into creative crafts, as kids get older, they're more likely to need someone to guide them. Chun also helps students create digital presentations for English and History classes with video, music, and their voice, as opposed to a typical essay or PowerPoint. In another example, students used iMotion and created scripts and sets.

So what's the real difference between a makerspace and a media center? Some people think it's just a matter of the *branding*. So much of American culture is driven by branding and brand awareness. For example, the term *Fab Lab* was developed as an MIT outreach project, and today there are more than 1,000 of them around the world. It's a franchise of sorts, where programs often include a 3D printer, wood shop, and computing toys. At the Fab Foundation's website, a budget is provided for starting up a Fab Lab with the cost coming in at just under $400,000. When a *makerspace* is positioned as a form of workforce development to help people get job-related skills, energy companies like Chevron have provided funding as part of their commitment to STEM education.

Scholars have noted that a key feature of makerspaces is the practice of iterative design; this practice of proposing an idea, developing it, receiving feedback and evaluating it, and then revising it is a classic feature of apprenticeship learning.[7] In the library world, the term *community informatics* is sometimes used to describe the many different ways that community enrichment occurs through the provision of information technology resources and popular education. In *community media centers*, the key feature is more likely to center on creative expression, youth voice, and citizenship, with the heart of the idea revolving on the idea that personal expression is a political act because having the courage to present your ideas and make them visible to others is the first step in becoming an engaged citizen.[8] All of these terms are conceptually rooted in the belief that, through creating and collaborating, people learn.

IDENTITY ISSUES FOR MEDIA CREATORS

Educators, technology specialists, and school librarians all make decisions to engage students in creating film and video for learning purposes only if they feel it really matters. Generally, such educators want to activate learners' media literacy competencies or advance community connectedness. But when school librarians are themselves digital authors, they often have a broader, deeper appreciation of the creative process and recognize the potentially transformative impact that such learning experiences can have. They often become passionately committed to including media creation activities into their library programs.

Some librarians bring their prior experiences as media makers or performing artists with them into the profession. For example, before he became a school librarian, Brien Jennings worked as a cameraman for the local Providence TV news channel, and from this he acquired a sophisticated understanding of the process of constructing broadcast news. As a school librarian at the Narragansett Elementary School in Rhode Island, Jennings brings his expertise in television production into the school library through the development of a media literacy program for children in grades K–4. When he started the job, the school had a traditional library program where students selected books for pleasure reading and gathered information for research projects. Although his work with the younger children focused on literacy and library skills, students in Grades 3 and 4 were eager to engage in media production activities in the school library's media center.

The media production studio in the school library includes a green screen. Children at the Narragansett Elementary School work in teams to create videos to represent what they are learning in their classrooms. In one video, children explained the mathematical concept of place value by counting Cheerios. The video starts with simple counting. But then we see the use of a zero to indicate tens, hundreds, and thousands as children playfully pile up lots of little bags of Cheerios into a giant plastic bowl.

All the children in the elementary school take delight in creating media. In one video, two special needs students create a "how-to" video by demonstrating how to make holiday ornaments using a mixture of cinnamon, applesauce, and cookie cutters. Editing is used to speed up the mixing and rolling process, and the time-lapse function enables viewers to see the finished product after the ornaments had dried for 2 days. How proud those children were of their production!

Although Jennings wants young students to be critical of advertising, news, and stereotypes, his primary focus is on empowering students to be media creators themselves. He said, "Kids can be critical thinkers and creative media makers. When they get this chance, their learning never ends."

But children at Narragansett Elementary School don't make media only in the school library. Elementary teachers use media production activities in the classroom, using simple drag-and-drop digital platforms to make multimedia productions, as Figure 3.2 shows. For example, students explored Buncee, a creation and presentation tool for students and educators to create interactive classroom content, allowing learners of all ages to visualize concepts and communicate creatively. In a videotaped interview about the merits of the platform, children explain that they like selecting and customizing animations, adding voice and drawings "to make book reviews and solving math problems the fun way."

The powerful energy of media production has helped contribute to a community of engaged and effective communicators. Teachers began exploring digital literacy by organizing a faculty book club reading and discussion program. Then with leadership from Narragansett Elementary School principal Karen Dandurand and support from Brien Jennings, elementary teachers created a video to introduce parents of the community about digital learning in the 21st century. In it, teacher Chris Cochran described how students now use laptops, iPads, and Google platforms to create and share information both inside and outside of school. Karen Festa introduced parents to the resources on the Common Sense Media

Figure 3.2 Students create media to demonstrate their learning.

website, demonstrating the use of the website and inspiring parents to explore it. Brien Jennings was thrilled when Capstone Press invited him to author a series of media literacy books for emerging readers in Grades K–2. Books like these help librarians, parents, and educators introduce media concepts to young learners. At Narragansett Elementary School, digital and media literacy learning experiences are conceptualized as everyone's responsibility—not just the librarian's.

Student-centered video production projects often thrive when teachers, librarians, and instructional technology support staff all work together. School librarians can help teachers design projects that align with learning goals and are structured in ways to ensure student success. Sarah Levin, a high school librarian at Urban High School in San Francisco, works with a Spanish language teacher on a major class project where students research the life of Che Guevara and create a Ken Burns–style documentary.

To get this project done, students meet in the library for a brief research-skills session to explore some print resources they'll need to gather facts about Guevara's life. They also explore multimedia sources, and the librarian recognizes that students often require assistance in evaluating websites. She points them to news archive sites where they may find video or audio resources to support their work. Then students create a voice-over script using their developing Spanish language skills using information they've found in print resources. Then they create a storyboard and produce the video using the images, video, and audio they have found online.[9] This project is made easier by the 1:1 laptop program, which the school has had in place for nearly 20 years. All members of the community are issued MacBook Pro laptops for school and home use. Students are expected to activate technology skills, multimedia design, digital literacy, and citizenship throughout the school day.

Students need a mix of creative freedom and creative constraint in order to create media. When a project is too unstructured, students struggle to focus their efforts; when a project is too structured, student projects all look alike. The creative spark never gets ignited.[10]

Respect for the process of creating information is key: It involves an iterative process of researching, creating, revising, and disseminating. It can be chaotic and messy at times—as creative projects always are. We like how the ACRL Information Literacy Frameworks emphasize the nuances of media creation as a set of competencies that include knowledge, skills, and dispositions. As explained in this framework, learners who are developing their information-literate abilities recognize the capabilities and constraints of information developed through various creation processes. They know that information may be perceived differently based on the format in which it is packaged. They recognize how the perception of value may shift depending on the context in which it is received. Most important, learners develop, in their own creation processes, an understanding of how their choices impact the purposes for which the information product will be used and the message it conveys.[11]

Learning With Lynda.com

Once you have access to a digital media production tool, how do you use it? Learning to create media involves mastery of the use of digital tools, and the learning process can be aided with the help a tutorial demonstration. To support media creators, a number of public and academic libraries are sold on the value of Lynda.com. What is it? After Lynda Weinman taught herself how to be a special effects animator and worked as an independent contractor on a variety of Hollywood films, she began teaching computer graphics. She produced a variety of short "how-to" videos to support her students' learning. Fast-forward 20 years. Recently, her company, Lynda.com, was acquired by LinkedIn in a deal worth $1.5 billion. For people seeking to learn more about 3D and animation, audio, photography, video, and web and interactive design, Lynda.com is a dream come true.

Lynda.com helps people learn for a lifetime, which is why The New York Public Library makes the platform available to patrons through its own website. But it's not just used at large libraries. The Greene County Public Library in Xenia, Ohio, also makes access to the platform available to library patrons. The platform supplements curricula and supports a flipped classroom approach to just-in-time learning. A number of academic libraries make licenses available to support student and faculty learning. In 2008, at the Gelardin New Media Center at the Georgetown University Library, library leaders purchased site licenses to help the staff stay up to speed on new software applications. Only 4 years later, with the staff sold on the value of the platform, the university provided access to all Georgetown students, faculty, and staff.

What learners like best about Lynda.com is its concision and ease of use. Learners can watch, pause, and copy to practice new skills. They can skip ahead and learn in any order, using the platform from home or on campus. They can learn a lot of information that would be too much to cover in a classroom. Self-paced learning takes some grit, to be sure, but the results can be worth the effort.

SPACES FOR MEDIA MAKING IN COLLEGE AND UNIVERSITY LIBRARIES

Today, a growing number of faculty and librarians are committed to research-based, student-created documentaries (and other genres) as an alternative to the traditional academic research paper.[12] Glenda Insua and Annie Armstrong, librarians at the University of Illinois at Chicago, have shown how they supported students' visual literacy competencies as they transformed research findings into ethically responsible short films. Documentary production can be a powerful alternative to traditional research papers in order to engage students with a broad range of learning styles in the research process.[13]

But how do academic librarians learn how to support student learning with media production tools? Since 2006, at the Weigle Information Commons (WIC), located on the first floor of Van Pelt-Dietrich Library Center at the University of Pennsylvania, academic librarians have made a deep commitment to supporting student media creation as a dimension of their academic work. Today, some librarians distinguish between an "information commons," which is a cluster of networked resources, and a "learning commons," which is a more student-centered approach to providing learning spaces and services.[14] Back then, the WIC was one of the country's first Commons—a bookless area with technology-enhanced collaboration spaces. But because of a strong commitment to support the academic use of video creation, today the place is humming with students, faculty, and staff engaged in a variety of media production projects that support learning and scholarship.

A key feature of the WIC is the Vitale Digital Media Lab, a self-service space for digital projects. Lab staff—who might be educators, librarians, scholars, students, and artists—assist users with specific hardware and software questions. There's a large-format poster printer and an equipment rack that enable people to create a digital clip from a VHS tape. Individuals can borrow video cameras, audio recorders, microphones, and projectors for 3 days at a time. The WIC has purchased an academic license for students, staff, and faculty to be able to access Lynda.com, which offers a series of do-it-yourself "how-to" tutorials on a range of media production platforms and tools.

Working in collaboration with the Penn Language Center, academic librarians have helped language faculty members take advantage of digital tools that promote foreign language learning. They helped establish a Certificate in Instructional Technologies and Online Learning for language educators, tapping into the expertise of WIC staff members who provide regular instruction to classes working on online, video, or audio projects with software and programs such as Audacity, iMovie, QuickTime Player, Snapz Pro, Final Cut Pro, PowerPoint (voice-over and audio), Skype, YouTube, and Google Hangouts, and on hardware such as iOS devices (apps for iPad and iPhone), video cameras, and audio recorders.

Academic librarian Anu Vedantham, then at the University of Pennsylvania Libraries, conducted research on first-year undergraduates who engage in video creation as part of academic coursework. She found that the choice of a familiar platform, such as YouTube or iTunes, can make video creation more approachable. Simple tools are often best because learners can be intimidated by the use of complex video cameras and editing equipment that require formal instruction.[15] Looking at gender differences in online video creation, Vedantham found some differences between women and men in their experience with online video creation, finding that men report overall more participation in video creation and editing. Her work has helped librarians and faculty explore how best to support the needs of all students in learning how to create media. Now she's at Harvard, serving as the director of Learning and Teaching Services for the Harvard Faculty of Arts and Sciences Libraries.

Renee was lucky to get a guided tour from Vendantham about her most recent project, launching the newly renovated Cabot Science Library at Harvard University. You enter the library through the café and coffee shop, so that's surprise number one. The space is open and welcoming, with plenty of diverse seating and study spaces. To accomplish this, 80% of the physical print collection was removed for off-site storage. During the renovation process, Vendantham managed patron expectations and staff morale by creating a communication schedule that provided informational updates every 2 weeks, helping staff and stakeholders imagine the "bright future that nobody could actually see yet."[16] She helped break down silos across campus by bringing together library staff from across the 70 Harvard University libraries to be involved in the program planning and policies for the new space, a process which helped to reduce "library envy."

Library leaders and space designers like to talk about "breaking the rules" as a means to create innovative program planning for academic libraries. Vendantham thinks carefully about the relationship between space, technology, and facilities, and she is imaginative in how she supports professional development opportunities as she inspires informal experimentation among library staff, faculty, and students alike. She is bold about using library space to both support formal and informal sharing and learning. Right at the entrance to the library, and visible to all who enter the Science Center, the Discovery Bar is an open space for sharing and learning, both "a water cooler and a soapbox" type space where people can wander in to observe others sharing knowledge, including librarians, graduate students, and visitors.[17] The Discovery Bar sends a highly visible signal that knowledge sharing is a key feature of the library. Library events have included game nights and dance parties, co-sponsored by student affairs.

Of course, video production is also a key service feature of the Cabot Science Library. Twelve mobile media carts support active learning pedagogies, and an instruction room is flexible enough to accommodate 15 to 120 people. Two media studios and a space for video editing provide self-service production opportunities for students and faculty. Self-service scheduling of these rooms was not easy to accomplish—since this was not a traditional practice for Harvard Libraries where library space is generally tightly controlled. But it was a major accomplishment, and Vendantham's effort in promoting a team-based approach to staffing has helped build a sense of shared purpose and vision around the central value of providing access and ease of use.

Best Practices for Supporting Learning Through Student Media Creation

PLANNING

- Have a purposeful goal for the assignment or project.
- Help learners conceptualize an authentic target audience for their work.
- Encourage the use of planning tools like mind maps and storyboards.
- Develop intermediate deadlines for different phases of the project to help learners manage time.

CULTIVATING CREATIVITY

- Encourage learners to collaborate with a partner using "the power of two" principle to promote creativity.
- Take time for play and other breaks during production to support the creative process.
- Take advantage of deadline pressure to create positive stress.
- Don't overstructure or establish too many expectations.

DIGITAL SKILLS DEVELOPMENT

- Encourage trial-and-error exploration and independent learning with one or more digital platforms and tools.
- Support changes in creative plans that evolve during the production process.
- Model the practice of just-in-time learning to support skill development.
- Invite peers to help each other.

FEEDBACK AND REVISION

- Help learners to discover creative ideas during the process of making media.
- Use questions to gently encourage learners to think in new ways about their work.

MAKING WORK VISIBLE

- Create ways to showcase creative work through screenings, gallery walks, and other events.
- Support the learning experience by asking authors to reflect on their production process.
- Demonstrate respect for people's emotional investment in their creative work.

ONE-BUTTON STUDIO

One great example of library innovation in media production is the One Button Studio. When Renee first observed the One Button Studio at Penn State University in 2014, she was impressed—and jealous. What a genius of an idea! Students and faculty use it to offer mini-lectures, practice their oral presentations, conduct videotaped interviews, and create promotional videos for student clubs and organizations. Until 2014, student access to video relied on the use of the FlipCam, an inexpensive video camera. Access to professional lighting, green-screen, and audio recording technologies were limited to those with technical expertise and access to the media studio. But when the One Button Studio was created, it included a simple process that automates the lighting, microphone, and camera, making it possible for students and faculty to create video simply, storing their creative work using a thumb drive to create a digital file. In only 2 years after its installation, it was used by 10% of the main-campus student body, reaching more than 8,000 users. Now all seven campuses of the Penn State University have One Button Studios. As of 2018, hundreds of other colleges and universities installed similar facilities, taking advantage of the ability to create their own studios because Penn State has made the software available for free from the Mac App Store.

Learning by Creating

WHEN LIBRARIANS CREATE MEDIA

Librarians create media as well as facilitate the creative process of others. At the Hayward Public Library in the San Francisco Bay area, librarians created their own historical film highlighting a long-standing event for gay teens. With support from a $10,000 grant from Cal Humanities, a nonprofit cultural arts foundation, librarians created "Now We Can Dance: The Story of the Hayward Gay Prom," which chronicles the 1995 creation of the gay prom.

Having a traditional high school prom for lesbian, gay, bisexual, and transgender youth gave teens a chance to have their own prom. Librarians teamed up with teens who learned how to shoot video, conduct interviews, and do research. The film features interviews with prom goers, volunteers, and even a protester. Laurie Willis, the adult services and electronic services manager, was inspired to create the film after the event was mentioned in another library video project.[18] She worked with co-producers Shawna Sherman and Sally Thomas, the youth services librarians, and the adult services librarians, and they received additional assistance from filmmaker Debra Chasnoff, who won an Academy Award for a short documentary about General Electric and environmental issues.

More and more librarians are creating "how-to" video tutorials to communicate key ideas about database search, the research process, and other information literacy competencies. At North Carolina State University, librarians have created short animated videos themselves to address common conceptual problems in information literacy. For example, many students see library research as a linear, not iterative process. Using simple video animation, librarians created "Picking a Topic IS Research," as shown in Figure 3.3. This video nicely explains how topic selection is a research process that involves a recursive process of moving from broad to narrow and back again.

Librarian-created videos like this one have received hundreds of thousands of views on YouTube, suggesting their perceived utility to beginning researchers. Today, film and media faculty, working with media librarians, continue to innovate in what and how they teach, offering courses that enable students to make short movies with their cell phones, study the representation of fascism in films from across the 20th century, or explore the rise of informal media criticism on Tumblr, just to name a few of the many topics examined by film and media scholars and librarians.

Alyson Gamble describes a project she developed at the University of South Florida, where she introduced the basics of information literacy by creating a video

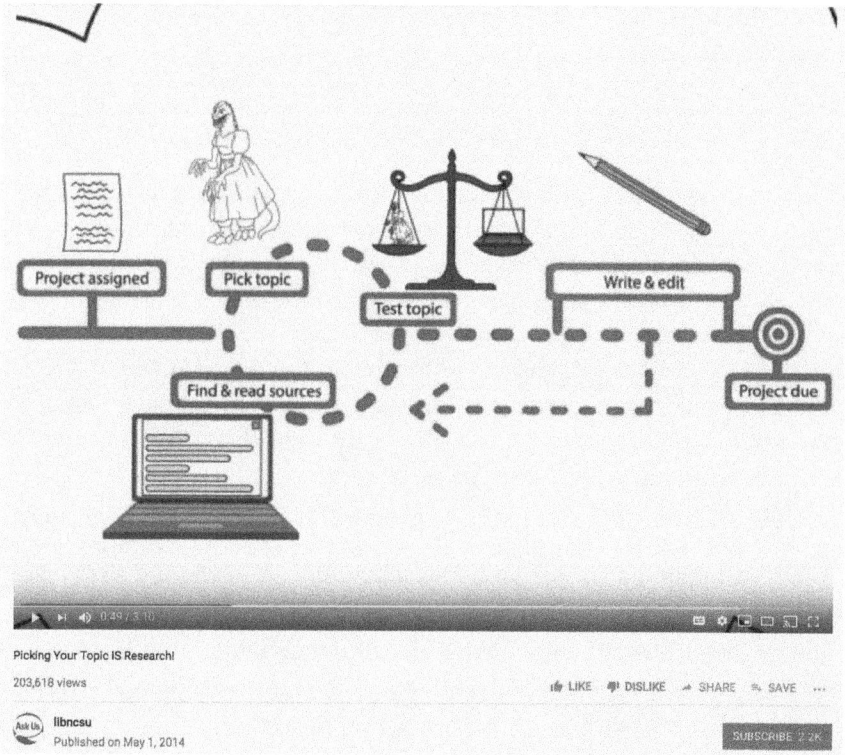

Figure 3.3 Picking your topic is research.

to introduce students to search and evaluation procedures, using the resources at the Clark College Libraries. In the video, she demonstrates the use of the ASPECT checklist, and she has created other videos that include topics like copyright and creating a digital presence.[19] She describes the many benefits of video creation to the academic librarian, noting that the time it takes to create media "is saved by avoiding repetitive lessons with the same students having to attend all of them, or in presenting to small or nonexistent audiences at poorly attended workshops."[20] Of course, another important outcome of this work is the ability for researchers to better understand the current and emerging social norms among academic librarians in their approaches to teaching information literacy.

Such amateur educational media productions are becoming more substantial and academic in tone. There is a whole genre of *short form media* devoted to conveying key ideas in the serious study of film. For example, film scholar Karen Pearlman at Macquarie University collaborates with professional editor Seven Pape to create engaging YouTube videos that illustrate film theories using film clips from both popular and classic films. One such video, "Why Action Movies Are Spectacular . . . and Boring," explores the structure of action films, using concepts from narrative theory and phenomenology to explain how action films may discourage empathy with characters and disrupt narrative flow. With more than 30,000 views in just 2 months, it's clearly an example of the expansive power of film theory to reach global audiences.

WHEN UNIVERSITY STUDENTS CREATE TO LEARN

The *create to learn* spirit is developing on college campuses. But just as academic librarians and faculty are discovering the power of media making to support student learning, students themselves are creating media as part of their academic coursework, and not just in the context of professional courses in film and media. Today, academic librarians are actively working with faculty and students to create and share information. For example, at the North Carolina State University (NCSU) Libraries, one librarian explained that "students consistently amaze and delight us with creative and high-quality productions." In a previous book, Renee has dubbed this hands-on, minds-on pedagogy "create to learn."[21]

Creating media can be important for advancing self-expression and learning, but it is also a time-honored way to deepen media analysis skills. Lisa Patti, a professor at Hobart and William Smith Colleges, uses an assignment that involves her media studies students in creating a set of bonus features for a film they have been assigned to analyze. Students work collaboratively to create a website, a DVD case, and a set of archival bonus features that enables students to demonstrate forms of textual, industrial, and cultural analysis learned during the semester.

In this project, university students write an essay about the film and create both a trailer and a commentary track for a scene from the film. For example, one group of students designed a Criterion Collection edition of *Singin' in the Rain*, directed by Stanley Donen and Gene Kelly in 1952. They collaborated to produce an original commentary track for the scene featuring Debbie Reynolds's performance of "Would You." In their work, students offered a formal analysis of the cinematography and sound design in the scene and explained the history of Hollywood's silent-to-sound transition period. This assignment was theoretically grounded, professional, and practical—and it helped develop competencies that contribute to students' future career success.

TEEN FILM FESTIVALS

The longest running youth-produced festival in the country is the Do It Your Damn Self Film Festival, which was founded in 1996 by teens in Cambridge, Massachusetts, who felt misrepresented in the media and wanted to do something about it. The program draws over 800 youth and adults to public screenings that champion social justice and issue- focused youth filmmakers who want to see change and make it happen.

We tried to track down the oldest, continuously running teen film festival hosted by a public library. The San Mateo (CA) Library has hosted a teen film festival since 2008. The Kent County (MI) Library has hosted a teen film festival since 2013. At the Dallas Public Library, the Teen Film Fest offered a creative twist: they required patrons to produce 3-minute videos shot entirely on cell phones, addressing the question, "What was your most significant moment of 2016?" They received 17 entries from a diverse array of students, including a delightful entry from Shelby Doroshow of Royce City High School, which features her hilarious and heart-warming adventures in learning to drive.

But the Ocean County (NJ) Library seems to be the longest running film festival in a public library, hosting its first festival in 2005. At the 13th annual film festival in 2018, a wide array of categories for submission is available for high school filmmakers to select from, as shown in Figure 3.4. Categories include the following:

> **Animation:** An illustrated or computer-animated film featuring a story or a plot. The visual technique provides the illusion of motion by displaying a collection of images in sequence. Limit 3 minutes.
>
> **Commercial:** An advertisement for a company, local business, or product. The object is to create an interest in the promotion of the advertisement and should be targeted to the public. Limit 90 seconds.
>
> **Documentary:** Primarily for the purpose of education, instruction, or historical record, documentaries cover a broad category of subjects intended to highlight some aspect of reality surrounding an issue, topic, or person of importance. The film should add value and promote discussion by bringing

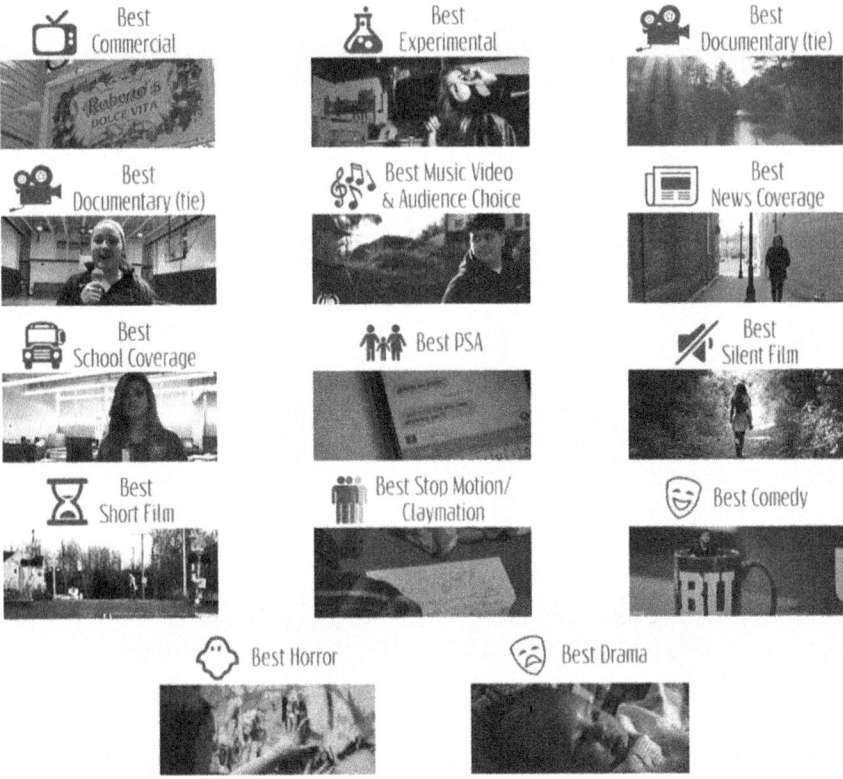

Figure 3.4 Submission categories for the Ocean County (New Jersey) Library Teen Film Festival.

in new information, identifying unrecognized problems, providing or suggesting new solutions, or offering a unique perspective. Limit 5 minutes.

Experimental: The film should be characterized by abstract or avant-garde techniques, a poetic approach to a film's construction, or the absence of a linear narrative. Limit 5 minutes.

Music Video: A film integrating a song and imagery created for artistic purposes. The film should represent the artist's original work and emphasize the relationship between audio and video. Limit 5 minutes.

News Coverage: A segment that brings attention to an important issue ranging from local to global. Limit 3 minutes.

OCL Promo: Make us a social media video! Create a piece that features why the library is important to you and the community. The winning video will be pinned on the library's Facebook and You Tube pages. Limit 2 minutes.

(PSA) Public Service Announcement: Create a message, with the objective of raising awareness or changing public attitudes and behavior toward a social issue. Limit 2 minutes.

School Coverage: An informational segment about something happening at your school, such as academics, a sporting event, a play, and so on. Limit 3 minutes.

Short Film: It should be an original film that emphasizes a story. It should include character development, conflict, and resolution with creative storylines that strive to keep the viewer engaged for the full length of the film. Subcategories include but are not limited to action, adventure, comedy, drama, and horror. Limit 5 minutes.

Silent Film: A film that contains no synchronized soundtrack and no spoken dialogue. It should emphasize a story. It should include character development, conflict, and resolution with creative storylines that strive to keep the viewer engaged for the full length of the film. Subcategories include but are not limited to action, adventure, comedy, drama, and horror. Limit 5 minutes.

Stop Motion/Claymation: Limit 3 minutes.

Many libraries host teen film festivals and by the design of the competition, librarians try to make these events both fun and educational. When librarian Coleen Bornschlegel decided to start the Teen Short Film Festival at the Prescott Valley (AZ) Public Library in 2017, she admitted that it's been a little more work as it's the first time the library has ever done something like this.

Some teen film festivals began as an outgrowth of the librarian's own expertise in filmmaking. For example, 10 years ago, teen librarians at the Greenwood (IN) Public Library got plenty of experience creating book trailers as a type of multimedia readers' advisory program. Emily Ellis describes the steps in the process of making a trailer as she persuades librarians that book trailers provide an opportunity to support patron interests by bridging the gap between technology and literature.[22] The teen film festival has been a smashing success. When it started, as a collaborative effort with the local high school media specialist, it has grown from 373 people in 2009 to and 768 people in 2010.[23]

Working collaboratively with the Johnson County Public Library system, in 2016, Ellis decided to engage young patrons in opportunities to showcase their own creative work. Now in its third year, the Teen Film Festival invites high school students to submit documentaries, feature films, music videos, or a book trailer. The application notes, "All entries must be G or PG rated." Community members judge entries, using a rubric developed by Ellis and her team. All filmmakers get recognized at the festival event, with the winner receiving a prize of $400.

One short film, submitted to the 2017 festival, captures the creative energy of a group of teens who use video making as a form of play and learning. In *The Righteous Dudes*, created by Luke Wiley from Center Grove High School, we're introduced to a group of teen boys who have X-Men-like superpowers. Then we see the boys as they plan an elaborate heist, *Oceans Eleven* style. The film features plenty of scenes of backyard sword and (fake) gun play and computer hacking, and there are some cool special effects (including explosions, of course). The story depicts a real test of loyalty, trust, and friendship, culminating in a dramatic rescue scene, leading the narrator to conclude that the world needs protection from the righteous dudes.

When the Louisville Free Public Library partnered with the Louisville International Festival of Films to create the Kentucky Youth Film Festival, they wanted to provide opportunities to all teens, including those just beginning to shoot video with their cell phones to those at magnet schools working with high-end video equipment. They knew that students would benefit from a more sustained and intensive learning experience, so in 2016, they collaborated with Beargrass Media and held a week-long film camp at the Main Library. Twenty teens came to learn and experience filmmaking, supported by media professionals from the community who came to teach sessions about acting, cameras, public speaking, field audio, and postproduction. The teens visited a radio station, a news station, and the local newspaper. We'll learn more about the value of such partnerships in Chapter 6.

The Power of Deadline Pressure

When it comes to media production as a learning experience, deadline pressure is an amazing creative force. Watching a group of children or teens create a meaningful film in 5 hours is a truly magical experience. It can be done!

For 7 years, Renee has been observing young media makers and their mentors at the Give Me 5 program, developed by the Rhode Island Film and Television Office in conjunction with the Rhode Island State Council on the Arts Education Program. The Media Education Lab at the University of Rhode Island has been an active partner of the program, thanks to leadership from Professor Yonty Friesem, now a faculty member at Columbia College Chicago.

In the free program, which is held on a Saturday, a group of about 30 children and teens get hands-on experience in creating media by generating, producing, and editing a 1-minute film in just 5 hours. Adults are available to serve as actors and a mentor keeps the team focused, providing support and instruction as needed. An amazing range of short films are created. When the films are screened at the end of the day, the pride is palpable, and everyone learns how the power of deadline pressure helps advance the creative process.

THE CASE FOR THE STORYBOARD

A stop-motion animation program can be adapted to most spaces, from inside a library to outside in a city park. At the Providence Children's Film Festival, it's been dubbed the Animation Creation Studio, and it's a pop-up style workshop that gives kids a crash course in animation using stop motion. There are four core elements to the workshop experience: (1) an introductory discussion and screening of short films or film clips for inspiration; (2) character making (using modeling clay, craft materials, or even found objects); (3) storyboarding to plan out a story; and (4) using a simple stop-motion application on a smart device to bring their stories to life.

In some of these workshops, coauthor Liz Deslauriers has coordinated a partnership with volunteers from Hasbro, Inc., the Rhode Island–based toy company, which has a well-developed volunteer program with a commitment to supporting children's organizations and programs in the community. It was a perfect fit to connect this volunteer base with PCFF's support needs. Many of the company's employees can draw on their professional expertise, especially those in creative roles, to guide young filmmakers through the workshop. This partnership has contributed to the overall success of the workshops, because having the volunteer support allows for more kids to participate in the program with guidance. On top of that, volunteers specialized in graphic design and storytelling have been involved in planning and creating materials that support the workshop, elevating the entire experience with custom set designs to serve as backdrops for kids' imaginations.

When developing ideas for an animation or short film, a blank storyboard is a simple and easy-to-use tool. It's just a sheet of paper with some boxes and a few lines beneath them. What it can become in the hands of even the youngest of creative learners, however, is a catapult for starting stories from scratch, understanding the basic structure of a film or story idea, and ushering creative expression in a visual format that supports collaboration.

Never overlook the power of storyboarding. Part script, part animation cell, this hybrid story-organizing tool is an entryway for anyone with a story to tell, whether they prefer writing or drawing. For the writers, drawing stick figures will do just fine to communicate action, while for artists, their detailed drawings just might communicate most of the story without a word. In either case, storyboarding allows us to easily put ideas on the page and begin creating, with no expensive or complicated equipment involved—just a sheet of paper and a writing implement.

Although coming up with an entire story might seem daunting at first, a storyboard makes starting a lot easier. Start with introducing a character, and go from there. What happens next with that character? What needs to happen to get from point A to point B, and from beginning to end? By providing a few staple prompts to fill in a narrative arc, anyone can create a simple story to share.

Another advantage of using a storyboard is that it allows us to visualize a story's structure. Of course, a story must have a beginning, middle, and end; a storyboard reinforces that sequence. Storyboarding allows one to plan the sequence of a single scene or an entire plot, and to see gaps in a story or lulls in action. This communication of plot in such a sequence also begins to inform the creator of the scope of the project. A storyboard also helps young authors simplify their message and estimate how long a sequence will take to film.

Storyboarding Q&A

This advice comes from graphic designer, Brendan Opiekun, who has volunteered his know-how to guide young filmmakers in creating storyboards during several Providence Children's Film Festival's stop-motion workshops. Brendan's expertise comes from art directing toy commercials and sizzle videos produced in a corporate studio.

Q: How long should a storyboard be?

A: With storyboards, you have the opportunity to briefly write out what's the sentiment, what's the thought, or what's the action that you're trying to capture in that cell or in that moment. Storyboards can be as simple as six or eight cells, or they could be 30 cells if you look at some commercials produced by a studio.

Q: What's been the best part about showing kids how to storyboard?

A: For me, it's seeing the satisfaction on the kids' faces and seeing all the creativity. Storyboarding has been amazing for stop-motion workshops because we have a foundation that helps us guide kids on what needs to happen in each frame to bring their story to life.

VIDEO BOOK TRAILERS

Make a film trailer about a book. It's a great activity stuffed with educational potential for learners of all ages. When coauthor Pam Steager was developing the Media SmART! Project in Providence Elementary Schools, the focus shifted away from violence prevention because the district had a new superintendent, and as Pam was told, "It's all about literacy now." Luckily, since literacy is media literacy's last name, it was an easy shift to make. One of the new schools where the project was now operating provided both office space and a closet off the library media center. To show their gratitude and to get the school community excited about the possibilities of having a media production addition, one of the AmeriCorps volunteers working with the project created a Day in the Life video that was shared with parents attending Parents Night and students in class via the school TV broadcast system. It worked.

Now it was time to see what students could do. The librarian and a few of the classroom teachers who had experienced the professional development program were also eager to put their new knowledge to use. A production studio was created in a nearby closet, and a decision was made to have students read recommended books and then create commercials for them. Their target audience: younger students. Students were invited to create a video that would interest younger students in reading the book. The students were divided into production groups, read the assigned or chosen book together, discussed their strategy, decided on production roles (camera operator, stage manager, production assistant, on-air talent, etc.), and created storyboards for how their 30-second commercial would progress. Their discussions included the techniques they would use to attract and hold attention, the points of view in the story and how they would be represented, and creating interest without giving the ending away.

A *book trailer* is a persuasive dramatization of a book synopsis using characters, ideas or scenes from the book in ways that leave people wanting more. Book trailers are made by professional companies for publishing companies as part of their social media marketing campaigns, and they are also sometimes created by learners of all ages as a media literacy education exercise.[24] The video book trailer has a long and distinguished history. Back in the early 2000s, media literacy educator Robert Kenney collaborated with Orange County School Media Specialists in Orlando to create Digital Booktalk. Kenney and his team were trying to motivate reluctant readers to select, read, and complete books. Undergraduate students from Florida Gulf Coast University produced book trailers, and in the process, they learned about instructional design, animation, visual storytelling, video recording and editing, audio recording, graphic design, website development, programming, and database creation.[25] In describing the value of book trailers and other multimedia projects, education professor Bridget Dalton wisely recommends that educators and librarians should try multimodal response to literature themselves, first as readers and composers and then with students and patrons.[26]

Scholars who have studied the video book trailers created by children and teens have noted the careful use of sound to evoke the narrative world of the book. Music and sound effects can capture dimensions of the characters, setting, and plot. As the authors put it, "Instead of just telling about these features, sound served as a conduit for the viewer to experience the book through aural senses and gain insight into the events of the book and emotions of characters." Students mimic the persona of different characters through the pitch and tone of their voices, capturing a distinct accent and even making animal noises to represent nonhuman characters. Children use cultural sound tropes as a bridge between the book and the language of popular culture, using colloquial expressions such as "Oh crap!"[27] The playful process of adaptation allows for enormous creativity as learners experiment with text on screen, sound effects, and narrative suspense.

Creative Communities

BOOKTUBERS ON YOUTUBE

BookTubers are an incredibly dynamic community, and every librarian should know about them. We like Joce, who goes by the name SquibblesRead. She had over 27,000 subscribers on YouTube in January of 2019. Because she has a 3-hour commute each day, Joce listens to and reads a lot of books. Some months, she reviews 18 or more books and creates short YouTube videos about her reading choices.

The BookTube community has not yet been carefully studied by academic scholars, but it seems to have emerged spontaneously in 2011 when people who make YouTube videos about books acknowledged each other and the community began to form. By 2014, participants began to reflect on the nuances of the community itself, identifying the strengths and limitations of the social norms that have developed over time.

BookTubers are critical thinkers, that's for sure. Some BookTubers even comment on and analyze the community itself including the phenomenon of getting paid to promote a specific book in a practice called *influence marketing*. For example, JotheGreat is an African American Booktuber with 3,500 subscribers as of January 2019. At her YouTube channel, she offers opinions and commentary about literary works. She enjoys making videos as a creative outlet and appreciates getting comments from viewers. In one video called, "The Truth about BookTube," JotheGreat pulls back the curtain on this genre of videos. She first acknowledges the hierarchies within the community, where reviews of fantasy and sci-fi books are watched more often than other genres. Now that the publishing industry has given financial support to Booktubers as a low-cost form of promotion, BookTubers have become more commercial as some are merely advertising books, not reviewing them. By problematizing this practice, JotheGreat articulates some tensions around emerging norms within the online community. Although BookTubers are not using synchronous face-to-face communication for their dialogues, they are members of a robust learning community that relies on the power of asynchronous video as a tool for the sharing of ideas.

BookTubers usually record themselves using smartphones, professional cameras, or webcams, and sometimes they use special effects to improve their videos. BookTubers may even use artistic production technology. For instance, to illustrate mood and tone, "the video might turn grey to represent doubts or questions about what is being said. They might cut sections of the video to avoid repetition or mistakes, to make themselves sound more fluent, or to provide emphasis for key ideas."[28]

But librarians and others should not overlook the power of the hidden YouTube algorithm, which the company tweaks constantly to shape public access to BookTubers' videos.[29] As algorithms shape and limit access to and transmission of information between human beings, both creators and consumers in the BookTube community are influenced. The visibility and meaningfulness of this online dialogic space is driven by algorithms that make certain videos more visible and others less so.

In the years ahead, a closer relationship between school, public, and academic librarians and BookTubers could help the BookTube community develop and grow. How wonderful it would be if talking about books via watching and creating YouTube videos could become an outlet for more young adults to engage in dialogue about literature in open, collaborative, and critical ways.

CELEBRATING THE PUBLIC LIBRARY WITH PATRON-CREATED PROMOTIONAL VIDEO

Sometimes the library can inspire young filmmakers simply by motivating them to create media through a contest or competition. When the Torrance (CA) Public Library celebrated its 100th anniversary, they decided to launch a video contest by inviting the community to explain why the library is important to them. Librarian Dana Vinke began by assembling a team to develop the application forms, the contest rules, the timetable for the project, the promotion, judging, and awards. They accepted entries over a 5-month period and, not surprisingly, they received many more entries from youth than adults. They received 14 videos and awarded three $500 cash prizes. By reaching out to local film instructors at community colleges and high schools, they hoped to find the next Steven Spielberg, who was making short films at the age of 11.

The videos serve to showcase how community residents see the value of the library. In a music video entitled *Find What You're After*, a rock anthem features a boy who finds peace of mind in a library. In another narrative video, a kid finds adventure in a library. In the video, we see a young teen who is fighting with his mom who is convinced that he's been playing too many video games. Mom says, "Go to the library—and take your sister." The kids ride their bikes to the library and while there, the boy encounters a magical book that transports him to a strange land with characters including Little Boy Blue, Wee Willy Winkie, and Robinson Crusoe. Soon he jumps into another book, where he encounters a scary murderer. Finally, he encounters Tom Sawyer and Huck Finn. Clearly, in this narrative, the adventure of reading has become a replacement for the adventure of video gaming. "Do you think we can come back tomorrow?" he asks his sister. Clearly, this patron-created video helps viewers appreciate the value of the library for igniting the imagination.

THE ART OF ADAPTATION

Films matter because they raise illuminating questions that offer insight on the human condition. As a student of English Literature and Film Video Studies at the University of Michigan, Renee remembers reading George Bluestone's classic work, *Novels into Film*, which urged readers not to position literature at the top of some artificial hierarchy, where a film's quality is evaluated on the principle of fidelity or similarity. Instead, we must appreciate the integrity of each form of expression and communication on its own terms.

As you have already discovered, the *reciprocal relationship* between books and movies is a key topic in this book. Movies can inspire interest in reading, and reading can inspire interest in viewing. But as we discussed in an earlier chapter, educators and librarians alike can often get caught in the trap called "the book is always better." For more than 50 years, scholars of literary adaptation have urged us not to judge the success of a literary adaptation based only on its supposed faithfulness to the author's intent. As literary scholar George Leitch reminds us, books and films are valued not just for aesthetic reasons—a film adaptation cannot be seen as working merely in service of the book. In considering the relationship between books and the movies inspired by them, Leitch suggests some provocative questions:

- Can a movie serve as a transcription or an interpretation of its source?
- How does a movie depart from its literary source because of new cultural or historical contexts it addresses?
- How are movies and books both subject to cultural and historical recontextualization?
- How do we understand the concept of fidelity in adaptations of fiction and nonfiction texts? Can a movie betray its literary source?[30]

School librarians often support the development of critical viewing and reading skills by helping learners make connections between film and literature. Figure 3.5 shows a school library display that features eight young adult books that are on track to be made into feature films. (Here we hope that the #thebookisalwaysbetter hashtag which accompanies this tweet is a playful, not a literal one.) As we mentioned earlier, believing that the book is always better reflects a particular fallacy of thinking that film and literary scholars have long pointed out. Differences between literary and cinematic texts are not simply a matter of the essential properties of their respective media.[31]

It's simply wrong for librarians or educators to claim that books activate the imagination more than films, or that films inherently emphasize action, or that literature features interior monologue—all because of the bias of the media formats. These erroneous beliefs interfere with examining the genuine complexity of the many particular and complex choices made by both writers and filmmakers. We invite librarians and others to notice and gently point out the flaws of this kind of distorted and self-serving reasoning wherever they encounter it.

One idea about the study of adaptation is centrally linked to the practice of media literacy education. As one scholar puts it, "Every text offers itself as an invitation to be rewritten."[32] When we encounter adaptations based on books, we must consider the choices that were made by the authors. Because adaptations construct and reconstruct narrative, looking at what they include and what they omit from the source text sheds insight on how meaning is constructed through choices.

SLRI @SchLibRI · Jan 13

RT @shunicke At least 8 **YA books** will be made into movies in 2018. How many have you read? #thebookisalwaysbetter #phspatriotslibrary #bookstomovies

Figure 3.5 School library display features young adult books to be made into upcoming movies.

Perhaps the best way to deeply explore the genre of literary adaptations is to create one. Students can create imaginative adaptations that connect the past and the present. In their book *Teaching Literature to Adolescents*, Richard Beach and his colleagues describe the work of a student teacher whose students read *To Kill a Mockingbird* and imagine a movie version. Students take on the roles of casting director, dialogue director, director, soundtrack designer, and storyboard artist. Working collaboratively, they produce a concept for an adaptation, using sticky notes to identify parts of the text that related to their production role. For example, the casting director uses sticky notes to mark the passages that refer to the descriptions or personalities of specific characters.[33]

A number of young producers are creating literary adaptations in the form of YouTube vlogs. The most famous of them is the *Lizzy Bennet Diaries*, a web series based on Jane Austen's *Pride and Prejudice*. Developed by Bernie Su and Hank Green, the adaptation immerses fans into Austen's timeless classic through original episodic video and multiplatform storytelling. This was the first YouTube series to win a Primetime Emmy, receiving the 2013 Primetime Emmy Award for Outstanding

Creative Achievement in Interactive Media-Original Interactive Program. As a form of transmedia storytelling, it uses YouTube, Twitter, Tumblr, and Pinterest to tell the story of the three Bennet sisters as they cope with school, student loans, and underemployment in the gig economy. Jane Austen scholar Lori Halvorsen Zerne notes how the important shift in focus from a privileging of romance in *Pride and Prejudice* to a favoring of career in *The Lizzie Bennet Diaries* does not interfere with delivering the happy endings in which the heroines attain both love and financial security, portraying a successful balance between financial stability and romance.[34]

When teachers and librarians create adaptations, they deepen their respect for and understanding of the creative work that is involved. We're fans of those creative and dedicated college and university faculty who collaborate with elementary and secondary teachers to create rich learning experiences. For high school teachers, advanced study of literary adaptations can be transformative, especially when participants get to connect the dots between the practices of critical reading and multimedia composition. Two faculty members at the University of Arkansas are exploring just that. At the University of Arkansas, Sean Connors works with preservice and in-service English teachers in the context of a graduate secondary teacher licensure program. Working with a colleague in the English Department, Lissette Lopez Szwydky, they developed a 2-week summer institute for K–12 English teachers, including elementary educators, media specialists, language arts, foreign language, music, art, and theater teachers. The 2018 program was entitled "Remaking Monsters and Heroines: Adapting Classic Literature for Contemporary Audiences." It was supported by a grant from the National Endowment for the Humanities.[35]

The program skillfully blended theory and practice, which may account for why teachers who attended found it valuable. While mornings were spent examining adaptation from different theoretical perspectives, afternoons were devoted to actively engaging in the work of adapting texts. This structure was reflected in the guest speakers who participated in the program, including academics whose scholarly work focuses on adaptation, as well as writers, artists, and musicians with experience in adapting texts.

According to the faculty who designed the program, many secondary English teachers place primary importance on the use of "original" texts, even while understanding that often that content was too far removed from their students to engage them adequately. The unfamiliar cadences and vocabulary of early modern English can be daunting for people who are unfamiliar with it. Those who worked with younger students or those in arts-focused areas such as theater, music, and art had a different perspective. They didn't feel the same pressure to address the printed text in its original form. Because teachers encountered a variety of different perspectives among their peers, they got a chance to reflect on their own beliefs and assumptions about adaptation. This helped participants to reflect on the purposes of literature instruction and the merits of making space in the school curriculum for digital composing. In exploring the topic of adaptation with learners, educators may have a variety of different motives and purposes, each of which can provide valuable learning experiences.

Surprisingly, the University of Arkansas program did not only focus on film adaptations of literature, but instead included film among a wider set of adaptation forms such as theater, song, picture books, graphic novels, and more. Although most educators expected they would be creating lesson plans as part of the professional development program, instead they created an original adaptation, using the digital tools that were explored during the Institute. Their projects took many forms, including recorded radio plays, podcasts, video forms, animation, musical scores, comic books, digital picture books, paintings, and multigenre texts. Through technology workshops in podcasting (using Audacity, a sound editing platform), video (using Shotcut, a free and open-source cross-platform video editing application), and graphics (using Comic Life, a graphic design software tool), teachers developed confidence as creative media makers.

By creating an adaptation themselves, educators deepened their awareness of the level of thought and attention this work demands. As an art form, adaptation requires an enormous range of decision-making and problem-solving practices. As Lissette Lopez Szwydky-Davis explained, "Some teachers expressed skepticism or discomfort about the prospect of working with media or modes they weren't familiar with. We used these opportunities as teachable moments insofar as we invited the teachers to view them as opportunities to experience what some of their students likely feel when they are asked to tackle problems and assignments that challenge them to take risks and which push the boundaries of what they perceive themselves as doing."[36]

Challenges of Sustaining Community Media Initiatives

Working on a creative media project can be complex and time consuming. When you involve children, you must multiply the complexity exponentially. If you then engage with community partners, you will need patience, tenacity, and stamina. But when community media projects involve collaboration not only with partners from outside the organization, but also from within an organization, these initiatives can become unpredictable and a bit fragile. As with most things, stresses can cause things to come apart at the seams.

At the Thompson Middle School in Newport, Rhode Island, a team of educators developed a community documentary project involving all sixth graders in the community. Started in 2013, it was inspired by a Digital Literacy challenge created by Jaime Crowley, the school principal, who wanted teachers to find ways to get students more engaged in the community. Reading teacher Tina Brownell developed the idea for the Newport Documentary Project, where students, working in a team of five or six members, created short videos to share their learning about the community.

Jen Robinson, the school librarian, provided technology support and brought her expertise in the area of digital literacy. According to the principal, "She is the 'go-to' person in the building when it comes to technology implementation. She is deeply committed to staying ahead of the curve with the use of technology in her classroom and also training others."[37]

Working together, they developed a plan. During the month of April, students learned about their community and developed short scripts, with assistance from classroom teachers Lisa Olaynack and Sue Dunbar and with support from both the school librarian and Amie Shinego, the technology teacher. With intensive coordination by Lisa Olaynack, local community members generally came into the school and students interviewed them on video, using Flip cameras to capture their subjects on video. Students used their original footage with remixed clips from other sources, writing a script to synthesize the information they have gathered. Finally, they used editing software with their teachers to produce the final documentaries. To support students' independent work, Jen Robinson created a LibGuide and screencast video tutorials to help learn new technology skills of video editing.

Teachers wanted students to experience the thrill of having a real audience for their work. So when the projects were completed, in early May, 25 of the short student videos were screened at the local independent cinema, where students walked on a red carpet to view their production on a big screen. An emcee playfully announced each production, and student achievement was acknowledged by presenting awards for best student work in various categories, modeling the format of the Hollywood Oscar Awards. Parents and community leaders attended the event, proud of the work that their students had done.

Each year, as they implemented and assessed the Community Documentary project, participating educators made efforts to improve and elaborate on it in order to make it more truly educational for learners and to manage the limitations of time and technology access. They tweaked the project theme, which varied from year to year. One year, the theme was It Takes a Village, and the students explored topics such as historical buildings, homelessness, foster care, ghosts of Newport, Save The Bay, or other local causes important to the future of the city. One year, the theme was Truth or Dare, and the students explored the fact-based and demonstrable truth behind stories and perceptions about various topics of community importance.

The team also worked hard to ensure that community members participated in the film screening event. For example, some the people who were interviewed in the films made award presentations to the prize-winning student teams. One year, David McLaughlin, co-founder of Clean Ocean Access, presented the award to students for the "Best Environmental Film." Alan Bernstein, the School Department's director of the arts, gave another group of students an award for "Most Creative Film." Housing Hotline community organizers Barbara and Jimmy Winters presented an award to students for their short documentary on homelessness. This creative strategy promoted the development of a real relationship between teachers, students, and community members, and it tapped into people's deep-seated need for recognition and visibility.

It is commendable that teachers made a great effort to connect students with people in the local community, but this feature of the program was not without controversy. Some students focused their attention on small businesses started by local graduates and entrepreneurs. One year, students interviewed Neil Toracinta, a graduate of the Newport Public Schools who parlayed his love of surfing and his penchant for design into a custom-crafted surfboard business. One documentary featured interviews with the high school basketball team, which had won the state championship. Managing the scheduling and timing of these interviews fell to teacher Lisa Olaynack. Students would sometimes be pulled out of their regular classes to interview a community member. During the month of April, so many community members were entering and leaving the school building that some teachers found it to be disruptive to school routines. To some, it seemed that building community relationships was of more value to the staff than to the students themselves.

Limitations of time and technology also proved to be major stresses for the project. When the State of Rhode Island required annual testing using PARCC assessments of students' math and English skills in 2015, the time required for the assessments disrupted the spring schedule. In 2016, when students took the PARCC test online, it displaced all educational use of technology for learning purposes. There simply weren't enough computers in the building for both testing and learning. The computer labs where students usually worked on their videos were now restricted for use with PARCC testing only. Rescheduling the project and figuring out how to access computers to get video editing done was a big headache for teachers and librarians.

Tensions about the strategic goals of the project also served to add stresses to the team. Teachers had a variety of motives and goals for the Community Documentary Project. Tina Brownell wanted to find a way for students to experience the power of being digital authors. She made sure that there was a real audience for students' creative work, contracting with the Jane Pickens Theatre to have the films screened in a special event for students, parents, and community members. Lisa Olaynack wanted students to work in diverse collaborative teams. Because the school uses homogeneous ability grouping, or tracking, to group students according to their perceived ability and achievement levels, students at the school are placed in high, middle, or low tracks in an effort to provide them with a level of curriculum and instruction that is appropriate to their needs. Olaynack recognized that this model is especially detrimental to low-income and minority students, and she wanted students to encounter the genuine diversity of the local community by having students collaborate across the ability groups. It was difficult to accommodate all the goals that teachers had for this project.

Still, students, teachers, and librarians all learned a lot from the experience. The learning that resulted from this initiative included the following ideas:

- Connecting with community members is a powerful experience for staff and students alike.
- Celebrating student work with an authentic audience during a public event enables students to learn about the community, about collaboration, and about themselves.
- Stakeholders must have buy-in on a shared vision of the project's value. The team may need to educate administrators, colleagues, and students about the value of cross-curricular learning.
- Juggling many elements of a program requires an extraordinary blend of precision and flexibility. Knowing when to utilize each element requires a team of master planners who collaborate effectively.
- Consistent access to reliable, current technology is needed. When technical difficulties compound the complexity of the project, frustration can affect both students and staff alike.
- Being mindful of colleagues and the curricular demands on their instructional time is vital to the success of the project. Scheduling and mutual respect are key.

The heroic effort involved to develop such a big and multifaceted event eventually took its toll on team members. After 4 years, the Community Documentary Project ran out of steam and the project was disbanded. In reflecting on the reasons for the program's demise, Jen Robinson, the school librarian, explained, "In the end, there seemed to be too many pieces to the puzzle. We tried to make them all fit, but some of the most important pieces fell to the floor."[38]

MUSIC VIDEOS SPEAK TO THE HEART

In the end, despite the challenges of creating media, it's really the boundless creativity that makes us love creating media as a form of lifelong learning. Sometimes the creation of a video can take the world by storm, deepening the connections between librarians, patrons, and communities.

When the staff of the Nashville Public Library decided to set a goal of increasing library card ownership to 70% of the city's population in 2014, they knew they would need to develop a comprehensive social media and marketing campaign. They wanted to communicate the idea that the library is a fun place filled with fun people. So when Meghan Trainor released her hit pop song "All About That Bass," librarians collaborated to create their own parody version of the song, entitled "All About the Books." The video features many members of the staff (including the library director who plays the maracas). The playfully nerdy rendition of the song is adorable and, according to staff, there have been nearly 1 million views when hits/views from links to the song on local news websites and on Facebook are included.[39]

Sometimes a parody music video can address the deepest values of librarianship. We were entranced by a video created to celebrate Banned Books Week in 2017 by the librarians and patrons of the Homewood (IL) Public Library, who collaborated to create a parody music video entitled *Leer Despacito - Banned Book Week Parody of Despacito by Luis Fonsi w/ Justin Bieber*. They adapted the visual look and music of Luis Fonsi's Spanish-language dancehall song "Despacito" (which means Slowly). This song was a global sensation, becoming the most viewed video in YouTube's history, with 4.5 billion views. Figure 3.6 shows a screenshot of the Homewood Public Library's parody video. In this black-and-white film, we see young readers who

Figure 3.6 Music video parody created at the Homewood (Illinois) Public Library.

encounter banned books by Hispanic authors. Captioning in English and Spanish makes this film a treat for a wide range of viewers:

Welcome to our banned book collection
So thankful for this
It's such a blessing, yeah
I'll take a second just to show my affection
These books are the sunrise when they're throwing shade
Tryna' keep people far away
Make me want to read each little word so slowly
They say things some just don't like so they shut it down
Lots of reasons why they wanna take em out anyone can read them if they take the time to find
Look around and find 'em right here in the room now . . .

Tu puedes leer los libros que elijas. (You can read the books of your choice.)
Elegir es una libertad. (Choosing is a freedom.)
Muchos libros han sido desafiados. (Many books have been challenged.)
Tu puedes leer los libros que elijas. (You can read the books of your choice.)
Elegir es una libertad. (Choosing is a freedom.)

Leer un libro que ha sido desafiado. (Read a book that has been challenged.)
Leer despacito. (Read slowly.)
Lectura de libros prohibidos (Reading prohibited books)
Es estandar no un privilegio (is the standard, not a privilege)
Y estos son autores cuestionados . . . (and these are questioned authors . . .)
Leer despacito. (Read slowly.)

La casa en mango street de Sandra Cisneros (*The House on Mango Street* by Sandra Cisneros)
Francisco Rosales" libro "Chicano" (Francisco Rosales's book *Chicano*)
Loverboys escrito por Ana Castillo (*Loverboys* written by Ana Castillo)
Leer la casa de los espiritus y Paula (Read *The House of the Spirits* and Paula)
Isabel Allende autora (Isabel Allende, author)
Solo mira un poquito. (Just look a little.)
Preuebe este libro escrito por el autor (Try this book written by the author.)
Gabriel Garcia Marquez (Gabriel Garcia Marquez)
Grandes cosas esperando. (Great things waiting.)

The video's black-and-white format and the playful relationship depicted with patrons and librarians make the art of reading come alive for the next generation of new Americans. Reading classic and contemporary works of Latino/a literature that express the complexity of human experience and capture the imagination has never seemed so cool!

As this chapter has revealed, creative media production ignites the imagination, builds a sense of community, and reveals the uniqueness of the human heart and mind. Through exercising their own creativity and collaborating with colleagues, school, public, and academic librarians support and extend the power of learning through creating spaces for creative work to occur, fostering dialogue about books and movies that matter, supporting lifelong learning, and celebrating human creativity. In the next chapter, we'll consider the role of media in the lives of children and youth and examine the power of learning practices that deepen insight on the constructed nature of knowledge.

4

Learning

Questions Answered in This Chapter
- Why should librarians and educators be knowledgeable about how television and video influence children's language development?
- What are the major concerns about film and video as they affect young children?
- How do educators and librarians integrate media literacy across the whole K–12 curriculum?
- How do media literacy competencies emerge in young children?
- What is the pedagogical value in encouraging learners to ask questions?
- How do media reinforce or challenge gender stereotypes?
- What is close reading of media and how does it support literacy development?
- How can teaching about popular film trailers promote learning?
- What are DVD special features and how can they be used for learning purposes?
- How can film and video be misused in the classroom?
- Why is it so important for learners to interrogate the authenticity and authority of image-based media?
- How are academic librarians advancing the digital literacy competencies of college and university students?

A father calls down the stairs to his toddler watching TV in the basement family room to come up for breakfast. On his third attempt, the father gets more specific. "Alex, turn the Pooh movie off now and come eat your pancakes!" Little Alex is equally specific in his reply. "I'm not watching a Pooh movie, Daddy. I'm watching the little commercial trying to sell me the next Pooh movie!" Now that's obviously one media-literate 3-year-old!

Such children may be rare in our media-saturated culture, where little ones are swiping cell phones and tablets before they are toddlers and grow up surrounded by videos in the family car, the kitchen, and even the doctor's office and the preschool classroom. But parents can help children to gain vital media literacy competencies during the early years. For example, simply by introducing words like *film, TV show, animation, comedy, drama, news, reality TV,* and *commercial,* parents can help children be aware of some of the many forms and genres of media that are part of their everyday life.

Later on in the day, little Alex might call his grandmother using Skype to chat as dinner is being prepared. Of course, it took some practice for grandma to figure out the new technology, because she didn't get much exposure to computers during her working career. But she learned how to use digital media because she was motivated by her desire to keep in touch with all of her grandchildren, some of whom live far away.

In nearly every family, the tablet is the third screen, where, along with the television and the cell phone, digital devices serve up entertainment, information, and important social connectedness to grandparents, aunts and uncles, and other relatives and friends. Our screens offer families distraction from boredom, topics of conversation and shared experience to enjoy together, opportunities to be alone and separate from others, and background noise to life.

Early childhood specialists tell us that the preschool years are a sensitive period in the development of cognitive, sensorimotor, and socio-emotional competencies that contribute to future academic and personal success. But there has been a fascinating shift in perspectives about the perceived risks, dangers, and benefits of media use for infants and young children. Nearly every library has a stack of *Baby Einstein* DVDs, still popular among some parents who believe that exposure to classical music stimulates children's brain function. Millions of parents buy pretend cell phones for babies that blink and make sounds when little fingers press the buttons. And even children under the age of 2 quickly discover the fun of using a real cell phone, watching YouTube videos, and playing with apps like Busy Shapes 2 or The Robot Factory by Tinybop.

But not every family is actively socializing children to use media. In some families, parents avoid using their digital devices in front of their children and screen time is more limited. Indeed, parents, teachers, and librarians may consider the following:

- Should we think of children today as "at risk" due to the pull of the many screens in their lives and the potential impact on academic, social, and emotional development?
- Or is the youngest generation at an advantage as compared to the generations before them, given their easy, instantaneous access to information and entertainment content?

There's no right response here, and we might answer "yes" to both of these questions.

When we consider the potential of digital media for people across the lifespan, including adults and senior citizens, it's obvious that cell phones and tablets provide opportunities for more frequent social interaction with family members and friends. Moreover, when people are able to engage with media and technology for information, they may make well-informed healthcare decisions as well. As we, as a society, navigate forward—for there is no rewind button on technology—parents, teachers, and librarians are well poised to acknowledge and understand the challenges and opportunities that a world of connectivity presents for young and old alike.

Why is learning *with* and *about* film and media so important for librarians and educators? The emotional power of moving image media appeals to people of all ages, nationalities, and cultures. Because it provides intense pleasure, novelty, and thrills, people may not always be aware of how film and media communicate ideologies and values.

In this chapter, we take on the complex *love-hate relationship* that librarians, teachers, and parents have about life in a world of mass media and digital culture. We start by exploring children's media and technology uses. As we will see in the pages that follow, helping people reflect on their media use choices is a vital literacy competency needed for work, life, and citizenship. We consider the impact of audiovisual media on children's language development and concerns about media's role in shaping attitudes and behaviors through stereotyped depictions, the valorization of consumer culture, and media violence. We then take a look at how whole-school integration of media literacy is supporting the educational and socio-emotional needs of young learners. We consider the power of inquiry learning to disrupt gender and racial stereotypes and document how the pedagogy of close analysis of audiovisual texts supports literacy. There's much of value in the use of film trailers and special features on film DVDs to engage learners in meaningful dialogue and discussion. But we know that popping in a video can sometimes be a lazy form of teaching, and we confront the misuse of audiovisual media in the classroom, which has led to the rise of hyperrestrictive policies regarding its use. Finally we conclude by considering the value of using photos and audiovisual content in more explicit ways as librarians take on the challenge of teaching information literacy in a world where photo manipulation and fake news are rampant. As we will see, there are many pedagogical practices for using audiovisual media in ways that support learning.

Influence of Children's Media and Technology

There's no road map for raising children in a digital age, and there never really has been. Each generation must figure out for themselves how to maximize benefits and minimize risk. When Pam was raising her children, she paid $3.25 a month for the first basic cable television that brought some New York City channels into central Pennsylvania, where there had previously been poor to no broadcast reception. When Renee was raising her children, there were 500 cable TV channels from which to choose. Although channel surfing with the remote control had become normative in many families, Renee refused to have a remote control in the household. To change the channel, family members needed to get up from the couch and touch the television's cable box directly! When Liz was a teenager, the cell phones only a few of her friends had were exclusively used for making phone calls. Her own child, however, is growing up in a wireless broadband household where every member of the family has multiple digital devices.

What advice can librarians and educators offer people about managing Internet use in the family? At the turn of the millennium, the advice was relatively simple: Keep the computer in the kitchen or family room, where it could be monitored by parents looking over their child's shoulder. Today that advice seems a bit quaint. Growing up with the ubiquitous use of tablets and smartphones, members of the family may be using Google Home, which enables people to access the Internet using voice commands. Many young children watch their siblings and parents use interactive mobile devices such as cell phones and iPad-style tablet devices and naturally, they want to use them, too.

Compared to some countries in Europe, we know relatively little about the media and technology choices of children and youth. You may be wondering why Americans don't have access to high-quality annual data about the media use patterns of American children and teens, given the rapid rate of change in this sector. Sadly, the US government does not have any agency responsible for collecting data about children's media use. The Kaiser Family Foundation, a philanthropy that had previously supported annual data collection on children's media use, stopped funding research reports in 2010. Fortunately, children's media researcher Vicky Rideout occasionally develops nationally representative surveys under contract from Common Sense Media, working in association with philanthropies or media companies to provide evidence of changing trends for children and their families. In many countries, the government media regulation agency collects data on children's media use to inform policymakers and the public. In the United States, such data are collected privately by marketing research firms and sold to candy companies, clothing firms, and gaming startups.

In England, there is a strong government regulatory tradition that is attentive to the media use of all its citizens and where regular data are collected to understand the fast-changing nature of these trends. The British Office of Communication (OFCOM) was created in 2003 by the British parliament to unify all forms of communication regulation, including TV, radio, video-on-demand, telecommunication, mobile use, and postal service, as well as the airwaves over which wireless devices operate. Accountable to citizens, the agency is funded from industry fees and government tax revenues. Each year, they produce a report documenting the attitudes and behaviors of adults, teens, and children in Great Britain, with a special focus on examining attitudes and behaviors associated with media literacy. In the next few pages, we offer some basic information that we think all librarians should know about media's influence on child development.

MEDIA'S INFLUENCE ON LANGUAGE DEVELOPMENT

Every parent has experienced nestling with spouse and baby in front of the TV. This kind of media exposure is often delightful—as parents get a moment of relaxation in their busy schedules. It's a type of media use called *incidental exposure*, and some studies have found that up to one third of all media exposure to children under the age of 2 consists of shows designed for adult audiences. With giant flat screen TVs in nearly every room of the house, children grow up with a lot of incidental exposure to audiovisual media.

Children's language development may be diminished by constant media use in the home. For toddlers ages 2–4, incidental viewing has been associated with a decrease in linguistic ability. Korean toddlers, like American and British children, generally watch for 1–2 hours per day. One in three watch for more than 2 hours per day. In one study, children who watched the most TV had 2.7 times more risk of language delay than those who viewed less than 1 hour and "the risk of language delay increased proportionately with the increase in TV watching time."[1]

Early TV exposure can have far-reaching impact on language development. Developmental psychologist Cathy Hirsh-Pasek and her colleagues observed 14 pairs of young children under the age of 2 with their parents while they watched television together. She found both the quality and quantity of parent speech significantly declined while the TV was on, and especially when the infants were watching.[2] Another longitudinal study found that children's heavy TV use at age 3 was associated with lower levels of reading at age 7.[3]

Some evidence shows that heavy use of screen media does affect children's interest in reading. For example, in assessing the developmental impact of heavy-television households on infants, toddlers, and preschool children, researchers have found that 5- and 6-year-old children read less in these homes.[4] Unfortunately, many studies show that such media use has a negative impact on attention, cognition, and language outcomes. What explains the findings? During TV watching, as both parents and children direct their attention to the screen, the quality and quantity of parents' talk tend to decrease. Media use seems to interfere with parent–child interactions and the quantity and the quality of play.[5]

When researchers first began studying programs like *Sesame Street*, they realized the complex process at work as children extract and comprehend educational content from television programs. Watching and comprehending television involves a process of paying attention and remembering. To learn from television, children must first selectively attend to certain aspects of the visual and verbal content, including both the narrative and the educational content.[6] When content is too complex, attention cannot be sustained. When content is not novel or complex enough, attention also lags.

Understanding the genre of a television program has an influence on how it will be processed in terms of its value for learning. Although the ability to distinguish reliably between reality and fiction does not fully develop until about the age of 11, children develop ideas about reality and fiction in television along with more general fantasy/reality judgments. Sometimes children believe that fictional events are real, but they can also mistake real events as fictional. As children grow, they develop story schema, an idealized internal representation of the parts of a typical story and the relationships among those parts. Researchers have been studying how children's story schemas affect reading, listening, and viewing comprehension for many years. Some evidence shows that story schemas can transfer across print and television formats.[7] Children with greater story schema skills are easily able to comprehend narrative content, which, in turn, helps them focus attention on processing educational content. Thus, understanding story structures helps children learn more from educational media.

CONCERNS ABOUT MEDIA INFLUENCE AND THE NEED FOR PROTECTION

For nearly 100 years, researchers have studied the potentially negative impact of audio and visual media on children and youth. Media researchers have examined the role of racial, gender, and ethnic stereotypes on viewers and looked at the relationship between media consumption patterns and obesity. Hundreds of studies have found that exposure to media violence has both short- and long-term effects on attitudes and behavior.[8] Although proving causality is extremely challenging using social science research methods, there is some important evidence that suggests that media use should be limited—and not just for children and youth, but for people of all ages.

Developmental psychologists have examined the impact of media use on cognition, finding that time spent using media replaces or substitutes for other activities that are beneficial for children. This is called the *displacement effect*.[9] For example, time spent watching YouTube videos is time taken from such activities as motor skill development and learning through playing with people and objects. Time spent viewing media can decrease the opportunity for social interaction.

When digital media use becomes a primary form of entertainment and play, children develop skills for using digital tools but may not acquire other life skills. As younger children are increasingly exposed to screen time through the use of parental cell phones, researchers are beginning to evaluate the impact of this on the preschooler. In the United Kingdom, teachers have found that as preschool children spend more time using screen technology, both language and motor skills are affected, including using building blocks and writing with pen and pencil. And the digital media that young children encounter are strongly commercialized, dominated by Disney, with easily recognizable logos and separate branding for little girls and little boys, so that many of the lessons children learn by using media are inextricable from learning how to consume.

For these reasons, since 1999 the American Academy of Pediatrics (AAP) has recommended that parents consider both the benefits and risks of their media use, and teach children and adolescents how to make good choices in their media consumption. Exposure to educational media and prosocial content can help children develop empathy, racial and ethnic tolerance, and interpersonal skills such as sharing and respect for the needs of others. After 15 years of recommending that parents keep children under 2 away from *all* screen media and limiting screen time of entertainment media to less than 1 or 2 hours per day and keeping screens out of kids' bedrooms, they modified their policy in 2016.

They created an online tool for parents to develop a Family Media Plan to make media use more strategic and intentional for all members of the family. They have encouraged pediatricians to ask about media in the bedroom and to challenge the entertainment industry to create positive content for kids and advocate for regulation about how food and other products are marketing to children.

Media and Young Minds

From the policy statement by the American Academy of Pediatrics, 2016:

Evidence is sufficient to recommend time limitations on digital media use for children 2 to 5 years to no more than 1 hour per day to allow children ample time to engage in other activities important to their health and development and to establish media viewing habits associated with lower risk of obesity later in life. In addition, encouraging parents to change to educational and prosocial content and engage with their children around technology will allow children to reap the most benefit from what they view.

As digital technologies become more ubiquitous, pediatric providers must guide parents not only on the duration and content of media their child uses, but also on (1) creating unplugged spaces and times in their homes, because devices can now be taken anywhere; (2) the ability of new technologies to be used in social and creative ways; and (3) the importance of not displacing sleep, exercise, play, reading aloud, and social interactions. Realistically, pediatric providers will need to know how to help parents find resources finding appropriate content, tools for monitoring or limiting child use, ideas for play or activities in which to engage rather than digital play, and how parents can limit their own media use.[10]

But not everyone sees the need to limit, monitor, or regulate children's media use. Sociologist Annette Lareau points out that only a small subset of families see childhood as a time when children are carefully cultivated through active parenting strategies and access to special learning experiences in sports, music, and the arts. Many parents adopt the position that children develop naturally through being part of ordinary family life and culture and do not need such special cultivation.[11]

Another factor shaping public attitudes is the rise of the digital media and learning community, which has challenged the dominance of the public health paradigm on media effects. They don't find correlational survey research or experimental studies to be persuasive or useful. Scholars like Jim Gee have noted the potential value of games as a means to support student learning and, in general, the belief that playing video games supports problem solving, fine-motor skills, and collaboration is widely held.[12] Others have emphasized the potential cultural value of violence in entertainment media, noting how it both reflects and shapes the values of American society. For example, Henry Jenkins points out that American culture incorporates violence into storytelling for a lot of complex reasons. He writes, "We need our art to help us make sense of the senselessness of violence in the real world, to provide some moral order, to help us sort through our feelings, to provoke us to move beyond easy answers and ask hard questions."[13]

There are many factors that contribute to violence in society and public health researchers acknowledge that media violence is but one small part of a larger cultural phenomenon. But researchers have found that exposure to media violence can lead to reductions in helping behavior and increased willingness to inflict punishment in an experimental setting. Children have been observed to imitate behavior, when the behavior depicted features an attractive perpetrator. Exposure to media violence also increases the perception that the world is a "mean and scary place," a phenomenon that one researcher has labeled the *mean world effect*.[14] Under some conditions, viewing can inspire imitation. For example, when violence is paired with sexual content, viewing it can increase the likelihood that male viewers will behave aggressively or physically assault females who have provoked them.[15]

Media violence has accelerated with the process of globalization. To compel the attention of viewers, filmmakers use representations of violence that are increasingly vivid and gory, as compared with previous eras. Because children and youth gradually learn to distinguish between real-world violence and pretend fictional violence, adult viewers "tend to read media representations against our perceptions of the real world and discard them if they deviate too dramatically from what we believe to be true."[16] That's why news violence—including eyewitness accounts of school shootings and police brutality—can be the most terrifying kinds of media violence that people of all ages can experience.

The Digital Worlds of Toddlers and Young Children

In 2017, Common Sense Media and the British government each surveyed parents, children, and teens to learn about the development of their media use and media literacy competencies. Some key findings include the following:

Among American Children Aged 0–2:
- 43% are read to, for an average of 21 minutes per day.
- 35% watch TV or videos, for an average of 40 minutes per day.

Among American Preschool Children Aged 2–4:
- 27% watch music videos often or sometimes.
- 43% have their own tablets.

Among British Pre-School Children Aged 3–4:
- 21% have their own tablets.
- 53% go online for an average of 8 hours per week.
- 48% watch YouTube, watching cartoons and unboxing videos.

Among American Children Aged 5–8:
- 11% use a computer every day.
- 28% use a mobile device at least once per day.
- 22% play social media games such as Club Penguin, Animal Jam, or Minecraft.

Among British Young Children Aged 5–7:
- 35% have their own tablet.
- 95% watch TV for an average of 13.5 hours per week.
- 66% play digital games for an average of 7.5 hours per week.
- 71% watch YouTube, watching cartoons and funny videos or pranks.

Developing Media Literacy Competencies in School

WHOLE-SCHOOL INTEGRATION

Elementary school is where students first learn how to learn. At the Mark Day School in San Rafael, California, elementary school is an intentionally designed learning community, where people can feel comfortable trying new things, asking questions, and making mistakes. Under the leadership of headmaster Joe Harvey, the school has built a Learning Commons and Creativity Lab, a new campus space that enables the library to function as a multimedia learning center.[17] This school is replete with creative approaches to integrating media and information literacy into the curriculum. It's a priority for the school librarian and technology specialist, of course, but it's also significant for many teachers and department heads.

Bonnie Nishihara, assistant head of the school and director of Educational Design and Innovation, has been helping the faculty to integrate media literacy into the K–8 curriculum for more than 10 years. She knows how media and technology support teaching and learning, as active creators and engaged learners use their skills and talents responsibly in the world, making an impact on the local community and larger world.

As a part of their faculty professional development program, they have identified four literacies that are woven into the entire curriculum: (1) critical thinking is activated through a focus on media and information literacy; (2) cultural competencies are activated through cross-cultural literacy; (3) socioemotional and ethical literacy is embodied by the process of meeting daily challenges and navigating human differences with a well-developed sense of social responsibility; and (4) stewardship of the environment is embedded in the concept of ecological literacy.

As an exclusive independent school outside of San Francisco, it's a near-ideal situation for whole-school integration of media and information literacy to thrive. At the Mark Day School, teachers are expected to integrate these literacy competencies in their own creative ways, with support from staff, including the technology specialist and school librarian, and stemming from their expertise, passions, and sensitivity to student needs.

Whole-school integration of media and information literacy is not something that just happens. It must be an intentional practice that is cultivated over several years. Mark Day School school leaders knew that many faculty were engaging students' media and information literacy competencies in different ways. But they didn't have a clear sense of the scope and depth of the work.

One simple practice helped the faculty better understand how media and information literacy were embodied in the daily practices of teaching and learning. To share and reflect on media and information literacy learning experiences across the school, Nishihara developed a Google Form for faculty to help them document examples of informal and formal learning in media and information literacy. From this, they discovered how often these concepts and practices get embedded in the curriculum. Some examples include the following:

- *Book Making.* When Grade 1 students explored worms, they began to understand their role in sustaining the health of garden soil, and ultimately of the vegetables and fruits that sustain us. To demonstrate their learning, children composed a book about worms in the garden that became part of the school library collection.

- *Designing a Cereal Box.* A lesson on advertising and marketing engaged children in examining how cereal, yogurt, and other products appeal to specific target audiences by using images, languages, and stories to create a brand. Students demonstrated their learning by creating their own cereal boxes for specific target audiences. Figure 4.1 shows a bulletin board that invites passersby to "guess the target audience" by looking at the design and packaging that students designed.
- *Digital Identity.* Children used an iPad app in a lesson on reputation to generate words describing how they want to be seen. They took photos of themselves and created images with the words they came up with.
- *History Research.* Students completed a "Research Ready" sheet by gathering information using their history textbooks to provide a starting point for keyword generation that would lead them into their own research. Through this, they discovered that one of the topics was not covered in the textbook: the Salem witch trials. Teachers and students discussed why this topic might be missing from the textbook. The information that appears in them reflects choices made by the textbook company. Those choices may be motivated by a number of factors. Students learned that textbooks are media—they are constructed messages, and all media messages are selective and incomplete.

Figure 4.1 Students design cereal boxes for different target audiences in a media literacy lesson on advertising and marketing.

- *Identifying Stereotypes.* Sometimes students take the lead in making connections between the curriculum and contemporary society. For example, the study of ancient civilizations in sixth-grade history led students themselves to examine perceptions and stereotypes about the Middle East today. By making connections between what they are learning in the classroom and the issues facing our communities, culture, and society, intellectual curiosity was sparked.

Tools for Transforming Video Into Active, Deeper Learning

VIEWPURE (WWW.VIEWPURE.COM)

This website displays YouTube videos on a spare white screen, without all the visual clutter. Because the comments section and the related videos are removed, the visual field is less distracting and less likely to contain "inappropriate content."

CAPTIONS

Turning on the caption function for video content is a widely accepted educational practice, and research shows that captions increase comprehension and support reading skills. Captions also help people recognize the strategic and intentional choices made by writers and speakers as they express meaning.

VIDEO ANNOTATION

When students engage with video by pausing and writing questions or comments, they are more likely to engage in critical analysis. Tools like Video Ant (www.ant.umn.edu) and Vialogues (www.vialogues.com) help learners engage in close analysis activities. When learners collaborate on annotating a video, they discover that multiple interpretations of video occur because people interpret media using their life experience, background knowledge, and worldview to make sense of what they see.

For whole-school integration to advance, teachers benefit from learning more about what kinds of learning experiences are occurring across the building and across the community. Librarians and technology specialists can coordinate to collect examples of film education, visual literacy, digital and media literacy learning, and other innovative practices, which can help to identify areas of strength, overlaps, and gaps.

EARLY EVIDENCE OF MEDIA LITERACY COMPETENCIES

When Renee and her graduate students started working at an urban elementary school in Philadelphia, they could see evidence that some—but not all—children had an emerging awareness of media messages. Even in their informal play with images, language, and sound, some children demonstrated evidence of thinking that was informed by exposure to ideas about authors and audiences, messages and meanings, and representations and reality.

To explore this, we asked children to draw a picture and explain their reasons for liking a favorite television show, video game, and song. We were able to compare academically gifted 9- to 11-year-olds to students in a regular education program. Some children were unable to describe why they liked their favorite TV shows, games, or songs, writing only "It's funny" or "It's cool" or "It's the best." Other children offered detailed reasoning for their media preferences. For example, one child wrote: "It is hilarious and some of the boys on there are cute and funny and it has my favorite t.v. stars." Another child wrote, "It's funny and the cartoons can sometimes be so clueless and at other times can be so evil." Describing a favorite video game, one child explained, "It has awesome graphics, great characters, and cool super attacks."

We noticed that children demonstrated active reasoning if they:

➢ Recognized the genre or type of message
➢ Made an explicit link between two elements of the composition (e.g., lyrics + beat, beat + dance)
➢ Described a compositional element
➢ Identified the message's purpose or meaning
➢ Referred to some social aspects of using media
➢ Described an emotional response plus one other element of the message

When talking together about media, adults and children may make statements to connect ideas, using both clues from the media text itself and the speaker's own background knowledge. Media-based activities support literacy development when they strengthen oral language, inference-making, and reasoning skills. Critical analysis of media involves inference making, where readers construct mental representations by identifying meaningful relations among text elements and between text elements and their own opinions and knowledge.[18]

Even very young children can demonstrate some basic skills that support media literacy learning. For example, researchers in Germany developed a simple test to measure the media sign literacy of even younger children. Working with 4- to 6-year-olds, researchers found that children with higher levels of media sign literacy learned more from educational television. Measuring media literacy among children who cannot read can be challenging, but these researchers use a creative approach with simple, age-appropriate questions. They ask children to match a presented voice with its corresponding character. Children hear the voices of a dwarf, fairy, bear, and wizard and must choose the picture of the character that was speaking. They are also asked to recognize how scenes look when portrayed from the point of view of different characters. Children see a landscape scene from the perspective of animals of different sizes and are asked: "Was this photo taken by the tiger, by the elephant, or by the ant?" They are asked to recognize symbolic representations on maps, including symbols for mountains. They are asked to demonstrate their knowledge of computer user interfaces, such as recognizing when an X symbolizes the exit function. Children are asked, "Where would you click if you wanted to exit the game?"[19]

The implications of this research are noteworthy. Parents can support the development of early media literacy competencies by pointing out the things on TV that are not real—and calling attention to content that depicts real people and real events. As media researcher Eric Rasmussen notes, "Children can notice when the weather reporter is really standing in front of a green screen, not a weather map. They can learn the difference between TV shows and advertisements," and questions can be used to gauge their comprehension of character emotions, motivations, and behaviors.[20] We think that individual differences in children's ability to comprehend and learn from media may be due to their differential levels of media literacy.

THE POWER OF QUESTIONS FOR INQUIRY LEARNING

To learn for a lifetime, the most practical competence is the ability to ask good questions and get answers in order to make good decisions. But often in schools, this skill is not given the attention it deserves. Angie Miller blogs about her experience as a high school librarian. In one story, she tells about a health teacher who came into the library with her students as they worked on a research project. The students arrived with a list of questions to answer. As they searched for answers, they put them into the form of a PowerPoint presentation.

Angie couldn't help herself. As she observed and consulted during the process, she asked them other questions such as "What is surprising about this?" or "Is there any stigma to this illness?" But kids were confused. Those questions were not on the worksheet. To her surprise, students simply didn't know how to engage with the learning experience enough to formulate a personal response.

The next semester, when Miller suggested to the teacher that the students generate their own questions, the teacher was concerned, wondering, "But what if they don't come up with the right ones?"[21]

That's a natural fear that comes from a teacher who feels obliged to cover content. But when students are empowered to design their own questions and take a journey of inquiry, students can be counted on to develop important, original, and meaningful questions that propel their intellectual curiosity and activate a sense of ownership over their learning. Renee's colleagues Amanda Murphy and Erica DeVoe from Westerly High School first introduced a way to help students generate questions using the methods offered by the Right Question Institute.

Questioning is a way to organize thinking around what you don't know—and that can be liberating once you free your mind to do it. Collaboration can support the question generation process. Here's an approach we've used that works well: After creating a focus statement on a topic of interest, students work with a peer. One student generates as many questions as she or he can, without discussing, judging, or answering the questions. The other student writes down every question exactly as stated.

If a student gets stuck, he or she turns statements into questions, using the classic question starters: why, how, what, where, who, what if, could, or should. Then the list of questions is reviewed to classify the questions as "open" (many possible answers) or "closed" (one right answer). They discuss the advantages and disadvantages of each type of question. Then they choose the three most interesting, important, or useful questions and begin using a variety of search strategies to gather information to explore and learn more.

Thanks to the school librarian's fine coaching, her health, history, and Spanish students were all able to develop their own research questions, gathering information to create a mini-TED-like talk. It does take more work to generate questions than it does to simply answer them, of course. Teachers and librarians need to model the process of question formulation; students need to practice and get feedback. But ultimately, as Angie Miller explains, "students not only ask the same questions we would have, but they actually ask better ones." The active process of learning to formulate good questions is an essential life skill that school, public, and academic librarians can help to develop in learners and patrons alike.

DECONSTRUCTING GENDER AND RACIAL STEREOTYPES

We often overlook the way in which identity is shaped by the books, movies, TV shows, and music we encounter as part of everyday life. Gender stereotyping is deeply woven into the fabric of consumer culture. Rebecca Hains, a college professor at Salem State University, is intensely aware of the power of gender stereotypes, having written about "girlie-girl culture," where feminine identity is marked with pink and glittery princesses. In her book *The Princess Problem*, Hains offers support to parents who want their children to be able to think critically about media messages.

She uses a technique she calls pop culture coaching, where through conversation starters, children learn to resist marketing, recognize attractiveness as a type of bias, and see through the gender and racial stereotypes.[22] Cinderella, Sleeping Beauty, and Barbie and Bratz dolls all reinforce gender stereotypes, beginning with young children, who may internalize a set of attitudes as they wear pink clothing and pose for the camera. Boys also experience stereotypes when they are given camouflage clothing, light sabers, and plastic dinosaurs to play with. Such stereotypes affect children's attitudes in ways that reinforce power and privilege. For example, heavy-viewing 4-year-old boys are more likely than other children to believe that others think boys and men are better than girls and women.[23]

Gendered media stereotypes are everywhere: in literature, news, magazines, advertising, television, videogames, and music, on social media, and in cartoons and films, too. Stereotypes influence men and women for the long term, influencing people's choice of lifestyles and careers, their attitudes about romantic and sexual relationships, and even their views on sexual harassment. Anxiety over appearance intensifies during puberty and 6 out of 10 girls stop doing something they love during adolescence because of concerns about how they look.[24] Teen boys also feel pressure to achieve a muscular physique, and studies show that many are highly concerned about their weight and body image, with anxiety about this well correlated with depression, binge drinking, and drug use. Some media content targeting African American teens, for example, contains higher-than-average levels of sexually objectifying portrayals of women.

When high school students get a chance to critically analyze older, children's animated films, they can sometimes spot cultural stereotypes more easily than in current popular films. In one Texas classroom, high school students viewed *Happy Feet*, the 2006 animated film directed by George Miller. They recognized the very human racial and gender stereotypes embedded in this film about a penguin who cannot sing. Learners noticed how the characters and their behavior reflect cultural values and stereotypes, appreciating that younger children might not recognize these stereotypes.[25] Critics have also noted that many children's films "depend on voices that are funny only because they exploit ethnic and racial stereotypes."[26]

Librarians in school and public libraries have done amazing work in paying attention to stereotypes that exist in children's literature. They call attention to books that provide positive and realistic representations that celebrate diversity. Librarians can also help parents unpack and reflect upon the stereotypes offered in children's television shows, movies, and games.

Close Reading of Media Texts

More than any other activity, close reading is the core pedagogy of media literacy. Through critically examining a text, students see the deep structure of the way the text has been constructed. Media literacy educators like to emphasize, "All media messages are constructed."[27] How does a close reading work when it comes to different forms of media?

- With a *book*, this might include the organization and structure of the work, the language use and vocabulary, and the strategic use of details, arguments, evidence, and inferential meanings.[28]

- With a *film*, this might include the representation of the characters, the choice of setting and time period, and stance toward the action, the use of dialogue, music, and camera and editing techniques.
- With a *photo*, this might include decisions about what to include inside the frame, how subjects are positioned, and the use of color.
- With a *website*, this might include a careful look at the content and headlines, examination of author expertise, and analysis of images and hyperlinks to help identify the author's point of view.
- With a *video game*, this might include a consideration of how users are positioned within the narrative activity, what choices are available (and not available), how the enemy or villain is depicted, and how users are rewarded for playing, advancing or winning the game.
- With an *app*, close reading would include consideration of the actions or choices offered to users and the nature of the rewards, plus careful analysis of the visual, musical, and interactive elements that make the app "sticky" or hard to stop using.

Close reading of media builds a habit of mind that promotes awareness of and sensitivity toward the rhetorical purposes of informing, entertaining, and persuading, whether it is print, video, or web-based content. This habit of mind takes a lifetime to master. The technique of close analysis relies on the power of repeated viewings to reveal layers of meaning through close examination of the constructedness of the audiovisual text. It's nearly impossible to critically analyze audiovisual content after a first viewing. There's simply too much going on in the text.

Sadly, in schools, close reading of video is not as common as close reading of print. In many schools, video viewing is sometimes used as a mere engagement device simply to get kids' attention or convey content.[29] For many teachers and librarians, it's not considered important enough to take time to critically analyze video or film. In too many high school English classrooms, close reading is often restricted to classic literature. Video is used as entertainment, reward or as a break from learning.

We've observed close reading of video in many public, independent, and private schools. But at the Mark Day School, where video is used as a significant tool for learning and close analysis is a valued skill, we've learned about the many ways that media literacy competencies are developed with very young learners in this K–8 school. For example, in one class, young children viewed a Brain Pop video to get an introduction to their science lesson in geology focused on the layers of the Earth. But the animated video wasn't just used for engagement purposes to capture the interest and attention of the children. It was object of inquiry. Through close analysis, the video because a stimulus for transforming passive viewing into active, critical analysis. It accelerated the development of children's critical thinking skills.

How did close viewing of video occur with young children? Students viewed the Brain Pop geology video three times, each with a focused goal:

➤ On the first viewing, learners watched to gain content knowledge and key ideas, including the many different names for the layers of the Earth.
➤ On the second viewing, learners watched a part of the video with some detailed content, and the instructor paused to check comprehension of key ideas by asking students questions.
➤ On the third viewing, learners focused on the constructed nature of the video, including specific metaphors, visual and linguistic features, and forms. They discussed the use of characters, the way humor is used, and they talked about the drawings and the other kinds of art used in the animated video. They discussed why the creators used features like the zoom to offer a close-up of the diagrams and show how they are labeled.[30]
➤ When the close analysis was completed, students then drew their own geology diagrams to display in their digital portfolios. They demonstrated their understanding of geology by creating media themselves.

Of course, a lesson like this takes time. But by slowing down the viewing and discussion process and incorporating simple note taking and media creation activities, students bring their creative minds into the learning process. They learn to focus their own attention. The pedagogy of close analysis helps them gain content knowledge while increasing their awareness of how media messages are constructed, enabling them to gain insights that improve their own skills as digital authors.

Students need plenty of practice across the K–12 spectrum to internalize close reading competencies. But such close reading competencies with multimedia are articulated in the Common Core State Standards. For example, in Grade 7, students are expected to compare and contrast a written story, drama, or poem to its audio, filmed, staged, or multimedia version, analyzing the effects of techniques unique to each medium (for example, lighting, sound, color, or camera focus and angles in a film). In Grade 11, students are expected to evaluate the advantages and disadvantages of using different media (for example, print or digital text, video, multimedia) to present a particular topic or idea.

Close reading of film can be a transformative experience for learners, resulting in significant changes to the way they view. Starting with an idea suggested by media literacy expert Frank Baker, Professor Bill Kist of Kent State University has used the opening sequence from the television series *Lost* without providing any introductory comments. Then students break into small groups, and each group is provided with a description of a film element (lighting, camera angle, editing, dialogue, music, costume, setting, etc.). Students discover how all the elements are used to advance the central idea about the tension between good and evil. Kist notes that his preservice students uniformly experience an "aha" from viewing the video clip in an entirely new way, saying things like "I didn't notice that sound effect the first time we watched the scene," or "Looking just at the editing made me realize how carefully the scene was planned." Media literacy educators are familiar with the nature of these kinds of student feedback—it's a common theme that close analysis changes the nature of the relationship between the reader and the text.

Practitioners and researchers are learning that the competencies involved in close reading may transfer across media forms and genres. For example, after analyzing a film sequence, Kist shifts to look closely at a print text. After reading aloud a scene in a print text, students break into small groups to concentrate on just one particular element—for example, the author's use of descriptive words, action verbs, dialogue, metaphors, character, or setting.[31] Close reading can help learners examine the author's purpose and to explore the genre, point of view, and multiple interpretations of the text. [32] The use of digital annotation tools (described in the boxed text) can also help promote an active stance toward reading.

Close reading demonstrates the ways that meaning are encoded in the text and interpreted by the reader. Modeling the practice of close reading can activate deep insights on human nature and the power of symbolic expression. But it's important to help students become both critical and sympathetic viewers. Tracy Cox Stanton writes, "The films I most enjoy teaching, the ones I am most beholden to in my own education, are those that require us to slow down and really see, hear, and feel a new reality."[33]

Reflecting on her experience teaching film, Cox Stanton observes that students are sometimes hesitant or hostile toward ideas that are foreign, unfashionable, or potentially unsettling. To counterbalance the "critical" perspective, she reminds us of the work of writing teacher Peter Elbow, who writes, "Our best hope for finding invisible flaws in what we can't see in our own thinking is to enter into different ways of thinking."[34] Even young children can come to understand the importance of reading with empathy, becoming aware of our limitations as readers, and opening ourselves to flexible thinking that helps us to discover new interpretations.

Some Other Pedagogical Strategies for Media Literacy

TEACHING FILM TRAILERS

Although in the United States, the film and media industry is barely involved in media education, in England, there is a long tradition of involvement of the British film industry in film and media education. Founded in 1985, Film Education was active in curriculum-based teaching resources, teacher training, and cinema-based events across the United Kingdom. Since 2013, the program that influences British media education is called Into Film. They offer teacher education and film clubs to nearly 50% of all UK schools and provide resources and activities that extend young people's understanding of film.[35] They also created a free massive open online course, Teaching Literacy Through Film, that introduces teachers to the pedagogy of media analysis and production in a 12-hour independent learning experience.[36]

One of the most interesting British initiatives we've seen is called Teaching Trailers.[37] Each year, primary and secondary teachers in Britain get access to a set of age-appropriate film trailers to explore the topic of persuasion. The genre of the trailer is a near-perfect resource for media literacy education. Trailers are designed to persuade audiences to see a film, and its short duration and strong visual content are carefully designed to activate emotion and create desire. Students discuss the features of persuasive texts, analyzing the impact of certain devices through looking at three different versions of a trailer for the same film. They examine different movie trailers to come up with a list of criteria for persuasive texts and explore the language used in the trailer alongside the film language. Finally, learners plan and develop their own trailer, applying what they learned in their own creative production.

In one lesson, children in Grades 3–6 learn about why film companies release trailers. They gain knowledge about the work that film distributors do and learn about the major elements of a film marketing campaign, including posters, trailers, radio and television advertising, social media channels, online communities, websites, and digital advertising. They look at three different trailers for *Cars 3*, a 2017 animated film directed by Brian Fee. They discuss why the producers created three different trailers for the same film. Students learn that trailers are released at different times prior to the film's release, to build excitement and anticipation. Students work in three groups to analyze one of the trailers. They are encouraged to notice the following elements:

1. **Shots.** What types of camera angles are used?
2. *Sound.* What can you hear? Music? Dialogue? Voiceover? Sound effects?
3. *Sequence.* How are the shots put together? Is the editing pace fast or slow? Why are the shots put together in this way? What is the effect?[38]

Teachers are encouraged to ask "how" and "why" questions in responding to students so that they are encouraged to use reasoning and evidence to defend their claims. It's important to point out that trailers are not simply mini-films. A trailer is a persuasive genre with its own set of easily recognizable features and conventions. Students can generate a list of conventions which make a trailer distinctive. In the curriculum, the authors note, "In some ways watching a trailer is like doing a jigsaw puzzle—we're given some information as to plot and character and our task is to fill in the missing pieces in the time available. The style in which the information is conveyed is fast moving and requires our attention

100% of the time."[39] In another lesson, students read three scripts from trailers from *Despicable Me* and learn to recognize the exaggerated language that is used in persuasive texts. After students analyze film trailers, they are encouraged to write a persuasive voice-over for one of the *Cars* trailers. Children are encouraged to include a question, a tagline, or a quote.

For middle school and high school students, critical analysis of trailers can be a powerful learning experience. In one lesson, students analyze the trailer for *Dunkirk*, the highest grossing World War II film of all time, which was written, directed, and produced by Christopher Dolan in 2017. The film portrays the evacuation of soldiers from three perspectives: land, sea, and air. It takes repeated viewing to unpack the complex, poetic trailer. Students look for specific evidence in the trailer to answer these questions:

➤ What sequence of images is included to arouse viewer interest?
➤ What information is provided about the storyline?
➤ How are we introduced to the main characters?
➤ What sense are we given about the film genre?
➤ What idea is suggested about the film?

In another activity, students work with a partner or in a small group to agree or disagree with statements such as:

➤ Trailers are produced for fun with money left over from a film's main budget.
➤ Trailers are a form of advertising.
➤ Trailers are simply a shorter version of a film.
➤ Trailers and film posters are designed to complement each other.

In determining their level of agreement or disagreement with these statements, the activity helps make students' tacit knowledge become explicit. Many students have substantial amounts of tacit knowledge about film and media because of their experience growing up as media consumers. Opportunities to discuss and analyze film trailers help students verbalize what they know, which builds student confidence.

REFLECTING ON AT-HOME MEDIA CHOICES AT SCHOOL

Gathering data about the home media use habits of students can create a powerful learning experience that advances both mathematical and media literacy competencies. After watching the documentary *Screenagers*, middle school math teacher Norm Lyons at the Mark Day School in San Rafael, California, invited his seventh and eighth graders to develop a plan to create data to understand the role of media and technologies in the lives of young people. They were lucky enough to engage with Dr. Mike Robb, the director of research at Common Sense Media through a Google Hangout, where students had the opportunity to ask questions that included, "How can we best confirm that the answers we collect are honest?"

Students then identified different variables they wanted to explore as they engaged children in Grades 2–7 to learn more about the time they spent with digital devices and, more important, the choices they make. Analyzing the data required students to use charts and tables to discover patterns; they had to summarize their findings using language and images to "tell the story" of their data. In doing so, students discovered interesting gender differences between girls and boys when it comes to texting, for example. Faculty appreciated the opportunity to learn more about students' at-home media and technology use. "Many students realized that how they worded survey questions, for example, affected the data they received," said Beth Bonzell, a math teacher at the school. "They reflected on how they could have improved those survey questions to make the data analysis easier and more accurate."

Every school should conduct a media and technology use survey with children and teens in the building. Students, teachers, and parents should be involved in developing the questions. Information from the survey can be used as a part of a whole-school professional development program and support parent outreach efforts, too. Although this is not yet a core pedagogy in most public schools, participating in a survey can help raise parents' awareness of the importance of monitoring children's media and technology use.[40]

DVD SPECIAL FEATURES AS A TOOL FOR LEARNING

Although many films are now available via streaming services, Pam occasionally prefers to borrow DVDs from her local library so she can check out the Special Features. Also called Bonus Features or Extras, these sections on many DVDs and Blue-Ray films often contain overlooked resources for anyone interested in film education as they provide further context to a film. They can include director and actor commentaries, deleted scenes, making-of videos, or behind-the-scenes access to filming techniques or a director's vision.

Pam often finds hidden treasures for adding interest to film discussions among the extra features. They can provide interesting starting points for discussion or critical analysis. For example, the 1997 animated film *Anastasia*, directed by Don Bluth and Gary Goldman, features the only surviving child of the Russian royal family who joins two con men to reunite with her grandmother, all while trying to avoid the evil Rasputin who seeks to harm her. In the Special Features section on the DVD of the Fox Films movie *Anastasia*, you can:

- Get an art lesson from animator Don Bluth on how to draw Anastasia, Dmitri, Rasputin, and Bartok.
- Listen to Anastasia's Music Box favorites.
- Sing along with the songs with lyrics over scenes from the movie.
- Hear commentary on the film by directors Don Bluth and Gary Goldman.

In the "How To Draw Anastasia" feature, animator and director Don Bluth reveals his stereotypical attitudes about the lead character when he says, "I know that part of what girls like to do is put on a little bit of make-up, so I put on a little bit of make-up. So I have the lashes here, so this gives her kind of a sexy look."[41]

This comment might provide a stop-and-pause opportunity to ask your audience if that seems like a true statement for all girls. Or it might lead to a discussion about authorship and the research process these middle-aged late 20th-century male directors and animators used to understand the life and times of a 10- to 18-year-old Russian aristocratic girl in the early 20th century. Sometimes there are answers to those questions in the director's commentary or in press interviews.

Sometimes the DVD special features reveal information that helps us appreciate literary works in a new way. For example, in the bonus features for the 2003 family film *Where The Red Fern Grows*, directed by Lyman Dayton and Sam Pillsbury, there's an interview with book author Wilson Rawls's widow Sophie, who explains that she was her husband's chief critic, proofreader, and editor. She tells the story of how he burned all the original manuscripts of his stories because he was embarrassed about exposing his lack of formal education. She explained that Rawls wrote back to children who wrote to him, at least "the first hundred or so." For animal lovers, the DVD offers a short film featuring the animal trainers and their animal "actors," which provides children and young people with a great behind-the-screen look at this fascinating profession.

The DVD version of one of Pam's favorite movies, *The Whale Rider*, directed by Niki Caro in 2002, includes an interview with Maori novelist Witi Ihimaera. In this story, only males are allowed to rise to be chief of a Maori tribe in New Zealand, but when the child selected to be the next chief dies at birth, his twin sister tries to claim her birthright when she comes of age. Niki Caro explains how the book influenced her imagination, and members of the cast share their insights about the process of bringing this story of cultural tradition, family, rebellion, and love to the screen. "I'm always reluctant to disclose the details of the special effects of movie-making," producer Tim Sanders shares in discussing how the scenes with whales were created. "For me this is like the magician revealing his secrets. But I think for the DVD, we are allowed to give a little more detail."[42] These glimpses of behind-the-scenes filmmaking provide context to support the deep reading of film texts and also provide an introduction to possible careers in the media industry.

Best Practices in Using Film and Media for Learning

KNOW YOUR AUDIENCE

- Be aware of the media environment that learners experience at home by gathering information about their media uses, attitudes, and technology habits at least once a year.
- Use this data to make wise choices of film and media content, considering student interest as you select topics and areas of focus for inquiry learning.

USE INSTRUCTIONAL PRACTICES TO DEEPEN LEARNING

- Select shorter media texts to ensure you have enough time for discussion and reflection after viewing.
- Incorporate close analysis of media texts into learning activities and ask critical questions to help students identify author, purpose, and point of view.
- Offer a structured note-taking tool to help students document what they are seeing, hearing, and learning while viewing.
- Model the critical viewing process by viewing, pausing, commenting, and questioning, making your interpretations explicit.
- Use repeated viewing experiences to explore both the content and form of film and video.

SUPPORT STUDENT MEANING-MAKING

- Encourage diverse interpretations of media texts. Help older learners to comment responsibly on a media text while viewing using a backchannel tool like "Today's Meet" or even a shared Google Doc.
- Encourage learners to suggest examples of film and video related to the topic or issue under examination and have them create a curated list of videos.
- Never screen media in a classroom that you have not yourself personally viewed beforehand.

Challenges

TURN ON, TUNE OUT

It's a painful subject to have to bring up, but there are nonoptimal pedagogies regarding the use of media in the K–12 classroom. There's the history teacher who shows a succession of films throughout the semester in a darkened room with little discussion of what's being viewed. There's the elementary school teacher who uses viewing of children's entertainment videos as a reward for good behavior or in place of a substitute teacher. There's the science teacher who relies on YouTube chemistry lab demonstrations in nearly every class.

Educational films and media have been part of the teacher's tool kit for more than 100 years now. A growing number of teachers rely on digital video as a fundamental part of the teaching and learning process, with nearly every teacher using them at least once during the school year and most using them an average of once per week. Curtis Chandler, an education professor at Brigham Young University, remembers picking his son up from school and learning that he had seen video clips in four out of five of his classes that day. In an informal tally based on his school visits, he found that more than 35% of the teachers he visited reported using video *often* (three to five times a week) during class.

As a new teacher himself, Chandler admits that he had occasionally overused video. He tells a story of intending to use only 3 minutes of the film *Napoleon Dynamite* to his high school students to illustrate the concept of dramatic irony. But, as the class unfolded, he showed quite a bit more because it was so enjoyable. And then a parent complained.

When teachers use YouTube to make students laugh, fill up extra class time, or as a reward for good behavior, Renee has called this behavior *nonoptimal use of video in the classroom*.[43] She asked undergraduate students to interview two of their favorite teachers from their K–12 years and ask them about how frequently teachers use video without a clearly identified instructional purpose. Eighty-five percent of the teachers responded in the affirmative. In a follow-up question, teachers were asked how common this practice was in their current school, on a 4-point scale from very common to not common at all. More than half (51%) of teachers indicated this practice was very common (11%) or common (40%). Only 12% indicated that these practices were uncommon, giving the lowest ranking on the 4-point scale.

Teachers have different perspectives on the use of video in the classroom. Some teachers stated that the occasional use of entertainment media in the classroom for entertainment purposes is educationally appropriate—and that having fun can and should be an acceptable motive for using media in the classroom. One teacher pointed out how important it is for students to enjoy reading, for example, and that pleasure in viewing is no different from pleasure with other texts. Others mentioned the patterns in group dynamics and bonding which help to create an effective learning environment. Some teachers even encourage students to suggest examples of film and video for screening in the classroom, with students voting for their favorite choices.

Most teachers in our sample were well aware that the noneducational use of video is a routine dimension of many school environments. Without stepping into the role of enforcing or policing classroom video use, librarians, school leaders and tech directors can collaborate on leading conversations to help faculty come to a shared understanding of the optimal use of YouTube, film, and video in the K–12 classroom. These conversations inevitably bring forward the complex relationship between play, entertainment, motivation, and engagement as dimensions of authentic learning. Unfortunately, because of abuses of video in schools, some districts have adopted policies that mandate how videos may (and may not) be used in the classroom. For example, at one KIPP Colorado elementary school, video can only be viewed for no more than 15 minutes per session for no longer than 30 minutes per day.[44] Such policies put hurdles in the way of using videos, decreasing the likelihood that teachers will use video at all.

Many schools require teachers and librarians to get parental permission before screening any movies rated over G. Letters to parents should include a description of the film and details about the rating and the content. A rationale for the educational value of the film should be provided along with examples of learning experiences to accompany the viewing experience. For parents who may consider opting their children out, a short description of an alternative learning experience is needed. Such letters may encourage educators to be strategic and intentional in their use of Hollywood films.

When math and history teachers were first discovering the power of Khan Academy videos for demonstrating how to solve math problems and gain historical knowledge through a lecture, the concept of the *flipped classroom* was introduced by Jonathan Martin. Teachers produce videos designed to be viewed at home, as homework. Thus, with the rise of the Internet, "content delivery" could be shifted to nonschool time, leaving time during the school day for tackling difficult problems, working in groups, researching, collaborating, crafting, and creating. Importantly, researchers who investigated this pedagogy found that it was the active learning component of the class (not the video portion) that contributed most significantly to increases in student learning.[45]

In many schools, because parental permission is not required for YouTube, teachers' use of video clips may not always be so strategic and intentional. This is why educators and librarians must reflect on their motives, asking the question, "Why am I using video right now?" When video is used only to engage learner attention, it's unlikely to be effective in promoting deeper learning. Teachers' reflective discourse on these issues, done collaboratively in school-wide communities, can nurture a sense of consensus about the range of appropriate and less optimal strategies for using media in schools.

Restrictive policies like these, often developed by well-meaning school boards or superintendents, can wreck plans to develop media literacy competencies among learners. Rather than use policies like these to regulate the use of video for learning purposes, we think it's better to promote constructive dialogue among educators and librarians to develop a shared consensus about the optimal use of video for learning purposes. By reading and discussing portions of *The Library Screen Scene* in a study group, faculty and librarians can explore appropriate pedagogies and practices for the use of film and video in their school community. They can make a shared commitment to end nonoptimal uses that position students as mere receivers of visual stimulation.

Hyper-restrictive School Policies for Video

In many school districts, outdated policies are still on the books that limit teachers' ability to use film and video for learning purposes. Such policies include the following:

✓ Defining quality or educational relevance too narrowly as in "fair and accurate representation of the facts" or "critical acclaim of the work" or "reputation of the writer, director, or performer"
✓ Disallowing videos that contain the presence of inappropriate language, depictions of violence, or inappropriate behavior
✓ Disallowing commercial movies made for entertainment purposes
✓ Mandating that a graded assignment accompany all viewing activities to "hold students accountable" for the material
✓ Rigidly applying Motion Picture Association of America rating systems to determine age suitability
✓ Rigidly limiting how much time is used to screen or view films, as in "limit the total use of AV time to one class period per unit"
✓ Requiring that all video or AV material be submitted to the building principal and/or superintendent as a list at the beginning of the school year
✓ Requiring the superintendent to report a list of approved movies to the school board
✓ Requiring teachers to notify parents of films that will be shown in the classroom and providing a lesson alternative for children whose parents have opted them out

---

Critical Perspectives on Information and Entertainment

ASSESSING CREDIBILITY

When teachers and librarians talk about the importance of assessing the credibility of information, they're talking about a special type of close analysis of nonfiction texts. As a result of the so-called fake news crisis, this topic got national attention in the media during and after the election of President Donald Trump. Unfortunately, in some school and academic libraries, examining issues of credibility focuses exclusively on the written word and rarely includes the genres of visual propaganda or moving image media. In the library world, there is also a predisposition to examine the credibility of static websites, not dynamic social media.

When education researcher Sam Wineberg compared how fact-checkers at reputable news outlets evaluated live websites as compared to other smart users, he found that both professors and university students perceived websites to be authoritative simply because they had professional-looking graphics, official logos, and statements of nonprofit status.[46] Whether we like it or not, visuals help make information memorable—they are not mere decoration.[47] Most people base their judgments of the credibility of a webpage largely on the graphic design. Communication researchers Andrew Flanagin and Miriam Metzger found that perceptions of credibility appear to be primarily due to website attributes (e.g., design features, depth of content, and site complexity).[48]

Many librarians ask students to evaluate websites using worksheet checklist, considering sites with an.edu or.gov extension as more credible than other sites. Other librarians suggest to students that scholarly articles are better than blogs. Sadly, these approaches deny the genuine complexity of credibility, which is inherently situational and contextual. Such approaches also ignore the important changes that are underway in how information circulates through social media networks, where source information is stripped away as information snippets are shared on Facebook.

But librarians are pioneering new approaches to teaching about credibility. As the Association for College and Research Libraries (ACRL) Framework notes, "Information resources reflect their creators' expertise and credibility, and they are evaluated based on the information need and the context in which the information will be used. Authority is constructed in that various communities may recognize different types of authority. It is contextual in that the information need may help to determine the level of authority required." Learners should do the following:

➢ Define different types of authority, such as subject expertise (e.g., scholarship), societal position (e.g., public office or title), or special experience (e.g., participating in a historic event).

➢ Use research tools and indicators of authority to determine the credibility of sources, understanding the elements that might temper this credibility.

➢ Understand that many disciplines have acknowledged authorities in the sense of well-known scholars and publications that are widely considered "standard," and yet, even in those situations, some scholars would challenge the authority of those sources.

➢ Recognize that authoritative content may be packaged formally or informally and may include sources of all media types.

➢ Acknowledge they are developing their own authoritative voices in a particular area and recognize the responsibilities this entails, including seeking accuracy and reliability, respecting intellectual property, and participating in communities of practice.

➢ Understand the increasingly social nature of the information ecosystem where authorities actively connect with one another and sources develop over time.

By acknowledging that authority is constructed and contextual, learners, educators, and librarians can begin to apply more granular reasoning about the credibility of particular information sources. Such efforts will inevitably involve developing knowledge about the content and topic and appreciating the limitations of how we know what we know.

ASSESSING STUDENTS' ABILITY TO EVALUATE DIGITAL INFORMATION

The Stanford History Education Group developed assessment to examine the online civic reasoning competencies of middle school, high school, and college students. They include the following:

Article Analysis: Students read a sponsored post and explain why it might not be reliable.

Comment Section: Students examine a post from a newspaper comment section and explain whether they would use it in a research report.

Evaluating Evidence: Students decide whether to trust a photograph posted on a photo-sharing website.

Facebook Argument: Students consider the relative strength of evidence that two users present in a Facebook exchange.

Claims on Social Media: Students read a tweet and explain why it might or might not be a useful source of information.[49]

A set of 15 tasks like these were used to examine how teens critically analyzed information. The assessments were administered to more than 7,800 students across 12 states, including urban and suburban schools. One assessment required middle schoolers to explain why they might not trust an article on financial planning that was written by a bank executive and sponsored by a bank. Many students did not make any reference to the author's identity or the bank sponsorship. They did not stop to ask the question, "Who is the author and what is the purpose of the message?"

Another assessment asked middle school students to look at the homepage of *Slate* and identify content on the page as either news or ads. Students were able to identify a traditional ad easily. But of the 203 students surveyed, more than 80 did not recognize sponsored content, mistaking it for news. Sponsored content looks like news because it has a headline, an image, and magazine-style text and sometimes, as in this case, it was clearly labeled "sponsored content." But the label is ineffective if the students do not know what that phrase actually means. In making an assessment of this online content, these students did not know how to tackle the critical question, "What type of message is this?"

Analyzing how photos are used in informational text is an important life skill. Students in the Stanford study examined a photo posted on a photo-sharing website. The prompt read, "On March 11, 2011 there was a large nuclear disaster at the Fukushima Daiichi Nuclear Power Plant in Japan. This image was posted on IMGUR, a photo-sharing website in July 2015." Figure 4.2 photo shows the image that includes the verbal claim that the deformed daisies have "nuclear birth defects."

Figure 4.2 Evaluating photos as evidence.

Students were asked, "Does this post provide strong evidence about the conditions near the Fukushima Daiichi Nuclear Power Plant? Explain your reasoning." Among the 170 students who completed this task, most considered it trustworthy due to the compelling nature of the visual image. Approximately 40% said that the photo provided strong evidence because it presented pictorial evidence about conditions near the power plant. Some students argued the post did not provide strong evidence because it did not depict animals and other plants that may have been affected by radiation. Fewer than 20% of students composed responses that questioned the source of the photo.

Teaching Information Literacy With Media and Pop Culture

Struggling to create high-interest, memorable learning experiences can be a challenge when teaching information literacy. Academic librarians often are required to "deliver" library instruction to thousands of students in one- or two-shot doses. Yet most students have little interest in getting an introduction to library resources when it is disconnected from a specific and relevant academic purpose. That's why media literacy is a type of "low-hanging fruit" for librarians who are charged with the responsibility of helping learners in the process of critically analyzing information.

Some academic librarians are using media literacy principles as part of information literacy programs. John Watts and Emily Scharf, librarians at Webster University, have found that it's useful to teach information literacy competencies by using images and ads. These librarians teach about concepts, including audience, authorship, purpose, and perspective, in order to illustrate these concepts and show how they apply to *all* information sources. Academic librarian Eamon Tewell uses clips from popular television shows in his information literacy classes at the university library. He's used segments from *Parks and Recreation, The Colbert Report*, and *30 Rock* to introduce students to topics including resource evaluation, plagiarism, and information ethics. His research shows that students who were randomly exposed to popular culture video clips in the context of information literacy instruction showed improvements in learning as compared to a control group which did not view videos. Researchers explain: "Student familiarity with IL concepts rose as a result of the use of television comedies as scaffolding for their learning. The experimental focus group was generally able to give more specific examples of resource evaluation when compared to the control focus group. Experimental focus group participants referred to timeliness, point of view, and context when they asked how they evaluate websites."[50] Easy-to-recall characters and stories from television comedies may have helped students remember and apply these concepts.

Representations of Libraries in Film

Films that feature libraries and librarians often address complex issues of fear and control. In the 1985 film *The Breakfast Club*, directed by John Hughes, students face an all-day detention in the school library. When one of the stars of that film, Emilio Estevez, read an essay by a now-retired librarian from Salt Lake City about the challenge of meeting the needs of the homeless who use the public library as a respite from the grueling challenge of living on the streets, he knew he wanted to create a movie to address the issue. Written, directed, and produced by Estevez in 2018, *The Public* tells the story of the patrons of an urban public library, many of whom are homeless and mentally ill. When the weather turns extreme, patrons turn the library into a homeless shelter for a night, raising questions about the moral imperative of public librarians to help people in need.[51]

The trailer for *The Public* provides a great discussion opportunity to consider the representation of libraries in popular culture. When Professors Gary and Marie Radford analyzed the representation of libraries in fiction and popular culture, they found that themes of power and humiliation recur in fiction, films, and television programs that feature libraries and librarians. "The discourse of fear is a cultural form," they explain.[52] The work of Michel Foucault helps elucidate the discursive practices within the library, the rituals and rules, and methods of behavior that are institutionally controlled there. By critically analyzing representations of libraries and librarianship in film and media, the Radfords promote the value of reflecting upon some assumptions that are baked into institutional and professional norms.[53]

PROFESSIONAL DEVELOPMENT EXPANDS DIGITAL LITERACY COMPETENCIES

Like the rest of the university, academic libraries have become ever more siloed, with a proliferation of disparate staff, programs, and services that don't always connect together. That's why events, including workshops, seminars, and symposiums, can be a powerful way to build relationships—among and between librarians and including faculty and instructional technology staff as well.

When it comes to digital literacy in academic libraries, there are some standout programs emerging in the United States. In the fall of 2017, academic librarians at Virginia Tech hosted "Explore, Create, Connect," an event designed to advance the university's interest in empowering students as both critical consumers and active producers of a variety of digital knowledge. Julia Feerrar, the librarian heading up this initiative, is helping the community develop a shared understanding of digital literacy.

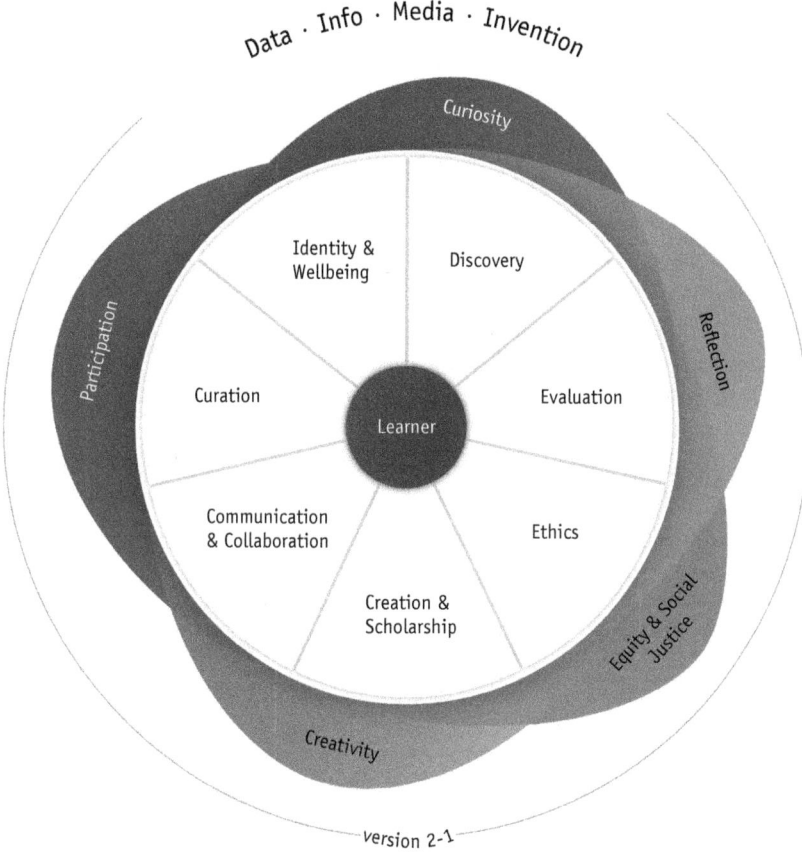

Figure 4.3 A conceptual model of digital literacy at Virginia Tech.

She designed an inaugural event to promote conversations and community among faculty, librarians, and instructional technology support staff. It took the form of a series of short talks and workshops, which enabled people from within the community to get to know each other and to brainstorm new ideas for teaching and learning. Figure 4.3 shows the conceptual model Feerrar developed as she developed new services and programs for students, faculty and staff. It includes these key questions:

Discovery: What are the questions driving your creative, academic, or professional work? What kinds of strategies and tools can you use to explore and access data, information, media, and other content?

Evaluation: What criteria do you use to assess and select digital content and tools? How does this criteria change in different contexts?

Ethics: Who has access to certain information, data, media, or tools and how does this access shape its use? How can you use digital content and tools most ethically? What kinds of standards guide your work? What guides the ways in which others use your work?

Creation and Scholarship: How do you synthesize learning and research in order to create something new? What are your rights and responsibilities when participating in a scholarly, creative, or professional community?

Communication and Collaboration: How can you participate in online environments and collaborative projects most effectively? How do you package communication for particular audiences? How do you build networks with collaborators?

Curation: How do you organize and save your data, information, media, or other creative outputs? Where and how do you manage and share content for others to use?

Identity and Well-being: Who are you online? How do you create, curate, and assess this online identity in order to tell your story? How do you manage your privacy? When do you choose to disconnect from digital environments?

The Virginia Tech library hosts a variety of programs aligned with these themes to support the community, including sessions entitled "Organizing Your Digital Life," "Online Collaboration and Teamwork," and "Shaping an Online Identity." These programs attract students, faculty, and staff who are all wrestling with some complex issues in the new ways that we communicate and work online.

Academic libraries promote digital and media literacy learning in many different ways. As we have mentioned earlier, contests sponsored by the library can be highly effective in raising awareness and visibility for the value of digital and media literacy education. While at Penn, Vedantham created the Annual Mashup Contest beginning in 2007 and continued the program for over 10 years. The contest was responsive to a real problem: Although many Penn faculty recognized the importance of helping students use research, evidence, documentation, and reasoning to support their ideas, they also knew that it can be harder to create a good 3-minute film than writing an academic paper. Lack of knowledge about copyright and fair use was interfering with pedagogical innovation. Many faculty were unclear about the scope of student rights and responsibilities for using copyrighted content to create transformative new work. By designing, implementing, and assessing a variety of initiatives, events, programs, and contests to encourage experimentation with digital media, academic librarians have helped increase awareness and visibility for copyright and fair use—among both faculty and students—as part of media literacy education.

Programs, events, and dialogues like the ones just described can also help to generate "ahas" that lead people to take more action. In considering the role of digital literacy in higher education, there are a range of topics and issues that are meaningful to explore, including approaches teaching and learning, the digital identity of the college professor, and social networking as a means of scholarly communication. To promote teaching and learning with digital media tools, Vedantham developed a program entitled "Engaging Students through Technology." This symposium attracted more than 150 faculty and staff attended from all 12 Penn schools. [7] The symposium highlighted topics including the use of video for homework (the "flipped classroom") and the use of Facebook Groups in class. One year, the program included an undergraduate student panel where students were on the stage and professors asked them questions about how they learn best. According to Vendantham, "This annual symposium helps faculty understand the pedagogical objectives of new media assignments, how partnering with the library is a good strategy for achieving them, and the impact of such assignments on student learning."

Of course, to get the appropriate mix of hands-on activities and robust dialogue, it takes more than simply announcing the event and hoping for people to show up. By intentionally selecting participants based on criteria that enable people to feel valued as active participants, events move from "preaching to the choir" and offer wider, more robust and more unpredictable learning experiences for all.

After all, the process of developing the event itself becomes a key vehicle for relationship development. At the University of Rhode Island's Media Education Lab, we have found that digital literacy events are successful when they bring together (a) people with more and less experience with digital media, including digital skeptics as well as enthusiasts; (b) faculty, academic leaders, instructional technology staff, and librarians from across the K–20 spectrum. We have found that faculty gain new perspective on their work while in dialogue with elementary and secondary teachers and librarians. The most important ingredient, however, is (c) time for hands-on interaction with digital tools, in small concentrated time periods of 30 minutes or less, working individually, with a partner or in a small group. In Chapter 8, we'll learn more about the role of professional development programs and services in advancing the needs of the library learning community.

Paradigm Shift: Unanswered Questions

We still have much to learn about what kinds of institutional and pedagogical support structures help learners take full advantage of audiovisual media for learning purposes. Just as we teach the process of writing an academic paper, students also need support to critically view and create moving image media. When faculty members understand the steps involved in video production, they can design assignments that activate student learning. But when students create media that engage with authentic audiences, new challenges may result. For example, when

Professor Susanna Lee wanted her students to create media as part of her Digital History class, her students got the opportunity to investigate and understand 3D scanning and printing technologies and their potential for local museum artifact presentation and preservation. When students visited the North Carolina Museum of History, they brought with them 3D scanning software (downloaded to their phones and laptops) while museum staff had gathered an assortment of artifacts, concentrating on those with intriguing features and stories.

The students worked collaboratively to scan the items they were interested in, sharing their digital scans and writing research papers that explored the historical context and importance of their artifacts. But this project raised unanswerable questions for librarians about the use of external sources from the community. They wondered, What are the legal consequences of using third-party materials from the museum in a visualization project that involved 3D scanning of material that may include copyrighted expression or trademarked content?[54]

The whole academic community benefits when students share their works with a wider audience and when their work is preserved as a part of institutional history and culture. A number of academic librarians provide access to streaming faculty- or student-produced videos, with most libraries hosting them locally and some hosting through a vendor platform.[55] And in an increasingly competitive work-place, many students appreciate how media creation learning experiences create opportunities to build a portfolio of unique works.

But when librarians host video content, they do sometimes struggle with copyright concerns and thus unintentionally limit the services they provide. For example, in a survey of academic librarians, one librarian at a private postgraduate Massachusetts library said in response to this topic, "We are very careful about not ripping commercially available DVDs as that violates copyright. The locally streamed content is content taped at [the] university that is produced by the university."[56] This librarian may lack a solid understanding of the concept of transformative use and may be unaware of the efforts made over many years to expand the provision of fair use to enable legal "ripping" by educators and students through the DMCA1201 exemption.

Among librarians and faculty, there are differing perceptions of the relative value of student-created media productions, and unanswered questions remain about whether (or not) they are important to the research enterprise and the scholarly communication ecosystem. Today, student work is often produced for a grade, with the teacher as the sole audience. But increasingly, librarians are enabling student work to be placed in online repositories. And of course, students are more and more likely to place their own work on the open Internet.

But when students don't want their creative work to circulate online, librarians can help with that, too. Librarians note that students have sometimes expressed "concerns about theft of—or embarrassment because of—their work, and therefore the possibility that they might not want these works discoverable on a long-term basis."[57] Academic librarians discuss and debate whether (and how) they can be responsible for preserving, storing and protecting student-created media works. In the next chapter, we'll consider the role of librarians as leaders in helping curate and collect media and video resources that advance knowledge and promote understanding.

5

Collecting

Questions Answered in This Chapter
- How do librarians curate content to meet the needs of their community?
- How do patrons discover the films that are available on streaming video services?
- Could digital platforms replace the need for librarian curators?
- How has the "scarcity mentality" affected the quality of film and media education in school libraries?
- How are librarians using YouTube in innovative ways?
- Why can't college students browse the DVD collection in many academic libraries?
- How can the specialized knowledge and skills of a media librarian support the needs of educators and patrons?
- Why do people value film and media reviews?
- Why are ratings systems controversial within the library community?
- How common is illegal downloading of film and media?
- Why do some librarians hate Netflix?
- What is the future of online streaming in libraries?

It was one of those nightmares that only a college professor dreams about: when a vital teaching resource seems to disappear right in the middle of the semester. The first time Renee taught a new course in propaganda to undergraduate students, she was teaching it in a fully online format. Her students were engaging in weekly videoconference class meetings using Zoom, an online video chat room. Many of her students were living on or near campus, but some lived far from the university because of work or family situations. So she needed resources that could be delivered to students in a digital, asynchronous format, where students could view a film at a time and place convenient for them.

As part of the learning experience, she wanted students to view and respond to *Forbidden Films*, a 2014 documentary by Felix Moeller that chronicles the story of the Nazi propaganda films that are still illegal to view in Germany outside of an educational context. Nearly 70 years after the end of the Nazi regime, more than 40 of the most heinous propaganda films remain in a highly protected special storage building that preserves the risky and potentially explosive nitrate film.

Interviews with German film historians, archivists, and filmgoers enable viewers to understand the ideological purpose of entertainment film from the Third Reich. The documentary includes clips from these films and documents several screening and discussion events where students and citizens in Munich, Berlin, Paris, and Jerusalem analyze and interpret them. The filmmaker engages viewers with the question: Should Nazi propaganda films still be banned?

The first time Renee taught the course, it was not difficult to find the film's distributor, Zeitgeist, and to invite students to purchase the title for $1.99 from iTunes. Students purchased the license to view the film at home, and online discussion was robust. The question of whether films should still be banned elicited a variety of thoughtful responses from students, because Moeller's film demonstrated that, even today, well-made historical propaganda can be highly effective. When propaganda evokes strong emotions, simplifies complex information, appeals to people's values, and cultivates and perpetuates stereotypes, it can promote misinformation and activate us-versus-them thinking that can be truly dangerous to democratic societies.

But the second time Renee taught the course, just 1 year later, the film title was nowhere to be found. Renee searched the University of Rhode Island academic library with no luck. A Google search revealed that there was an illegal digital file of the movie available through BitTorrent, an application that enables peer-to-peer file sharing. Renee did not want to download illegally or encourage her students to violate copyright law. Did the university library offer streaming media? It took some searching to find the place on the university's library website where streaming media services were listed, but there was no search bar to access these resources efficiently. Furthermore, it seemed like the distributor had moved the licensing of the film from iTunes to Alexander Street, a company that offers streaming video to academic libraries. But unfortunately, Renee's university did not subscribe to this service. However, Renee requested special access to a 30-day free trial of Alexander Street and just in time, she received an access code that enabled her students to view the film. University of Rhode Island librarians later purchased a license to make the streaming film available to students when the trial period ended. What started as a nightmare had a happy ending.

As we have seen so far in this book, using film and video in the classroom can engage learner attention and deepen learning by activating critical thinking and communication competencies. But it takes time and energy to find appropriate film and video content that helps to increase the knowledge and competencies of students and enables them to debate and discuss controversial decisions, like the German government's historic postwar decision to restrict access to so-called dangerous propaganda.

Renee's experience with *Forbidden Films* is not an isolated experience. When it comes to classroom video content, college faculty and K–12 teachers generally make their own choices, with librarians generally not involved in facilitating classroom access. As budgets have increased to include video collections in physical and streaming formats, librarians may be more proactive in informing faculty about the many available and relevant titles. But often, educators select videos without consulting academic librarians, and librarians make choices about video streaming services without significant input from educators. No one is satisfied with this. In a 2015 survey of 1,046 educators and academic librarians, educators report frustration with the library's development of the collections in support of course curricula.[1] For example, "development of a discipline-wide collection" received particularly low scores, even though it was identified (by both librarians and educators) as among the most important services. Humanities faculty were the most frustrated group in this regard.

Let's face it: an educator's request like Renee's wish for streaming access to *Forbidden Films* is both very specialized and expensive. Librarians can't always afford to purchase access to a whole streaming platform just for one's professor's need for a single film. Given diverse, competing needs and priorities and limited budgets, how do academic librarians decide which audiovisual content and services are best for the diverse needs of their community? And how can educators' interest in streaming media services be cultivated and encouraged?

As we will see in this chapter, while many school librarians face challenging times and some are vulnerable to the negative impact of school budget cuts, they have helped educators and students use audiovisual resources in numerous creative ways. Online streaming services provided by third-party vendors enable people to have 24/7 access to media content and PBS still serves a large and diverse audience of viewers. As YouTube is becoming a staple fixture of the American classroom, librarians are finding creative ways to use it to promote intellectual curiosity. Making clips of media is essential to many forms of student learning, and legal use of copyrighted content for creative expression relies on the ability to understand and apply the doctrine of fair use.

In this chapter, we learn how effective curation depends on access to reviews and reviewers, and how viewers themselves can be empowered to read and provide reviews. Although parents may use the Common Sense Media website to determine whether a particular movie is too violent, or rely on the TV or MPAA ratings systems for guidance, we learn why these various ratings services and systems can be controversial. We learn how educators access films and videos for learning purposes and how students rationalize their decision to engage in digital piracy using sites like Pirate Bay. Finally, you'll be fascinated to learn why some academic librarians hate Netflix and the questions that emerge as we imagine the future of streaming film and video as it continues to develop in the years ahead.

The Visibility of Film and Media Collections in the Library

Public and academic libraries often collect a mix of Hollywood, global, and independent films. Less often, they include short films, experimental films, and amateur films. School collections have a substantial nonfiction focus, especially in history and science, with some fine and performing arts content. Understanding the terms used to label films can be challenging because filmmakers are continually reinventing genres. But here's a brief overview:

Hollywood: Films made by major motion picture production studios. Production budgets are big, major stars are featured, special effects are common, and the expectation for profit is high.

Independent: Films with character-driven stories and smaller budgets. Filmmakers may have more autonomy in relation to filmmaking conventions or content.

Shorts: Television commercials, music videos, promos and movie trailers, digital billboards, corporate videos, and pretty much anything else with a running time under 60 minutes.

Experimental: Some films explore cinema's capacity to manipulate light, motion, space, and time, and/or express the filmmaker's personal artistic vision.

Amateur: Nonprofessional, personal, or hobbyist filmmaking, including aspirational directors and actors as well as home movie recordings of family and leisure activities.

Educational: Content including interviews, performances, simulations, or procedures created by faculty, media instructional staff, or students and used for instructional purposes.

Although librarians make decisions about which of these (and other) types of film and video to collect, we haven't seen a rich description of these strategic choices in the scholarly or professional literature in librarianship. Thus, we can't say for certain why some public libraries are stuffed with Hollywood titles and other libraries include more specialized collections of independent, educational, and amateur fare. We're not always sure why, in some libraries, DVD and sound media are right at the front entrance and in other places, they are tucked in a corner, far away in the back.

It's clear that librarians are making decisions about balancing the creative, informational, and cultural needs of patrons for film and media, but we don't know much about their methods, strategies or rationales. Collection development policies may emphasize currency, relevance, authority, and accuracy, but how do these concepts get applied to choosing DVDs for the public library collection? There are probably a host of historical and practical reasons for the many differences that we see in both the content and the physical display of film and media collections in school, public, and academic libraries that next generation of library researchers could explore.

In a review of library collection development policies, some researchers saw evidence that librarians took into account *user demand*, but little evidence in the policies explained how demand was assessed or how need could be inferred from circulation statistics. As researchers note, "Explaining how collection priorities are balanced enables a more targeted evaluation of the collection as a whole."[2] But with little disciplinary transparency about strategy and goals, it's hard for us to offer useful ideas about how to evaluate the quality of a library's film and media collection. Given the rise of streaming media and other format options, librarians should carefully document (and reflect upon) their decision-making processes in collecting film and media in public libraries. By sharing knowledge on this topic and adding it to the rich LIS literature on collection development, the field overall will be strengthened.

CHOICES, SO MANY CHOICES

When it comes to audiovisual media, many choices are available today with the flick of the remote control, a few taps on the keyboard, or a simple voice command. According to Nielsen ratings, Americans collectively watch around 1.25 billion hours of TV each day. Cable television and satellite providers reach more than 85% of the population. Despite talk about the "cord cutters" who are viewing media using only the Internet (without using pay TV services), it's a business that rakes in $100 billion annually in North America alone. However, it's important to note that not many forms of audiovisual media are available free to people in the home. The three largest and most important free providers of audiovisual content are broadcast television networks, YouTube and PBS. But sometimes the value of these important free resources may be overlooked.

The landscape for collecting audiovisual materials in school, public, and academic libraries is complex and dynamic. The scale of innovation in Silicon Valley has produced a plethora of new ways to view and interact with visual media. Today, librarians think carefully about the user experience as patrons navigate online environments to access and analyze movies and media. We consider curation as a literacy practice that is now becoming important for ordinary people, who find the need to organize their many photos, music, and documents. Through the media we consume, we express our personal and social identity. In fact, curriculum is coming to be thought of as a series of curated choices that students read, view, and interact with, often in playlist format. But today's librarians can't just be good collectors, though. They must also help learners and patrons develop their own curation competencies to select media for themselves as they support access to audiovisual content in many forms.

HOW MANY CLICKS TO FIND FILMS?

There's no universal standard for how public libraries guide people's access toward (or away from) films, videos, and streaming media. That's probably because of the enormous diversity of public libraries in the United States and around the world. In the design of the physical space of the library, librarians may consider the flow of traffic and the logistics of the space needed to showcase and house a media collection. In the design of library websites, librarians also make choices about how to structure user choice based on the perceived needs of their patrons. In reviewing dozens of library websites to see how users could find and access the media collections, the authors of this book generally liked it when the words Read, Listen, Watch, and Learn are clearly presented on the library home page, making it easy for patrons to browse the print, audio, and media collections and see what events and programs are coming up.

The design of library websites shapes how patrons access materials. It's an important job and usually the process of developing a library website is done behind closed doors. That's why we were thrilled to learn more about that process when we found an 11-minute video created by the Darien Public Library that was shared on YouTube in 2016. As the librarians explain it, the old library website was a river of content, driven by librarians as content creators. But the metrics showed that patrons didn't click on this content. Now, simplicity is driving the design of their new website. In the video, we see the careful efforts of the whole staff in the website design and planning process; we learn how the design of the new website affected every staff member in some way. We see the way that the new website integrates e-books, streaming media, and other digital content from third-party providers.

Since our focus in this book is on film and media resources, we simply used a quick-and-dirty strategy by noticing how many clicks it takes us to browse the DVD collection and access and watch a streaming film or video when using a library website. Sometimes we experienced failure when we tried this test. Other times we were pleasantly surprised by what we found. For example at the Sachem Public Library in Holbrook, New York, the home page includes the library hours, featured programs, and downloadable materials. In two clicks, the user is viewing a list of recently acquired DVDs. We couldn't easily find the catalog to scan the entire collection, however. At the tiny Beaver County Pioneer Library in Oklahoma, it takes five clicks to access the list of 375 DVDs, using the Visual Search function and the Materials by

Type link. Here the film collection is largely targeting adults; only 12% of the film collection is aimed at children or teens, with titles like *The Polar Express*, the 2004 film directed by Robert Zemeckis, and *Anne of Green Gables*, the Canadian television series produced by Kevin Sullivan.

At the website of the Providence Community Library, the words *watch, film,* or *video* do not appear on the home page. Clicking under Library Services and Info, we learn how to borrow a Kindle or get a library card, but not how to access streaming media. When we type the word *film* into the catalog search bar, a list of books about film is presented. After five clicks, we still couldn't figure out how to find the DVD collection or learn whether the library offers streaming media services or not.

At the Billings Public Library in Montana, in only two clicks we moved from the Browse link to a link to DVDs, which takes us directly to a rather unfriendly-looking catalog, with a search bar, where it seems that there are 1,700 DVDs available for circulation. There doesn't seem to be a browse function. But there's a link called RB Digital, which links to a third-party platform that distributes e-books and audiobooks. The Recorded Books platform provides audiobooks and digital media to schools and libraries, but this library does not provide access to the IndieFlix service that offers access to streaming film and video.

At the Chicago Public Library, the website looks amazingly like an Instagram page, with boxes filled with interesting pictures that feature library programs and events. The menu offers only two choices: Browse and Events. When we click on Browse, a menu comes up inviting us to browse by format, audience, and more. There we see Movies and TV, which presents a Netflix-type visual display of films (organized by genre) showing available and forthcoming DVDs. There's even a box titled "The Chi: What Else to Watch," which lists movies about Chicago for fans of the popular 2018 Showtime series created by Lena Waithe. It's clear this design reflects librarians' awareness that their patrons live in a digital and media-saturated world. On the side menu, the words "Hoopla Audiobooks, Music, Video, and eBooks" take us to Hoopla, the 3rd-party digital media service that makes streaming and downloading available to anyone with a library card.

Clearly, there are no established norms for how users access film and media content via library websites. Based on the design of library websites, we can infer that in some communities, providing access to film and media is considered very important. In other communities, providing access to film and media may be much less important or not even considered a core part of the library mission. We understand how budget and staff constraints may shape digital media collections, but we strongly recommend that every school, public and academic library take a close look at how the design of its website enables the discovery of film and media resources.

BEST OF TIMES, WORST OF TIMES

Many school librarians can identify with the famous opening line, "It was the best of times, it was the worst of times" from Charles Dickens's historical novel, *A Tale of Two Cities*. While in some communities, the rise of interest in digital learning has made the work of school librarians more important than ever before, in other communities, school librarians are sadly considered nonessential personnel as school library budgets are being slashed. When money is tight, school districts look at personnel budgets by distinguishing between essential personnel and nice-to-have staff, which generally includes art and music teachers as well as school librarians. In Shawnee, Oklahoma, the school library received zero dollars for book acquisitions in 2016. In Wichita, at three public schools, clerks replaced high school–certified librarians. According to the Kansas Department of Education, in the last 15 years the number of certified library media specialists has dropped 31%. Chicago Public Schools are facing an equally dire situation, as the number of librarians in the district dropped 35% just since 2012.[3] California, however, has the worst record in the country. In Oakland, 30% percent of its 80 school libraries have closed, mostly at the high school level. Three of 17 high school libraries in the Oakland Unified School District are open, staffed only by teachers or volunteers.[4]

It's worth reflecting on just how and when perceptions of school librarians began to shift in the eyes of educators and the general public. One of Renee's favorite school librarians is Doug Johnson, whose Blue Skunk blog is a source of inspiration at the intersection of media and information literacy. When Johnson began his career as junior high librarian in a small school in Iowa, he had access to a small computer lab with two Apple II computers—the only ones in the building. At the time, they were precious resources indeed. He has observed that despite the increased access to technology, "the scarcity mentality remains, especially among school librarians. After decades of small or non-existent budgets, resources— books, computers, space, supplies—are viewed as precious commodities that need to be tightly controlled and reserved for 'school use only.'" The spirit of scarcity has led to the public perception of librarians as stingy and controlling. For this reason, Johnson emphasizes the need to apply the philosophy that "It's better to wear out than rust out."[5]

We're not playing a blame game here. We are the first to admit that school librarians, of all the education professionals, are most vulnerable to the negative impact of school budget cuts. A most poignant story of loss comes from Mary Jane Waite, who found herself in the Franklin (Massachusetts) High School library, with its extensive collection of DVDs for educational use. She moved the films to open shelves in the front of the library and educators and students alike were stunned at the size of the film collection on topics relevant to their curriculum. The library contained films about "American government, grammar usage, verb tenses in foreign languages, atrocities of the Holocaust, life under Jim Crow laws, how to conduct yourself in an interview, marketing strategies, examples of physics in real life, and how to search databases and search engines." She held meetings with educators to suggest videos and invite her colleagues to browse the collection, placed catalogs in mailboxes, encouraged new requests, and even designed a viewing space for the library. But then came the Great Recession of 2007, when the position of librarian was eliminated by the school district.[6] Mary Jane Waite lost her job.

When Renee's friend, colleague, and coeditor Paul Mihailidis told her that his mother, Valerie Diggs, the department head of school libraries for the Chelmsford Public Schools, was fired from her job due to school budget cuts, the issue hit close to home. Diggs, who served as president of the Massachusetts School Library Association, was responsible for the complete transformation of the Chelmsford High School library to a learning commons. In 2009, *Teacher Librarian* spotlighted her impressive program. Renee learned about her work when she collaborated with her son on an article titled "From Information Reserve to Media Literacy Learning Commons: Revisiting the 21st Century Library as the Home for Media Literacy Education."[7] Fortunately, Diggs was able to fight the decision and with support from the community have her position reinstated, but it is indeed ironic that the position of school librarian is both more essential and more insecure than ever before. Today, the lines continue to blur between the roles of teacher, library, and instructional technology support staff. As an expanded conceptualization of literacy becomes increasingly part of everyone's learning experience, librarians are key resources for the future.

YOUTUBE AS A SOURCE OF INFORMATION

You don't have to look very far to find someone in your social network who is a YouTube fan. Today, people are spending more time watching YouTube than ever before. Users watch (on average) 1 hour of YouTube per day just on their cell phones! YouTube, the social media website for sharing videos, is owned by Google and funded by advertising. They generated $4 billion in 2014.[8]

YouTube is a truly democratic form of broadcasting because anyone can upload and share video content. Four hundred hours of content are uploaded every minute as of 2017, and YouTube is the second most popular website in the world, after Facebook. On YouTube, the genre of "how-to" videos encompasses more than 36 million videos. Search for "vlog," the video genre where people document their daily life by talking personally to the audience, and you'll find 95 million results.

We know that patrons, students, educators and librarians search YouTube to find videos to meet their information needs. When they have to repair a chair, prepare a mousse, recall a special formula for Excel spreadsheets, or even learn how to apply glittery, decorative rivets on that old but beloved cardigan, librarians search on YouTube for a how-to video. But in their professional capacity as librarians, it sometime seems that YouTube barely exists.

Library land has not yet discovered YouTube, it seems. We searched high and low for examples of how reference librarians use YouTube searches to support the information needs of some patrons. We asked reference librarians: Do you offer tutorials or guidance on searching YouTube? Do you use YouTube to answer patron queries? We searched numerous books for and about reference services to no avail. There's no mention of YouTube in Linda Katz's 2014 book, *Managing the 21st Century Reference Department*. Scott Lanning's third edition textbook, *Reference and Instructional Services for Information Literacy Skills*, has only a short acknowledgment of YouTube, presenting it as a place to host videos, not as an information resource where patrons may discover content that meets their information needs. There is little about YouTube in either the professional or the scholarly literature of library and information science. It seems that apart from the small number of librarians who are creating videos, YouTube's capacity as an information resource has been largely overlooked among school, public and academic librarians.

Fortunately, YouTube is becoming a staple of the American classroom, from kindergarten to graduate school.[9] Educators make extensive use of YouTube, often searching for hours to find the right content for their teaching needs. They may do this at home because school networks sometimes disable YouTube or limit it using content filters. To play YouTube videos in class, many teachers use a simple digital platform to easily download a YouTube video as a digital file. This enables them to play back the video in a classroom even where Internet access is slow, unreliable, or nonexistent.

We think librarians should help everyone to understand how YouTube Search works and be aware of its structural limitations. Notice that on YouTube, you cannot search YouTube creators by geographical location to find the people in your community who are creating and sharing videos. This is a pity. You can, however, use YouTube's search tool to filter results in particular ways, by upload date, length, view count, and rating. As librarians make more active use of YouTube, they could consider requesting the company to increase the range and depth of search options or work with technology entrepreneurs using the YouTube API to build new applications that include a more diverse range of search strategies.

Librarians should also help people better understand how YouTube works when we search it. In a video produced by YouTube Creator Academy, the company explains how algorithms are used to match viewers to the videos they are most likely to enjoy. Remember that Google owns YouTube; thus, if you use Gmail, the content of your emails and the content of any attachments you share become part of the data used to customize your YouTube search. Data about a particular

YouTube video—including its title, the creator, how much of the video is generally watched, and how many people are commenting—is used to align with the anticipated needs of the YouTube user, which includes what kinds of videos you have watched in the past, how long you have watched them, and what times of day you are watching.[10]

In the face of increasing political polarization in our communities and around the world, librarians should help patrons understand the economics of digital platforms like YouTube. Like any business, YouTube wants to keep engagement high. To keep people online for longer periods of time, the company uses algorithms intentionally to serve users more and more extreme and controversial videos that compel human attention. For example, if you watch one modestly anti-immigration video, you'll be presented with others that offer even more virulent and hate-filled content. Because humans are attracted to sensational content, this algorithm works to advance YouTube's business goals while at the same time increasing exposure to more extreme ideologies. And with the release of more than 50 million Facebook records to the political marketing firm Cambridge Analytica on behalf of the Donald Trump presidential campaign, surely we are just beginning to learn how machine learning and curation can have unintended negative effects on individuals and society. YouTube has been criticized for pushing people toward sensational and unreliable content. Now claiming to understand their social responsibilities to reduce exposure to disinformation, they have tweaked the algorithm to stop recommending miracle cure videos and conspiracy theory 9/11 deniers.[11]

LIBRARIAN-CREATED VIDEOS

Librarians are learning to increase their visibility on YouTube. The most active and popular library YouTube channel, The New York Public Library, had 679 videos as of 2018, including recordings of live events as well as specially produced films. Still, it has only 10,000 subscribers, as compared with John and Hank Green's (aka vlogbrothers) 3 million subscribers or Crash Course (their educational channel), which has over 10 million subscribers. At the University of Alabama, academic librarians have created 46 videos since 2011 to support the information literacy curriculum, with videos on search and evaluation processes among other topics. Even the tiny Boxford Library in Massachusetts experimented with YouTube in 2013, creating a series of 30-second book reviews, where patrons of all ages offer short reviews of books they are reading. But such programs may not be sustainable without dedicated library leaders who recognize how YouTube relates to their educational mission.

Colleen Theisen is one of the most innovative academic librarian YouTubers we were able to find. She is a special collections librarian who uses YouTube to engage her community in the mysteries of the academic library special collections at the University of Iowa Libraries. Her YouTube channel, Staxpeditions, is a real treat to view. The channel features a number of videotaped library explorations into the rare book stacks. Figure 5.1 shows a screenshot of an episode.

We love her work so much! In one video, Thiesen uses the Library of Congress call letters FML to explore the mysteries of what's in the collection. YouTube viewers see her searching a box that contains a handmade art book called *Soundings*. In another, she explores PN6700 to find a nonfiction graphic novel called *Cravan* about the real life of Arthur Cravan (actually Fabian Lloyd, the nephew of Oscar Wilde), a poet, journalist, pugilist, and 20th-century man of mystery. In this episode, the unique International Dada Archive is showcased, which is a scholarly resource at the University of Iowa for the study of the historic Dada movement.

What makes these videos so addictive? The video series piques intellectual curiosity about the topics explored in the videos by depicting the joy of discovery. These videos may even inspire educators or librarians to make their own "search and find" videos to document their own library discovery processes. Obviously, Colleen sees YouTube as a powerful tool for lifelong learning and as a valuable resource for advancing public awareness of and appreciation for the

Staxpeditions 28: DA 300-512

60 views

Figure 5.1 Staxpeditions by Colleen Thiesen, University of Iowa Special Collections.

cultural value of a library's special collections. You simply have to watch one of Colleen's videos to find out what makes them compelling to watch. It's the power of mediated face-to-face communication, which has been "fine-tuned by millions of years of evolution," according to Chris Anderson in a TED talk in 2010, noting that "what Gutenberg did for writing, online video can now do for face-to-face communication."[12]

Curation as a Digital Literacy Practice

Librarians, archivists, and museum professionals have long understood the professional practice of curation, which includes the practices of collecting, cataloguing, arranging and assembling for exhibition and display. Professional curation requires a high level of metacognition, because, in making selections of what to include and what to omit, a keen awareness of one's own bias is needed. But ordinary people also engage in curation. Long before the rise of digital culture, people have created collections of favorite record albums, audiotapes, CDs, and DVDs and created mix tapes with careful selections of music to express certain ideas and relationships. Today, people find the need for curation as part of leisure, work, and citizenship. Curation is a vital dimension of digital literacy.[13]

The blurring of boundaries between professional and amateur creates new ways to think about curation in relation to digital and media literacy education. One of the reasons why curation is so personally important is because of the way in which our choices of media content are tied to our personal and social identity.[14] Our choices express ideas about what we value. That's why some scholars see curation as a literacy practice that has some parallels to writing, speaking, and media making.[15]

Historically, one of the most important things that libraries do involves developing collections that meet the needs of the people they serve. Public librarians collect DVDs to meet the entertainment and informational needs of patrons in their communities, and they may (or may not) choose streaming media services. School librarians may recommend or select films that align with the curriculum and address social, cultural, and political issues relevant to the school community. They may create playlists of video resources for units of instruction or offer how-to tutorials that can be accessed from the library website.

Professor Joyce Valenza at Rutgers University has helped us to appreciate the many ways in which librarians are engaging with social and digital media tools and platforms to support the practice of curation. She has examined how library professionals define and engage in social media curation. She discovered that while librarians value free digital curation platforms, they are also quite loyal to LibGuides as their preferred platforms for curation work. LibGuides is a commercial platform used by thousands of libraries worldwide.

As professional curators, librarians begin by (1) collecting or gathering content, moving gradually to (2) connect content and resources for specific purposes and target audiences. Sometimes, they (3) add value by providing context and commentary. Finally, they (4) share their collections with others and empower the community by providing opportunities for collaboration.[16] Curation skills clearly overlap with other competencies valued by people with interests in digital literacy. With new terminologies emerging for the variety of competencies needed for thriving in an information age, some scholars struggle with the "nomenclature challenges" associated with the "sometimes overlapping and sometimes diverging cluster of terms centered on technology skills—information technology (IT) fluency, technology literacy, computer literacy, digital literacy, and others."[17] To address this problem, some library scholars have created yet another new term, a reframing of information literacy they call *metaliteracy*.

This term aims to be responsive to the challenges of helping learners thrive in an era where so many choices of information and entertainment are available. Some dimensions of metaliteracy include the ability to evaluate user feedback that is provided using ratings systems found on social media platforms like YouTube, Goodreads, and Yelp. When people recognize the context in which user-generated information is created, they are better able to evaluate dynamic content like comment thread and online forums critically. To be metaliterate, people should also produce original content in multiple media formats. As they decide how to share their ideas with audiences, they must understand personal privacy, information ethics, and intellectual property issues.[18]

We're not keen on creating new names when there are already a plethora of names out there, but we do see metaliteracy as a worthwhile attempt to bring media literacy and information literacy into closer alignment, reflecting the more fluid and flowing nature of digital participation today. Because the term metaliteracy emphasizes the value of a metacognitive perspective, learners are encouraged to reflect continuously on their own thinking and strategies in the use of various media and digital technologies. As scholars across the various disciplines of library and information studies, education and human development, and media and communication studies increase their collaboration, it's possible that shared understandings will obviate the need for new terms.

Some Platforms for Curating Digital Media Content

E-Link (https://elink.io/). You can turn links into visually appealing webpages and share curated content with others.

List.ly (https://list.ly/). Curate and publish links and media for class projects, assignments, and homework and enable anyone to contribute.

TES Blendspace (https://www.tes.com/lessons) This online learning platform lets users curate websites, videos, blogs, and more into learning playlists.

THE POLITICAL ECONOMY OF CURATION

In a world with "too much information," curation offers much added value, and there is a complex economy developing around curated access to content of all kinds. Some librarians are including links to open educational resources and content created by patrons in their local communities. Others, such as high school librarian Michelle Luhtala at New Canaan High School in Connecticut, are curating a significant collection of how-to videos created and shared on YouTube by the members of the high school community to accelerate learning through social networking.[19] Figure 5.2 shows a screenshot from a time-lapse video that depicts a typical day at the library. This, along with hundreds of other videos, offers insight on the ways that video is used at the school to promote a spirit of sharing knowledge and a sense of community. To get a sense of the amazing quality of this high school library, check out the video entitled *We Trust You 2012*. It is an engaging, fun-to-watch library orientation video for freshmen students created to help them understand that with the freedom to use social media in school come some important responsibilities.[20]

Librarians and technology specialists have been on a steep learning curve in trying to figure out how to support student engagement with digital content.

Figure 5.2 Just an average day at New Canaan High School Library.

Online databases and platforms for the school market, although they are changing rapidly, are can be clunky and hard to use compared with the ease and simplicity of Google or Google Scholar. Many school librarians teach students how to download and configure apps to use Destiny Quest, an interface created by Follett that enables students to search for books and other resources in the school library collection. High school and college students are generally surprised to learn that Google does not generally provide access to scholarly works that are restricted by academic publishers behind academic paywalls.

Some school librarians are concerned about how changes in the digital marketplace may compromise their ability to make curation decisions. Michelle Luhtala reflected on some of the challenges of developing guidelines to help school librarians make decisions about digital content acquisitions. She recognizes that the rapid changes in the marketplace may create pressure for librarians to rely on a single distributor, thus limiting their own ability to make careful selection of content based on school and community needs. Could digital platforms replace the need for librarian curators? She writes, "If we relinquish these responsibilities to commercial interests, we literally sell out our own profession. We will be perceived as disposable. It will always be cheaper to buy prepackaged content than retain a librarian. This is a slippery slope, and it sets a precedent that will be very hard for economically challenged school districts to ignore."[21]

As more and more schools move to a 1:1 ratio of student to digital devices, some educators strive to make digital content easily available to learners in ways that create high levels of customization or personalization. For example, a language arts teacher might create individual playlists of assignments to complete. A playlist might contain links to videos, online articles, or interactive lessons—or even traditional reading and writing assignments. Students complete these work at their own pace, and the teacher monitors their progress.

Although some teachers create these playlists themselves, a variety of companies have stepped in to provide this service, either free or at a cost. For example, Summit Public Schools, a charter school management organization (funded by Facebook founder Mark Zuckerberg and his wife Priscilla Chan), uses a digital platform where all the content knowledge standards for the year are laid out for students on a dashboard. Academic content comes from companies like Khan Academy and BrainPop. Because the program receives money from venture capitalists, the company is eager to grow, and they have made attractive offers to school districts that sign up to launch the program.

But there are risks to ceding responsibility for academic content to giant corporations. This content may or may not be appropriate for the students and the community. That's why it's wise to look at the quality of the online instructional materials that are actually provided by the program.

Best Practices of Curating as Pedagogy

LEARNERS CAN

GATHER

- create a list of "favorite" examples of music, movies, athletes, videogames, or TV shows
- select a current events topic (like immigration/migration, income inequality, or climate change) and create a list of content designed to use the power of narrative storytelling to explain the issue
- create a small collection of digital images to express an idea, mood, or feeling
- find examples of digital content on a specific topic, using a variety of search strategies, keywords, search engines, and databases

EVALUATE

- create a rank-ordered collection of articles, images, videos, or websites based on a "credible to incredible" ranking system
- select a sample of digital content for a particular purpose, target audience, or learning situation

ADD VALUE

- offer justification for their choices, reflecting on their decision making about what they included and what they omitted
- offer comment and critique of the particular content selected

SHARE

- make their curated collections public and encourage others to add to it, comment, or critique

Reviews and Reviewers

If you're a film fan like we are, you may rely on critics and reviewers to support the process of deciding which films you want to see. You probably read book reviews to decide which books you might be interested in reading next. But how many students learn about book and film reviews and reviewers in their high school English classes? How often do we reflect on the quality of the reviews we rely upon for deciding what to read or view? How could reviewers be showcased or featured in library programs? What criteria distinguish a great review from just a so-so one? Librarians should help patrons and learners of all ages to appreciate the value of reviews and reviewers and empower people to take advantage of this important form of public service.

Whether you need help on where to start with picking a film, or you've had success with film programs and need to keep your selections fresh, film reviews are essential for library film programs. There are many types of film reviews out there, including fairly neutral, descriptive summaries written specifically for librarians and published in *Library Journal* or *Video Librarian*, which offers an extensive set of reviews for independent film. There are film reviews that may also include critical or cultural commentary in publications like those found in *The New Yorker* or in scholarly journals like *Cinema Journal*.

If you're going to choose movies, you're going to need to find film reviewers that you can trust and respect. One of the most famous film critics in the media literacy world is Rose Pacatte, who reviews films for the *National Catholic Reporter* and hosts the National Film Retreat under the auspices of the Pauline Center for Media Studies in Los Angeles. As a media literacy expert who is also a Catholic nun, Sister Rose takes participants on a journey using film viewing and discussion for collaborative reflection on the spiritual dimensions of human experience. After all, good films explore our profound longings for emotional connection. Sister Rose's work aligns with Georgetown professor Theresa Sanders, who in her book *Celluloid Saints*, wrote: "If we think of theology as rooted in story, it should come as no surprise that some of the most profoundly theological works of the past century have been movies."[22]

The authors of this book each have their favorite film critics. Pam likes most of the current reviewers in *The New Yorker*, especially Anthony Lane, but misses heavy-hitter critics like Pauline Kael, Judith Crist, and Janet Maslin, who provided honest, witty film criticism through female eyes. To fill the gap, she seeks out female reviewers online and she also submits all films to the Bechdel-Wallace Test created by cartoonist Alison Bechdel. She evaluates the representation of women in a film by asking this question: (1) Does it have at least two women (who have names) who (2) talk to each other, about (3) something other than a man? Pam also loved the online octogenarian YouTube film reviewers and former film industry professionals Marcia Nasatir and Lorenzo Semple, aka Reel Geezers, and aspires to that role herself.

Renee relies on A. O. Scott of *The New York Times*, who has been a film critic since 2000 and a distinguished professor of film criticism at Wesleyan University. In his book *Better Living Through Criticism*, Scott notes a critic is a person whose interest can help to activate the interest of others. Scott is aware that film criticism is a type of conversation, as the critic engages in an imaginary conversation with both the filmmaker and the audience.[23]

While A. O. Scott reaches an influential audience, there's a whole genre of YouTube film reviewers who reach a more diverse audience. One of them is Chris Stuckmann, who has 1.2 million YouTube subscribers.[24] Stuckmann's reviews are both informative and entertaining. After describing the plot and characters, Stuckmann identifies themes and uses clips from the film to illustrate his points. In some cases, he describes how audiences react to the film and comments on their behavior. He describes his own experience as an active reader of films, noting both the form and the content, and sharing his own emotional responses. Learning more about film critics can help you appreciate their values. On his website, Stuckmann offers a philosophy that reflects his passion for film:

> For as long as I can remember, I've been in awe of movies. . . . As I grew older my love for movies turned into a love for the art of film. I began to examine them, thinking about the director, the writer, the cinematographer. I tried to get inside their headspace and discover why they made the film they did.[25]

Stuckmann is among the film critics whose work on YouTube has inspired the development of aggregation review services, including Rotten Tomatoes, Metacritic, and Independent Movie Database (IMDb). Rotten Tomatoes was created in 2000 (and since 2016, it is now owned by Fandango, the website that sells movie tickets). The website tabulates a score based on a summary of reviews from more than 3,000 certified reviewers. In doing so, its ratings offer a kind of critical consensus.

But film critic aggregation websites are controversial in part because of the role of film reviews in movie marketing. Here the underrepresentation of women in film criticism has long been recognized as a problem. More than 80% of journalistic film critics are men.[26] Analysis of the aggregation websites shows that, not surprisingly, men and women rate TV shows differently. In particular, on the IMDb website, Walt Haney found that male users were more likely to rate television shows with a female-heavy audience lower than female users rated male-centric television. It's important to be aware of this form of bias. In one well-documented case, men gave particularly low scores to *Ghostbusters 3*, the all-female remake of the classic comedy directed by Paul Feig in 2016.[27]

How are library patrons empowered as film critics? One of our favorite stories about film critics in the library came from Daylily Alvarez, who posted this photo on the #ALATT Facebook page. Figure 5.3 shows the work of an anonymous patron who composes his own film mini-reviews on Post-It notes and attaches them to DVDs in the library. This is a public-spirited impulse, and not a "problem" to be solved. Readers and viewers are happy to share their recommendations about works that were meaningful to them. Perhaps librarians could productively channel the creative energy of patrons like this and other budding film critics who can be found in every school, public, and academic library.

Figure 5.3 Film critics in the library.

COMMON SENSE MEDIA: MAKING GOOD CHOICES

Parents make choices on behalf of their children from birth until they reach adulthood (and sometimes beyond), providing a home environment, selecting nutritious food, and helping children develop good self-care habits. Parents greatly influence the child's choice of hobbies, activities, and interests. Parents may determine whether and how a child will get access to a library.

When it comes to books, music, TV, movies, and games, the scope of these choices can be overwhelming. Many parents want to be intentional and strategic about making good choices of media just as they make good choices on behalf of their children's health care and emotional needs. Jim Steyer founded Common Sense Media in 2003 to give parents some help. He created a website media review service for parents, rating movies, TV shows, and video games in terms of age-appropriate educational content. The company has grown to include a focus on digital learning and policy issues relevant to children, media, and technology.

Today, they offer a Common Sense Seal to identify high-quality movies and TV shows and games that offer families an exceptional media experience. Programs get selected if they spark family conversations, entertain families of all types, or make a lasting impact on the culture as a whole. For example, in 2017, the website featured *The Man Who Invented Christmas*, a film which features a fictional story about how Charles Dickens may have written *A Christmas Carol*. According to the website, this film includes positive messages about charity and empathy.

Common Sense Media also gives a positive review to *Wonderstruck*, a 2017 film by Todd Haynes based on author-illustrator Brian Selznick's award-winning novel, which follows two deaf 12-year-old characters from two different time periods as they run away from home to New York City to look for family members. The Common Sense

Media review seems aware of parents' interest in details about potentially problematic content, noting, "There's not too much iffy stuff (other than the 'running away' situation, of course)." Potentially upsetting scenes include "nightmares about scary wolves," an angry-looking father yelling, a boy losing his hearing after being electrocuted, and a young character getting all his money stolen in New York City. Characters smoke, and there are a few uses of words like 'shut up' and 'oh my God.' "[28]

When Common Sense Media reviewed *My Life as a Zucchini*, the Oscar-nominated French-Swiss animated movie about an orphaned boy who goes to live in a group foster home, they provided some guidelines to help parents determine whether some of the content might be problematic. Figure 5.4 shows an example of the graphic organizer used by Common Sense Media to describe the movie. The film offers some mature subject matter, including the death of Zucchini's alcoholic mother and references to sex, abuse, violence, suicide, deportation, and other reasons children end up in state care. Parents are thus encouraged to be sensitive to the positive messages of the film and the positive role models and depictions, as well as references to sex, violence, consumerism, drinking, drugs, smoking, and language.[29]

Today's parents may also appreciate that Common Sense Media reviews YouTube channels, including those for popular YouTube celebrities like Tyler Oakley, Bethany Mota, Joey Graceffa, and PewDiePie. To develop a rating for a YouTube channel, reviewers watch 1 or 2 hours of programming to get a general idea of the themes and content featured. In general, Common Sense Media reflects an ideology that is progressive and liberal, a common stance among upwardly mobile, affluent Americans with more money than time.

But Common Sense Media offers more than film and media reviews. They also provide curriculum resources on digital citizenship and media literacy to schools and offer professional development programs for teachers. Their advocacy arm addresses important political issues including privacy and online safety. Common Sense Media helped sponsor the Eraser Button bill, a California law that requires websites and apps

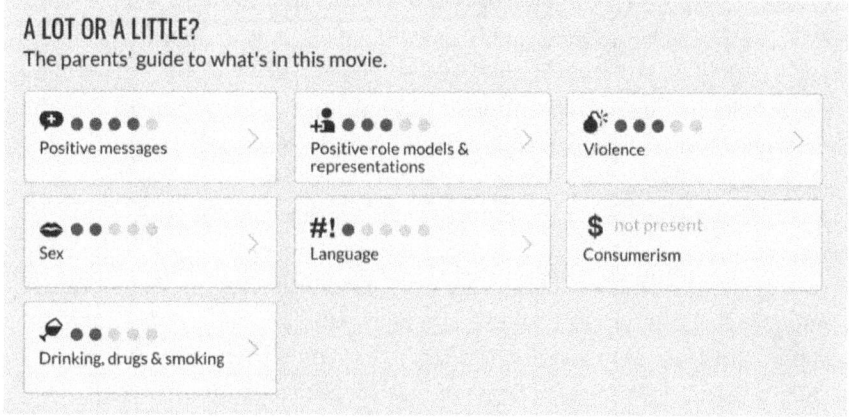

Figure 5.4 *My Life as a Zucchini* review chart from Common Sense Media.

to permit users under 18 to remove content they've personally posted and prohibits all advertising of harmful products that are illegal for minors to purchase (such as alcohol, tobacco, and guns) on websites and apps targeted to minors.

For these reasons, today the organization has been called "a political dynamo . . . influencing billions of dollars in government spending on education-related technologies, like classroom broadband access, as well as teachers' choices of learning apps." Along with financial support from individuals and foundations, funding from media companies helps finance Common Sense Media, which is now the largest nonprofit organization dedicated to children's issues. Critics have also noted how the group's growing political influence reflects the increasing privatization of American public education and "the complicated financial interrelationships that are developing as education technology proliferates."[30] It's noteworthy that the organization has demonstrated little interest in partnering with the National Association for Media Literacy Education (NAMLE), the national membership organization that hosts the National Media Literacy Week and offers a bi-annual conference for educators, librarians, youth media leaders, and college educators. As Common Sense Media has grown larger, smaller grassroots groups struggle to keep up. For example, Media Literacy Now, a policy organization charting media literacy legislation, also aims to bring a critical mass of advocates and initiatives to advance media literacy education for wider audiences, but with only a tiny fraction of the financial and human resources available to Common Sense Media.

Ratings Systems: A Library Controversy

Ratings systems can bite. Although the American Library Association (ALA) respects the freedom of organizations to create and develop ratings systems, they are built upon an explicit authority hierarchy that "presuppose[s] the existence of individuals or groups with wisdom to determine by their authority what is appropriate or inappropriate for others." Even more troubling, according to the ALA, "rating systems also presuppose that individuals must be directed in making up their minds about the ideas they examine." That's why the ALA has made it abundantly clear that libraries do not engage in providing ratings and that ratings systems in libraries present distinct challenges to the principles of intellectual freedom embedded in the Right to View.

Ratings systems can become a substitute or a shortcut for personal judgment. That's when they can become dangerous. Because the ALA values the rights of individuals to form their own opinions about resources they choose to read or view, libraries and librarians are discouraged from formally adopting or endorsing ratings systems. But the ALA takes pains to point out that librarians should not attempt to remove or destroy the ratings that are placed there by the publisher, distributor, or copyright holder because this action itself could be considered a form of expurgation—which is another form of censorship.[31]

RATINGS SYSTEMS: VIEWER DISCRETION ADVISED

"Viewer discretion advised" is a type of content warning. You may have seen this phrase pop up when you're watching a TV show or a movie. Maybe you have always known that it means the content might be racy, violent, or gross. It turns out that many Americans, especially those for whom English is not a first language, are not sure about the meaning of the phrase. The word *discretion* is confusing to some people. But there's another reason this phase can be confusing.

In most of the 160+ countries around the world, a strong broadcast and media regulatory tradition has shaped the content of what is shown over the airwaves. In some countries, the mere appearance of a particular show on television provides a kind of imprimatur of government and social approval. But in the United States, a weak regulatory tradition has prevailed. The economic imperative to make the maximum profit leads media companies to make programming decisions that emphasize controversy, sensationalism, the silly and the superficial. Cable and broadcasting television networks and local stations make independent decisions about what to air and when to air it based on their judgments about profitability—and the size of the audience is the primary metric for profit.

Who rates movies and TV shows? Is it a group of parents or child development experts? When public pressure to mitigate the violent and sexual content of the movies intensified in the 1960s, the Motion Picture Association of America staved off potential government regulation by issuing a voluntary self-rating program. In Kirby Dick's 2006 documentary about the Motion Pictures Association of America's film rating system, *This Film Is Not Yet Rated*, we learn that many ratings board members do not have young children in the home and seem to treat homosexual content differently than heterosexual material. In fact, raters are deliberately chosen for their lack of knowledge about media literacy or child development.

In the 1990s, broadcast and cable television providers faced criticism from the public about increasing levels of media violence and sexuality. The TV ratings system emerged as part of the passage of the Telecommunications Act of 1996, which mandates the inclusion of the V-Chip, a device built into most television sets to allow parents to block out programs they don't want their children to see. The V-Chip can't work without ratings being placed on shows.

You may be surprised to learn that television producers make their own determination of a rating for the shows they create. The concept of ratings is based on the principle that viewers (not government regulators) are responsible for deciding what to watch. Only entertainment shows get ratings; news and sports are exempt from the TV ratings system, and advertising, religious, and home shopping programs do not carry a rating. But some companies choose not to participate in the self-regulation of their content by providing viewers with a rating. For example, NBC is one of the largest media companies that refuse to participate in rating their shows as a matter of principle.[32] The company perceives any ratings system as a slippery slope that might interfere with their First Amendment rights of free expression.

Ratings and content warnings can create problems, researchers have found. They can have unexpected effects on some young people, as ratings notifications can help increase (not decrease) the appeal of programming among middle school and teen viewers, especially among boys.[33] It's the forbidden fruit effect. When something has a rating that makes it seem more "adult," some teens will be eager to get their hands on it.

Policy Issues in Media Curation

PBS AND YOUTUBE: DEMOCRATIZING ACCESS AND INFLUENCING POLICY

Librarians love public media. PBS and National Public Radio are considered to be cultural treasures by many. Librarians often identify with public broadcasting and its historic mission to meet the informational needs of citizens. Nationally distributed shows like *All Things Considered, Frontline, PBS News Hour,* and *Sesame Street* are widely known by librarians. Less well known is the local public programming created to serve local communities. For, example, *Georgia Traveler* is a travel show produced by Georgia Public Broadcasting and made available across the state. *Basic Black* (formerly titled *Say Brother*) is a long-running talk show produced by WGBH Boston to serve the needs of the African American community. WNET produces *Treasures of New York,* a documentary series featuring New York City architecture and cultural institutions.

There's much to love about public broadcasting. Fifty years ago, when Congress created the public broadcasting system, it fully recognized the limitations of commercial media, with the profit motive influencing decisions about all content. The government aimed to encourage the growth of radio and television broadcasting for instructional, educational, and cultural purposes. The goal was to serve the needs of people in particular localities and throughout the United States with diverse, high-quality programming, especially in meeting the needs of unserved and underserved audiences, particularly children and minorities. Today, public broadcasting is under threat from those who say that with the explosion of cable and satellite channels, federal funding is no longer required.

If you're a younger person, you might imagine that children and old people are the primary viewers of public television. But actually, public television has a very diverse audience socioeconomically. A recent study found that half of the public television audience is poor and lacks access to Internet services in the home.[34] Congress imagined that a robust public broadcasting system would ensure that all citizens of the United States (even in poor and rural communities) have access to learn from the power of broadcasting. The Corporation for Public Broadcasting receives support from "viewers like you" as well as about $500 million in annual federal funding. In Chapter 2, we learned about the significant effort that PBS puts in to reach audiences and accelerate the social impact of their documentary and children's programming. Less well known is the effort by documentary filmmakers to influence federal, state, and local policy.

The Center for Media and Social Impact (CMSI) led by Professor Patricia Aufderheide leads the field on this topic. When documentary filmmakers arm themselves with knowledge about the policy-making process, their films can have substantial impact. For example, the 2011 documentary *Semper Fi: Always Faithful*, directed by Tony Hardmon and Rachel Libert, tells the story of a Marine whose daughter died of a rare type of leukemia. Trying to make sense of what happened, he discovers one of the largest water contamination incidents in US history. After nearly 20 years of effort by the Marine and only 1 year after the documentary film premiered, Congress passed the Honoring America's Veterans and Caring for Camp Lejeune Families Act of 2012, which was signed into law by President Barack Obama. The law provides healthcare for the Marine Corps veterans and their families who lived or worked at Camp Lejeune and who have a condition linked to exposure to the toxic chemicals as listed in the legislation.

Clearly, this example illustrates a key theme of this book: Film has enormous power to activate the emotions and spur actions that contribute to social change. Documentary filmmakers captured the personal story of this grieving father to create "a powerful, emotional force that brought facts and statistics to life for policy leaders, advocacy groups and the public."[35] Documentary filmmakers tell true stories because they want to inform, persuade, and entertain, using the power of communication and information to make a difference in the world. Because of their profound emotional power, recognizing the opinion and point of view presented in a documentary is an essential life skill.

Should Video Propaganda Be Labeled?

Documentaries can be a powerful form of propaganda. As the "fake news" crisis exploded in 2017, YouTube executives wanted to demonstrate their social responsibility. So they came up with an idea to label video content that receives government funding. Under the plan, YouTube viewers will see labels on videos, just above the video's title. After the backlash that Facebook and Twitter received about their handling of Russian propaganda in the 2016 election, YouTube is trying to combat the negative use of state media.

But under this designation, some PBS documentary clips found on YouTube may receive the propaganda label because member stations receive a small percentage of their funding from the federal government. To be sure, PBS is not a state broadcaster akin to BBC or Russia Today. YouTube's proposed labeling could wrongly imply that the government has influence over PBS content, which it does not. If YouTube's intent is to advance public understanding of propaganda, we see this as a step in the wrong direction.

CLIPS MATTER

Despite the prevalence of YouTube, educators still sometimes need to make digital clips of films and videos in order to limit the amount of time it takes to cue up a DVD, or where short video clips are used. Want to use film clips to promote close reading? Want to use clips for digital authorship? Clipping media is essential to many forms of creative expression as well as teaching and learning.

The DMCA exemption process, created by the Digital Millennium Copyright Act of 1998 and administered through the Library of Congress, has gradually expanded the rights of teachers, librarians and students, who can legally make digital clips even from copy-protected DVDs. Teachers are empowered to make film clip compilations, using scenes or short portions of films for classroom use. The most common way to accomplish this is through the use of Handbrake, a digital video editing tool. After downloading Handbrake, you simply select the destination where you want your file to be stored and then start digitizing. Then use the MPEG Streamclip video converter to select short portions.

To create clips from longer films and documentaries, some users use VLC, the free and open-source media player. Developed by VideoLAN, this software was developed by a French nonprofit organization that began as a student project at the École Centrale Paris. Today, developers from around the world help make all forms of video and media accessible to millions. VLC is constantly being improved to meet changing times. Now it even enables you to rotate video you shot in a vertical format and lets you play it in a horizontal format!

Strategic clipping of video content can be a form of hands-on pedagogy, as some librarians and college faculty have discovered. One innovative approach to advancing the ability of educators to make effective use of media resources comes from the Media Resource Center at the University of California, Berkeley. Faculty learn how to compile clips with support from the Media Resource Center in collaboration with the American Culture Center's Multimedia Teaching and Learning Initiative. Faculty fellowships allow educators and graduate students to create a unique clip collection from the DVDs in the library collection. Fellows receive a small stipend for identifying relevant clips from feature films, educational documentaries, or audio-based media from the library collection. In doing so, they develop familiarity with searching, clipping, metadata, and annotation features, and they learn how to embed film and media clips into a learning management system.

For example, in the Critical Race and Sociocultural Media Literacy Collection, educators and librarians have selected short film clips from documentary and narrative films that open up important topics related to gender, race, and culture. In the *She's Beautiful When She's Angry*, the 2014 documentary by Mary Dore, one clip offers a 4-minute overview of the origins of the women's movement. In *Race: The Power of an Illusion*, the 2003 PBS series directed by Christine Herbes-Sommers, a

4-minute story documents the case of *Takao Ozawa v. United States*, the 1922 case of a man denied citizenship because of his race.

Film and Video Collections in Academic Libraries

Not all educators use film and video, but many rely on it as a key part of instruction. Although the sciences have been generally slow to adopt video as a learning tool, many humanities and social science educators use video frequently, as do those from disciplines such as communication, business, and education. But where and how video collections are supported varies from one college and university to another.

Organizing a video collection within an academic library can be a complex endeavor. Is it better to use a local classification system or Library of Congress classification? In a small academic library, media cataloging responsibilities can be onerous. A survey of academic libraries in 2004 found that most video collections were catalogued separately, apart from the main library collection. When videos and films are not fully catalogued, patrons miss out on important resources. After Keene State University library inherited nearly 2,000 DVDs and videos, they managed the complex process of physical relocation, cataloging, processing, shelving, and establishing borrowing policies, placing the collection in open, browsable stacks.[36] It takes a team of academic librarians working collaboratively to get this work done.

At the University of California Santa Barbara, the Instructional Development department, a service organization supporting the instructional mission of the campus, handles film and video ordering. Educators are allocated a subsidy of $50.00 per quarter for acquiring titles from off-campus vendors, libraries, and rental agencies (which must also cover shipping charges). Films with higher costs are charged to the academic department.

Some higher education faculty members make active use of film and media. A study of 250 Rutgers educators conducted by Jane Johnson Otto, the Media and Music Metadata Librarian at Rutgers, the State University of New Jersey found that virtually all respondents used moving images in the classroom a minimum of once or twice per academic year, and the majority used it six or more times during the year. Eleven professors said they showed moving images in almost every class session. Most educators said that they assigned students to watch video as an out-of-class assignment at least once a semester.

It's a topic that is poorly understood: How do teachers and librarians find and use film and video for classroom use? In general, educators perceive that documentaries, YouTube videos, and fiction films are most useful for the purpose of teaching and learning. To find resources, educators use YouTube, word of mouth from people in their networks, and their own movie and television viewing experience. As Figure 5.5 shows, the library catalog, reviews, and personalized recommendations from Netflix are perceived by educators to be less useful.

Although academic libraries may have created tools to support educators' selection of media resources, at many colleges and universities, educators are not aware of the availability of these materials. For example, at Rutgers, more than 90% of 250 educators surveyed were unaware of the Rutgers Media Collections Research Guide or the Online Syllabus Exchange, which librarians and instructional staff had prepared to support educators. These resources have little practical value if educators are unaware of them.

At some colleges and universities, there is a dedicated media librarian who can help educators and students who are looking for specific films in DVD or streaming video formats. In other places, media librarians can help ensure that video used for educational purposes is captioned or subtitled, enabling full access to students with disabilities, and supporting the creation of clip compilations. Sometimes they can

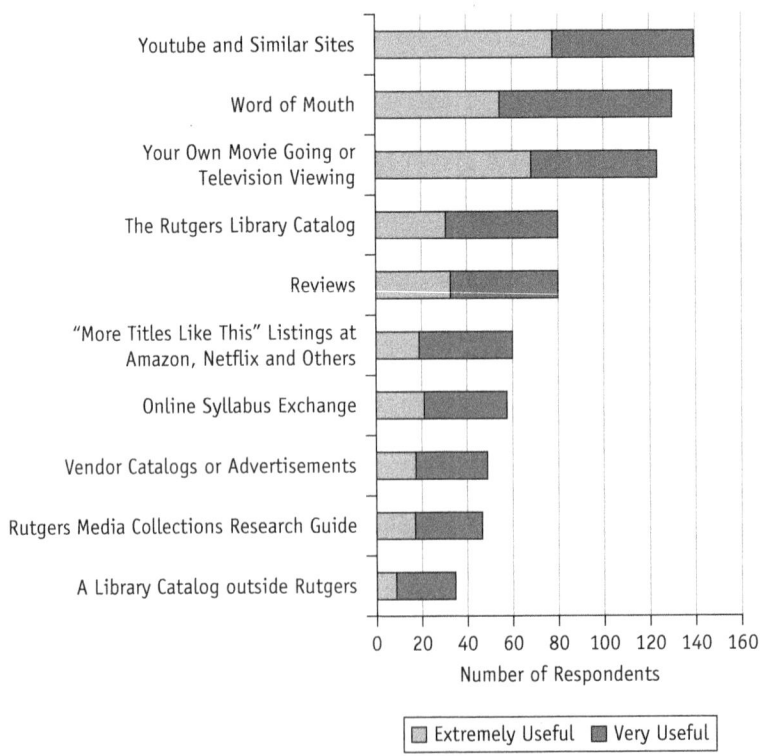

Figure 5.5 How useful are these discovery tools for film and video? Perceptions of university educators.

Source: Otto, J. J. (2014). University faculty describe their use of moving images in teaching and learning and their perceptions of the library's role in that use. *College & Research Libraries*, 75(2), 115–44. doi:10.5860/crl12-399.

provide assistance with converting or upgrading VHS tapes to a digital format or lending a portable DVD player.

Academic librarians have unique approaches to collecting film and media based on the kind of specialized academic programs offered at the college or university; obviously, if an MFA program in film is offered, the library will need far more specialized film and media collections than those at a community college or small liberal arts school. Scott Spicer is Media Outreach and Learning Spaces Librarian at the University of Minnesota and he has examined the role of instructional video in higher education, showing how historical practices concerning access to video have affected contemporary interpretations of fair use among college faculty and university librarians.[37]

Another academic librarian, Gary Handman, the legendary former director of the Media Resources Center at the University of California Berkeley has deep insight on the field: he describes video collection development as falling into one of two types: *just-in-time* and *just-in-case*. Just-in-time collection happens based on educator requests and at the point of need. Just-in-case collection is when selection is based on anticipating future teaching, research, and institutional needs.[38] Some libraries even have separate budgets for these two types of acquisition in order to differentiate between films and videos selected by librarians and those selected by teaching educators. For example, at the Morris Library at Southern Illinois University Carbondale, two funds exist for purchasing videos. The video collection there is primarily intended to support teaching and research needs in film and media studies and, to a lesser extent, to support acting and performance studies through feature, documentary, experimental, and animated films purchases. The collection policy states that it is not intended to duplicate films that are readily available through video rental sources.

At many university libraries, academic video collections tend to have a heavy focus on the disciplines of the fine and performing arts, communication, and media studies and sociology. The media librarian is often charged with supporting the programmatic needs of the communication faculty. At the Johnny Carson School of Theater and Film at the University of Nebraska-Lincoln, the video collection supports the teaching, research, and service activities of the entire university community, with special attention to undergraduate and graduate curricula for theater arts and film. The collection policy emphasizes practical filmmaking, actors and acting in films, and the applications of digital media and digital arts in film. Research needs of educators and students are supplemented through Interlibrary Loan. At some universities, librarians acquire specialized knowledge about video collection development from practical experience over time.[39]

If you're not in higher education, you may be surprised to learn that many video collections in university libraries are held in closed stacks. It's not possible to browse a closed stack to see what the collection might hold. Instead, you must use the catalog to request a specific item, and generally there are specific rules for circulation that are more limited than for content in open stacks. Because the scholarly and professional literature on library media policies is so limited, we don't know much about how these policies meet user expectations. Who benefits and who is harmed by closed stack media content? In a review of the literature, Rachel King comments on the lack of emphasis on nonprint materials in the professional literature and in library school curricula, noting that most of the knowledge we have about this topic comes from a single issue of *Library Trends*, published in the winter of 2010.

Without documentation and scholarly analysis, "confusion and inertia can take hold."[40] In many places, it's just a matter of "we've always done it this way." But because noncirculating collections and closed stacks cannot be browsed, this is a significant handicap for students and teachers alike. When faculty members are hired at a university, how can they see what in the film/media collection may be relevant to their courses or research? How likely is it that students will make recreational use of a DVD that they have to search for at the computer terminal? For many users, relying on keyword search can be far less efficient than simple browsing.

Media librarians justify closed stacks by pointing out that DVDs can be fragile and expensive to replace. But when academic library leader Nora Dimmock purchased items for a video collection at Brown University, she explained that for her, the biggest challenge was philosophical, because "librarians and library administrations have historically viewed collections of popular materials as inappropriate, unsuitable to academia, and/or as 'special' collections in isolation from the collection as a whole."[41] The inferior status of film and media within academic libraries is easy to spot when you try to search a university library website, as we described earlier in this chapter. Often, it's just not easy to find out where to find film and media content.

But change is in the air. Online video streaming is changing the way people use film and video in the home. Today, people are getting familiar with live streaming, where content is broadcast as it happens via a video webinar, music, public speaker, or sporting event. As early as 2010, Handman recognized that the future of library video collections was in streaming media, which makes access to video content available upon user demand. He observed that its advantages are significant by the following:

> ➤ Enabling people to access video content anytime, anywhere
> ➤ The ability to preserve deteriorating content in now-obsolete formats
> ➤ Eliminating need for multiple copies or the purchase of replacements
> ➤ The easy integration with learning management systems like Blackboard or Sakai[42]

Since most people use streaming media online in the home, this presents important new opportunities and challenges for school, public, and academic librarians, and for patrons and learners alike.

Questions About Using Film and Media for Learning

Q: Can I show a DVD in class?

A: Yes, you can. Section 110(1) of US Copyright law grants a specific exemption for the showing of performance or display of any lawfully acquired copyrighted content by instructors or pupils in the course of face-to-face teaching activities of a nonprofit educational institution, in a classroom or similar place devoted to instruction.

Q: If I have a DVD, can I make digital clips of short portions for use in my online class?

A: Yes, you can. As a result of the DMCA Section 1201 exemption process, K–12 and college educators are allowed to use clips from DVDs for purposes of criticism and commentary. You can use film and television clips or short segments to support lectures or to stimulate discussion and dialogue. To digitize clips, you can use Handbrake, an open-source video transcoder that enables you to "rip" content to a digital file and use MPEG Streamclip to edit clips.

Q: Can I make a digital copy of a VHS tape?

A: Maybe. If you have a VHS title that you need a DVD copy of, the library can help you find out if a commercial DVD copy is available. If the title is commercially unavailable or out of print, it is legally possible to make a digital copy provided you follow certain procedures. Informed by Section 108 of the Copyright Act, a librarian can help you conduct the due diligence needed to make a replacement copy.

Q: Can I make a screen-capture copy of digital content I find on CNN.com or other websites?

A: Yes, you can. When your purpose in making a screen capture of copyrighted works is to educate, comment or critique, the use of screen capture images is considered a fair use.

Q: Can I create an original creative work using bits of copyrighted content?

A: Yes, you can. When you use clips of copyrighted content in your own creative work, or in a remix, you'll want to aim for a transformative use of the material. Ask yourself: Am I using the copyright content for a new purpose other than that of the original? Am I using only the amount I need to accomplish my purpose? If the answers to these questions are yes, you can claim fair use.

Q: If I teach an online course, can my students view a film as part of their coursework?

A: Yes, they can. Many documentaries and other forms of educational media are available to learners via online streaming media available through the library. Instructors may also ask students to purchase the film via a subscription service such as Netflix or Amazon.

Streaming Media Services

The rise of digital streaming is perhaps the most exciting and potentially transformative way to make film and media widely available. No longer must a physical copy of a film be on a shelf; today, the digital file of the film makes it available from any device. Consumers are familiar with media streaming due to the rise of platforms like Netflix, Hulu and Amazon Prime. But many people are still unfamiliar with library streaming platforms, which are free to anyone with a library card.

One of the largest streaming media platforms for public and academic libraries is Kanopy, which is used by over 4,000 public and academic libraries worldwide. They provide digital streaming access to over 30,000 films and videos from a wide range of distributors. There are no commercials on Kanopy. They charge public libraries via a patron-driven acquisition model: that's a pay-by-use model where public libraries pay a fee each time a user watches a film. For example, using their library card to access the collection, patrons of the Philadelphia Free Library can view up to four films per month from the Kanopy collection. Alternatively, academic librarians can select individual titles from the Kanopy collection to license through a traditional 1-year, 3-year or permanent licensing model. Filmmakers receive 50% of the revenue generated. Librarians also receive specific and granular information about which films are viewed, for how long and on which devices, and they even receive detailed information about how users find and select films.

The most amazing films are available on streaming media platforms. At the Alexander Street platform, I learned about *My Millennial Life*, a 2016 film directed by Maureen Judge about the young adults who are struggling with high unemployment, underemployment, and uncertainty. The film presents the dreams and disappointments of the millennials who experience love, life, work, and becoming a grown-up at a time of great uncertainty. To facilitate careful study, the platform makes available a full transcript and collateral print material. At the Film Platform website, you can screen *Under the Gun*, a 2016 documentary by Stephanie Soechtig about the national debate on gun control policy in light of the rise of dramatic mass shootings across the country. *World Class Kids* is a 2010 Israeli documentary by Netta Loevy about Grade 2 students in Tel Aviv who are painfully aware of the conflicts in their society. We watch as the Gaza War upsets the social dynamics in the classroom, and we see the painful identity issues that result. At the Kanopy platform, viewers can see *The Red Pill*, a 2017 documentary by feminist Cassie Jaye who explores the men's rights activism movement, which raises fascinating ideas about domestic violence, gender bias, stereotyping, and other topics. Kanopy Kids offers a well-curated set of children's films and television programs for kids of all ages. The Story Time collection offers 190 short videos, 8 to 12 minutes in length, that introduce children to delightful works of children's literature, including *Hansel and Gretel* by James Marshall and *Creepy Carrots* by Aaron Reynolds.

Streaming video is a great convenience to both students and educators because the content is available anytime and anywhere. Links can be embedded in a course Blackboard or Canvas learning management platform, too. The digital format also removes common librarian worries about wear and tear, loss, or theft.[43] For media literacy educators like Renee, who is teaching online undergraduate and graduate courses, streaming video is a godsend.

Some Third-Party Streaming Video Services

- **Hoopla**: Hoopla provides entertainment media products and services to public libraries across North America. They offer patrons a selection of movies and TV shows, music, audiobooks, e-books, and comics; and patrons may borrow content immediately online.
- **Kanopy**: Originally supporting the needs of Australian universities, this company moved to San Francisco to support universities with film and video streaming of more than 30,000 titles to over 4,000 colleges, universities, and public libraries.
- **Alexander Street**: The largest provider of academic streaming media to libraries, owned by ProQuest, this company launched in 2000 and now offers more than 60,000 video titles across all disciplines. Users can create clips of films, assemble custom playlists, and access full texts of underground comics and graphic novels.
- **Swank Motion Pictures**: Feature-length Hollywood and independent films can be licensed through this service to access Disney, Miramax, and NBC Universal films for public performance.
- **Films on Demand**: A curriculum-focused video subscription providing unlimited access to videos, which can easily be added to LibGuides, distance education courses, and learning management systems. These films provide public performance rights, too.
- **Film Platform**: Curated films for academic use can be streamed on and off campus and easily integrated into the library's catalog. This firm offers exclusive film study guides and arranges Skype conversations between filmmakers and college classes.
- **Can I Stream It?** Instead of searching dozens of streaming services, type any film name into the box, and you will get a list of all the streaming services where the title is available, including instant streaming, streaming rentals, films available for digital purchase, and even Xfinity on-demand video.

Streaming video enables educators to "offer classes online that were impossible in the DVD era," according to one Michigan public university librarian.[44] Streaming video can be used in a class, at home, or in the library, and multiple students are able to view the same content simultaneously. Educators can ask a large group of students to watch the same film and all can access it independently, viewing anytime that it is convenient to them.

How do educators and students learn about the fabulous film and streaming resources available from the academic library? Many libraries offer some sort of streaming video content with an emphasis on documentaries, movies, and TV programs. But the issue of patron discovery is a substantial and ongoing challenge. There are no recommendation engines like the sophisticated ones offered by Netflix and Amazon that rely on individualized user data to offer suggestions.

WHY ACADEMIC LIBRARIANS HATE NETFLIX

Today we take streaming media for granted because YouTube, Netflix, Amazon, and Hulu bring a world of choice into our living rooms. YouTube provides videos that support learning on a very wide range of topics. You can learn about topics in computer science, nursing, literary theory, architecture, anthropology, economics, management and much more. A study of university anatomy students in Ireland found that 78% of students use YouTube to study anatomy, with a large preponderance of them finding anatomy videos to be useful or very useful for learning.[45] A systematic review of the literature found that university students report that lecture recordings make it easier for them to understand content, helping learners to fill in gaps where information was not comprehended fully or as a refresher to prepare for exams or as a substitute for reading.[46] Of course, this last purpose is likely to give both teachers and librarians the chills.

Sadly, both Netflix and Amazon have terms of use that explicitly are biased against institutional use of media. Moreover, as Michelle Kraus notes in her paper "Why Academic Librarians Hate Netflix: Digital Copyright and the Challenge of Acquiring and Providing On-Demand Streaming Media for Classroom Use," some are concerned that the terms of the agreement of home streaming services may limit the legal rights of teachers to use video for learning purposes. For example, when educators at Emory University wanted to develop a screening series on Black Television, they found it difficult to find licenses for some of the content they wanted to show. Public performance rights were not available for some TV shows they wanted to use in the series.

Some of the language of these terms of use have troubling implications for educators and librarians.[47] It doesn't seem right that fair use does not apply to a Netflix member who wants to stream Netflix videos for educational purposes. But when Netflix or Amazon users agree to the terms of use agreement, some courts have claimed that such agreements supersede copyright law. Look at the language used to see how these user agreements limit use:

Netflix's End User License Agreement: Software is for your own personal, non-commercial use, and cannot benefit any other person or entity.

Amazon: Use is restricted to non commercial, private use which means a presentation of digital content for which no fee or consideration of any kind (other than that which you pay to us) is charged or received, which takes place in your private home or apartment or, if outside your private home or apartment (e.g., in a hotel room, dorm room, office, or airport waiting lounge), is limited to a private viewing for you and your invitees. This specifically excludes any public presentation (e.g., a presentation in a dorm lounge) and any presentation by a place of public accommodation or other commercial establishment (e.g., a bar or restaurant), even if no fee is charged for viewing.

Despite this scary legal language, legal experts Jonathan Band and Peter Jaszi provide encouragement by noting such language is not likely to be legally enforceable. They explain that "librarians and instructors should not be intimidated by statements on a purchased film's packaging or at the beginning of the film itself that the film is for 'home use' only. These notices have no legal effect, and do not override the section 110(1) classroom performance exception. Similarly, librarians should not pay additional costs to acquire a performance right if the only expected showings of the film are consistent with Section 110(1)."[48]

Although academic librarians have experimented with Netflix's recommendation engine as a discovery tool for film and video, they have been discouraged from using it to support the learning needs of students and educators.[49] Librarians are sometimes overcautious about these stated terms of use even when librarians and teachers report cases where Netflix representatives offered verbal agreement to librarians who contacted the company.

It's a mistake to think that all digital learning must rely on the restrictive provisions of the TEACH Act. The American Library Association's copyright guru Carrie Russell has helped the academic library community contextualize the TEACH Act restrictions on the performance of "dramatic works" as part of distance learning, which states that educators may use only "reasonable and limited portions" of the work. She writes: "Fair use is a critical part of the distance education landscape. Not only instructional performances and displays, but also other educational uses of works, such as the provision of supplementary materials or student downloading of course materials, will continue to be subject to the fair use doctrine."

Librarians all over the country benefit from experts like Carrie Russell. As a result of her deep understanding of the evolution and context of the law as it has changed over time, Russell explains that educational institutions do not really need the TEACH Act to lawfully use digital content and technologies for distance education purposes. She writes, "In fact, many educational institutions chose not to implement TEACH at all, and instead rely on fair use."[50]

Fortunately, as streaming media services become more competitive, media companies themselves may realize the futility of trying to restrict access through convoluted terms of use. In 2017, Netflix proudly announced that *13th*, a film about racial inequities in the American criminal justice system, could be streamed in the classroom for educational purposes. We would like to remain optimistic that, perhaps in the future, the market will correct itself to ensure that copyright confusion does not interfere with the rights of teachers and librarians to make full use of streaming media for educational purposes.

According to James Steffen, an academic librarian at Emory University, the legal and financial barriers to accessing streaming audiovisual content represent a significant danger for the future of media education. He explained, "A larger and larger percentage of content is not available for educational use because of the licensing practices of streaming services like Netflix and Amazon Video. This is a type of information inequality—and in my view, it is as dangerous as income inequality in terms of the future of our democracy."[51]

Other Challenges

DIGITAL PIRACY AMONG COLLEGE STUDENTS

Whether we like to admit it or not, some college and university students have been downloading films illegally since middle school. Bit Torrent and Pirate Bay are among the most common sites where students access music, movies, and TV shows. Growing up with YouTube and Vimeo, many students expect film and media to be free, even as more and more media consumption experiences online are fee based.

Research with samples of college students have found that nearly half of them have illegally downloaded digital content within the past 2 months.[52] For example, many college students watched the seventh season of *The Walking Dead* on the AMC network, but many more also watched it via illegal methods. According to the piracy-tracking site Texcipio, the episode was illegally downloaded 600,544 times in the 24-hour period after it aired on the network. A large-scale study of movie piracy around the world shows that 32% of Americans had viewed an illegally downloaded movie, but only 4% were currently highly active in illegal downloading (by engaging in the activity within the past week).[53]

College students are particularly active in acquiring video content through illegal downloading. One study from students at Utah Valley University found that 85% of undergraduate students are aware that downloading, selling, and sharing of copyrighted media without permission of the copyright holder is against the law, but 6 in 10 students see it as a victimless crime. Most college students in this study did not have a sense of fear or guilt about illegally downloading media.[54]

For students on a budget, renting and buying films are the least popular methods of accessing video content. Another study of undergraduate film students at a Canadian university found that 40% were familiar with cyberlocker applications as well as peer-to-peer file sharing software like BitTorrent and sites like Pirate Bay. Among these students studying film, only 14% report that they rent DVDs occasionally. Most students in this survey did not value seeing the special features on DVDs. Although most students did not feel that it was important to own the movies they watch, more than half said that it was extremely or very important to store the film on a personal device for future use during the course.

At some universities, efforts are made to control student illegal downloading. In England, one Bristol University student had her access to Wi-Fi blocked because she downloaded an illegal copy of *Chicken Run*, the animated film produced by the British studio Aardman Animations. The student used BitTorrent to download the film, but she was caught by the university's IT department and blocked from using the university's Wi-Fi for 20 days.[55]

Among some film educators and students, there is a "Don't ask, don't tell" policy regarding the use of illegal downloads. In the study of undergraduate film students in Canada, one faculty member said, "I have made it my policy not to ask HOW the students are viewing the films, since I know most are doing so illegally. I do not encourage this, and I ensure legal access is available, but many students are so used to illegally downloading media that their first instinct is to view the films that way."[56] Academic librarians could play an active role in helping educate students and faculty about the importance of respecting intellectual property.

FINDING STREAMING FILM AND VIDEO RESOURCES

Despite the substantial investment in streaming video services in academic libraries, many educators remain completely unaware that the libraries purchase videos and make them available for classroom viewing. A survey of academic libraries conducted in 2017 by *Library Journal* revealed that librarians experience some challenges as they try to integrate streaming video into their catalogs. Ensuring that patrons are aware of these resources is an even bigger challenge.

In the Rutgers study, 50% of respondents did not know where the Rutgers Libraries' films or videos were listed. Many educators didn't recognize the library catalog as the tool for discovering potential film and video resources. According to Otto, "There were over twenty responses suggesting educators were not sure how to search the catalog for moving images, didn't know it was available for this purpose, or had simply never tried. A few said they wouldn't look in the catalog—period."[57]

The lack of awareness among educators about streaming media services is a formidable obstacle to the innovative pedagogical use of film and media education in higher education. In a study of educators' awareness of streaming video at Washington State University, two thirds of the educators who participated in the survey were unaware that the library even offered streaming media services. Among those who were aware, several noted the difficulty of finding video content through the library's website. One wrote: "I have tried numerous times to even find the WSU DVD archive and have never been able to find it. Could you all please make it easier to navigate to it from the WSU Library's main page?"

Other concerns were with the burdensome nature of streaming technology, as in the comment from one instructor who noted, "I don't like to use the library for any streaming video—the videos I use are widely available online, typically from public sources, and don't require multiple extra steps like downloading special plug ins (e.g., Microsoft Silverlight)— or the incredibly frustrating library require-ment to 'check out' the video for only a limited period of time." Evidence from the Washington State University study also suggests that some educators are unsure of their legal rights to use home streaming media for educational use, as in the faculty member who wrote, "Sometimes I want something that is commercial, like a TV show episode, and use my personal HULU subscription. I have wondered whether that's kosher."[58]

To address this problem, some academic librarians have created easy-to-use sup-port materials that help educators to find and use media. Jared Seay, head of Media Collections at the College of Charleston, created a LibGuide for the Addlestone Library that offers easy access to many different types of media, including DVD, streaming video, and streaming audio. Video streaming services for libraries can be pretty complicated and are not yet a turnkey service in many institutions of higher education. And video streaming services offer a maddening array of licensing options. Some films are licensed for perpetual access while others offer a license for a specific period of time.

As media streaming business model grows, it seems to be biased in favor of indi-vidual users in ways that may limit the ability of academic libraries to provide cost-effective access to instructional content. For this reason, academic librarians are sometimes conflicted about how to support the needs of educators and students, especially when films are available on commercial streaming services but not avail-able to academic libraries. For example, on the VideoLib listserve, one university librarian was contacted by an educator who wanted to use the 1995 film *Dead Man*, directed by Jim Jarmusch. The film is a psychedelic Western with original music by Neil Young. Once available via streaming media from Swank, the film is no longer available from that company. It is now available from VUDU, a content delivery company owned by Walmart. The rental fee is $2.99 per user. Although the educator did not want to ask 100 online students to each pay $2.99 to watch this film, it is the most realistic option until (and if) the film is acquired by a service that provides streaming media to academic libraries. But this example reveals much about why some streaming media content providers may be loathe to engage with academic librarians. It may be simply more profitable to bypass libraries.

Reviewing the academic and professional literature on the issue of helping faculty get access to film and video, some tensions are clearly evident. Some librarians blame educators either for their lack of interest in video or for their often unreasonable demands. According to Jennifer Leffler and her colleagues at the University of North Carolina, "Educators often have misconceptions about streaming video, such as an assumption that all materials are available in a streaming format; a belief that ripping video from DVDs is always acceptable; and the idea that a week's notice is all that Technical Services needs to process a streaming video request."[59] It's natural for librarians to feel slighted when educators do not make use of the academic library's high-quality DVD or streaming collections in their courses, preferring to use YouTube to show clips in class.

One approach to dealing with streaming video in academic libraries may occur right at the point where educators are engaging in the process of instructional design, using learning management systems like Blackboard or Canvas. At the University of North Carolina, for example, when a professor requests a streaming video from this office, a librarian contacts the professor and "explain the ins and outs of streaming video licensing and permissions." Librarians report that "it has been a struggle to find a balance" between the job of the librarian and the job of the instructional designer, however. Sometimes misunderstandings emerge as educators interact with library staff (about placing reserve videos online) without full knowledge or appreciation of the complexities involved.[60]

As we conclude this chapter, we are cautiously optimistic about the future of video streaming in libraries. When the Louisville Public Library started its 6-month trial of Kanopy in January 2019, they budgeted for 1,000 downloads per month, restricting users to five films per month. The High Plains (CO) Library offers 10 films per month to library patrons. Perhaps new economic models will continue to emerge to accommodate institutional licensing to libraries, helping to fuel the quality and diversity of streaming media content available to all Americans through the public library.

But it's also possible that the industry "hopes to create a market of individual subscribers that sidesteps the library entirely."[61] According to Rachel King, that's why academic librarians should continue to develop media collections that include both DVD and streaming media by leveraging the strengths of both tangible media and streaming video subscriptions.[62] In thinking about the shift from collections to programs across all of library land, we also wonder about whether librarians will embrace streaming collections, which are largely delivered by third-party vendors. The future of streaming media in school, public and academic libraries is undoubtedly deeply tied to the attitudes, knowledge and beliefs of librarians. These questions concern us:

> ➤ Will librarians engage so deeply with collecting film, video, and digital content in the absence of a physical object?
> ➤ What will happen when librarians are no longer responsible for selecting individual titles because third-party vendors now perform this function?
> ➤ Will streaming media services for libraries be able to compete with the many services available to individual users in the home?
> ➤ Will film and video streaming be used by ordinary patrons or become a narrow niche area for specialists and those already in the know?

Fortunately, many librarians like Scott Spicer, serving as the Media Outreach and Learning Spaces Librarian at the University of Minnesota Libraries, have inspired the authors of this book to be optimistic. Spicer works hard every day to create a media services program that is fully capable of supporting faculty and students' identities as media consumers and creators. He knows that it takes a suite of services to "provide instructors, students and researchers with the tools and support they need to easily locate, reformat, store, catalog, deliver and repurpose content through whatever traditional or emerging channel is most appropriate for their teaching, learning and or multimodal scholarship needs."[63] When it comes to changing media and technologies, of course the future is unknowable, but we have confidence that all those who care about film and media—viewers, filmmakers, scholars, educators, and librarians alike—will find a way forward.

6

Connecting

Questions Answered in This Chapter
- How do film viewing and discussion events align with community needs?
- How can film and media education promote cultural understanding?
- Why do filmmakers and librarians need each other?
- How does film media education connect across the generations?
- Why is experiential learning transformative?
- What enables library–community partnerships to thrive?
- How do planning, promoting, and assessing programs relate to partnerships?
- How can film and media education reduce polarization and mistrust?

It's a cold, late November school night in a mostly middle- and upper-middle-class Providence neighborhood. We're feeling a sense of surprise at the increasing stream of people still coming in to the community room of the Rochambeau branch of the Providence Community Libraries just before the start time. Everyone is hustling to register people; rearrange the food, drink, and information tables; and add more chairs to accommodate the eventually standing-room-only crowd.

The event is a special screening of locally produced videos made by ethnically or economically marginalized teens about their personal life experiences. It is a partnership between the library, the local neighborhood association, and Everett, a multidisciplinary performance arts incubator who created a filmmaking program as part of a citywide summer youth employment initiative.

Following the screening of the short films *Pink Matter*, about a boy coming to terms with his sexual identity, and *Dear Mom*, about facing the illness and death of a parent, the youth filmmakers formed a panel to answer audience questions. Students were asked what they had learned about their neighborhood, filmmaking, and themselves in the process. After the panel discussion, the host organizations made pleas for more community support for disenfranchised youth. Local youth and family-serving organizations were invited to share a 30-second description of their resources, upcoming events, and contact information with those gathered. Ten individuals did so, sharing brochures, booklets, and event flyers on an information table. Participants learned about the local YMCA and their next-door recreational and day care facility, a health center, an elementary school, a college and career program for young adults, several churches, a media literacy initiative, and a homework help and enrichment program.

During the meet-and-greet after the program, an elder attendee commented, "I've lived in this neighborhood for 40 years, and this is the most diverse and community-oriented program I've ever attended."

A man standing in the back of the room asked the young people sitting in front, "How many of you have been to this library before?" There was an awkward silence and some giggling, and then one girl raised her hand. "I came once a couple years ago to check it out," she said, "but it seemed kind of dead and there was nothing to do."

While the library can be commended for hosting a vibrant and well-attended community program that night, it also sounded like the library staff or board members in the room received some vital feedback about a gap in their youth services that they may not have received when surveying their active patrons. Most of the time, of course, it is difficult to get much information from nonusers about how our libraries are doing in fulfilling their social contract.

In this chapter, we'll learn about the ways in which libraries are connecting to the communities they serve. We learn about the role of partnerships between librarians and media professionals as a key to impactful and sustainable programming. We learn about how sometimes film screening events can align with community needs in ways that advance civic, environmental, and social responsibility and build a sense of local history.

And because filmmakers need librarians as much as librarians need filmmakers, we explore the complex economics of independent film and consider potential approaches to deepen a win-win relationship with these stakeholders. We look at how school librarians mobilize partnerships in relation to their professional standards and show how future librarians get experiential learning in public and school libraries when they learn to create partnerships that advance film and media literacy. We look into a bit of the history of library marketing and promotion; then we explore the various program planning, promotion, assessment, and evaluation methods that can be employed, as well as the many resources available in books and online to do so. We provide information on why thinking about promotion, assessment, and evaluation of a program should begin as soon as program planning begins. We provide real-life examples of planning, promotion, assessment, and evaluation efforts that worked and why, and how a well-designed process from start to finish can help with library strategic planning and development as well. We explore the value of including partners in the earliest steps of program planning in creating and maintaining meaningful community connections. We share some best practices in promoting and marketing a film or digital media event, as well as the benefits of effective program planning, including film and venue selection, determining your target audience, the many resources available to help with this process, and how community partners can do some of the heavy lifting.

What is the point of all this connecting? Film and media literacy in libraries helps to create communities where ongoing sustained dialogue helps us talk and listen to each other. When we share our interpretations of media messages, we come prepared to listen to the interpretations of others. And as we model respectful ways of talking about movies and media, we know that these vital civic competencies can transfer to the home, the family, the workplace, and the community.

Making Community Connections

Librarians in school, public, and academic contexts have all been more outward-facing in their outreach efforts over the past 15 years. There have been programs that connect academic libraries and public libraries as well as specialized outreach to labor unions, day care providers, and high school students.[1] But the term *outreach librarianship* may be little more than a matter of marketing and adaptation for survival. After all, if patrons won't come into the library, the librarian can come to the patron.

Such outreach efforts can be a transformative life experience for people. In the short YouTube video *The Bookmobile*, we learn about the power of the bookmobile for children of migrant workers in a powerful first-person narrative developed by Story Corps.[2] Terms like embedded librarian and liaison librarian offer a "troubadour approach to reference," where a librarian sets up shop in settlement houses, community centers, student unions, residence halls, and academic buildings and departments. It works brilliantly because, as one scholar put it, "The entire foundation of outpost librarianship rests on the supposition that in a digitally dominated environment, there is still inherent value in the personal encounter."[3]

When it comes to film and media outreach, we learn that space and place matter, too. It's been called *library-as-place*, the idea that the physical aspects of the library attract communities of users who value the space and the programs that are offered there.

Public film screenings enable public and academic libraries to meet the needs of all people in the community—including those who can't, don't, or don't like to read. They enable libraries to magnify their influence, through active efforts at community outreach that takes the pulse of all citizens, young and old. As Nancy Dowd, coauthor of the American Library Association's best-selling book, *Bite-Sized Marketing*, clearly states in *Library Journal*, "Plain and simple, libraries that are valued by their communities involve the people, local groups and government agencies in developing services and programs. If you don't have the right programs and services, people won't care. If people don't care, they won't pay attention. And if they don't pay attention, they'll just keep thinking the library is doing the same things it was doing last time they visited."[4]

LOOK OUTWARD, ANGEL

Collaboration is not always easy, and librarians must sometimes "kiss a lot of frogs" before they find a community prince. Actually, unsuccessful collaborations can be a vital learning experience. Renee believes that perhaps more learning occurs through failure than through success. There is much to value in the process of rapid prototyping or "fail fast" strategies where librarians work with partners, make limited progress, learn from the experience, and try again. In education and social science fields, this is also known as action research—action taken "to assist the 'actor' in improving or refining his or her actions."[5] You can think of every programming partnership attempt (when you're starting out, and even when you're very experienced) as research. Who knows how to do research better than librarians?

A great example of that kind of action research is to be found in the unique partnership between a local library and Arc of the Ozarks, a nonprofit community organization whose overall goal has been "to bring about a significant change in attitude towards individuals with developmental disabilities," and whose mission is "to support individuals with disabilities in directing their own lives as valued members of the community."[6] As reported by Kathleen O'Dell in Library Journal, staff at the Library Station branch of the Springfield-Greene County Library District in Missouri first joined in the Arc's efforts in 2013 by providing a monthly storytime for the Arc's population. But the storytime event fell flat. After receiving feedback from Arc staff, however, the monthly sessions eventually became rebranded as the Explore program and included more "craftivities," media, and multimedia production experiences.

Soon, viewing and discussion programs were added, including, in 2015, a monthly Explore Movie Club. There, participants screen and discuss independent films through the library's IndieFlix subscription. [7] When the authors learned about this program, we were reminded of the marvelous Academy Award–nominated 2016 documentary by Roger Ross Williams entitled Life, Animated, featuring Owen Suskind, an autistic young man who found his voice through Disney films and went on to host his own Disney film club.

Films connect us to others in part by providing a rich array of characters and stories that enable us to make sense of our own complex lives. But connecting to others takes courage, grit, and perseverance. Rather than seeing collaboration as a marketing opportunity, it's better to think of it as a two-way street. Why? The ALA National Impact of Library Public Programs Assessment lists the advantages of collaboration in relation to the possible benefits for our collaborators as well as for libraries. Each partner brings a potentially different segment of the community to learn about the library. Partners offer complementary skills, but they may also have services, locations, technology, and other assets that may have a lasting impact on the library. Partnerships may help libraries better respond to demographic shifts in the community; they can also sometimes energize and inspire staff. Most important, partners have "fresh eyes," offering input from different perspectives that helps libraries recognize and respond to community needs.[8] When librarians embrace the mentality of "engage, experiment, fail, and try again," they may discover parts of their community that were previously unknown.

In teaching future school librarians, school library leader Susan Ballard emphasizes the importance of librarians as school leaders. Sometimes librarians are reticent to accept that leadership role, preferring to stay on the sidelines. But the process of keeping on top of new resources and nudging people to experiment and try new things involves taking on a leadership role.[9] When librarians are territorial about "their" library, this can interfere with developing a sense of community connectedness. When people from different parts of the library don't share information or when librarians are not intellectually curious about the interests and needs of the other educators in their school, this can interfere with partnering. But when librarians use inclusive language, recognizing that everything they do supports the learning process and that their work helps learning, then that sense of shared purpose is communicated to colleagues. From there, partnerships can grow.

We've already shown how some film and media literacy education programs and services are not sustainable over time. Indeed, as we document in this book, some even fail. Some are stillborn. In 2014, the troubled Adams Memorial Library in Central Falls, Rhode Island, hosted a fundraiser starring Alec Baldwin of *30 Rock* fame (now known for his *Saturday Night Live* impressions of President Donald Trump). But the detailed plan developed to bring a library media center into the community did not materialize. Despite the high-visibility fundraiser, there were too many more important needs for this urban library to address, like paying the staff and keeping the electricity on.[10] Cultivating partnerships can seem like a luxury when all hands on deck are struggling to stay afloat.

PHILANTHROPIC PARTNERSHIPS

As Chapter 7 will reveal, there's a long history of philanthropic support for film and media programs in libraries. In schools, media literacy education initiatives are generally self-sustaining; in libraries and nonprofit organizations, they are often reliant on federal and/or philanthropic funding. Tracking down the full role of external funding in the development of media arts centers and digital media labs is beyond the scope of this book, of course, but it's safe to say that the rise of some of the film and media programs described in this book would have been impossible without investment from the philanthropic community. When the Providence Public Library needed significant funding for a needed renovation and update, the Rhode Island Council for the Arts provided $200K to upgrade the media capabilities and quality in their almost 300-seat auditorium, providing another venue for community arts events. Executive Director Jack Martin also procured another grant from the city to create an Education Lab with makerspace, classrooms, and office space for community partners providing important services to residents and patrons.

For more than 10 years, the John D. and Catherine T. MacArthur Foundation played an indisputable leadership role in advancing digital learning programs in libraries. When Connie Yowell, former associate professor of education at the University of Illinois at–Chicago, became program director at the MacArthur Foundation, she began exploring media education and digital learning in 2006 with a large-scale ethnographic study of youth media practices developed by Mimi Ito, a cultural anthropologist. According to Ito, when online, youth were not just watching YouTube videos and sharing text messages with their friends. Many were engaged in informal, networked learning. In the 23 case studies and 440 pages of her book, *Hanging Out, Messing Around and Geeking Out*, Ito and her colleagues documented the use of digital media for play and learning. The work demonstrated the value of informal learning activities driven by the interests of teens themselves. When youth interact with mentors and peers, they develop competencies and confidence through both online digital and face-to-face activities.

But these many case studies barely mentioned the kinds of risky and problematic uses of media that Professor Sonia Livingstone was documenting in her large-scale survey research with children and teens in Europe. It seems that Ito wasn't focused on uncovering youth engagement with the "dark side" of the web, including teen use of pornography, unwanted interactions with people online, bullying, and the wide array of digital scams, malware, malicious advertising, and more. However, among children and young people, these risky behaviors were prevalent enough that Livingstone developed a typology of risk, noting how content, context, and conduct could all pose risks for children and teens who used the Internet. Livingstone recognized that many of the empowering benefits of Internet use had to be considered in relation to the potential harms.

But the MacArthur Foundation's focus was not on exploring potential harms of the digital environment. With a focus on interest-driven networked learning established early on, Yowell also decided that focusing on implementation in public schools was not the way forward. As a scholar of education, she knew about the many obstacles to innovation there. She had participated in the evaluation of a large-scale $50 million Annenberg Challenge grant, which aimed to support local school improvement in 210 public schools. Efforts were made to improve curriculum and instruction, teacher professional community, school leadership, student learning climate, and social services for students and families, and to develop parent and community support for local schools. Unfortunately, the Annenberg Challenge had not been able to establish that the program had an impact on student learning outcomes.[11]

However, schools are "just one node on a young person's learning network," Yowell pointed out. She wondered, "Are classrooms with blackboards and textbooks and teachers up front really the best learning environment we have to offer?" She explained:

> Historically, the emphasis has been on teachers and schools as the source of information and the nexus of how young people learn. New digital media are chipping away at the old teacher-centric information push model by making what happens at the edges more visible to the center. The shift to the new knowledge co-creation model entails expanding our notion of where "school" is on the map of students' lives—and designing an infrastructure to support the interest-driven, participatory networks that are so much a part of their daily lives. Such networks already are leading to the democratization of ideas. That is, anyone can contribute from anyplace they wish, in any format they wish to contribute in. The idea is that everyone has something to contribute—given the right environment—and that one learns by contributing.[12]

Informal learning at the library, with support from media artists and technology professionals, enables teens to gain valuable technology and workforce development skills by creating a variety of digital media projects, including music, videos, blogs, and podcasts. At the Tacoma Public Library, the Digital Media Labs (originally called Story Lab) were founded with a grant from the Microsoft co-founder Paul G. Allen's foundation. Another investment group, the Hive Digital Media Learning Fund, also invested $875,000 to New York City organizations, including Global Action Project.

Today's philanthropies have a very hands-on and strategic approach to funding. In previous eras, creative people came to philanthropies with good ideas for projects and funders evaluated them to decide which ones to support. The idea was that people in their communities knew best how to identify and address social and educational needs. But now many of the largest foundations create elaborate competitions on highly focused topics of their choice. Would-be grantees must adapt to meet the stated goals of the funder. For example, when the MacArthur Foundation announced the Project: Connect Summer Youth Programming Competition in 2013 as part of the Digital Media and Learning Competition, they had a very clear set of goals and objectives in mind. Grant applicants had to demonstrate how they could achieve goals, including bridging social and cultural differences, by using hands-on making and learning experiences based on the Connected Learning principles.[13] For this particular competition, more than

266 applicants from 41 states applied, and MacArthur ultimately gave out sixteen $10,000 grants to museums, libraries, and nonprofit institutions to engage young people in the development of apps, badges, curricula, and other tools to "make the online experience more civil, safe and empowering." Grantees were selected on the basis of their capacity to actively contribute to the goal of "a more equitable, social, safe, and participatory web for all." A big priority was for "the development or testing of new digital tools and learning programs."[14] (In this particular competition, only one library, the Philadelphia Free Library, was a recipient, with the rest of the funding given to universities and nonprofit organizations).

Libraries and museums seeking support for innovative programs and services depend on federal funding from the Institute for Museum and Library Services (IMLS), established by an act of Congress in 1996. This federal funding program helps promote innovation in library services. From 2002 to 2011, the Grants to States program supplied $980 million to libraries and museums to increase access to digital information. They also promote dialogue that identifies problems and generates solutions. IMLS library leaders foster an attitude of discovery, helping librarians build capacity, increase access, and transform communities by generate new and practical ways to increase lifelong learning. In fact, the book you are holding in your hands was inspired by a 2014 IMLS-funded project called Media Smart Libraries, which was a National Leadership Grant to the University of Rhode Island's Graduate School of Library and Information Studies (GSLIS), in collaboration with the Providence Children's Film Festival, and the Rhode Island Office of Library and Information Services (OLIS).

Some funded initiatives result in books like this, while other projects may continue after the funding runs out as the work gets institutionalized within organizational practice. However, despite elaborate plans for sustainability, some initiatives that get supported by external funding simply end when the money runs out. For 6 years, the Sundance Film Festival got federal funding from IMLS and the National Endowment for the Arts for a program called Film Forward, which used film and conversations with filmmakers to introduce a new generation to the power of story, while fostering a global community. Each year, eight independent films got screened at universities, film and cultural centers, museums, libraries, and other community, educational, and cultural venues. Until 2016, when it closed, Film Forward was a touring program designed to enhance greater cultural understanding, collaboration, and dialogue around the globe by engaging audiences through the exhibition of films and conversations with filmmakers.

Funding for innovation matters. A variety of federal funders have also supported film and media literacy education programs. Pam's proposal for the Media SmART! Project in Providence Public Schools in 2000 was one of ten projects nationwide funded with a combination of US Department of Education and National Endowment for the Arts (NEA) funding. Although a full examination of the issues, opportunities, and challenges of fundraising for film and media education are beyond the scope of this book, it's clear that establishing meaningful relationships with funders is part of the process.

Partnerships Through the Year

Small-scale partnerships can support the quality of film viewing and discussion events. Today there are numerous seasonal recognition days, weeks, or months. For example, National Media Literacy Week occurs in November and the members of the National Association of Media Literacy Education (NAMLE) offer hundreds of programs and events during that week to increase awareness of media literacy education.

Recognition days also provide opportunities for interesting and inclusive programming and community outreach, including displays of films on a particular theme or topic. While there are now far more recognition themes than there are days in a month, almost all have a connection to the community, and the plethora of options lets you pick and choose the ones most relevant to your area.

For example, in looking at the February list at the National Day Calendar website, there are 21 national monthly observances, 41 weekly observances, and from two to six national observances on every day of the month. You may not want to jump on National Cabbage Day, National Condom Week, or National Snack Food Month, but we can easily see National Girls & Women in Sports Day, American Camp Week, or National Heart Month inspiring community connections for fun and unique film programming. Figure 6.1 shows an example of a film display for African American month at the Providence Athenaeum library.

Librarians already create book or bulletin board displays and newsletter, blog, or website mentions for cultural heritage months. It's not much more extra work to include films about those cultures, too.

CULTURAL PARTNERSHIPS CONNECT DIVERSE COMMUNITIES THROUGH FILM

Going a step or two beyond displays inside the library, however, can take a week- or month-long cultural exploration to a whole new level. In their blog about Hispanic Heritage Month in September, the Charlotte Mecklenburg Library in North Carolina, with 22 branches, mentioned their planned events and suggested related reading and films, including *Food for the Ancestors*, directed by Jan Thompson in 1999 and part of the PBS Video Collection.[15]

Documentaries like this are obviously a great way to learn more about a culture, but so are many dramatic films. Because librarians love stories, they also

Figure 6.1 At the Providence Athenaeum: African American Month film display.

recognize the power of narrative to engage and inspire audiences. For example, consider *Quinceanera,* a bittersweet Latina coming-of-age story, which was made in 2006 on a $400,000 budget by Richard Glatzer and Wash Westmoreland, who won big prizes for it at the Sundance Film Festival. It's a crowd-pleaser for people of all ages.

Screening films in the language of a culture represented in the community can be one way of making neighbors whose ancestry is from those cultures feel welcome. Even more important, cultural screening and discussion events can also increase understanding between new immigrants and other groups. The use of language subtitles enhances access for nonnative speakers of the language. When using subtitled films, try to make sure the subtitles are easy for all to see, as some flat-floor screening spaces in library community rooms may not be set up for optimal film viewing, especially for a clear view of the bottom of the screen. As we discussed in Chapter 2, when local cultural groups partner in film programming, they help orient the program's design to meet the needs of the community. Suggesting they share some delicious food, dance, or other cultural traditions, as well as personal or local insights about the issues raised in the film, helps to acknowledge community leaders and attract new audiences.

Since Providence, Rhode Island, has a large Latino population representing at least 18 ethnicities, the Providence Children's Film Festival has screened many family-friendly films from Spanish-speaking countries and includes Reel Connections with corresponding cultural groups in the community. The 2018 festival included a film about a Honduran family who are undocumented immigrants living in Mexico, titled *The Other Side of the Wall*, directed in 2017 by Pau Ortiz. Another one that charmed us was *Hero Steps*, the 2016 film by Colombian writer-director Henry Rincon which tells the story of Eduardo, a 10-year-old boy who has suffered through poverty and conflict and is missing a leg as a result of stepping on a landmine. With help from a teacher and friends, Eduardo aims to participate in a children's soccer tournament. Screened at the Barrington Public Library, this film and the Reel Connection that followed promoted cultural understanding and disability awareness, and it made urban-suburban connections as well.

Sometimes partnerships can yield unimagined benefits for local libraries and community organizations. Reaching out to public officials can be a matter of ask-and-you-shall-receive. For example, when the film festival selected *Jeffrey*, a family drama directed by Yanillys Perez in 2016 about a young windshield washer on the streets of Santo Domingo who dreams of being a reggaetton singer like his older brother, Pam approached the Guatemalan-American mayor of Providence, Jorge Elorza, at a fundraiser. She talked about the many Latino films in the lineup and asked for whatever help his office could offer in making the best connections with Latino arts and cultural leaders. The mayor's office compiled a very thorough list of names and contact information of local community leaders that will be beneficial for years to come.

COMMUNITY ENGAGEMENT LIBRARIANS

The Portland (Maine) Public Library is located right smack in the middle of the town and they are dedicated to being a robust community-centered organization. Rachael Harkness, programming director for the library, believes in bringing art, programs, and other opportunities to the community. She even runs an art gallery inside the library. As with many other communities, the Portland library benefited when a local video store closed its doors and donated their collection of over 18,000 DVDs.

When Harkness started the job in 2010, there were a few programs in place but little community outreach. The library's Health Team was doing three programs a year and many programs were poorly attended. Because of her background as a cultural arts administrator, Harkness knew how to interface with a variety of local community organizations. She worked with librarians to canvass the community in search of potential partners. Over time, their successes grew. In 2017, the library's health team offered four to six programs a month.

"The partnership with organizations is key to effective programming," Harkness says, "because they bring expertise, knowledge, and a focused audience." The Portland Library has invited their partners to serve on a Sustainability Council, which helps identify and bring speakers for their monthly events as well as with promoting programs and events. Harkness also sees her role as helping librarians to choose their partners well, including how to weigh the benefits and downsides of partnering with for-profit companies. This is another aspect of the trust issue between libraries and their patrons. She occasionally reassesses the amount of programming, and now they even have the luxury of "getting picky" about the partnerships they develop.

Meaningful partnerships between public libraries and film festivals create win-win visibility and provide robust learning experiences, too. For example, since 2016, several Rhode Island public libraries have hosted stop-motion animation workshops both during the week of the Providence Children's Film Festival and at other times during the year. Youth attending the workshops are encouraged to view animations and then create their own stop-motion films with help from the nearby Hasbro toy company, local arts organization creative staff, and volunteers. The films are later compiled and posted on both the festival's and the library's website, bringing more viewers to the additional resources available there. The goals of this community outreach include using film and filmmaking to encourage young people to see themselves reflected on the screen, to have them become media makers so they can share their own stories, and to introduce them to potential careers in media production.

What's in it for the public libraries that participated in the program? The payoff is the number of new patrons who enter the library for the workshops. Many people visit the library for the first time to attend film and media programs. Word-of-mouth marketing grows over the years. There have been times when parents were asked to leave the activity room to make room for more youth participants, which of course left the adults to wander around the library while they waited for their young media makers to complete their projects.

The Aspen Institute Dialogue on Public Libraries *Rising to the Challenge: Re-envisioning Public Libraries* reinforces this idea, noting, "public libraries, library directors, library staff and their supporters must forge new partnerships and collaborations in the community and align their work with the community's goals.

But libraries and their supporters are only one part of the equation. Re-envisioning the public library is a broad effort that requires the community and its elected leaders to recognize their stewardship of this valuable public asset."[16]

Film Festivals as Community Engagement

It takes a village to create a film festival. It's a year-round process that involves finding partners to provide funding and other forms of support, soliciting filmmakers to submit films, screening and selecting them, developing a multimedia marketing campaign, and then hosting multiple days of screenings, sometimes at multiple venues.

One of the most exciting film festivals we found in a public library context comes from the Princeton (New Jersey) Public Library. Susan Conlon has 15 years of experience in developing film festivals in public libraries. The Princeton Student Film Festival provides youth filmmakers an opportunity to screen their work to a broad audience, with lots of appreciation and lively feedback. There is no admission to attend the screenings, which are intended for a teen and adult audience. But it was the annual Princeton Environmental Film Festival, founded in 2006, that captured our interest and imagination. To develop this film festival, Conlon worked collaboratively with her library colleagues, including the youth services technology librarian, Amanda Chuong, and the community engagement coordinator, Kim Dorman. They recruited community leaders from the local schools and universities, and together they recruited a variety of partners, including speakers with expertise, venues, and program promotion, and have included D&R Greenway Land Trust, the Northeast Organic Farming Association of New Jersey, a local art cinema, and more recently, Princeton University.

Founded in 2006, the film festival shares exceptional documentary films and engages the community in exploring environmental sustainability from a wide range of angles and perspectives. For 11 consecutive years, attendance has been free to moviegoers, a rarity in the world of film festivals. The festival has been a smashing success. In 2012, they library reported 70,000 in attendance for programs, a 25% increase over 2011. The screening of *Antarctic Edge 70° South*, the 2015 documentary by Dena Seidel, packed both the library and the Princeton Garden Theatre. Figure 6.2 shows the crowd in the library for this event. In 2017, they aimed to increase the total user base, increase library visits, and improve volunteer engagement. They increased the number of programs by 5% and the number of attendees by 10%. They also set a goal to increase multimedia circulation by 3% and measure and increase patrons' use of programs, collections, and services devoted to language and cultural and environmental literacy. With its solid track record of success, we have complete confidence that this talented team will continue to reach its goals in ways the benefit the community they serve.

Figure 6.2 Screening of *Antarctic Edge 70° South* at the 2015 Princeton Environmental Film Festival.

SCHOOL LIBRARIES CAPITALIZE ON LOCAL FILM FESTIVALS

Sometimes film festivals can promote civic, environmental, and social responsibility through school outreach. At the 2016 Providence Children's Film Festival, their Reel Connections program connected global and universal issues in the films with individuals, organizations, and efforts within the local community. In one case, they reached out to librarian Holly Nagib at the Henry Barnard Laboratory School, one of the first laboratory schools in the United States, which is located at Rhode Island College. Educators there coordinated a film screening for children in grades 3–5.

The children read the illustrated picture book *Ada's Violin* by Susan Wood and Sally Comport, and then they watched *Landfill Harmonic*, the 2015 documentary by writer Alejandra Amarilla about a musical group of Paraguayan children playing instruments made from garbage. Then, children themselves made music out of trash, designing their own instruments from recycled materials, and they even shared their progress with members of the Recycled Orchestra via Skype. Figure 6.3 shows the immersive project which culminated in the "Extravaganza de Español" concert, which also features plays and songs in Spanish.

"There is a growing body of research that underscores how music engages critical thinking skills essential for academic success," says President Frank Sánchez of

Figure 6.3 School children have a Skype dialogue with members of the Recycled Orchestra of Paraguay.

Rhode Island College. "Through this innovative project, students at Henry Barnard Laboratory School are learning music, Spanish, technology education and library arts, in addition to the social and emotional benefits of engaging directly with young musicians from another culture."[17]

VIDEO ORAL HISTORIES SHARE COMMUNITY STORIES

In some communities, locally created oral histories on video bring people together to share stories, and this form of digital media has cross-generational value for both current and future residents. At the small Everson Branch Library in the state of Washington, the warm and inviting space of the Nooksack Valley Heritage Center (NVHC) continues to fulfill its purpose of actively engaging community members around their own local history.

Volunteers use digital technology to help patrons digitize documents, cassettes, and VHS tapes, and to record their own personal life stories. Volunteers are available to help with genealogical research on Ancestry.com, a database made available throughout the Whatcom County Library System branches. Another volunteer oversees and updates the display cabinet, refreshing the historical artifacts every quarter. At any time, the cozy space occupied by the Center invites laptop users and informal or formal meetings of various sorts. "It really is an attractive focal point for our library," Library Director Eileen Shaw states.

Figure 6.4 Nooksack Valley Heritage Center documents living history on film.

The community's embrace of the dedicated library space is roundly evident in the volunteer-driven NVHC committee of local history enthusiasts. They conceived NookChats, a monthly program hosted by local historian Jim Berg and featuring special guests who talk about Nooksack Valley heritage. The chats attract 30 or more people per session. The center's rocking chairs, a DVD of a crackling fire, and refreshments all contribute to the relaxed, homey atmosphere, as Figure 6.4 shows. Audience comments and questions are encouraged. "People connect and reconnect at these heartwarming gatherings," says Shaw. "We hear many expressions of enthusiastic gratitude."[18] The Chats are videotaped and made available on YouTube, thus augmenting the Nooksack Valley historic record by creating and preserving oral interviews. Raw footage is uploaded to YouTube; edited sessions are also shown on local TV.[19]

FILM FESTIVAL PARTNERSHIPS WORK BOTH WAYS

Film festivals are everywhere. Sure, it might help to live near Hollywood to partner with an established film organization, but according to our last count at the New York Film Academy site, which claims to have compiled one of the most accurate and current film festival databases available,[20] there are currently 477 film festivals taking place around the United States. In the small state of Rhode Island, there are at least 14 film festivals every year, and even people in the most rural areas can get to them all within an hour or less.

Partnerships with film festivals can take many forms, including offering a suitable library space for a prefestival event, screening, filmmaking workshop, postscreening, or festival discussion, or just offering free patron passes to select movies at the festival and promoting the festival at the library. In Providence, youth services librarians created a complementary reading list of books in the library collection for filmgoers who might be interested in exploring the topics, issues, or locations introduced in the festival films. As Figure 6.5 shows, Tanya Paglia, the teen librarian at the suburban Barrington Public Library, created a book display table based on the films for the days the festival came to her library and beyond.

For an understanding of how film festivals operate in conjunction with independent filmmakers, and the film selection process, we turn to Anisa Raoof, executive director, and Eric Bilodeau, director of programming for the Providence Children's Film Festival (PCFF). Films find their way into the festival in myriad ways. The festival puts out a request and then accepts submissions for films based on set criteria that fit with that festival's particular lens. The festival directors also actively seek out the best of children's cinema by attending other film festivals as well as simply taking note of what other festivals are showing. In making selections, Bilodeau looks for what's relevant to kids of all ages and what speaks to kids on

Figure 6.5 Film-to-book display at the Barrington (Rhode Island) Public Library.

different levels. He also considers how a film might become part of a bigger conversation and experience beyond the film, whether through film talks or other workshops or performances in local libraries.

The festival circuit is an important revenue generator for independent filmmakers, but perhaps more so, it is a vital was to build awareness and recognition. As Bilodeau well understands, "Filmmakers want their stories told."[21] In working with a filmmaker and getting his or her film into the festival lineup so that story can be told, every situation is unique. Some filmmakers request a fee negotiated directly with the festival, and some filmmakers have signed their license to a distributor, in which case the festival must work with the distributor.

Unfortunately, in some cases distributors can actually hinder a film from being part of a film festival if they are unwilling to negotiate, whereas direct negotiations between filmmakers and festivals can often be more flexible. This creates another opportunity for librarians. Just like a film festival, librarians can contact and work with independent filmmakers for the rights to screen a film. Much like a film festival, librarians can be film curators for the patrons of the public library.

Local film festivals can be excellent partners for librarians who are looking to develop a film program. As a result of their increased partnerships with libraries across Rhode Island, PCFF received funding from the Rhode Island Council for the Humanities to create a directory of all past festival films in their online Film Hub resources for the specific purpose of providing libraries, schools, and the community at large with access to information about them, including which films are now available through their statewide Ocean State Libraries network. It's likely that every community has individuals or organizations ready to support and help inspire film programming in public libraries.

Seeing a partnership develop is a joy to behold. We've seen the most charming evidence of a library and film festival partnership at PCFF Jury Nights held at the Providence Athenaeum, where children and adults gather to screen and select films for the festival. On one mid-November evening, we observed as youth and adult jurors grabbed some pizza, popcorn, a ballot and pencil, and took their seats in front of the big screen in the large downstairs Reading Room. As they settled in to preview and vote on films that were submitted for the festival, Eric Bilodeau welcomed the gathered crowd and set the agenda for the evening. He helped them appreciate the important curation and judgment process involved in selecting films for a film festival. The audience, which included young and old, and past and future festival attendees, was riveted by the important decision-making process before them. It was magical!

The film festival staff love this part of the film selection process because it happens after submissions for the next year's festival have started arriving but long before the stresses associated with pulling off a 10-day festival have set in. Athenaeum library staff love that these jury nights continue to grow along with the festival itself. The jury process itself, as a series of events, provides more evening opportunities for families to frequent the library together, creating a win-win situation, as most good partnerships are.

Best Practices for Film and Media Partnerships

MEET-AND-GREET

- Join existing community coalitions and networks.
- Plan meetings with community leaders to determine local needs and resources.
- Target local journalists, broadcasters, filmmakers, and arts groups to gather ideas about their work and interests.
- Identify local groups and potential community partners working on issues where film programming might be used to promote dialogue.
- Start small: build from existing relationships and add more over time.

GATHER INFORMATION AND INVITE

- Conduct focus groups to stay aware of community needs and identify film preferences and programming.
- Organize a Film Programming Committee with staff, film aficionado patrons, media professionals, and interested others. Include responsible and interested library representatives and individuals and organizations that are well connected to the community.

BRAINSTORM AND FOCUS

- Meet face to face with partner decision makers to brainstorm and discuss possibilities.
- Using collaborative brainstorming and decision-making processes, find a project that appeals to all partners.
- Develop a clear goal for each partnership. What do you want it to achieve? What does each party bring to the table? How does each partner benefit?
- Use bullet points, simple language, and no more than 10 points to describe your vision and purpose.

TAKE ACTION

- Identify the responsibilities and expectations for each partner.
- Use the most effective communication strategies for the group (email, shared planning documents, online or in-person meetings, etc.).
- Communicate your progress and share your perceptions with partners.
- Celebrate the accomplishments of your partners.
- Plan internally about next steps for the relationship.
- Thank your partner in writing, in meetings, in public, early and often!

WHY INDEPENDENT FILMMAKERS NEED LIBRARIANS

Filmmaker Eugene Martin has helped us understand why filmmakers need librarians as much as librarians need filmmakers. Now a professor and chair of the Department of Media Arts at the University of North Texas, Martin works fluidly between narrative and documentary forms, and often combines techniques from both in his work. His films have been screened internationally in more than 25 countries. His work has aired on national PBS, The Sundance Channel, and the BBC. His films have been screened at the Directors Guild of America, the National Gallery of Art, and at more than 100 film festivals internationally. Martin created the 2001 docudrama *Diary of a City Priest*, starring David Morse who plays a White Roman Catholic priest in a North Philadelphia congregation struggling with the stresses of poverty and unemployment. His 2012 documentary, the *Anderson Monarchs*, is about an African American all-girls soccer team competing, living, and thriving in Philadelphia. Martin has helped us go behind the scenes to understand the economics of independent cinema and what it takes to get a film made and seen.

Most independent filmmakers are primarily concerned with finding an audience for their films. Even before filming starts, filmmakers are thinking carefully about who will see the film and how their audience will learn about it. To see any financial return on the production of a film, the film will need buyers. Most of a film's upfront funding, if they are lucky enough to have it, is likely going toward paying a film editor and covering music licensing costs. The filmmaker might not actually get paid for his work until the film is finished and a distributor agrees to distribute it. Martin said, "For independent filmmakers, making money through distribution is challenging in a digital landscape."[22] That's an unsettling problem in an industry where digital is increasingly not just in demand, but the new norm.

To distribute a film digitally, filmmakers typically need what are known as *aggregators*. Think Netflix and all the other big subscription and rental streaming services. There are various smaller aggregators in the business as well. Big or small, these aggregators purchase rights to the film in order to distribute it digitally.

And here's the opportunity we want to highlight: libraries can be aggregators, too. Libraries stand to be an avenue for independent filmmakers to distribute their films. There is a case to be made for developing partnerships between independent filmmakers and public librarians that enable them to directly negotiate the rights to own and screen films under license.

Judith Dancoff coaches independent filmmakers on how to approach the academic library market. She cautions them not to jump into major distribution deals too soon, as the return for filmmakers ends up being only pennies for each rental or private screening. While that may amount to a substantial amount of money if it's seen by hundreds of thousands of viewers, it may be wiser to market directly to the academic market first, where the individual license fee might be far greater. In negotiating with academic libraries, Dancoff advises:

Can you really make enough on Netflix, Amazon, Distribber, et al, to equal eight or more academic sales per month—at $2,000 per month? And even if you can, how much time and social networking will that require? Once a librarian sees the Amazon price, he may be unwilling to pay for the licensed film, even though he knows he should.[23]

This is helpful information for librarians as well. If the filmmaker is acting as her or his own distributor, he or she may be looking for the highest fee possible. If you can promise good publicity and a big audience, the filmmaker might be more willing to cut a deal based on your available funds or shrewd bargaining skills.

Pam had an interesting experience while working on this book when she attended a sneak peek screening of *First Man*, directed by Damien Chazelle based on the book *First Man: The Life of Neil A. Armstrong* written by James R. Hansen. The film was a free premiere presented by the Ivy Film Festival at Brown University, and it was preceded by a short piece featuring Ryan Gosling, who plays Armstrong, thanking the audience for seeing the film on a large screen in a theater "the way it was intended to be seen." That led Pam to wonder if this was both a marketing effort and a film education lesson targeted at this college audience used to watching movies on smaller screens—another consideration for librarians wanting to connect great films and young audiences.

Taking the Show on the Road

The Mobile Film Classroom in Los Angeles, originally an enrichment program of the Mary Pickford Institute for Film Education developed in 2006, is now a nonprofit organization based in Los Angeles. They partner with over 60 Southern California school districts, charter schools, juvenile justice centers, and community-based organizations, including the County of Los Angeles Public Library and The City of Los Angeles Public Library. They offer three age-appropriate filmmaking courses and professional development opportunities.[24] Take a look at their stated values to see the deep connection between them and the core values of librarianship:

1. **Diversity:** We value voices that help us to understand different perspectives and life experiences.
2. **Storytelling:** We believe in the power of storytelling to connect us as human beings.
3. **Access:** We believe every child should have access to arts education, technology, and skilled teachers.
4. **Authenticity:** We believe each student has a unique story to share.

FILM CONTESTS: THE 90-SECOND NEWBERY

The compressed narrative is a genre of storytelling that entertains and delights. When James Kennedy first got the idea for the 90-Second Newbery Film Festival, he was trapped in a work meeting back in 2011. Bored, he wanted to try to write a quick script that summed up Madeleine L'Engle's 1962 classic book *A Wrinkle in Time* in just 1 minute. He was already familiar with the compressed narrative form and recalls the pleasure of viewing the student projects created by British schoolchildren as part of the British Film Institute's *60-Second Shakespeare* project. In that project, which ended in 2014, curriculum resources helped teachers develop a short film project with students, and these efforts received support from filmmakers and media literacy educators.

Since Kennedy loved his written short story version of *A Wrinkle in Time*, he got his nieces and nephews together with their friends and they shot it in a day. Kennedy had never made a video before. When he published it on YouTube, with a call for more projects, he was astonished to receive more than 100,000 views in just a few weeks!

Now the 90-Second Newbery contest has spread across the library world, and in a few cities across the United States, there are community screenings of the student-produced films. In North Carolina, the Asheville Public Library's 150-seat auditorium was filled to capacity when they developed a partnership with a local filmmaker and the Asheville Community Theater where a group of kids created short films. In another project, kids at the Aurora Public Library in Illinois made a version of Avi's 2003 Medal-winning *Crispin: The Cross of Lead* in the style of a black-and-white silent movie.

Key Elements of Library Film/Media Program Development

When librarians work collaboratively, the visibility and quality of their work improve. School librarians were proud to unveil the new AASL library standards in 2017. The standards were developed over a 2-year process through a collaborative effort, which included input from survey questionnaires and focus groups from school librarians and other stakeholders. Librarians were pleased to see how well the new initiative was received by school administrators and department heads. Susan Ballard, past-president of the AASL and former president of the New Hampshire School Library Media Association, helped to develop the new standards.

The AASL Standards theme "Help Kids Learn" includes four action verbs (Think, Create, Share, and Grow) and six shared foundations. They emphasize student-centered ways that incorporate cognitive, socio-emotional, and developmental approaches to learning and teaching. With the new standards, teacher librarians say, "We are teachers, too" and the document seems designed to help librarians better tell their own story and articulate their role in the school community. In developing the new standards, Ballard wanted to emphasize the importance of using a shared vocabulary that resonates with teachers and school leaders. She found that the term "school library program" is a problematic concept because school administrators often think of the word "program" as a very specific type of commercially-purchased education content. Library programs are essentially a set of scaffolded learning experiences. When it comes to promoting school library programs, Susan Ballard informed us, awareness comes first. Teachers and staff need to become aware of the services and support for learning that librarians can provide. Next comes understanding, followed by a commitment to making change happen. Only then can you move to develop a strategy to take action and move things forward.[25] This seems like wise advice on building lasting partnerships to meet the learning needs of the students in public, private, and parochial schools.

A GOOD FILM/MEDIA PROGRAM DEPENDS ON GOOD PLANNING

In the planning stage of programming, it's best to start with asking pertinent questions. What specific film, issue, or topic do we want to address? Who is our target audience? Who can we enlist as partners? What are our goals for our media education program? How will we best achieve them? After the program the questions change. What worked? Were our goals met? What did we learn along the way? Planning, promoting, assessing, and evaluating media education programs can provide valuable insights into both the worth and impact of the programs, but also point to ways in which future efforts might be improved.

It's good to remember at the outset that you don't have to do film programming alone. As has been mentioned earlier and often, start by finding your allies. Look close to home to begin, by seeking out movie-loving library staff, patrons, and community members. Then search farther afield. What are local high schools doing around film? Do they have a media production course or club? Is there a tech school, college, or university with a media production or film studies program or course whose resources you can tap into? Are there any nearby film festivals? Enlist the support of your local or state Arts and Humanities Councils to help identify filmmakers or council staff who might be willing to lend their expertise on your committee, including funding support, if needed.

As public librarian Kati Irons states in her book *Film Programming for Public Libraries*, "The more thoughtful planning you put into your film programs, the more your patrons will enjoy them, and you will enjoy the benefits of a popular program."[26] Approaching event planning as a creative process means being an alert event consumer yourself. Think of both the best and worst programs and events you've attended over the years. What was it that made the good ones good? What were the bad ones missing?

As we mentioned earlier, failure is part of the process of developing library programs. School librarians sometimes face stiff competition when planning and implementing afterschool programs. At Pawcatuck Middle School, pre-service librarians planned a screening of the award-winning Australian independent film *Paper Planes*, directed in 2014 by Robert Connolly. The fictional film features a boy who discovers his unique talent for building paper airplanes. They planned to host a film discussion, paper planes construction, and a paper planes competition in addition to screening the movie during the week before school vacation. They asked the school principal to announce the event each morning during school announcements. They placed a poster in the school library.

But on the day of the event, only two children showed up in the large school auditorium. What went wrong? There were a million reasons why, but mostly it was lack of awareness and sensitivity to the many other events and activities that were competing for children's time and attention at the same time. Getting people to come to your school library film event is not always easy, but the more you plan ahead, know your target audience, anticipate challenges, and put a lot of thought into the best promotion strategy, the better your chances for success.

Some film events draw audiences when they include local experts who have name recognition in the community. At the University of Dayton in Ohio, Communications and Outreach Librarian Katy Kelly suggests choosing your setting wisely and "casting" your hosts. For the latter, she draws heavily on the experts within the university—people who are both knowledgeable and passionate about the topic to be discussed. She also tries to reach beyond the college walls whenever possible. For example, Kelly brought in a local spoken word artist to introduce the 2006 documentary by Henry Chalfant, *From Mambo to Hip Hop*, and the artist created an original performance for the occasion.[27]

Similarly, along with partnering with local libraries as venues, the Providence Children's Film Festival tries to create local connections for as many of their feature films as possible. Like Katy Kelly in Dayton, they cast a much wider net than just those who can speak after the film screening. With limited financial and staff resources, they engage a volunteer education committee that begins meeting in September to plan those "Reel Connections" for the February festival.

As they prescreen the films, they start looking for people or organizations within the community or state who can add value and a local perspective to the viewing experience for audiences. Those community partners are then contacted and recruited. They promote their participation in the festival to their audiences, and the festival gets closer to meeting its goal of the diverse audience they seek to view their community-curated independent and international films. They don't rely on the same familiar faces year after year, but instead make substantive efforts to make new friends through providing opportunities for local community leaders to engage with the audiences who attend the films. PCFF's partnerships with local libraries includes providing both free and ticketed events in neighborhoods around the city and in other towns around the state, and this expands their reach to those diverse audiences—in urban, suburban, and rural communities—who might not otherwise attend the festival. Skillful partnering with community organizations can help increase the diversity of participants who attend a film screening.

ICE ICE Baby

School librarians recognize the core competencies for lifelong learning in their new National School Library Standards:

Inquire. Build new knowledge by inquiring, thinking critically, identifying problems, and developing strategies for solving problems.

Collaborate. Work effectively with others to broaden perspectives and work toward common goals.

Engage. Demonstrate safe, legal, and ethical creating and sharing of knowledge products independently while engaging in a community of practice and an interconnected world.

Include. Demonstrate an understanding of and commitment to inclusiveness and respect for diversity in the learning community.

Curate. Make meaning for oneself and others by collecting, organizing, and sharing resources of personal relevance.

Explore. Discover and innovate in a growth mindset developed through experience and reflection.

Source: American Association of School Librarians National School Library Standards.

MANAGING TIME

Not all people who develop film programs have the luxury of months of planning, a healthy programming budget, or generous donors. When Pam started out to plan her first-ever library film education program, it was with two graduate school classmates with only 6 weeks to plan and and execute the event. Given the constraints of an academic semester, she and the other Rhode Island member of the team met in person in early March to start planning a mid-April event. Prior to meeting, they had each written down their personal goals for the event to compare and discuss when they met. Then they created a task list and started dividing up tasks. Because they'd been doing a lot of reading and discussing about what made for a successful film education program, even in that early stage of planning, team members knew they wanted to create an engaging, fun, and interactive program, and to do so in collaboration with multiple community partners to increase their reach for both audience and influence. Their consolidated goals followed the model provided in the ALA *One Book, One Community* guide, which includes goals for the program, the audience, the collection, and the community.

The first goals the team considered were goals for the program itself. Taking time to reflect on goals for a program is a key dimension of program planning because "By setting goals you will be able to articulate your plans, your needs for assistance, and the impact that you hope this program will have on your community." Setting goals helps librarians communicate their vision for the program to your supporters, colleagues, sponsors, partners, and the general public.[28] As they discussed their ideas, Pam's team identified goals for participants focused on engaging and informing children through film screening and discussion. For the community, they wanted to promote the use of film and media literacy. For themselves, as learners, they wanted to create a professional portfolio item and a model for future programs. They also wanted to enhance their own learning through teamwork.

MARKETING AND PROMOTING LIBRARY PROGRAMS

As we have shown, when two organizations collaborate on promotion, it can expand the scope of a program's visibility and influence. When three organizations partner up, that can make it even better. There are a myriad of ways to do promotion, from the lowly and reliable in-house poster to getting the most out of social media, from do-it-yourself promotional materials to professionally created collateral.

The Princeton Public Library hires a professional producer to create a festival trailer for their annual Environmental Film Festival. Librarian Susan Conlon feels that this has produced the best results in drawing in their audience, and she has often heard patrons say the trailer made them want to see all the films highlighted.[29] They also promote the festival through the local press, the library website, the festival Facebook page, and a quarterly print publication.

Want to get some national exposure for your film program? One way is to join the POV Community Network and sign up to host a screening of one of the documentaries available from the lending library of this award-winning series on PBS. It will then be listed in their Upcoming Events listing, and it might be mentioned in a blog post. There are many benefits to having your event listed and marketed on a national outlet because it increases the likelihood that a local journalist will be interested in writing about or attending your program.

While social media might allow you to post frequent updates about what's going on at the library, there might be a bigger story that you want to tell your public. One of the ways some libraries are doing that is through a visual storytelling media like video. The 2016 Best Library Story winner of the TechSoup Storymakers 2016 campaign, Daviess County Public Library in Owensboro, Kentucky, takes the thinking that libraries are obsolete and turns it on its head in their creative fundraising video *Libraries Transform Teaser*.[30] In this video, old footage from 1950s library promotion films are humorously repurposed to show the many new services that libraries offer, with phrases like "Libraries are streaming" and "Libraries are social." When viewers see the phrase, "They aren't always quiet," viewers see fingers on a MIDI keyboard, images of live musical performances and DJ remixing in the library. When you see a patron checking out a guitar, it's obvious that this video disrupts stereotypical beliefs about libraries in an engaging way.

We are such big fans of the Nashville Public Library, and in a previous chapter we mentioned our love of their YouTube music video parody, *All About the Books*. Creating this parody of Meghan Trainor's 2014 pop hit song, "All about the Bass" was indeed a brilliant move on the part of these creative and talented librarians. They took a pop song and made a parody extolling the glories of books. In their own words, they explain: "We had a little bit of fun showcasing how easily Nashvillians can borrow, download, and stream books, music, and movies with a free library card. Currently, just 48% of Davidson County residents have a library card, and we want to grow that number to 70%. That means 195,000 new people, so we need all the help we can get!"[31] According to Andrea Fanta, special assistant for marketing and promotion at the library, the response to the video was overwhelmingly positive. It didn't cost the library anything to produce, and the mostly senior library and resident puppet troupe staff had fun making the video.[32] What we loved best about the song parody as a marketing idea was the involvement of library staff, books, puppets, and toy instruments. We also loved the simple production values. If imitation is the highest form of flattery, then the Nashville video crew should be flattered because there are now 50+ similar song parody videos created by librarians in the same vein.

Of course, some library promotion videos have been professionally produced, and we love them, too. One video for the Orange Public Library, called Bruno Mars Uptown Funk Parody: Unread Book, features snappy lyrics and a large cast of singing and dancing librarians (including one dressed as Bilbo Baggins and another dressed as Katniss Everdeen from The Hunger Games). Figure 6.6 shows a still frame image from this video. Partners for this project included both a local digital marketing consultant, a video producer, and nearby Chapman University. Made for the 2015 National Library Week, this video has received more than 550,000 views. With such efforts, libraries are reaching new audiences and potential patrons, changing people's stereotypical attitudes about librarians and libraries.

We celebrate librarians who take on new roles in their communities and realize their full potential as community connectors. The Aspen Institute recognizes the future of public libraries in their report *Rising to the Challenge: Re-envisioning Public Libraries*. They write, "Public libraries are poised to play a leading role in helping individuals and communities adapt to this changing world. Many libraries already are linking individuals to information and learning opportunities, driving development and innovation, and serving as community connectors"[33]

Bruno Mars Uptown Funk Parody: Unread Book

549,784 views   👍 3.4K   👎 235   ➤ SHARE   ≡₊ SAVE   •••

Ventucators
Published on Apr 11, 2015   SUBSCRIBE 575

Figure 6.6 Unread Book, a Bruno Mars parody.

TARGETING MULTIPLE AUDIENCES

During the planning of Pam's program at the Fox Point Library in Providence, her team realized there were multiple audiences they wanted to reach in some way, and each audience needed a unique promotional strategy, so they developed and executed the following plan:

> *Marketing to youth aged 9–15.* Since the team was confident that 20–25 youth from the library and the Boys & Girls Club would attend the program, they didn't think a widespread marketing effort was necessary for this target audience. Instead, they hand-delivered copies of the event poster one member had created to both organizations, to be posted in strategic locations. They also sent both partners the digital version to share via their online communication, and the registration sheets created for help with sign-ups.

> *Marketing to parents.* The team originally wanted to try to get some parent involvement as well. Due to suggested audience size, capacity limitations, and the decision to hold the event at a time when most parents are working, they decided to focus on youth and youth-serving staff as their primary audiences, and to provide some handout resources that youth participants could take

home or parents could pick up at the library and Boys & Girls Club. Parents interested in having their children attend the event could learn about the program via the event posters at key sites, including the parents' room of a nearby elementary school; its online presence; on the Providence Community Library online calendar of events; and on the calendar at KidoInfo—a Rhode Island online family activities website, now a part of Rhode Island Parenting magazine.

Marketing to older students and community partners. One of the event goals aimed to have cross-age and community collaborative aspects to the film education event. Both were sought, along with spreading awareness about the event, to selected community partners—the closest middle school after-school program, an alternative high school with a media arts center, and an inner-city educational center, including an Academy of International Studies. This marketing was done via email and in-person communication with key personnel at these youth-serving organizations. The team also contacted potential funding and other contributor sources, and they were able to get a $100 gift card for healthy snacks and paper supplies from a neighborhood Whole Foods store, and free books for their Gift Table from another local library about to hold a book sale.

MAXIMIZING SOCIAL MEDIA PROMOTION

Even if your library doesn't have a staff person or consultant who's responsible for marketing library services and programming, if you've got a staff member under 50, an older one or a patron who is a social media whiz, or one who works in the technology biz, your library can be using social media to its best advantage in no time.

After all, social media is all about connecting. Through it, you can get a sense of the rich diversity of talents in your local community and region. You can also share ideas with people from around the world. The *Social Media and Libraries Learner Guide* lists eight forms of social media libraries can use—Facebook, Instagram, Twitter, YouTube, Pinterest, LinkedIn, Snapchat, and Medium, but we're going to assume that more will have changed besides Snap's new name by the time you are reading this book.[34] In writing it, we relied on social media as a research discovery tool to find many of the creative promotional and marketing strategies used by school, public, and academic librarians. To the many librarians already using social media as a professional networking tool, we thank you.

Still, if you're new to using social media as part of library programming, *The Social Media and Libraries Learner Guide*, which includes a three-part webinar series, is a useful resource for providing an understanding of social media platforms and purposes. Created by Tech Soup in partnership with Web Junction, it walks librarians through a brief strategic planning process for determining your needs and goals in this regard. Ask questions like: How often will you post? Who will manage the social media channels? How will you track progress?

TWEET YOURSELF TO SOME PROMOTION

Rita Dove has said that poetry is language at its most distilled and most powerful. Just as poetry is all about packing a lot of meaning into a small number of words, there is both skill and art involved in making the most out a small space on Twitter. Luckily, in November 2017, Twitter doubled the word limit from 140 to 280 characters, but for whatever reasons, most Twitter users have not expanded their tweets to fit the new, expanded space. Also, you don't have to be a poet to start tweeting away, but if you're writing on behalf of your library, it might be a good idea to give it a bit of thought before you put fingers to keyboard, or at least before you hit the Tweet button.

At the University of Rhode Island's annual professional development program for K-12 teachers, librarians and college faculty, the Summer Institute in Digital Literacy, the motto is: "Everyone learns from everyone." Social media is a powerful way that people can collaborate in learning. Librarians in the IMLS-funded Media Smart Libraries initiative advanced their digital and media literacy skills of school and youth librarians through professional development focused on five core competencies, including the meaningful and effective use of social media. In one session, Catherine Damiani, emerging technologies librarian at the Weaver Library in East Providence, offered sessions to help librarians learn to use Twitter.

Beyond the basics of getting an account, however, it takes some practice for people in library land to learn the art of Twitter promotion. Look at the following examples of promotion via library and school Twitter accounts, shown as Figures 6.7–6.10. These questions might inspire your analysis and reflection: Which ones catch your eye? Which ones make you want to know more? Which are least effective and why? Can you identify the author and purpose? Do you notice any techniques used to get your attention? What are the values represented in these tweets? How might these tweets be interpreted differently? What's left out that would make a particular tweet more informative or useful?

What caught your attention first in looking at the tweet shown in Figure 6.7? How has the author attempted to engage the audience? What do you think was the purpose for sending this tweet? What various parts of the library collection are referenced? Was anything omitted that could have improved its impact?

What about the tweet shown in Figure 6.8 from the Yokohama International School Library in Japan? Who is the target audience and what is the purpose of the author? What techniques were used to capture attention? What purpose do the hashtags play here? What do they tell us about the author or the attitude of the school staff toward the value of magazines and films?

Figure 6.7 #MovieTitleMonday tweet from the Toledo Public Library.

Figure 6.8 #YISlearning tweet from the Yokohama International School Library.

Hmm . . . what would have made the post shown in Figure 6.9 more informative and eye-catching? Where can a user go to learn more? Anyone who has used social media knows that a post with an image has a greater chance of being seen by a larger audience. When we review these and other library promotion tweets, we notice that only a few of them contain a link to a URL so that people can learn more or see what else is happening at the library. Why is a URL missing in so many of these posts?

In Figure 6.10 we see how seventh-grade English teacher Dayna DiVenere promotes the work of her students by showing their group reflection activity after viewing *Wonder*, the 2017 family drama directed by Stephen Chbosky and based on R. J. Palacio's book of the same name. After viewing, children reflect on the film's narrative and theme as they consider the heartwarming story of a fifth-grade boy with facial differences who attends a local elementary school for the first time.

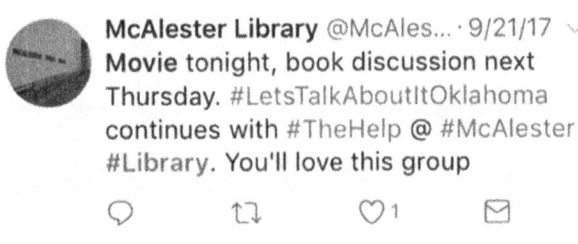

Figure 6.9 #McAlester Library event promotion.

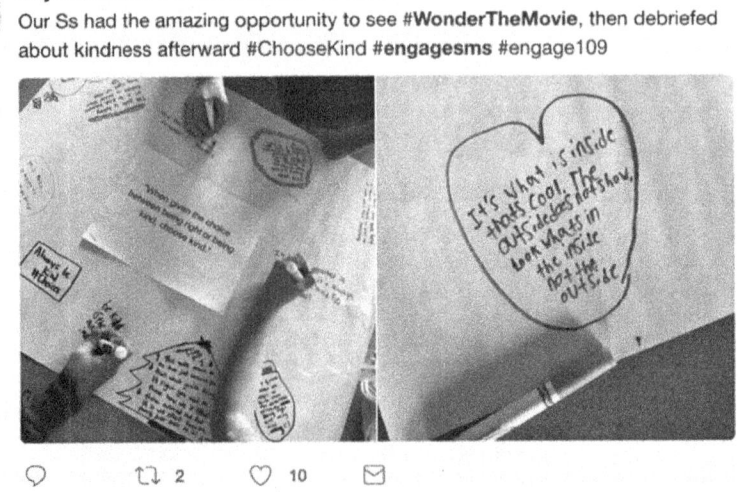

Figure 6.10 After viewing #WondertheMovie, students reflect on the film's theme.

Through strategic use of hashtags, her tweet informs her own school community at the South San Antonio, Texas Alan B. Shepard Middle School, and it also inspires other teachers to try the activity. Furthermore, the use of the film hashtag links out to inform the many fans of the film that children are learning to identify and discuss the importance of kindness. What a great way to deepen respect and appreciation of the uniqueness of each individual!

Character Day

How do people come together to discuss socio-emotional learning and global change? One of the most charismatic connectors we know is Emmy-nominated filmmaker and founder of the Webby Awards Tiffany Shlain. Her film studio, Let It Ripple, developed Character Day, an event that unites people from all over the world to discuss and reflect upon the role of character in making society more just and equitable.

Shlain creates short films that are designed to bring people together and provoke dialogue. *The Science of Character* is an 8-minute film that introduces the different values that human beings hold as important for living "the good life." Another film, *The Adaptable Mind,* a 10-minute film about the competencies that are needed for thriving in an unknown future: curiosity, creativity, initiative, multidisciplinary thinking, and empathy. In 2017, she developed *50/50,* a short film about gender inequality.

Let It Ripple's mission to use film to promote discussion and deepen a sense of community connectedness is well aligned with the core themes of this book. Libraries can host live and virtual events to engage people in conversation and action around the many complicated political, economic, and social issues that are now reshaping our lives.

We appreciate Shlain's artistry in using "cloud filmmaking" to create films through collaboration with people all over the world. Most of all, we appreciate how the films themselves help to start conversations about topics that matter.

ASSESSMENT MATTERS

From our research in writing this book, we've learned that you can see and feel the success of a library film program by the way the audience talks and behaves. As the presenter or master of ceremonies, though, it's not always possible to observe people so carefully. That's why Pam likes to query other adults who attend her programs; she invites them to share what they noticed about the experience through a questionnaire and an informal interview. With a 10%–15% average response rate for surveys, additional routes to getting this valuable information are worth exploring.

One strategy is simple: engage an observer to watch the participants and take notes. After one of Pam's library film education events, an educator who was present remembered what most impacted her about the program and why she was convinced it was a success. She said, "I loved seeing the responses of the young people to the skateboard movie. They noticed that the message of the movie was made without dialogue. I also loved the excitement of the kids when they were able to ask the filmmaker questions. I was most impacted by the way these youth responded to being respected enough to question the filmmaker. They had good questions."

This educator was attentive to the interaction of the children whose behavior during the program indicated that this was a highly meaningful experience for them. The youth services specialist at the library also noticed the children's good behavior. She said, "I thought it was great that your team was able to get the boys engaged and involved in the hand clapping as well. One little boy even stayed after to learn some hand clapping games on YouTube with me."

To assess the impact of this particular program, Pam's team also used a feedback activity they called "Write It Down and Stick It Up." Children were given sticky notes and asked to write down their comments that could then be looked at later. They placed these on a large sheet of paper at the end of the program. Motivation for doing this and other school-like requests during a school vacation week came in the form of small gifts on a prize table. Children who completed tasks or participated in discussions got tickets to choose a small prize. Most were inexpensive school or art supply items and donated books. Little rewards for participating in discussion or giving written feedback proved to be a strong motivator for paying attention and being an active participant in the workshop.

It's important to know what you want to know, and what might be the best route for gathering that information. Formal measurement of the outcomes of library programs may involve clear identification of what can be measured. At the Hennepin County Library, Teen Tech Squads include teen workers who receive training on a variety of software programs and tools and collaborate with the librarians on the planning, implementation, and assessment of workshops and programs. Guided by the logic models used by the W.K. Kellogg Foundation, they decided to focus on three measurable outcomes that the teen workers in their programs are most likely to achieve. They decided to use a mix of open-ended and closed questions. Questions formulated as "yes" or "no" enabled them to easily count responses while open-ended questions provided specific details and anecdotes that helped them tell the story of the program's value to participants, as Figure 6.11 shows.[35]

In the service design approach articulated by Joe Marquez and Annie Downey of Reed College, partnerships help to assess and design current and future library services. Marquez and Downey describe a library design team that works in

OUTCOMES	SAMPLE INDICATOR	QUESTIONS
Youth increase technology skills and their ability to express themselves using technology.	Youth gain skills in sharing content and ideas.	Did you share any of your work with others today?
	Youth learn skills that they wouldn't be able to learn at school or at home	Can you use any of these tools that you used today at home or at school?
	Youth gain skills by using technology that interests them.	What digital tools were you most excited to use today?
	Youth gain confidence in their skills.	Do you feel more comfortable using these tools after today's workshop?

Figure 6.11 Measurable outcomes in a teen technology program.
Source: Genett, 2014.

partnership with both internal and external stakeholders. They advocate for the creation of a diverse user working group (UWG), for short-term projects or as ongoing consultants, to provide feedback from their different perspectives and help co-create services that are relevant to users. They write:

> Libraries are, by nature, service providers and are an environment that stands to benefit from implementing a service design approach when assessing, refining, and creating services. Even as libraries evolve with technological innovations and new methods of accessing information, the dedication to service is at the heart of librarianship, which highlights the importance of being constantly aware of how services are being provided to ensure the best user experience. The service design approach is particularly promising for libraries because of its holistic focus and co-creative process. With service design, library staff are encouraged to look at all services, how they interconnect as a whole, and from the perspective of users. This can open staff up to a level of understanding of their users that they may not have considered before, especially in light of the functional siloing that is common in libraries.[36]

It takes courage to engage with people who have different perspectives about the value and relevance of library services and gather information and feedback that helps improve them. But when library staff can see their work with fresh eyes, it can generate transformative insights that help advance the quality of programs and services and help them be more relevant to user needs.

Some Quick and Easy Ways to Collect Feedback

- State the value of sharing comments and ideas; then ask for responses and thoughts as soon as the program ends.
- Hands Up! Invite participants to "Raise your hand if..." and add a statement reflecting a potential response to the film that builds upon connections between the film and people's life experiences. Use three to five of these as a sequence to promote reflection and engagement.
- Take a Stand/Walk the Line activity: Invite people to stand and respond to three to five statements about the film topic. To indicate their opinion, participants stand on an imaginary or marked continuum line between Strongly Agree and Strongly Disagree. Invite people to explain their reasoning. Allow people to move along the line, if they are persuaded by new information.
- Invite people to contribute sticky note answers to complete the sentences: "I liked..." "I learned..." and "I wish..."
- Thumbs up or down bins: Participants put nametags, programs, and so on in one or the other to show overall assessment of the program.

Many of these approaches require thinking through the questions, statements, or prompts to get the assessment information you're seeking. Try to avoid asking yes or no questions. We like questions like these:

- What was something you liked about this film?
- What was something new you learned today?
- On a scale of 1 to 10, with 10 meaning "very likely," how likely are you to try one of the online streaming services for accessing video from the library?

Silence or lower numbers give you some indication that the program did not meet user needs. Pay attention to both active participants and nonparticipants. Both can provide valuable information about what is important to your audience.

FLIPGRID FEEDBACK

There are plenty of people, especially young ones, who want to have their 15 minutes (or seconds) of fame in front of the camera. Using the Flipgrid platform or app to capture audience members' thoughts after a program is a good way to get some spoken feedback. Participants can record their 60- or 90-second video either in the library or at home. They can even watch the videos of others before recording their own response, which might include a comment agreeing or disagreeing with someone else's thoughts. We are big fans of Flipgrid. We're thrilled that so many school librarians used Flipgrid during School Library Month in 2017. Ashley Cooksey, a library media specialist in Arkansas, asked her students to share what they like most about coming to the library. Ashley shares examples of student Flipgrid videos and gives her readers a chance to try it out for themselves. She encourages them to consider the possibilities of using this application for student self-reflection and library advocacy.[37] Similarly, Wynita Harmon provides easy-to-follow, step-by-step instructions for setting up a Flipgrid.[38] Distinguished teacher librarian and technology integration specialist Shannon McClintock Miller recognizes that even young elementary students can be excited about using this video communication and reflection tool, suggesting the many ways it could be used in schools and libraries, including for book talks, reflection on a field trip, reciting poetry, recording a speech, creating a news show, singing a song, or interviewing someone in their family at home or an older student in school.[39] It takes practice to become a confident communicator, and tools like Flipgrid give students opportunities to become more comfortable using their powerful voices for learning.

FILM AND MEDIA PROGRAMS: A MANDATE FOR COMMUNITY CIVIC ENGAGEMENT

The reason why people love film and media is because it reaches both our hearts and our heads. Now, as never before, ongoing sustained dialogue where we talk to each other about our interpretations of media messages is needed in order for democracy to thrive. As we model respectful ways of talking about movies and media, these skills can transfer to the home, the family, the workplace, and the community.

Libraries build community through connecting people with ideas and experiences. The library mandate for community engagement is stated clearly in the ALA Policy Manual:

> The broad social responsibilities of the American Library Association are defined in terms of the contribution that librarianship can make in ameliorating or solving the critical problems of society; support for efforts to help inform and educate the people of the United States on these problems and to encourage them to examine the many views on and the facts regarding each problem; and the willingness of ALA to take a position on current critical issues with the relationship to libraries and library service set forth in the position statement.[40]

At a time in our history when examining the facts, views, and positions on current critical issues in our communities, nations, and world may be more important than ever, many outward-facing libraries and librarians have been taking this goal to heart, and to the heart of their programming, and know that film programs, especially when they include community partners and effective evaluation, can play a key role in supporting that effort. As you have seen in this chapter, the payoffs for making connections with your staff, your collections, your community, and your programming data as you integrate films and other visual media more fully into your educational programming are numerous.

Part II

PAST, PRESENT, AND FUTURE

7

Past

Questions Answered in This Chapter
- Why were film screenings first used in public libraries?
- How was film censored at the turn of the 20th century?
- What were common 20th-century fears about film viewing among community leaders?
- How did film companies try to appeal to educators and librarians?
- How did people first begin to think of films as having educational value?
- How did the rise of film viewing and television affect library circulation?
- What factors led to the rise of film discussion groups around the world?
- How and why did libraries first start collecting films?
- When did educators start analyzing film in the classroom?
- When did children first start making films in schools and libraries?
- How did librarians react to a controversial 1977 film about intellectual freedom?
- What special collections are available for the study of media literacy history?
- Why did libraries begin circulating VHS tapes?
- What factors shaped the development of film collections in university libraries?
- Why is the preservation of film and video so important?

As we have seen in previous chapters, film is a ubiquitous part of library collections and programming, even if it may not always be a top priority for librarians. All year round, patrons check out DVDs from public libraries across the United States and librarians host screening and discussion events for their patrons. For example:

➤ In February 2018, at the Carol Stream Public Library in Illinois, patrons attended a book club meeting where they read and discussed *The Immortal Life of Henrietta Lacks* by Rebecca Skloot, which tells the story of an African American woman who becomes an unwitting pioneer for medical breakthroughs when her cells are used for research purposes in the early 1950s. Two weeks later, they watched the 2017 film of the same name directed by George C. Wolfe. Viewers enjoyed the movie, and closed captioning helped seniors and new immigrants follow the story. After the movie, some patrons stayed to discuss and share ideas.

➤ At the Oak Lane Branch Library in Philadelphia, patrons were offered a weekly program entitled "How I Spent My Summer @ the Movies Series," with screenings of films, including *Moana*, the 2016 Disney animation; *Selma Lord Selma*, directed in 1999 by Charles Burnett, an African American independent filmmaker; and *Kubo and the Two Strings*, a 2016 stop-motion fantasy action film directed by Travis Knight.

➤ At the Hawthorne Public Library, a branch of the Madison Public Library in Wisconsin, patrons gather for the Hawthorne Anime Club, which was created to give people a place to gather, watch, and talk about Japanese animated films. Each meeting includes screenings of both classic titles and new releases.

It's only natural to wonder: When did such events first occur in public libraries? To understand the history of film and media education in school, public, and academic libraries, we started our journey in the archives of the Providence, Rhode Island, public library. If films were screened there in the early part of the 20th century, there is no record of it. We find no mention of film or media in the annual reports of the Providence Public Library until 1949, when the librarian notes, "The printed page is still our chief stock-in-trade. Nevertheless, we cannot disregard the place of recorded music, folk tales, and important historical and documentary records or film in today's world. As soon as resources are available, the beginnings of circulating collection of recordings and important historical, educational and industrial films would be desirable."[1]

Although the tone suggests a somewhat begrudging perspective, there is an emerging recognition that nonprint media may have some value. Television was the cause of declining library circulations, some believed. A Providence librarian noted in one annual report, "How much influence television has on interest in reading, nobody really knows, but that it is considerable, many suspect."[2] This issue probably reflected a typical perspective among many well-educated people of the time.

We had similar experiences in the Philadelphia Free Library in trying to trace back the roots of film screenings in public libraries. There, the archivist informed us that promotional materials for film screening events from the past were probably located in "the vault," an uncatalogued and inaccessible storage space. We also searched through the local historical pamphlet collection but to no avail. Looking at the scholarly literature, we were surprised to find only a slender set of articles on the origins of film screenings; film-book promotion; and the introduction of 16mm films, video, and DVDs into library collections.

Library historian Suzanne Stauffer of Louisiana State University puts it bluntly: "Library historians have essentially overlooked the medium, and academics and practitioners alike appear to be almost completely unaware that there is such a history."[3] Although there are a few scholarly articles on the topic, the library field as a whole lacks a comprehensive examination of how film collection and public programs developed in public libraries. In attempting to uncover the history of film in libraries, we found ourselves wondering a broader question: Why is there so little reference to film and media resources in the professional literature of the field?

Although it's never been particularly valued or appreciated by mainstream library professionals, the use of film in public libraries has a long history that is nearly as old as the medium itself. As collection manager for the Reserve Film and Video collection of The New York Public Library Elena Rossi-Snook works hard to keep 16 mm films, VHS tapes and DVDs in active circulation, helping ensure that these resources are actively used by the general public (and not merely preserved).

In exploring the history of film in public libraries, she explains, "The introduction of film into American public libraries could not have occurred without a radical departure from traditional library dogma."[4] During the 19th century, libraries were designed to meet the needs of scholars. But with the rise of immigration, public libraries reinvented themselves to serve the whole of American society, including children, newcomers, and the general public. Part of that shift in focus helped film and media resources to enter the doors of the library.

Why is the study of the library's past practices so important? With the many rapid changes in media and technology, forecasting the future is a challenge. Libraries continue to change and adapt to the needs and expectations of their users, and to the cultural environment of the times. We think that if we are to imagine the future of film and media in school, public, and academic libraries, we need to take a careful look at the past.

In this chapter, we'll learn how during the 1930s, libraries made important efforts to become relevant to the needs of the communities they served. Some libraries pioneered new approaches to service. Years later, as television was beginning to make an influence on people's leisure activities, librarians were beginning to get worried about the long-term impact of television on reading. With some notable exceptions, for a long time, most librarians studiously ignored film and media. As we will see in the pages that follow, over time, librarians and educators gradually adapted to changes in society as they began to recognize that we were shifting from a print to a visual culture. They recognized that these new media were truly empowering art forms that could function as powerful storytellers and truthtellers. Audiovisual media, including radio, film, and television, could promote learning. When Margaret E. Davis, a Wisconsin librarian, wanted to encourage children's librarians to use educational radio and television programming broadcast by the state's educational media network as part of children's library service, she noted, "Contrary to contemporary folklore, television and radio are not an evil menace insidiously dulling the minds of children and adults."[5]

In the Beginning

To cultivate an interest among children and teens in books and reading, some librarians were making innovative use of film programming as early as 1910. The Madison Public Library provided the first recorded use of film in a public library when a film was used in a children's story hour to illustrate the tale. Horne describes this practice as "book baiting," an old-fashioned term that refers to the use of films as a lure to attract young readers to books. Two librarians, Marion Weil and Harriet Imhoff, presented seventh and eighth graders with a mixed program that included live storytelling, an illustrated lecture, and short silent films.

Librarians emphasized the instrumental value of such programming as a way to promote the library. By 1915, the South Side Library in Milwaukee had a motion picture projector installed in the library auditorium, showing films as a way to promote interest in books. Some librarians even got into the act of creating short films. The Seattle Public librarians actually arranged to film a paper airplane contest conducted by one of the children's librarians. As a result of the success of this 1914 experiment, other activities were filmed and then shown in local movie theaters to publicize the library.[6]

Ina Clement, a film activist and reference librarian in New York, reminded librarians that they could use their curation skills to select a well-balanced film program to serve the educational needs of the community.[7] To cultivate the library habit and inspire an interest in reading, some librarians began hosting regular film events for children and teens. Apparently, these events were quite popular. At the Reddick Library in Ottawa, Illinois, in 1913, the librarian received help from the local Boy Scout troop who served as ushers and ticket-takers at the 45-minute screenings. As part of the program, children were given instruction on how to behave at the movies. After observing children's behavior during these screenings, the librarian advised others that programs that mixed educational films with comedy were more well received than those that included only educational films. To select films, librarians began to rely on regional "networks of expertise" to select "wholesome" films that did not stir up controversy.[8]

As film became the newest fad, some librarians began to think of themselves as in competition with the rising tide of film entertainment. By 1914, a librarian from the Los Angeles Public Library wrote that the picture theater was "the greatest competitor of the public library, and the very people whom the library serves the least are the mass of men and women who patronize these theaters." He argued that librarians need to do a better job of marketing and publicity, as well as improved collaboration with film exhibitors. Despite this enthusiasm, however, few American libraries during this time period saw film as a resource worth collecting.

To make sense of all these stories, it's important to recognize that, in the early part of the 20th century, librarians were themselves in the middle of a reform movement that was enabling the library to be a force for progressive social change. Some library leaders slowly shifted away from their long-standing focus on publishers and academics and toward becoming "an institution to actively develop society." By providing open access to shelves, creating children's rooms, providing user-friendly catalogs, and incorporating lectures and exhibits to reinforce and promote reading, librarians were becoming more responsive to the needs of the local community.[9] Many new innovations were developed during this period. During the 1920s, many public libraries had so-called foreign departments, where books in languages other than English circulated and citizenship classes were provided to introduce people to the library. Outreach to children and teens in poorer neighborhoods was initiated. For example, with the cooperation of public school leaders, the Providence Public Library supported summer book wagons, which were retrofitted trucks fitted with shelving providing "book service in the open air" to playgrounds.[10]

Film screenings were sometimes part of this wave of innovation. Love of books and movies, accompanied by positive attitudes toward public service helped to inspire some librarians to make a connection between the page and the screen. The new technology of film captured the imagination of many, and some librarians became aware of how film could inspire people's interest in reading. However, as much as librarians wanted to use this new medium, it was not easy to acquire films. Distributors sometimes looked askance at librarians' requests for films. Sometimes librarians arranged to have educational films screened at local theaters because of the challenge of gaining access to expensive film projectors.[11]

Meanwhile, Americans were flocking to the movies. The contemporary fascination with screens is nothing new. In 1926, people saw about 40 movies per year. Movie going was a weekly event for many. With a population of 117 million, there were 23,000 movie theaters in the United States with movie attendance of approximately 90 million every week.[12] To compare past to present, where viewing is now a daily part of everyday life, consider how much time people spend with Netflix. In 2015, Netflix members streamed 42.5 billion hours worth of programming, with each individual subscriber spending about 568 hours per year just watching Netflix (that's about 90 minutes per day).[13] Screen entertainment has become ever more central to daily life.

EARLY DAYS: FILM CENSORSHIP AND PROPAGANDA

Although there were a few pioneers who brought films into libraries in the early 20th century, most librarians were not so enthusiastic about the prospect of focusing on film. Librarians and educators have always had a complex love-hate relationship with moving image media. Films were not considered to be high-quality storytelling. Action-packed adventures of cops and robbers, and cowboys and Indians thrilled young people who were flocking to urban areas as industrialization transformed American cities. One of the most famous movies of the early 20th century was *The Great Train Robbery*, created in 1903 by Edwin S. Porter.

Early on, people could see the negative impact of these cops-and-robbers films on the children in their neighborhoods. In 1909, Jane Addams, often considered the "mother of social work," noted that some Chicago boys who had just seen one such film spent weeks carefully planning to lasso, murder, and rob a neighborhood milkman. Clearly, film inspired children to imitate what they saw, and magazine articles of the time referred to the ways in which viewing film made people "suggestible" and "impressionable."[14] As juvenile crime was on the rise in overcrowded tenement slums, it seemed to many that watching films was to blame.

During the early part of the century, there were concerns among parents, teachers, and librarians about the quality of messages being received by young listeners and viewers. Exposure to media violence, coarse language, and references to sexuality were noted by educators as early as the 1910s. With the rise of entertainment film, there were a host of critics who recognized film's potential to harm the public. Common fears about cinema viewing included concerns about the safety of the nickelodeon space, fears about children's eyes, and the risks of sitting for hours in a darkened room. The content of film also inflamed debates, as many stories featured conflict and aggression, alcohol and drug use, and other material deemed salacious by middle-class audiences. Film and media were also thought to displace time spent reading. As might be expected, "Debates over cinema's respectability . . . deeply influenced librarians' attitudes to film."[15]

Propaganda was a common feature of early 20th-century films. Movies could arouse people's patriotic feelings or inspire them to be aggressive, selfish and vain. During the time of the Great War, films became thought of as manipulative and propagandistic. Many films contained pro-war propaganda in order to inspire young men to march into battle. But during this time period, social reformers also tried to use film as a form of positive propaganda, promoting middle-class behaviors to the massive wave of immigrants entering the country. These so-called social hygiene films included frank and candid discussions of syphilis, sexuality, prostitution, and even depictions of live births.[16] Media historian Eric Hoyt has documented how the film industry recognized the need to archive and organize their work, creating film libraries as a business model and strategically limiting access to older works.[17]

By the 1920s, the industry helped create the cult of celebrity by inventing the concept of the movie star. Hollywood was considered an iconic place where rich men and fast women worked hard and played hard.[18] One term commonly used to describe Hollywood at the time was "unsavory," and it referred to both the people involved in the early film industry and the raucous content depicted on the screen. The 1921 trials of Fatty Arbuckle, a silent film star accused of raping and murdering actress Virginia Rappe, filled newspapers with stories of alleged Hollywood orgies, murder, and sexual perversion, which intensified public fears.

Because of the lurid content of early films, municipal censors were active and vociferous. For them, it was a simple matter of public decency. For example, in their first 6 months of operation in 1915, the three-member Pennsylvania State Board of Censors inspected 11,146 reels and found that 75% of films were melodramas offering lurid and sensational depictions of fighting and crime, and the rest were comedies "of a coarseness unknown at any time in the history of the American theater." According to the board's report, the earliest films depicted smoking cigarettes and drinking alcohol "out of proportion to anything known in real life."[19] These groups issued fines to local film exhibitors and sometimes banned films.

The film industry itself worked hard to shift public attitudes away from censorship, however. As early as 1914, self-censorship began to be recognized as means to protect the business model for the growing film industry. Strategists for the film industry suggested that coalitions between film distributors and librarians could help educational films get the attention (and circulation) they deserved. One such group, the National Committee for Better Films even urged librarians to develop cataloguing and classifying systems for films.

Public concern about the movies led to the expansion of state film boards, which rose up to solve the problem of film's problematic content—but these groups could be capricious. By 1930, eight states had censorship boards, which had the legal power of film censorship. Censors recognized the power of disruptive social narratives to challenge status quo social norms, and they sought to have those narratives removed from public view. According to the authors of *Censored: The Private Life of the Movie*, published in 1930, the Ohio board had a deeply Victorian sensibility: they cut scenes of a man in tight pants from a D.W. Griffith production and removed all reference to a female villain in a film adaptation of Victor Hugo.[20]

However, one New York City organization, the National Board of Review of Motion Pictures, started out as a censorship board but gradually began using a more progressive approach in shaping the quality and content of early films. Instead of beating filmmakers with a stick, they rewarded them with carrots—in the form of positive attention. They offered filmmakers awards and prizes, endorsing quality films and offering their official stamp of approval, "Passed by the National Board of Review." They published a film review magazine and demonstrated an appreciation for the new art form. Their underlying message to the public was one we still hear today: informed media consumers make better choices.

EMPOWERMENT AND PROTECTION

Like many middle-class people of the early 20th century, many librarians viewed both film and radio with suspicion. In the 1920s, there were few films produced for children—yet children were flocking to the cinema. In looking back at the first inquiries on media influence, it's clear that each new medium brings interest in questions about how children and young people may be affected. Consider this introductory paragraph from W. W. Charters, the chairman of the Payne Foundation Studies on media and children:

> MOTION PICTURES are not understood by the present generation of adults. They are new; they make an enormous appeal to children; and they present ideas and situations that parents may not like. Consequently when parents think of the welfare of their children who are exposed to these compelling situations, they wonder about the effect of the pictures upon the ideals and behavior of the children. Do the pictures really influence children in any direction? Are their conduct, ideals, and attitudes affected by the movies? Are the scenes which are objectionable to adults understood by children, or at least by very young children? Do children eventually become sophisticated and grow superior to pictures? Are the emotions of children harmfully excited? In short, just what effect do motion pictures have upon children of different ages?[21]

Back in the 1920s and 1930s, when radio and film were growing in social influence, researchers funded by the Payne Foundation gathered data about these new media which were rapidly transforming American culture. These studies, completed in 1932, examined film content in detail, finding that crime, sex, love, mystery, war, children, history, travel, comedy, and social propaganda were common themes. Because American children were attending movies unsupervised at least once a week, many middle-class people had concerns about the erosion of morality. They worried that children's values were being compromised by their exposure to films designed primarily for adults.

As a result of rising concern about potential risks of media use, researchers used cutting-edge social-scientific approaches (then in its infancy) to measure the effects of film on children. Researchers used surveys and questionnaires to explore how film viewing affected children's learning, attitudes, emotions, and behavior. Importantly, researchers discovered that children learned and retained information they received from movies.[22] In particular, children's attitudes concerning ethnic, racial, and social stereotypes were affected by movie viewing experiences as children became more exposed to cultural diversity through film. For the general public, the Payne Fund studies confirmed that film could have a powerful influence on children; this also inspired some philanthropists to explore the early potential of media education.

Still, by the end of the 1920s, it was clear that Hollywood had an image problem. Parents were so concerned about children's exposure to films that they tried to keep them away. Exhibitors were concerned about the loss of revenue at matinee screenings and started giving out toys and ice cream to boost attendance.[23] When Will H. Hays became the first president of a new trade organization called the Motion Picture Producers and Distributors of America, Inc. (MPPDA), his job was to "clean up Hollywood." To placate public concern about the content of motion pictures, they developed Production Code in 1930, which restricted certain depictions of violence, sexuality, profanity, obscenity, vulgarity, and other "repellent subjects."

In 1934, they produced a magazine, displayed proudly in the lobby of movie theaters, called *The Motion Picture and the Family*, which was filled with information designed "to help American families select their films wisely, and utilize to the full the social and cultural value of films." The industry also hoped that the magazine would help to develop in audiences "more discriminating standards of photoplay appreciation" and "increase demand for pictures that are worthwhile and wholesome."[24] Figure 7.1 shows an illustration from the magazine that suggests how movie promoters emphasized the deep connection between literature and film.

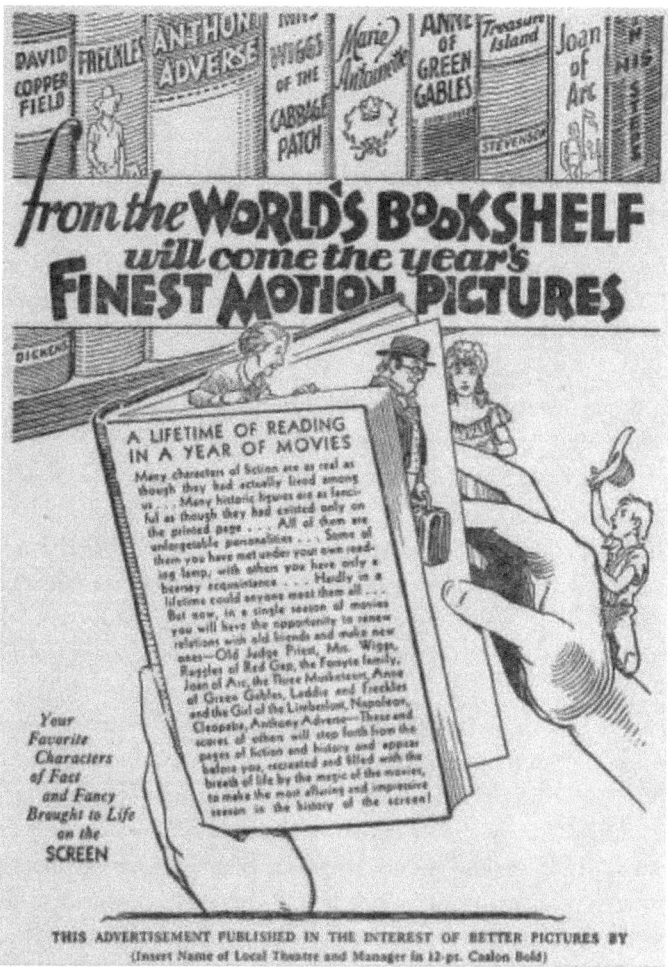

Figure 7.1 Advertisement from *The Motion Picture and the Family*, 1934.

Film companies began sending educational and promotional materials to high school libraries, and many school librarians reported that they had impressive educational value for students and also influenced library circulation. Public libraries also hosted research exhibitions about the art of film. These sometimes took the form of displays that took people behind the scenes of a production, akin to the "making-of" genre of short films that are common today. Sometimes these materials included up to 100 photographs, as in the display of photos showing the art of film makeup, which was displayed for 3 weeks at The New York Public Library in 1936.

During this time, high school English teachers in the United States were also developing a growing interest in film and media education, and teachers at the National Council of Teachers of English gave presentations such as teaching about film animation. Interest in educational use of film was growing in the United States and around the world. The European Educational Film Congress and other groups of film educators convened annually between 1927 and 1931 and after World War II as well.[25] A number of publications were developed to showcase the film education practices that were developing in schools across the United States.

ORIGINS OF THE CLEVELAND PUBLIC LIBRARY'S FILM PROGRAM

Films helped to promote a shared American culture among new immigrants. The Cleveland Public Library's St. Clair Avenue branch library hosted a motion picture event in the library's auditorium on June 29, 1911, co-sponsored by the Cleveland Independence Day Association. They wanted to encourage a "sane fourth" by promoting public safety and national pride by screening short films, including *Washington at Valley Forge* and *Stars and Stripes*. Acknowledging the value of films to promote a sense of shared cultural identity, librarians themselves wrote about the value of communal screening activities as part of their justification for acquiring films for the library collection. By end of the decade, some libraries had even begun to create film collections, working in collaboration with film industry organizations like the National Committee for Better Films, which advertised in *Library Journal* and issued lists of recommended films through magazines like *Exceptional Photoplays*.

Librarians began to notice how current films being screened in their community were affecting patron requests for books. In 1915, the director of the Cleveland Public Library informed librarians that the film adaptation of *Ramona*, the novel by Helen Hunt Jackson, would be coming to Cleveland. The story features a white woman who falls in love with a Native American. Librarians were informed: "Notice has been received that an unusually fine film of Helen Hunt Jackson's *Ramona* is in the process of making. If the attention of readers is called to this it may promote the circulation of the book. Librarians are reminded to look over their stock of *Ramona* to see if they are prepared to meet the probable demand when the film is released."

Remember that during this time period, movies were thought to be distinctly low-class. So it's quite impressive to think that the library staff had an awareness of the power of film to stimulate people's intellectual curiosity and motivate their interest in reading. When Linda Anne Eastman was hired in 1918 as the director of the Cleveland Public Library, she was the first woman to lead a big-city library. The Cleveland Public Library continued to pioneer library-film collaborations with local exhibitors to help librarians meet the needs of a new generation. In the early 1920s, under Eastman's leadership, the library inserted a bookmark into every checked-out book that listed the title of a film showing locally along with the titles of books to read before and after the screening.[26]

LIBRARY LEADERSHIP SUPPORTS FILM ADVISORY SERVICES

Some librarians believed that their role was to provide film reviews to patrons in order to raise the public's demand for quality film. For example in 1934, the Los Angeles Public Library developed a telephone service where people could call up and ask for details about the suitability of a particular film for young audiences. This information service was developed with support from a variety of women's clubs who produced a report every 2 weeks.[27]

While some librarians were enthusiastic about linking books and authors with current Hollywood film productions, others ignored film completely, fearing that the motion picture industry would cause films to become a substitute for reading. Still, with the film-viewing craze in full gear with the introduction of the 16mm format, by 1924, the American Library Association (ALA) developed the first Committee on Moving Pictures and the Library, with recognition that film in public libraries was a form of adult education. The committee recommended that urban libraries include information on sources of films and encouraged libraries to collaborate to acquire and distribute films. They also blessed the development of cooperative relationships with the motion picture industry.[28]

However, some scholars, looking back at this period, saw the ALA committee as the beginning of a national bureaucracy that reflected the "apathy and confusion" about the appropriate role of film in the public library.[29] After all, many librarians were deeply suspicious of film's popularity. For example, Melvil Dewey, the creator of the Dewey Decimal System, worried about film's potentially negative influence on the public's interest in reading. At the time, the idea of librarians as people who took care of books was well entrenched in the profession, and the concept of service through library programming was still a novel idea. Most librarians of the time saw their responsibilities in providing people with access to books through activities involving the selection and organization of collections. Still, even Melvil Dewey conceded that "The motion picture . . . is one of the greatest agencies for education man has yet devised."[30]

As film became more important as a cultural force during the 1930s and 1940s, librarians, policymakers and scholars wondered how educational films could help support the library's educational mission. The Tyrrell Public Library in Beaumont, Texas, began circulating a collection of 16mm films to meet the educational and recreational needs of its public as early as 1939.[31] With film, librarians could vastly expand their role in adult education, some argued. For example, T. R. Adam wrote in 1937, "If they are to circulate motion pictures for mass education, they must understand thoroughly the operation of all the agencies of adult learning in their communities, from women's clubs to trade unions."[32]

Marian the Librarian

In the 1962 musical *The Music Man*, created by Meredith Wilson and directed by Morton DaCosta, one scene takes place in a busy but supremely quiet 19th-century community library in Iowa where we meet Marian the Librarian just as she is operating a state-of-the-art lift to hoist a pile of returned books to the second floor of the building. She sees three young men, dressed in shirts of pastel spring, and they march in serious formation, one by one, to approach the library desk. Each young man opens his book in turn as Marian rapidly stamps the books with a due date stamp. Unexpectedly, in her stamping zeal, she stamps the hand of Professor Harold Hill, the new music teacher who has arrived in town. To analyze the representation of librarians and libraries in this classic musical, we can ask:

- How does Marian embody the stereotype of the librarian?
- How does she disrupt the stereotype?
- How does the director want us to feel about Marian?
- What do we learn about Professor Harold Hill in this sequence?
- How does the director want us to feel about him?
- What adjectives fit with how you see her personality?
- What do you notice about the physical space of the library?
- What do you notice about the depiction of checking out a book?
- What are some of the many ways that sexual tension is represented in this sequence?

Mid-Century Momentum

READ THE BOOK, WATCH THE MOVIE

Although librarians discovered that movies were stimulating people's interest in reading, they were sometimes shy about making connections between mystery and crime films and mystery book collections because, as one librarian put it, "There are so many mystery story readers already that they don't dare attract greater patronage." They felt similarly about making connections between films and children's literature. Of course, 1939 was the year when *The Wizard of Oz* premiered, a stunningly original film musical that catapulted the visibility of L. Frank Baum into the limelight and inspired librarians to think in fresh ways about the connection between film viewing and reading.[33]

In the 1930s, book clubs were starting to increase in popularity, and some librarians began experimenting with film clubs. Of course, book clubs were not new to the 20th century. Salons and private social gatherings to discuss books were a popular form of entertainment and civic action in the 19th century and even earlier. But in the 20th century, across the country, public groups became increasingly important. Because women were largely excluded from higher education, literary societies arose from women's reform groups, including church groups, the National Council of Jewish Women, and the American Association of University Women. When entrepreneurs recognized the opportunity to cash in on the trend, they founded the Book-of-the-Month Club and the Literary Guild, offering middle-class people a way to have a communal reading experience. Elena Rossi-Snook's excellent book chapter "Continuing Ed: Educational Film Collections in Libraries and Archives" examines the many ways in which films were acquired and used for "the betterment of society."[34]

Some social reformers were finding creative ways to bring film viewing and discussion experiences directly into the neighborhood community. At the People's Institute in Brooklyn, a community education center for working-class adults and immigrants in New York City, film discussion groups were hosted as a means to discover how people could learn to talk about, analyze, and appreciate films. In this experimental program, for 1 year, they hosted film discussion groups at people's homes, and in the process of documenting this new approach to adult education, they learned quite a bit about the promise and the limitations of film for public enlightenment. First of all, some groups were not keen on watching and discussing films—after all, they had chosen to participate in a group because of their interest in reading, not viewing. Librarians did their best to pair a book and a film, for example, reading Stella Morgan's *Again the River* with Pare Lorentz's classic documentary film, *The River*.

It seems people have always known that film discussion events can be spoiled by too much focus on the experts. At Northwestern University, an exploration of film discussion programs for adult education discovered that films about social problems yielded the most engagement. However, they commented on the challenge of using university faculty to introduce the topic of the film. Most of the faculty talked for too long and in too much detail, and their behavior interfered with the film screening itself.

All over the world, film discussion events were seen as a form of positive propaganda. During this time period, cineclubs brought film viewing and discussion experiences to Italy, the Soviet Union, Finland, and France. As America prepared to enter World War II, the government began to use public libraries to disseminate war-related documentaries, propaganda, and informational films. In big cities, libraries used their large auditoriums to screen the *Why We Fight* series of propaganda films developed by Frank Capra. To support the distribution of these films, the Educational Film Lending Library Committee was formed to assist federal agencies in distributing their films. But despite this robust experimentation with film discussion groups, by 1940, only a few public libraries used films as part of a book discussion series, according to a comprehensive report.[35] But the idea of supporting people's information needs with the use of film caught on in some places. For example, to support local job seekers, the Denver Public Library screened films about career opportunities, followed by a short lecture from a representative from the business community talking about job opportunities.[36]

During World War II, the military used films in earnest for training soldiers and as a form of positive propaganda to increase public support for the war. The ALA Film Forum Project was financed by a grant from the Carnegie Corporation from 1941 to 1943, and it jump-started a deeper interest in film screening and discussion programs in public libraries. As library historian Suzanne Stauffer notes, films were screened in more than 40 libraries, accompanied by book exhibits, guided discussions, and supplementary reading lists. During wartime, these screenings helped to introduce the public to political and social issues relevant to the war effort, shifting attitudes toward understanding the rationale for US involvement.

It was, after all, the shared group experience of viewing in a public setting that could influence large numbers of people and influence public opinion. Suzanne Stauffer, in analyzing the literature of the period, noted that librarians expected that "exposure to 'quality' films would have the same effect that exposure to 'quality' literature was intended to have, that of the 'development of the discerning eye, on the part of large groups, for the complex art of the cinema' which would 'inevitably result in a demand for better quality,' such that viewers would not 'ever again be really satisfied with pedantic or trite film treatment.'"[37]

THE DOCUMENTARY MOVEMENT INSPIRES LIBRARIANS

During the 1930s, documentary films were beginning to be recognized as a valuable new form of informational media. During the Great Depression, a federal government film program was started and filmmakers documented aspects of American culture. For example, Pare Lorentz produced *The Plow That Broke the Plains* (1936), which is considered a classic among documentary films. It shows the bad agricultural land use practices that helped to create the Dust Bowl, when drought and high winds led to massive crop failure and the westward migration of desperate farmers.

His next film, *The River* (1937), chronicled the history of the Mississippi River basin and the impact of the Tennessee Valley Authority, a civil engineering program which advanced flood control and irrigation throughout the region. Because the film was a commercial success, the United States Film Service was created in the late 1930s and was expanded to produce motion pictures and shorts for various government agencies.

John Grierson, one of the fathers of the documentary film, defined the documentary as "the creative treatment of actuality," and he saw the potential of documentary film to support civic engagement and democratic values. When he was invited to give an address to the ALA annual meeting in June 1946, he encouraged librarians to recognize the potential of film as an educational and artistic medium. In that speech, he pointed out that art, poetry, and information, by itself, could not solve the economic problems and the moral crises faced by people who had just lived through a harrowing world war. While in the ancient world, a community was the group of people who could hear the sound of a man's voice, film and newspapers and radio and television had brought all people "within range of each other's sight and hearing."

Grierson challenged the librarians, noting their absence in the growing film education movement. He warned them that if they did not embrace new forms of media, "that it will pass to people who have a less profound tradition of public service." He said, "I do not say that the day of the books is over, but the day of the books *only* is certainly over." According to Grierson, people could not transform their lives with information alone: they needed enlightenment, a spark that bridges the gap between the citizen and their hopes and dreams for the future.[38] An influential group of library leaders had invited Grierson and had hoped his message would resonate with the membership. But not a single publication in the library professional literature of the time makes reference to Grierson's speech, so we must assume that many librarians simply didn't see these ideas as relevant to their profession.

During the middle of the 20th century, the movies were shaping American identity and cultural values. Two well-known examples of the real or imagined influence of film on an entire populace both took place in the years surrounding and including World War II. The role of the Nazi propaganda films of Leni Riefenstahl in the 1930s and 1940s in the advancement of the Third Reich and the role of the artist in creating propaganda are still being debated today. In the United States, the fear that communism was infiltrating the country, and especially the Hollywood film industry, was fanned into a frenzy first within Hollywood, and eventually through the activities of Congress with the infamous House Un-American Activities Committee.

During the 1940s, librarians were paying somewhat more attention to film because a growing number of businesses were producing public relations, promotional or edutainment type 16mm films and making them freely available to libraries and schools. With the help of Hollywood, the government was creating propaganda, too. Some public libraries developed film programs that were designed to strengthen post-war civilian morale through screening and discussion activities. Librarians developed supplementary reading lists and book exhibits to accompany film screenings. As we will see in Chapter 8, this work set the stage for the long-term partnership between libraries and public broadcasting.

AN EDUCATION IN FILM APPRECIATION

Professor Edgar Dale of Ohio State University was among the earliest teacher educators to recognize the importance of teaching about media as a way to develop discerning viewers who would demand better quality programming. As a contributor to the Payne Fund Studies, Dale was perhaps the major proponent for empowering learners by helping them to develop higher standards of taste in the appreciation of motion pictures. He believed that more informed and thoughtful consumers would help Hollywood create better films. Dale used literary adaptations "to promote the cultural status of cinema at a time when it was facing increased criticism." Dale's 1933 publication, *How to Appreciate Motion Pictures*, led him to create film study guides on popular film adaptations such as *Romeo and Juliet* (1936), directed by George Cukor.

The New Haven public schools were among the first to explore the utility of Dale's approach to teaching film appreciation. The English department required at least 10 lessons to be devoted to the study of motion picture appreciation. Figure 7.2 shows a book cover that some teachers used to learn about film, the attractive and lavishly produced 1937 book, *Talking Pictures: How They Are Made, How to Appreciate Them* by Barrett Kiesling. A student group previewed films and recommended which ones should be viewed. Local cinemas reduced admission prices for school groups. By 1940, it was estimated that film viewing clubs were active in 3,000 schools and film study guides achieved a circulation of 100,000.[39]

In her analysis of the pedagogy of this early form of media literacy, Penny Chalk claims that the film appreciation crusade failed for two reasons: problems of access and problems of cultural hierarchy. Teaching film without being able to screen films in the classroom posed a real challenge for teachers. Teaching clips were necessary but nearly impossible to find and use. Then there was the cultural hierarchy problem. Some teachers thought that their pedagogical purpose was to persuade teens to prefer costume dramas to shoot-em-up crime stories, not to build critical analysis skills in appreciating film as art. Overall, Chalk writes that teachers of English inevitably "became trapped in a battle of cultural hierarchies in which the appreciation of film was always second to the appreciation of literature."[40]

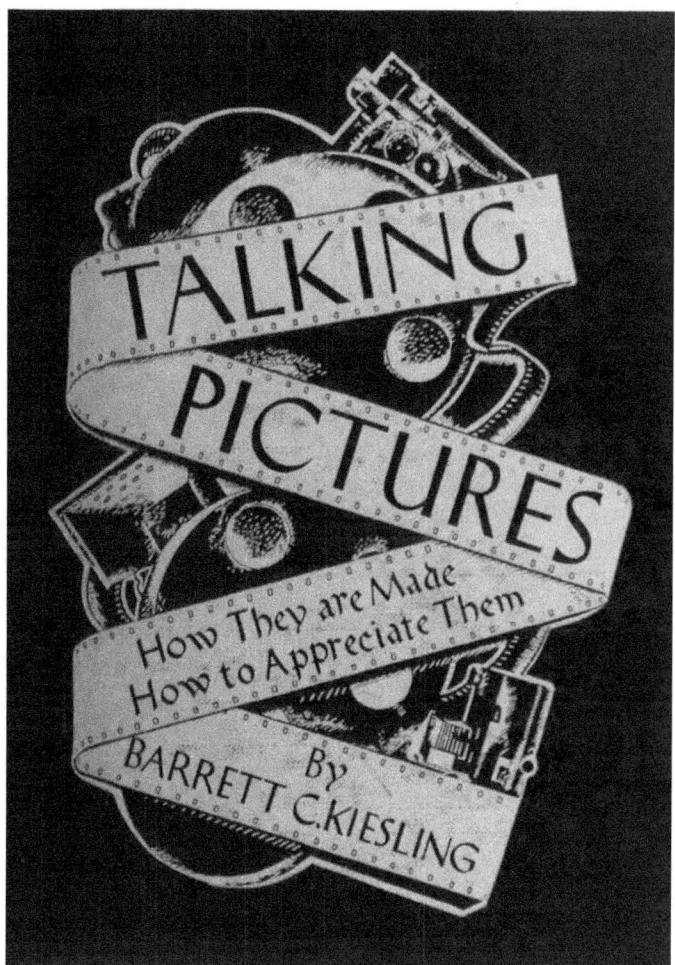

Figure 7.2 Books take readers behind the scenes of a film production.

PHILANTHROPIC SUPPORT FOR FILM EDUCATION IN LIBRARIES

During the 1940s, philanthropies embraced the idea that, through the strategic use of educational and informational film, social transformation might be scalable. As documentary, informational and educational films were beginning to become more available in the United States, an experiment in library film programming developed with support from the Rockefeller and Carnegie Foundations. In 1940, the American Library Association contracted with the Rockefeller Foundation, which provided the sum of $5,500 to support a small research initiative. The ALA published a report by Gerald McDonald, a librarian at The New York Public Library, which provided a comprehensive survey of audiovisual educational resources. This report helped educate librarians about the potential of film as a resource for their patrons.

Still, outside of a few exceptional libraries in big cities, films were not generally a part of most library collections, McDonald reported. And only three public libraries in the United States offered films for circulation. Why? Educational films were difficult to access, with complex procedures involved in identifying, curating, and purchasing them. "If books were as hard to get as films, there would be very little reading done in this country," he wrote. Most public libraries did not own 16mm film projectors or have librarians on staff who were familiar with the medium of film. Films were being used by labor unions, fraternal organizations, church groups, and business groups, but not by libraries, according to McDonald's study. Among librarians, there was not much knowledge about how to use films for adult education. There was little personal contact between film producers and distributors, librarians, and consumers. Then there was the question of how to train librarians and educators "in the intricacies of bringing films into widespread and effective use for educational ends."[41]

Cleveland Public Library director Clarence S. Metcalf and Russell Munn, head of the Adult Education Department, are the librarians generally credited with a vision to systematically include films in the collection, making Cleveland the first public library in a major city in the country to circulate films. By 1943, the collection included 244 informational films, including documentaries, historical films, and travelogues. Under the leadership of Patricia Blair, they instituted a regular Friday lunchtime screening at the Main Library. They established a Film Bureau, hosted library film viewing events, and began circulating films. According to the 1945 annual report, the Cleveland Public Library collection had grown to include 621 films, 4,000 slides, and 30 filmstrips. There had been more than 12,000 showings to 850,000 people.[42] After the war, Blair made a serious effort to update the film collection to include contemporary topics of interest such as religious and racial tolerance, which were issues of growing concern in the multiethnic community. She knew that film was an "ally to the book" and that it had the capacity to reach "two thirds of the population . . . which libraries have never reached."[43]

Blair also helped educate librarians to support film and media education in public libraries in ways that influenced people far beyond Cleveland. Librarians were able to answer reference questions about audiovisual education and to assist in the development of film bibliographies and strategies for film programming, supporting educators and librarians from around the country. Blair began film reviewing for *Library Journal* in 1946 and "warned librarians against free films which were nothing more than thinly veiled advertising for the sponsor."[44]

To accelerate the inclusion of films into public libraries, the Carnegie Corporation gave the American Library Association $42,000 to establish the Film Office in 1947, just one year after John Grierson's speech. The Cleveland Public Library's Patricia Blair was hired to run the office, and she traveled the country, helping librarians set up regional film collections. By mid-century, some librarians were beginning to embrace film as part and parcel of library service. Blair helped develop procedures for librarians to select, acquire, catalogue, classify, repair, and store films. Into the 1950s, the Carnegie Corporation continued to fund library film circuits in eastern and western Ohio, Tennessee, Detroit, New York, and other states. A survey of librarians during this time period shows that collections varied greatly. Some collections were tiny while others were considerable. Some librarians built collections entirely consisting of government-sponsored films. Others relied on commercially sponsored films by companies promoting their products. Still others selected largely independent documentaries. Travel and nature films were among the most popular subjects.

Patricia Blair helped create Library of Congress catalog cards for films and standardized the compilation of film circulation statistics. She was able to report some impressive shifts in library culture as a result of this initiative. For example, in 1947, only 12 public libraries in the United States circulated films, reporting about 8,500 showings to a combined audience of 462,000. By 1951, 114 libraries were circulating films, 103 of which reported over 48,000 showings to an audience of over 3.7 million people.

Librarians have long been effective in sharing resources in systematic ways. Colleges and university libraries with film collections also began getting more requests for school assemblies, luncheon clubs, and labor groups. During this time, the Educational Film Library Association (EFLA) was created by L. C. Larson of Indiana University along with leaders of state university libraries to facilitate the sharing of 16mm films. By centralizing the contracting and booking process, librarians made it possible to increase availability and access to a wide variety of films by creating efficiencies that minimized staff time.[45]

Film cooperatives also developed during and after World War II when thousands of 16mm projectors that were used in the war effort were being sold off to smaller libraries. Instead of acquiring films individually, regional film cooperatives, hosted by a central library, shared a bundle of films for a specific period of time, offering them to school and public libraries on a regular schedule.[46] This collaborative approach spread the practice of film screening into even the smallest communities across the United States.

At large public libraries, significant film collections developed during the 1950s and 1960s. For example, The New York Public Library has 6,000 16mm films, 5,000 VHS videocassettes, and 1,200 DVDs. The library began collecting films in 1952.

Its outstanding collection focuses primarily on independently produced works. The collection includes political, social, and cultural documentaries as well as experimental films and video art, short films, and films created by and for children and teens. While many large public libraries have eliminated their film collections through the process of deaccessioning, Elena Rossi-Snook help ensure that current and future generations of New Yorkers get to experience the thrill of screening film in formats including 16mm cinema, VHS tapes and DVDs.. Rossi-Snook engages in active outreach to the community to ensure that educators and citizens understand the cultural insights to be gained from film history. We were thrilled to discover a Facebook video where she explains how 16mm films are still being actively used to advance the media and visual literacy competencies of New York City school children.[47]

Some Challenges
TELEVISION'S INFLUENCE ON LIBRARY CIRCULATION

The rise of television contributed to changing patterns of library circulation. Frances Lander Spain, who served as president of the American Library Association in 1962, noted that librarians recognized the influence of television on children's reading habits early on. When the five-part television series *Davy Crockett* aired on ABC in 1954–1955, children's librarians noticed the impact immediately. There was a sudden demand for covered-wagon stories, histories of the Old West, pioneer yarns, and even folk tales of Paul Bunyan, as "all our books on every subject even remotely connected with Davy Crockett were called for and borrowed until our library shelves were bare."

The same effect was noticeable for young adults, although Spain explains that teens use the adult sections of the library just as they watch adult programs on TV. "A program on the Old West or the Civil War or Mark Twain stirs a ripple in the circulation of every book related to the subject." These patterns apply both to television and movies, Spain explains, noting that, in a large city like New York, "librarians can follow the course of a motion picture through the neighborhood theaters by the pattern of requests that come to the branch libraries."[48]

When Renee read this anecdote, she wondered: Had there been any systematic research exploring how movies and television affected library circulation? Indeed, there had been. In the early 1960s, Stanford professor Edwin Parker developed a fascinating study by taking advantage of a type of natural experiment that was currently underway in the United States. Because of the way that the FCC allocated television channels during the early 1950s, some communities received broadcasting in 1950 and others did not receive it until 1953. Parker could match 36 Illinois communities with similar demographics into experimental and control communities in order to examine changes in library circulation during the time one member of the pair was getting television. Many communities received television broadcasting in 1950 while many comparable communities did not receive television broadcasting until 1953. The group of communities without television served as a naturalistic control group for the potential influence of other variables on library circulation.

Parker compared circulation changes that individual communities experienced before and after getting TV. Parker found that public library circulation was lower after the widespread adoption of television than it would have been in the absence of television. He also found that the relative decline in circulation was greater for fiction circulation than for nonfiction circulation.[49] By bringing entertaining stories into the comfort of the home, broadcast television reduced the demand for fiction in libraries.

When TV Arrives in New York City, Library Circulation Declines

Circulation of both children's and adult books declined immediately after the introduction of television into the community, as reported by The New York Public Library. Table 7.1 offers some concrete evidence.

Table 7.1   **The New York Public Library Circulation Data**

Year	Children's	Adult
1949–1950	2,810,255	7,696,096
1950–1951	2,696,313	7,497,694
Loss	113,942	161,402

Source: Spain, F. L., & Scoggin, M. (1962). They still read books. In R. L. Shayton, *The eighth art: Twenty-three views of television today* (pp. 176–197). New York, NY: Holt Rinehart Winston.

HOLDING OUT FOR QUALITY

As more and more audiovisual content was available to people through broadcast television, the distinction between cheap entertainment and quality films was becoming more obvious. During the 1950s, librarians began to solidify their focus on providing quality films to their community. Although there were plenty of classroom and educational films about history, travel, and nature, librarians wanted films about serious nonfiction topics perceived to have relevance to the community; films about the American labor movement and films about music and regional folk culture were valued. This was the essence of the vision that John Grierson had urged librarians to embrace. Librarians sought out experimental films that used pixilation, animation, and other techniques to stimulate the creative imagination of children.

What librarians definitely did not want was commercial feature-length films produced by Hollywood. When patrons called the Cleveland Public Library about getting access to these films, librarians referred them to commercial distribution companies.[50] Many librarians simply did not believe that libraries should circulate films for recreational purposes. When libraries selected films, their choices reflected ideas about quality cultural or informational content— what people should know or value. As Rossi-Snook explains, in the 1950s and 1960s, there is "an unwillingness to collect or promote films that did not have a direct relationship to literature or the humanities."[51] Remember that librarians of this time period would have had little exposure to the formal study of film, as it had barely begun to be an academic specialty. The first academic group of film scholars formed as the Society for Cinematologists in 1959, renaming themselves the Society for Cinema Studies in 1968.[52]

Librarians saw their interests in film as distinctly different from the commercial movies and movie stars that were coming to dominate American popular culture. They did not want to compete with the local movie house. They wanted to provide a clear and distinct alternative to Hollywood. Although they had long discovered that a film program was most satisfying to audiences when it included a mix of information and entertainment, librarians felt more pressure to "preserve the distinctiveness of their institution as a place of learning." They were more fearful of film events becoming a "place for the mental passivity that is encouraged by the unchaperoned screening of narrative."[53]

MAKING SACRIFICES UNDER PRESSURE

After the invention of television in the 1950s, which had a dramatic influence on the leisure habits of Americans, librarians found that patrons' taste in film was changing. As they struggled to manage the soaring costs of personnel, materials, and technology, and since film programs could be relied upon to attract large audiences, librarians began to use popular Hollywood theatrical feature films to "get people into the tent."

Librarians had long hosted musical concerts and travel lectures to appeal to the public. In the 1950s, film programs became a common means of attracting audiences to come to the library and librarians began to use entertaining, noncontroversial, or familiar films to boost audience size. At this time, some local community members were nostalgic for those classic W. C. Fields comedies of the 1930s, which people had watched in the cinema as children. Libraries would screen 16mm prints of *Man on the Flying Trapeeze* (1935) and *You Can't Cheat an Honest Man* (1939) for older patrons who loved re-watching the films of their youth. But many librarians were not happy about such crass attempts to reach audiences. Rossi-Snook documents tensions about the shift in thinking among librarians by quoting Bill Sloan, head of the Donnell Library Center Film Library of The New York Public Library and founder of *Film Library Quarterly*, who noted with disdain, "Too often we turn to guaranteed crowd pleasers to fill up library auditoriums, and thereby build up impressive attendance statistics to show to directors, trustees, and city fathers."[54] Sloan urged librarians to be responsible when programming features and to create a balance "between giving the public what it wants and living up to our leadership responsibility."

A detailed focus on educational technology in schools is beyond the scope of this book, but filmstrips brought images and sound into the classroom, and the luckiest of children were sometimes selected to operate the film projection equipment. Figure 7.3 shows an example of a filmstrip from the time period. By the end of the 1960s, moving image media had become part of school and library programming. Some librarians and teachers loved documentary and educational films and created innovative programs using them. But as the 1970s arrived and popular culture intensified, movies became something not just to consume, but to create as well.

Figure 7.3 Filmstrips bring images into the school library.

AMERICAN LIBRARY ASSOCIATION FILM
CONTROVERSY: *THE SPEAKER*

It was a film that nearly destroyed the ALA. That's how distinguished library leader and winner of the Robert B. Downs Intellectual Freedom Award Ann Symons puts it.[55] In 1977, the organization premiered a new film commissioned and co-produced by the ALA's Intellectual Freedom Committee. Designed for the general public, *The Speaker*, directed by Lee Bobker, is set in a high school classroom where a controversial, racist speaker has been invited to campus to speak at an upcoming event. In the story, the community gets up in arms about the decision and the invitation is cancelled. The film was shot in a high school classroom where professional actors play students who partially improvise their lines. Figure 7.4 shows a

TheSpeaker ... A Film About Freedom

2,708 views   11   2   SHARE   SAVE   ...

ALA Office for Intellectual Freedom
Published on May 20, 2014

SUBSCRIBE 211

Figure 7.4 The controversial 1977 ALA film *The Speaker.*

still from the film, which was digitized by the ALA Archives at the University of Illinois Champaign-Urbana.

In the film discussion guide produced to accompany the film, it says: "At a crucial point in the discussion, the moderator should be ready to ask the basic question posed by the film: What ideas do you believe are dangerous? What restriction would you place on discussion of those ideas?"[56]

Because the film is rooted in the ideas of First Amendment absolutism as articulated by the constitutional lawyer Floyd Abrams (who served as an advisor to the film), the narrative concludes that the racist speaker should have been allowed to speak at the high school. The film is intentionally designed to lead viewers to a predetermined conclusion and the discussion guide puts it this way: "What the group discussion should show is that every controversial idea has its enemies, and that suppression of one controversial idea may lead to the suppression of all."

Sadly, this film does not invite a more nuanced look at the complex issues of freedom of expression. The film discussion guide omits any discussion of how the characters and their motives are represented and may be perceived. In the film, stereotypes are used to simplify characters. For example, the parents and teachers who object to the racist speaker are depicted as wimps. The African American students are depicted as irrational and unprincipled—they don't have ideas; they are merely angry.

The stereotypes presented in the film were infuriating to many members of the library community. At the time, the ALA's Black Caucus said, "The film does not do justice to either the First Amendment or intellectual freedom," noting that "the interjection of the issue of race relations destroys the intent of the film."

In analyzing what went wrong, most of the problem seems to be that the ALA did not exercise appropriate oversight of the production process. For example, members of the review committee did not receive a script until the film was completed. John Berry, editor-at-large for *Library Journal*, notes that the controversy was inspired by the poor quality of the film itself. He writes, "This cleverly manipulative film . . . suggests that racism is the price of freedom."[57]

Although the intended purpose of *The Speaker* was to invite librarians to examine their perspectives on intellectual freedom, that message was lost because of the oversimplified rendering of the First Amendment issues along with the oblivious and insensitive representation of the struggle of African Americans and other persons of color. It's possible that, among some leaders of the library community, perceptions of the usefulness of film as a tool for professional development were negatively affected by the controversy.

Freedom to View

The FREEDOM TO VIEW, along with the freedom to speak, to hear, and to read, is protected by the First Amendment to the Constitution of the United States. In a free society, there is no place for censorship of any medium of expression. Therefore these principles are affirmed:

1. To provide the broadest access to film, video, and other audiovisual materials because they are a means for the communication of ideas. Liberty of circulation is essential to insure the constitutional guarantees of freedom of expression.
2. To protect the confidentiality of all individuals and institutions using film, video, and other audiovisual materials.
3. To provide film, video, and other audiovisual materials which represent a diversity of views and expression. Selection of a work does not constitute or imply agreement with or approval of the content.
4. To provide a diversity of viewpoints without the constraint of labeling or prejudging film, video, or other audiovisual materials on the basis of the moral, religious, or political beliefs of the producer or filmmaker or on the basis of controversial content.
5. To contest vigorously, by all lawful means, every encroachment upon the public's freedom to view.

This statement was originally drafted by the Freedom to View Committee of the American Film and Video Association (formerly the Educational Film Library Association) in February, 1979. It was updated and adopted by the American Library Association in 1990.

Technology Brings Multimedia to the Masses

THE AUDIOVISUAL ERA

Film gained increasing influence as an educational tool during the 1960s and 1970s. In schools, the educational media movement brought a variety of forms of moving image media into the classroom. In his history of educational technology, Paul Saettler chronicles the hyped-up rush of "the new" in bringing educational media to schools. Renee remembers the glee she experienced when the black-and-white television set was wheeled into the school gymnasium so that children could watch the liftoff of the Apollo 11 mission to the moon in 1969. Pam remembers holding off her violence prevention session with some fourth-grade classes so everyone could watch the Challenger space shuttle liftoff with science teacher Christa McAuliffe aboard, and then having the teachers turn the class over to her after the explosion without any discussion about what had happened. Remembering that terrible experience, on September 11, 2001, Pam found herself contacting principals of the elementary schools she was working in to tell them to make sure TV sets were turned off until school staff could be briefed about what was happening. Educators needed time to offer children age-appropriate responses to help interpret the tragic events of that day.

Of course, the major film studios played an outsized role in the distribution market for 16mm films. In the 1965 Annual Report for Walt Disney, it states: "An estimated 55,000 different 16mm prints of Disney films are currently in circulation around the world. More than 2,000 clients rent or lease these films each year, including schools, public libraries, car clubs, universities, health departments, forestry and parks, financial institutions, industries and nearly 1,000 organizations. Disney 16mm films have been translated into 14 languages and exhibited in 56 countries."[58] But hundreds of smaller companies also promoted their wares to school districts around the country.

The audiovisual era was a major part of the 1960s and 1970s. As artists like Nam June Paik started experimenting with video as an art form, films got groovy and a new generation of librarians recognized their power to engage and inspire younger audiences and those who did not grow up in print-centric households. In 1967 the Providence Public Library mentions an "educational film program" in its annual report and in 1969, the library hosted a 6-week film series entitled "Of Black America." By 1970, there is mention of 500 films for use by groups and organizations through the Rhode Island Library Film Cooperative. In 1972 the library hired a part-time media technician to begin acquiring a basic collection of audiovisual equipment and materials, noting in their annual report that "these filmstrips, tapes, cassettes, and records are especially effective when used with children who do not relate to the printed word. When one hears youngsters asking for the beautiful picture book first seen on a filmstrip, or listens to children using a tape recorder to recreate the sounds of the Indianapolis 500, one realizes that the potential of the media is boundless."[59]

In the public schools, a variety of experiments in new forms of film and media education were underway during the 1970s. In the collection of the Chicago Film Archives, we found the film *Metro!!! The School Without Walls*, a short documentary directed by Rod Nordberg in 1970 about the Chicago Public High School for Metropolitan Studies (aka Metro). The film follows a diverse group of students and their teachers who learn outside the classroom. Filmmaking was considered an important way that young people could learn to be citizens. Figure 7.5 shows a still

Figure 7.5 Metro!!! The Schools Without Walls, 1970.

from the film that depicts teens showing their film cameras to teachers and school leaders.

Some Canadian public libraries began hosting animation workshops for children in the early 1970s.[60] Universities and colleges got very active in collecting films throughout the 1960s and 1970s. In fact, Renee was a member of the first graduating class of students at the University of Michigan to receive an undergraduate major in Film/Video Studies (in addition to her more traditional major in English Literature). Weekly viewing assignments included screening films in college auditoriums in the evening, outside of class time. As Karen Gracy has notes, "By the end of the 1970s, film libraries were a key resource in higher education," with the Consortium of University Film Centers including over 50 members.[61] In documenting the history of archivists and preservationists, she shows how the library world had developed into highly differentiated collections of films based on their functions for coursework, research, and media production. Among media librarians, we see this important shift in perspective along with growing levels of professionalization throughout the 1970s.

In George Rehrauer 's *The Film User's Handbook,* published in 1975, he addresses an audience of academic librarians responsible for film collections, emphasizing that film should not be used "merely to get users to read more."[62] He stated, "Film is unique unto itself and should not be relegated to a shill position. To show a film in order to get students to read is poor methodology. To link book, film, and other media together in order to provide a total experience is more desirable and honest. To use films to draw persons into a library so they can make use of the other services is once more to assign to film a burden that it should not have. Film should be shown for its own sake and not as a come-on for some other service that needs patron support."[63] The prominence of this comment suggests that the practice of "book baiting" was still occurring the context of higher education.

But film was coming into its own. During the 1970s, librarians' attitudes were also changing as most recognized that audiovisual media were truly valuable to patrons. More and more librarians began to be more open to multimedia as legitimate sources for leisure and learning. In a 1977 survey of Wisconsin librarians, only 3% agreed with the statement, "Public libraries are, and always have been, book places and we should stick to developing them along that line."

Yet, despite their openness to audiovisual media, few librarians got much exposure to it as part of their job. Researchers surveyed librarians in Wisconsin in 1977 and found that only 20% of system libraries even had 16mm films in their collection. Most films did not circulate to patrons directly. Instead films in the library collection were only used for programming occasional film events. Survey evidence shows that only about 15% of Wisconsin libraries had a dedicated budget for audiovisual resources. Throughout the 1970s, libraries did not have dedicated space for viewing or listening in the library and less than 2% of libraries in the state of Wisconsin provided workshops on the use of audiovisual materials. Only 15% of libraries reported any form of in-service training for library staff on the use of audiovisual resources.[64] Film was a luxury that, for the most part, only the big-city libraries could indulge in.

NATIONAL HOME MOVIE DAY

Home movies are a fascinating part of public culture. Before the advent of the mobile phone, people created home movies using film and video equipment. They used 16mm and 8mm film cameras, Sony Portapak reel-to-reel video, video cameras using VHS tapes, and digital video cameras. When Renee was growing up, her dad made films depicting the opening of presents on Christmas Day and the family's annual trip to the local Fourth of July parade. Renee made video home movies of her children's musical performances and birthdays. As a form of creative play, her children, Roger and Rachel, learned to create video claymation animation and performed in their own fictional action-adventure movies.

To increase awareness of the value of preserving home movies as a window onto our culture, a group of film and media archivists organized the first Home Movie Day in 2002 and the tradition continues to the present day. It includes a range of events in the United States, Japan, Canada, Argentina, Brazil, Australia, Germany, Italy, the Netherlands, and many other countries. For those of us who lack access to working projectors, we get to relive our family history by sharing our home movies for a community screening event. For film and media archivists, the event visibly demonstrates the value of preservation.

Home movies are at risk of being lost to history; thus, the public screening of them contributes to increase the visibility of film and media education. As a cofounder of Home Movie Day and a media cataloguer at Northeast Historic Film in Bucksport, Maine, Brian Graney points out that, unlike commercial films, home movies are one of a kind.[65] Public libraries are making such digitization services available for people to preserve their home movies, and regular screening events should feature home movies produced by members of the community.

THE VHS EXPLOSION

It was a 1980s craze that brought film and video to mass audiences and, when it began, it transformed the media habits of people all over the world. Within months, it seems, there were video rental stores in every neighborhood of every big city, and even tiny towns and hamlets had a video rental store within a short distance. Some local entrepreneurs even tucked a collection of rentable tapes in the back part of local convenience stores, hardware stores, and other businesses. In some communities, there were even VHS tapes for rent at the local gas station!

As early as 1978, public libraries were exploring the potential of videotapes as a resource for patrons. In Minnesota, the Anoka County Library initiated a videotape player rental program, including children's titles and a reference collection on topics such as car care, solar energy, and landscaping.[66] By the early 1980s, libraries all over the country were jumping into the business of loaning VHS tapes and even VCR machines. At that time, there were two competing standards: Betamax and VHS.

In many libraries, the immediate popularity of VHS tapes led them to circulate more than books. This caused some resentment and grousing among librarians. In some libraries, rental of VHS tapes accounted for 30% of all circulation.[67] One study found that in public libraries about 50% of the film and media collection included entertainment feature films.[68] Showcasing entertainment media increased library circulation. The Lansing Public library reported circulation of between 7,000 and 8,000 videotapes a month. Some libraries charged patrons differential costs, depending on popularity: Renting VHS tapes varied from $2 to free.[69]

But right away librarians also noticed that often patrons who came in for VHS tapes also checked out other materials. Naturally, the ambivalent attitudes of librarians toward movies and their sensitivity to the needs of their patrons affected their collection development policies, their approach to cataloguing the new materials, and their circulation policies.

Two general patterns emerged. Those librarians who made no distinction between print leisure reading and video entertainment were happy to purchase mass market print authors like Danielle Steele and John Grisham as well as acquire Hollywood films like *Erin Brokovich*, the 2000 drama directed by Steven Soderbergh. In other communities, some librarians were wary of competing with Blockbuster and the more than 15,000 video rental stores that were circulating titles by 1985. These librarians decided to adopt a *counterprogramming strategy*, acquiring more highbrow fare, including international titles, documentaries, and noncommercial video.[70] They weren't aiming to raise circulation data as their ultimate goal; instead, they wanted to provide people with an increased range of choices of video content.

There's no doubt that the inclusion of video changed the way that librarians thought about their mission in a number of different ways during the 1980s. Although they recognized the need to provide free access to all patrons, they also had to make complex decisions that sometimes conflicted with this core value. For example, librarians had to decide whether the video collection should be restricted by age so that children cannot take out films that are rated R. They had to decide whether the library collect films that are rated R, X, or NC-17. And they had to determine whether the library would charge fees for video rental or issue fines for late returns.

When the VHS boom took off in the 1980s, libraries took different approaches to collecting them. Some academic libraries were reluctant to participate in adding these resources to their collections. By this time, many academic departments, especially in the area of film and video studies, were acquiring video independently outside the academic library. Because videos were being acquired by media centers and academic departments, many academic libraries did not feel the obligation to add them to their collections, fearing duplication of resources. In reviewing this history, William Walters notes that, in 1977, the audiovisual collections of most Association of Research Libraries (ARL) universities were not managed by the library but instead by other units of the university.[71]

Archives for Studying Media Literacy History

The Elizabeth Thoman Media Literacy Collection dates from 1943 to 2010 and contains organizational records for the Media Action Research Center, *Media&Values* magazine, the Center for Media and Values, and the Center for Media Literacy. Also available are the founding documents and early archives of the Partnership for Media Education, the Alliance for a Media Literate America, and the National Association for Media Literacy Education (NAMLE).

According to Michael RobbGrieco, a media literacy historian, Elizabeth Thoman's landmark magazine, *Media&Values*, offers rare insight on the development of the field. Published for 17 years between 1977 and 1993, the magazine grew "from a newsletter promoting a communications ministry in Catholic religious communities to a magazine on media-related issues for thought leaders across many faiths, finally becoming an independent nonprofit corporation producing curricula for media educators directly."[72]

In the beginning, media literacy was conceptualized as a dimension of media reform. The magazine crafted a narrative of transformation for its readers "from victims of malign media influence to crusaders for public health, social justice and media reform." Then it emphasized the need to understand the nexus between representation and reality, problematizing the media's ability to shape and influence social reality and values through news, advertising, and entertainment. Finally, it addressed the pedagogy and instructional practices of media literacy both at home and in schools.[73]

Also housed at Temple University is the KIDSNET archive, developed by Karen Jaffe as the Clearinghouse of Information on Children's Radio and Television. In 1987, Karen Jaffe knew that educators could benefit from having more knowledge about the range of programming available. In the 1980s, there were Afterschool Specials, Saturday morning cartoons, evening sitcoms, movies of the week, PBS series, cable programs, radio shows, and VHS tapes, which was then sometimes called home video. The collection also includes numerous network TV study guides for children's programming that were produced and distributed nationally to school librarians and educators. These archives are vital resources for the next generation of scholars to better understand how media literacy and media education developed during the 20th century.

A HISTORY OF RESTRICTED ACCESS

As we discussed in Chapter 4, today educators generally rely on their personal collections, the resources available in their departments, and YouTube, and only when these are exhausted do they explore the available resources of an academic library collection.[74] What role did academic libraries play in collecting moving image resources for teaching and research purposes?

Back in the 1970s, some academic libraries participated in collaborative networks to facilitate sharing of 16mm films, and as a result, they developed a complex set of practices of making VHS videos accessible to faculty and students. As Barbara Bergman explains, many academic librarians treated VHS tapes as they had treated film, as a type of special collection. This led them to restrict access, hold titles in closed stacks, and not participate in interlibrary loan programs. For example, in 1993, a survey of academic libraries found that only 33% permitted students to check out VHS tapes and only 23% required videotapes to be viewed only in the library (not in the classroom or at home).[75] At some libraries, even members of the faculty could not even check out a VHS tape to preview it!

The special collections mentality toward VHS tapes had some negative consequences for academic librarians and their patrons. In justifying their policies, academic libraries emphasized that immediate accessibility for classroom use was considered more important than the mere convenience of home use. Videotapes were expensive, after all, and replacement costs were high. Many librarians wanted to avoid "wear and tear" on these materials, as some were irreplaceable.

Scholars exploring these attitudes have noted that, despite "a long history of sharing resources to advance scholarship and teaching, many librarians have yet to embrace fully the idea that information is information, whatever form it takes."[76] One survey found that although librarians were quite willing to request videos for their patrons through interlibrary loan, less than half were willing to lend their own video holdings to librarians at other institutions. Many had detailed restrictions as to what they would lend to whom. As we discussed in Chapter 6, even as late as 2009, 48% of academic libraries kept their video collections (now including VHS and DVD) in closed stacks.[77]

Fortunately, some librarians gradually adopted a different philosophy toward VHS lending. They simply moved away from the special collections mentality and started to treat VHS tapes like books, permitting free circulation to all patrons. These librarians believed, fundamentally, that access to information should not be limited because of format. Although they recognized that usage would lead to loss and replacement, they put the interests of patrons first. Not only were open circulation policies a good form of public relations, but these policies reflected the belief that decision making about access should always favor usage.

We like this idea: Film and video should be treated no differently from print collections, and policies should always favor use. By leaning away from outdated policies rooted in a preservation ethos towards encouraging open access, librarians fulfill their service mission.

Today, DVDs and streaming media in public, school, and academic libraries in the United States have replaced VHS tapes. But the change has been indeed slow. For example, only in 2017 did the University of Maryland in Baltimore County (UMBC) remove all VHS players from classrooms. As educational technology scholar Chareen Snelson explains, problems of cost and obsolescence have been a continual challenge for librarians and educators in relation to the acquisition of film and video throughout the 20th century.[78] Only with the rise of YouTube have the economics begun to shift.

Film/Media Preservation Matters

Collecting and preserving film and media is more important than ever before. The Association of Moving Image Archivists, founded in 1990, includes archivists, librarians, collectors, curators, students, educators, artists, technologists, researchers, and distributors who preserve and access a wide variety of film and media collections. It's a small group of people who know that the primary goal of preservation is the act of providing the public with access to our history and culture.

Today's archivists face the challenges of both the increasing volume of film and media texts as well as the rapid obsolescence of the technologies used to create them. But it's not just the physical objects themselves that need to be preserved. The practical skills of operating and maintaining old technology need to be learned as well. For someone to be able to watch the projection of a film print, there must be a librarian or archivist who knows how to find, use, and maintain a film projector.

When it comes to film and media in libraries, how we understand the past shapes how we move forward into the future. But experts point out that preservation is a term that is often misused. It refers to "the totality of things necessary to ensure the permanent accessibility—forever—of an audiovisual document with the maximum integrity."[79] This is not something that is a one-and-done activity. It's actually a never-ending management task, one that needs an ongoing stream of financial and human resources. That's why we hope that more librarians and educators reach out to archivists and become advocates like some of the individuals we profile in this book. It's why we were pleased to learn that a part of the latest Providence Public Library renovation includes a digitization lab, where they plan to digitize the donated archives from AS220, an arts organization that has evolved organically since 1985 in response to community needs and has dramatically changed the landscape of the city. People who use the power of communication and information can help to increase public awareness of the importance of memory institutions that help us understand the many ways that film and media contribute to society and culture.

PLANNING FOR OBSOLESCENCE

Academic media librarians have always been planning for obsolescence as film and media formats have been changing rapidly for over 100 years. That's why media librarians Scott Spicer and Andrew Horbal have recommended that librarians take seriously the need for internal planning for format obsolescence, working in collaboration with audiovisual support professionals at their institutions.

It's not only VCRs that are in the process of becoming completely phased out from most classrooms in colleges and universities across the United States. DVDs are looking increasingly imperiled as well. Today, most professors and students use laptops that do not have DVD playback capability. Students, who have grown up largely since the peak of DVD sales (way back in 2013), watching online is often their primary form of accessing moving image media. Many students do not even have access to a DVD player. DVDs may be watched at the parents' home, but when they are at college, "most students do not buy, rent, or watch films on DVD . . . because [f]or students studying film in the era of instant streaming, the DVD is an artifact of the exhibition habits of their childhoods, when they visited the local Blockbuster store on the weekends to rent the newest releases."[80]

Still, many academic librarians and instructional media support staff are beginning to recognize the increasing obsolescence of this format. In one survey of academic librarians responsible for media, half believe that DVD devices are being used less frequently and more than 80% mentioned that DVD and VHS players are becoming difficult to find. Of the hundreds of thousands of VHS recordings once in commercial release, many have never been released on DVD or in streaming format. Plus, most VHS tapes are likely to be unviewable by 2027, due to the age of the tapes, limited access to playback equipment, and the retirement of VHS technicians. As Spicer and Horbal warn, "Unless academic libraries take action now, significant portions of their video collections will no longer be able to be used to support instruction, the most likely reason they acquired these collections in the first place."[81]

Academic librarians faced some complex decisions with the transition from film to video, which occurred when the 16mm rental market collapsed in the 1980s. As Karen Gracy explains, university audiovisual departments adopted video as the primary format for viewing. She writes, "Few librarians saw the value in retaining old, fading 16mm prints, and often, even rare out-of-print materials were deaccessioned if the informational content was seen as outdated."[82]

Truth be told, many librarians have not made it easy for patrons to view films from the past. A few public libraries continue to maintain core collections of films on 16mm and VHS tapes. Yale University Library recently acquired 3,000 VHS horror movies from the 1970s and 1980s produced largely by amateurs for the direct-to-VHS market.[83] But because VHS players are no longer being manufactured, these films can be difficult to access. At the Enoch Pratt Free Library in Baltimore, patrons can still check out one or more of the 2,100 16mm films still in the collection, including Chuck Braverman's 1972 *Condensed Cream of Beatles*, a kaleidoscope of flashing images, music, and ideas from the legendary rock and roll group who powerfully influenced the youth culture of the sixties. For many baby boomers, this film was their first exposure to the genre of experimental film. However, because the public library does not provide access to film projection equipment, it's not clear how a patron would actually view the film. Making physical copies of media available without providing access to working technologies for their display is no access at all. Such challenges make digitization an attractive option in order to ensure that old films are available to the current generation of users.

SECTION 108 PRESERVATION

One of the most important ways to address the problem of obsolescence is to migrate content from one format to another. It is legal for libraries to make copies of copyrighted content to address format obsolescence. Under Section 108 of US Copyright law (US Copyright Office, 2014), nonprofit libraries can duplicate content that is lost damaged, stolen, deteriorating, or in an obsolete format. Section 108 requires that, prior to duplication, a reasonable search be conducted to determine that an unused copy of the title is not available at a fair price, and evidence of that search should be kept. That's why the late Deg Farrelly and other librarians responsible for the Due Diligence Project (originated at American University, Arizona State University, and William Paterson University) collaborated to document their research processes, looking at the original distributor's sales website, contacting the original distributor for information on availability or transfer of content to another distributor, searching Amazon.com for the title and searching WorldCat database of library holdings for alternate imprints of title.

There is so much content that is becoming obsolete—and yet is worth preserving. A key phrase of Section 108 of the copyright law empowers libraries to copy content from an obsolete format to make a preservation copy, provided they make a reasonable search effort to locate copies available at a reasonable cost.

Some people think that "reasonable search" means that it's important to track down the copyright holder and ask for permission. But retired media librarian Deg Farrelly didn't think that was what the law intended. He believed that the important criterion is the continued right to use and preserve the content previously acquired. The Due Diligence Project is a digital database (section108video.com) with results about the availability of several thousands of titles. One of the most exciting initiatives on VHS preservation will enable this project to grow and thrive far into the future. The Academic Libraries Video Trust, developed by the National Media Market, is designed to preserve commercial video content that is no longer in distribution. The Trust will leverage preservation and replacement exceptions for reproduction by libraries. Maintenance of the site and creation of secure technology has become the responsibility of the Trust, administered under the auspices of National Media Market and Conference.[84]

But audiovisual academic support staff can be cautious and risk-averse about digitizing VHS tapes in part because of their own lack of knowledge of online streaming combined with copyright confusion. Some may not receive frequent, regular professional development that is coordinated with media librarians and other academic support professionals. For example, when Scott Spicer and Andrew Horval asked audiovisual support staff at 49 universities what guidance they would offer an instructor with a DVD or VHS tape he or she wanted to show in a classroom that was not equipped with playback equipment for that format, 93% said they would tell the instructor to digitize the item using the library or encourage the instructor to digitize the video themselves. Only 61% suggested that they look for a streaming video version of the title. This finding made researchers wonder: are higher education educational technology staff fully up-to-date on video streaming services?

As Spicer and Horval note, the evidence suggests that some audiovisual staff might be unfamiliar with streaming online video services that may be available through the academic library. They recommend, "Academic libraries and classroom AV support professionals need to work together to ensure that instructors at their institutions are not being given mixed messages about copyright."[85] Because this could save time and effort, audiovisual support professionals are likely to welcome learning about streaming video licensing and digitization services offered through the library.

Small academic libraries are managing the process of digitization in ways distinctly different from large flagship universities. For example, in 2017, the Stonehill College Library in Easton, Massachusetts, published their official policy on digitization of VHS materials, which is based on individual item review and the teaching needs of the college faculty. VHS materials in faculty personal collections are eligible to be digitized if the faculty member donates these works to the libraries' collections and the material is cataloged prior to digitization. Prior to digitization, due diligence research is performed to investigate replacement options, and the original VHS tape is maintained by the libraries. Digital files are made available to students through electronic reserves for a set period of time. While it took several years to develop the policy and get it approved, this kind of proactive academic librarianship is vital to ensure the continued viability of film and media resources for teaching and learning.

Sarah McClessky knows that academic libraries in the United States have thousands of VHS titles that are rapidly degrading. She said, "No one makes the VHS players anymore, and regularly circulated tapes and players quickly degrade to the point of being unusable. The benign neglect that resulted in the loss of thousands of early motion pictures and early television recordings will happen with VHS recordings unless libraries undertake major preservation projects to protect them."[86] Media librarians, by investing in the important work, ensure that we can someday tell the story of the VHS era as we seek to understand this important part of media and cultural history.

MEDIA DIGITIZATION AND PRESERVATION

Interest in film preservation among librarians grew steadily in the 1990s with the release of the seminal US government report *Film Preservation* in 1993, which documented the growing need for funding and support. The Association of Moving Image Archivists (AMIA) grew to more than 900 members by 2012.

Among the many important film and media digitization initiatives, the one at Indiana University is pretty amazing. Holding one of the largest and most diverse collections of motion picture film at any university in the United States, librarians at the University of Indiana–Bloomington identified over 670,000 analog and physical digital audio, video, and film objects on campus, of which 41% are unique or thought to be rare. With leadership from academic librarians, the University Provost and head of the Bloomington campus appointed a task force and published a report, "Meeting the Challenge of Media Preservation: Strategies and Solutions" in 2011. As a result of this systematic and important inquiry Michael McRobbie, the president of the university, created the Media Digitization and Preservation Initiative (MDPI), with the goal of preserving all significant audio and video recordings within 5 years.[87] In 2017, they began digitization of approximately 25,000 film reels. The collection includes a large number of educational films that were rented to schools, libraries, and colleges across the country from before World War II as well as home movies, amateur films, local Indiana advertisements, and commercial films. What a treat to follow along with the excitement of the team on their blog as they digitized the rare lacquer disks of Orson Welles and the Mercury Theater of the Air.

STREAMING INTO THE FUTURE

Over a period of just 20 years, people all over the world have seen a profound shift in the way we access film and video. In 1995, DVDs became the medium of choice for viewing video and film, and the consumer market for DVDs was established. When Netflix started in 1998, they offered consumers a large selection of DVDs delivered by mail. Renee and Pam remember being truly addicted to the little red DVD envelopes that would arrive in the mail bringing an array of films for weekly viewing.

Users selected titles from the website to place their order. There were no late fines. Best of all, you could have unlimited rentals for one monthly price. By 2000, Netflix was gathering feedback from users about their perceptions of the quality of films and using the power of that data to personalize recommendations based on past choices. By 2005, they had grown to 4.2 million members and in 2007, they introduced online streaming, gradually expanding their services into Europe, Latin America, and Asia to become a global media company.

Still, despite the rapid growth of Netflix and other companies, in 2010, public libraries were the largest distributor of video and film in the country, lending out 2.1 million movies per day. That's pretty amazing, when you think of it. The Public Libraries Survey reports that in 2014, libraries offered 218 video materials per 1,000 people, including DVDs, VHS tapes, and downloadable video.[88]

Sadly, the most recent Public Library Survey from 2017 does not offer data about the circulation data regarding video and film resources. We wonder if they're hiding the bad news. It's likely that many libraries faced the same declining circulation statistics as North Madison County Public Library System in Indiana, which experienced declines in DVD circulation, with checkouts down 19% over the previous year.[89] YouTube and Netflix provide flexible, easy-to-use ways to access film and video with powerful search tools. Streaming media may make physical forms of film and video obsolete within a generation.

As we have seen in this chapter, the history of film and media in school, public, and academic libraries is a complex fascinating one, but researchers are surprisingly challenged to tell this story by the lack of information available in libraries about their own institutional history. Librarians must create and maintain their own historical repositories of their work to document the library's approach to film programming, circulation and collection development. This will enable the next generation of scholars to uncover this important dimension of library history.

The past matters. Because many library film and other public programs were not carefully described or documented by librarians in the library's annual reports or in scholarship, our knowledge of the past is irretrievably limited. The omission of this information may have reflected the low status or ambivalent attitudes of library leaders; thus, those negative attitudes have indirectly shaped our ability to understand the past. Certainly, this shows that an ongoing lack of interest in film and media by librarians can have far-ranging consequences.

Of course, to contribute to future scholarship, librarians need time to carefully document their own practices regarding film screenings and discussions and other film and media literacy education initiatives they develop. In the next chapter, we turn toward the present, looking at some of the many ways in which librarians develop their own skills and competencies in relation to using film and media to promote lifelong learning.

8

Present

Questions Answered in This Chapter
- How do librarians share their appreciation and respect for film and media?
- What do we know about how film screenings address civic competencies?
- How do patrons promote libraries on YouTube?
- Why do librarians use listservs for knowledge sharing?
- What factors are shaping the rise of media and information literacy globally?
- How does teacher motivation shape the practice of digital and information literacy?
- What features of graduate education best enable future librarians to support film, digital, and media education in libraries?
- How can librarians benefit from lifelong professional development opportunities that explore film and digital media?
- Why are information literacy competencies broadening to include visual media?
- Why do librarians love LibGuides?
- How are librarians helping people engage with films from the past?

Library graduate students who were assigned to watch *The Library*, a short film written and directed by Jason LaMotte, expected it would be another typical YouTube viewing experience. So many educators assign students to view YouTube videos, it's practically routine. But students were not expecting to be so emotionally moved by this film. The 20-minute short narrative film features the story of a 13-year-old British girl who encounters a mystery when visiting her local library when she begins receiving notes from a secret admirer. Set in a delightful, classic-looking country library in England, the film reveals her journey of discovery through literature and romance, and ultimately the short film culminates in a bittersweet personal history that connects past, present, and future.

Students were eager to talk about the film and share their feelings and thoughts about it. The quality of this particular film discussion experience very quickly became deep, personal, and intimate. One student, Megan, appreciated the mysterious secret notes that are at the heart of the love story. Another student, Robin, commented on the timeless quality of the film and observed how few words were spoken in the film. She noticed the highly visual nature of the narrative, and how little moments of action were used to reveal the characters' personalities. Coauthor Pam, then auditing the course, observed that with a stirring musical score, this film features many symbolic elements that create an evocative mood that resonates with viewers of all ages. "There are so many stories in a library," she concluded.

Bill, another library graduate student, picked up on that theme in his response, noting that in the film's climax, when the main character suddenly realizes who has been sending the messages, there is a tender moment that unexpectedly connects two of the characters. Every class member was engaged in reflecting and sharing their response to the film, and each person added something insightful and personally relevant to the conversation.

But as thoughtful and intense as this class discussion was, it wasn't happening in a classroom. All the people in the class weren't even contributing their ideas at the same time. Students were using Flipgrid (www.flipgrid.com), an asynchronous video-based discussion tool, which meant that each student contributed some ideas to respond to the film, listening and commenting on the ideas shared previously by students.

This particular online asynchronous discussion was simply mind-blowing. Britta noticed the sense of mystery and anticipation that is built into the story. Emily noted that the story reminded her of another science fiction romance that is set in a library, *The Time Traveler's Wife* by Emily Niffennegger. Were Emily and Ruth perhaps the same person? Was this a kind of time travel story or not? Other students comments on Emily's intriguing point, thanking her for the insight and building upon her ideas. The discussion experience itself was as magical as the film viewing experience. Until that very moment, Britta recalled, she hadn't *really* understood what it meant to really learn from a film discussion experience. All the members of the class discovered that, with video discussion tools like Flipgrid, people can interpret, discuss and respond to film even when they are not physically together in the same room. This particular way of learning through film occurred in the present, where today, many people have access to digital tools that enable them to participate in learning communities not bounded by time or geography.

Why do we focus on the present in this chapter? Because librarians and educators, right here and now, are lifelong learners, connecting people, spaces, and film and media resources in ways that delight, engage, and transform. Using innovative approaches to professional development, film and media literacy initiatives are now building capacity for even more ambitious and influential programs in the future. In the age of the Internet, librarians must continuously try to meet the fast-changing learning needs of people in their communities.

In this chapter, we imagine the small but important changes in the behavior and attitudes of librarians who work in school, public, and academic libraries as they embrace and value audiovisual and digital media as truly equal with print resources.

We examine research that looks carefully at how films are thought to engage civic awareness and action. We consider again the profound parallels between movies and books as works created by authors to express ideas about the complexities of lived experience. We describe various approaches to learning, including the active use of listservs that help people share knowledge in ways that support lifelong learning. We look at the global Media and Information Literacy (MIL) community to consider its potential for making a transformative impact. We describe our own experience of teaching (and learning) in a specialized graduate course in film and media education in libraries.

As we will see in the pages that follow, through lifelong learning and professional development programs, librarians can come to fully embrace the art forms of film and media and use them to help patrons, learners and community members better understand the complex world and our place in it. We conclude the chapter by considering how the interdisciplinary knowledge community dedicated to film and media preservation may inspire innovation in how we program film and media events in schools, public libraries, and in academic contexts. We want to build an understanding of the past and use the power of film and media history to help us understand the present and future changes that we see all around us today.

Learning to Value Film and Media in the Library

THE STEPCHILD STEPS UP

Even today, when most librarians love watching films themselves, and many look forward to the Academy Awards show each year, the DVDs in many of their collections are often treated as the unwanted stepchild—the Cinderella. For many librarians, films and videos in their collection are tolerated rather than loved. They have benefit, perhaps, but they are rarely appreciated or cared for like the "real" children of the library—the beloved books.

Imagine, if you can, a scene in which a child arrives at the circulation desk with three DVDs to check out—all mainstream Hollywood movies. Now imagine the possible thoughts swirling through the mind of the librarian behind the desk and the various things she or he might say to that child. Did any of them sound like this?

- It looks like you really like movies. Have you ever considered a career in the film industry?
- Sometimes these DVDs have special features that let you go behind the scenes and give you an idea of how the film was made. Have you ever looked at them?
- I see you like the Disney films with strong female characters. Have you ever seen *The Whale Rider* or *The Breadwinner*? I bet you'd like them, too.

- A fellow cinephile! What? Never heard that word before? It means film lover. You *are* a film lover, aren't you? Have you been to any of the local film festivals? They show amazing films from all around the world, and we have some of the ones they've shown in past years in our collection, too. Let me know if you'd like to check them out, and I can show you how to find them.

If those responses are similar to what you imagined, you get the fairy godmother award. You have already begun transforming the stepchild into the belle of the ball. If you had other, less film-supportive thoughts, it may be time to give the stepchild another chance.

THE PURPOSE OF CINEMA

Because film and video are so much a part of our culture, we take them for granted. The purpose of film viewing is not something we think much about anymore. In the 1933 book *How to Appreciate Motion Pictures*, Ohio State University professor and scholar Edgar Dale writes:

> The results of the investigations reported in companion volumes in this series demonstrate conclusively the effect of the motion picture on children's information, attitudes, and conduct. It is hoped that this volume will provide a necessary corrective to possible harmful results, and provide audiences for those films which sincerely and honestly convey significant interpretations of the world in which we live.

In reflecting on the purpose of film, Dale recognizes the depth of this question, noting, "The question of purpose is one that thinking people must ask, not only about motion pictures, but also about schools, churches, industry, about life itself." What, then, are motion pictures for? Dale asked a group of high school students this question, and these are a few of the answers that he received:

- They give the audience some fun and entertainment.
- They keep me from getting bored with life.
- They give people pleasure.
- They make you forget your troubles.
- It's somewhere to go when you have a date.
- It's a place to go at night.
- It's just a way to kill time.
- It's a way to learn about life.
- You learn what happens when you make certain choices.
- They show what people do under different circumstances.
- It gives you the artist's idea of life.

As we can see from the answers he received, many people think of movies as merely pleasant distractions from the daily grind of life. But there are some who look a little deeper. Dale observes those last four reasons offered by teens, noting, "I believe that the students who wrote these last four answers have a much clearer picture of what the motion picture might do than do the first seven. It is my own belief that the motion picture is an art as important as music, literature, painting, or the drama, and that a conception of the motion picture merely as idle entertainment for idle people is too limited."[1]

When we first started our journey to writing this book, we appreciated the Heartland Film's guide, *Teaching With Movies*, which offers excellent recommendations for parents and teachers.[2] Heartland Film is a nonprofit arts organization founded in 1991 with the mission to inspire filmmakers and audiences through the transformative power of film. Heartland Film offers a 10-day film festival in Indianapolis each October and awards the Truly Moving Picture Award for films with power to promote positive change in audiences' lives, and they also offer a high school film competition and various workshops and seminars.

At this point in the book, you must realize that the intellectual curiosity of librarians is boundless and that many of those who love film and media are eager to share their passion with their communities and with the wider world. One such librarian, William Chamberlain, has been supporting the needs of film lovers in Nashville for many years. As one reporter put it, "The library's free DVD/video checkout has long been a kind of secret handshake among Music City cult-movie aficionados, who know it as the only game in town if you want to find the likes of Samuel Fuller's all-caps gangster thriller *Underworld, U.S.A.*, Fassbinder's *The Bitter Tears of Petra von Kant*, Forough Farrokhzad's 1962 short *The House Is Black*, or Jacques Demy's gorgeous musical *The Young Girls of Rochefort.*"[3]

We simply love Chamberlain's Legends of Film podcast, which is hosted at the Nashville Public Library, where he interviews film directors and screenwriters whose work is being screened at the library. In one recent interview, director Michael Mann describes how the gritty texture and romance of the city of Chicago influenced his thinking about the 1981 action film *Thief.* Mann explains that the story offers insight on how we see our life experiences when actions and events collide with or contradict social norms. Based on the book *The Home Invaders: Confessions of a Cat Burglar* by Frank Hohimer, the hero gets into an exploitive relationship where he trades independence for financial security. As the filmmaker tells the story of how the film got made, the artistry and depth of insight of the authorial process are revealed. Because Chamberlain respects filmmakers as authors, he invites us to do the same. Podcasts are simply remarkable: what a delight to encounter the minds of these fascinating filmmakers through the power of recorded dialogue!

DO FILM DISCUSSIONS IN LIBRARIES PROMOTE CIVIC ENGAGEMENT?

POV is the United States' longest-running television showcase of independent documentaries aired weekly on PBS. These nonfiction films encourage viewers to think deeply about a wide variety of social, political, and cultural issues facing our country and our world, offering a distinctive point of view on issues of public concern.

So when we ran across the publication of a major study of a film and media community engagement initiative featuring the POV series, we were thrilled. Anthony Cocciolo studied the impact of film screening and discussion sessions in more than 276 libraries. The goal of the initiative was to increase community engagement through educational awareness and by connecting local audiences with important issues. Such community engagement and outreach efforts developed by POV have been in place for nearly 20 years, supported by a mix of charitable foundations who provide funding to increase visibility for the films at the local level.

Researchers wondered if participating in film discussions might contribute to civic engagement, which they defined as collective action, community service, and political involvement. Partnering libraries were required to hold a discussion after each film was screened or bring in a local expert to explore the issues in the film more deeply via a question-and-answer session. Librarians were provided with a discussion guide and a resource kit that includes suggested actions that individuals can take after the film screening to get more involved. They were also provided with surveys for patrons to complete at the conclusion of the event.

For a 4-year period from 2008 to 2012, 136 films were made available to librarians throughout the United States, and 436 film screening events in 36 states were held. It worked like this: Librarians initiated a request for particular films via an online form. They received a DVD, promoted the event, hosted the film screening, and gathered audience evaluation data. After the event, librarians themselves received a questionnaire to measure their perception of the civic engagement–related outcomes associated with the event.

From the 426 film events, 296 librarian surveys were returned, for a reasonable response rate of 70%. In addition to sharing their perceptions of the event, librarians were also asked to provide information about the demographic characteristics of the patrons who attended the program and describe the marketing efforts they used to promote the event.

Librarians were responsible for distributing surveys to patrons who attended the film screenings. Sadly, only a small number of surveys were completed and returned. We don't know why librarians were not able to return many of the patron surveys. Did they forget to copy or distribute the forms? Did they distribute the surveys but patrons refused to complete them because they were asked to provide their name and email address? Did people leave the room before the film was completed? Were they unfaithful partners in the PBS research process? The researcher is silent on this matter, reporting only that of the 7,227 individuals who attended a screening, 1,052 surveys were returned, yielding a response rate of 15%, which is a typical response rate for surveys that target external audiences.

The data clearly reveal that viewers who attended the library film screening learned from the experience, as 81% agreed that they learned something new from the event and nearly 60% agreed that the film deepened their understanding of the issues presented in the film. More than 57% agreed that they would discuss issues with friends and family, and half said they would encourage their family and friends to watch the POV documentary they had seen. However, less than half of the patrons said that the postscreening discussion was valuable.

For many people who attended the film screening and discussions, the experience did inspire their intention towards civic engagement. About one in five patrons said they would write letters or sign petitions (19%), join an organization working on the issues (21%), organize a screening or discussion (15%), organize a workshop or training (12%), or donate money to an organization working on the issues (22%).This research has important implications for school, public and academic libraries. Film screenings inspire people by increasing their knowledge and impacting their feelings.

But reading this study, we found something a bit startling about this research study: the perceptions of the librarians themselves. As Table 8.1 shows, when librarians were asked to identify the relative value of film screening and discussion programs, librarians strongly agreed that patrons learned from the documentary screening experience, developing a greater understanding of the issues raised by the program and increasing the audience's knowledge about the power of film as a tool for social change. When asked to describe the relevance of the film screening event to the library's mission, 62% said the film screening event raised the profile of the organization, and one in three librarians said it attracted new members into the library. But only 16% said it garnered press attention, and only 8% said it improved internal library organizational development and education. This leads us to speculate that the librarians responsible for these events might not have seen them as particularly valuable toward reaching library-oriented goals. For some librarians, sadly, film screenings and discussions like this may have been a chore, not a delight.

As we noted earlier, for half of those who attended the film events, the discussion after the film was perceived as not valuable. It seems that the ho-hum nature of some of these discussion experiences was a downer for librarians and patrons alike. Anthony Cicciolo, the researcher, is a library education leader, and he reflects on data that showed that half of patrons moderately to strongly agree that the discussion after the screening was valuable. He writes, "There is an opportunity for librarians to become more skillful discussion leaders and to think of new ways to provoke thought and engagement in participants beyond what is provided in

Table 8.1 **The Value of a PBS-Library Film Screening Program: Perceptions of Librarians**

	% Agreement
Patron Knowledge	
Fostered a greater understanding of the issues raised by the program	77%
Increased audience's knowledge of film as a tool for social change	48%
Patron Action	
Inspired action among audience members	21%
Connected audience to local resources	18%
Library Outcomes	
Raised organization's profile in the community	62%
New members	36%
Garnered local press	16%
Improved internal organizational development and education	8%

N = 296.

Source: Adapted from Cocciolo, A. (2013). Public libraries and PBS partnering to enhance civic engagement: A study of a nationwide initiative. *Public Library Quarterly, 32*(1), 1–20.

the documentary."[4] Library and information science (LIS) educators can support future library and information professionals in learning to facilitate discussions around controversial social, political, and cultural issues with relevance to local communities. For this to occur, they need to take time in the classroom to model this process either through face-to-face synchronous or digital asynchronous dialogue.

USING MEDIA TO PROMOTE THE LIBRARY

Librarians have long recognized the potential of video as a marketing vehicle. Many are exploring the potential of YouTube to advance the mission of the library. Yet most YouTube videos that feature the keywords "library," "libraries," "librarian," and "librarians" are not created by librarians themselves. Still, researchers Selene Colburn and Laura Haines, who measured libraries' use of YouTube as a promotional tool, found that library-created promotional videos were more common than those created for professional development or personal reasons, as Figure 8.1 shows. Some of the 379 video examples described by these researchers include content that might be considered a form of promotion or marketing for libraries.

We were delighted with some of the examples of library promotion on YouTube. When Roy Litwin, the arts and humanities librarian at the University of Minnesota-Duluth Library, founded a contest to encourage student patrons to design promotional videos for the library, he got some interesting submissions. In 2007, two students decided to create a video parody of *MTV Cribs*, a show that features tours of celebrity mansions. Entitled, *UMD Cribs*, the video accumulated over 20,000 views as of February 2018. In one scene, a student walks through the library as if it were a home and points out the artwork and the newspapers from all over the world. As the student moves through the stacks, he says, "Here is my book collection. I don't like to read but they're nice to have. Maybe they will go up in value some day."

Litwin uploaded the video to YouTube and embedded it on a web page announcing the winners. The link was promoted through the library newsletter, the library homepage, the library Facebook page, and a campus-wide e-mail list for staff. Some academic librarians might shiver to think about leaving library promotion up to the undergrads, but according to Litwin, it "hasn't been a problem and they've had fun with the library topic. We don't have control, but because we don't, the videos can speak to students in the way that we want. They're coming from students; it's not the library authorities telling them the library is cool and interesting."[5]

We love the idea that perhaps Rob and other academic librarians learned something from seeing how the students themselves perceive their collections and services. Sometimes the fresh eyes of the newcomer offer insight to the seasoned professional. Evidence of the promotional value and effectiveness of such videos comes from a quick look at the comments. One from a user named Twin Cities Fishing says, "This is cool. I'm only in 7th grade but I plan on going to UMD."

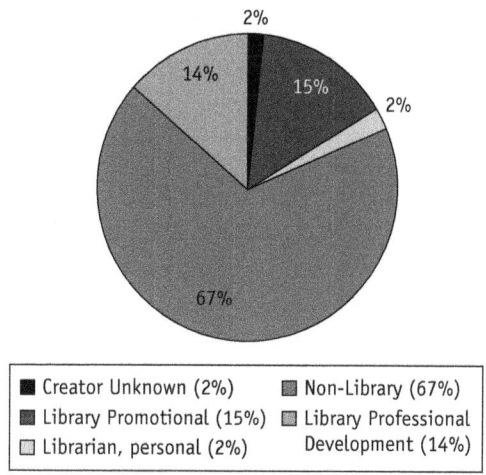

Figure 8.1 Library content on YouTube.
Source: Colburn & Haines, 2012.

A Lifetime of Learning for Librarians

LEARNING THROUGH LISTSERVS

People use the Internet all the time for self-directed purposes in seeking answers to questions. After all, that Google search bar is the stuff of dreams, a gateway into knowledge and learning. Sometimes our queries just help us find a new restaurant; other times, our searches generate the sharing of information that leads to thoughtful interaction and dialogue that inspires deeper learning.

Search and sharing are comingled at the roots, and they always have been. We rely on the kindness of strangers to meet our information needs. But let's not overlook one of the oldest forms of digital learning: participating in a listserv. Some readers may get a dozen or more notifications in their email box every day from listservs while other readers may have only the barest familiarity with listservs as a form of information sharing. Today, digital platforms like Reddit and Tumblr support knowledge communities that form around every imaginable topic from the most trivial to the most profound. Some would argue that within the education community, Twitter has replaced listservs to a large extent. For this reason, some younger people who primarily use digital platforms for knowledge sharing may not know that listservs emerged in the late 1980s and 1990s as a way to share information among groups of people via email.

For people whose digital skills are limited to email or for those who are too busy to learn to use new digital platforms, listservs are perfect. Some librarians we have met haven't bothered to explore other social media sharing platforms because they rely on listservs – in that sense, then, they're almost "too easy." There are other disadvantages to listservs as a means of information sharing. Getting a lot of emails about topics you're not interested in can be demoralizing and they are a rather disorganized way to share knowledge. Because knowledge is shared via threaded discussion, the subject line may not have anything to do with the informational content of the email. Also, some people accidentally send personal emails to a large group because they lack familiarity with the conventions of participating in a listserv. We have also observed librarians who use listservs as a form of lazy research, asking questions to the group that could have been easily answered by a simple Google search. Poor quality and inaccurate information is also sometimes shared on listservs and it takes courage to confront these problems. As a result, listserv communication can lead to rants and critiques that create misunderstandings and hurt feelings.

But listserv membership, like any online-networked community, offers a number of advantages as well. Listservs may foster a spirit of camaraderie and cultivates a community of practice and professional identity. Researchers who have studied the nature of the learning that results from participation in a listserv find that informal learning occurs through discussion, questioning, networking, mentoring, and observation. Even just lurking on a listserv (without contributing) can lead to learning.[6]

Librarians share information about film and media through listservs. To write this book, we spent a lot of time perusing listservs to see how librarians learn and share online. For example, we observed a conversational thread that developed in the Video-Lib listserv, an online community of subscribers to the *Video Librarian* magazine, which is edited and published by Randy Pitman. This thread of ideas consisted of a group of librarians who responded to a query that addressed the complicated status of ancillary materials associated with film DVDs. Ancillary materials may include the printed liner notes that accompany print packaging of DVDs. Some of these ancillary materials are quite impressive. These may include audio commentaries by filmmakers and scholars, restored director's cuts, deleted scenes, shooting scripts, and even storyboards and other artwork. A number of video distribution firms, including the Criterion Collection, provide physical and streaming access to classic and contemporary films. They publish ancillary materials to supplement and provide contextual information to meet the needs of collectors and to deepen learning.

In one email, Erin DeWitt Miller, media librarian at the University of North Texas, asked for ideas about how to handle oversized supplementary material that frequently comes with DVDs. She explained:

> There's no good way for us to shelve this material with the DVDs themselves (space limitations, etc.). Historic use rates have been extremely low (i.e. nobody ever checks any of these out) and with so much "supplementary" material now available online I don't know that it's worth cataloging and keeping hard copies on the shelf (but I don't reasonably have time to search for online versions before deciding what to keep). I'm wondering what solutions other libraries have come up with? Do you catalog supplementary material separately? House it with the DVDs or some other organizational solution? Throw it all immediately into the recycling bin? Digitize it and make a link available through the catalog? Something else?

Nineteen academic librarians from all over the United States weighed in to respond to this question over a period of just a couple of days.

Most librarians described the decisions they made about how to catalog and store these resources. For example, some place them nearby where DVDs are housed, noting that, unfortunately, they rarely circulate or get used. Dennis Doros of Milestone Film & Video added a perspective as one who produces these materials, noting that the ancillary booklet for the film *I Am Cuba*, the 1964 Soviet-Cuban film directed by Mikhail Kalatozov, "corrects a lot of the stories that have been written about the film elsewhere." And James Steffen of Emory University reminded librarians that "a great deal of thought and effort often goes into what materials and features are selected to accompany the film." He observes that while private collectors value these editions precisely for those features, "library circulation practices decontextualize the DVDs within the sets and make the content less discoverable and accessible." This conversational thread provided a lot of insight to all the librarians in the knowledge-sharing community.

Through exposure to diverse perspectives, readers of this particular listserv thread have gained a considerable amount of insight and new ideas about many issues related to film and media in libraries. You may or may not be a fan of listservs, but we found that informal learning through both listservs and digital platforms can provide potentially transformative lifelong learning experiences. The best librarian-centered online knowledge communities build upon a generous and open-hearted spirit of trust and respect.

MEDIA AND INFORMATION LITERACY GOES GLOBAL

Librarians have been involved in the media literacy movement since the earliest days. Most scholars and educators acknowledge media literacy using the definition provided from a report on a US National Leadership Conference on Media Literacy, which described a media literate person as someone who "can decode, evaluate, analyze and produce both print and electronic media. The fundamental objective of media literacy is critical autonomy in relationship to all media."[7] Participants at the conference pointed out that different media literacy programs might emphasize informed citizenship, aesthetic appreciation and expression, social advocacy, self-esteem, or consumer competence, and that the diversity and range of topics and issues under the media literacy umbrellas was likely to grow over time.

Today, media literacy has risen to prominence in Europe, partly as a result of the European Commission efforts to support media literacy through strategic initiatives, grant competitions, and coordination with member states on policies and best practices. They define media literacy quite broadly as "all the technical, cognitive, social, civic and creative capacities that allow us to access and have a critical understanding of and interact with both traditional and new forms of media."[8]

As a result of increasing global collaboration between librarians and educators, the concept of *media and information literacy* (MIL) has developed internationally to characterize the interrelatedness of the two paradigms. Figure 8.2 shows how MIL is linked to both the information and learning process (from data to information, knowledge, and wisdom) and the decision-making process, using appropriate resources and technology with the activation of critical thinking.

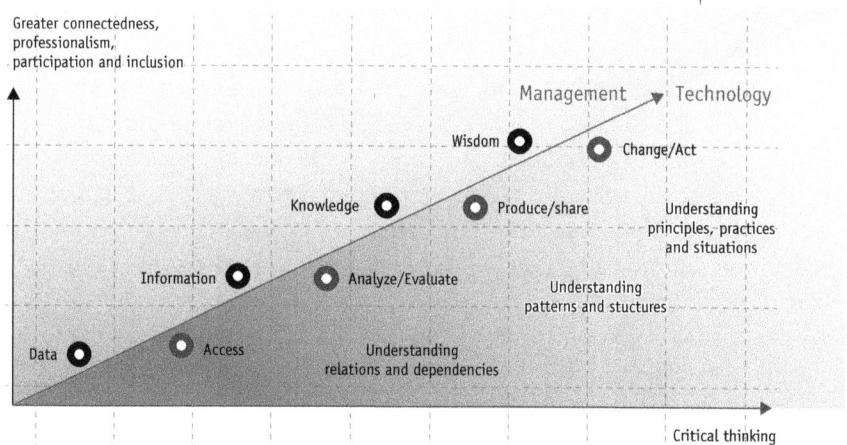

Figure 8.2 Relationship between cultural participation and critical thinking.
Source: UNESCO Global Media and Information Literacy Assessment Framework.

Organizations like the International Federation of Library Associations (IFLA) have also stressed the importance of media and information literacy for the social and cultural development of individuals, communities, and societies. Since 2012, the IFLA and UNESCO have been broadening the traditional scope of libraries on information literacy, defining media and information literacy in this way:

> a combination of knowledge, attitudes, skills and practices required to access, analyze, evaluate, use, produce and communicate information and knowledge in creative, legal and ethical ways that respect human rights.[9]

European policymakers and scholars acknowledge that even though this concept seems right at the heart of the profession, by and large, "the library profession and its academic counterpart, the library and information science (LIS) discipline, haven't devoted much time and money on the evaluation of concrete programs."[10] It is important to unpack the complex reasons why the global LIS research community has so far contributed relatively little to this important area of inquiry.

PROFESSIONAL DEVELOPMENT IN DIGITAL LITERACY

Teachers and librarians are lifelong learners, and many crave the chance to continue their learning in a social context. When Renee and her colleague Julie Coiro started the first Summer Institute in Digital Literacy at the University of Rhode Island in the summer of 2013, it was conceptualized as a week-long exploration of digital literacy in relation to the needs of K–12 teachers; college faculty; youth media professionals; and school, public, and academic librarians. As we saw it, digital literacy education practices must be integrated within existing structures of elementary and secondary schools, public libraries, colleges and universities, and academic libraries. Many other cultural organizations and institutions, including nonprofit organizations, museums, public health organizations, and social service organizations, can also play important roles. The media industry itself can be a stakeholder in advancing digital and media literacy education. The Summer Institute in Digital Literacy would be open to all and adopt an inclusive "big tent" perspective.

Unlike many who consider digital literacy to be largely activated in out-of-school, informal, interest-driven experiences[11], we situate our vision of digital literacy in the pragmatic context of formal K–20 education, where the uses of media and technology are inevitably situated in relation to institutional structures. As a result, we emphasize the use of inquiry learning with digital media texts and platforms. We reject a narrow tool-centric and skill-centered approach to teaching digital literacy.

Digital and media literacy encourages learners to have voice and choice in how they learn. When teachers and librarians experience agency through activities that involve reading, analyzing, and writing digital texts, they gain confidence in advancing their own students' digital literacy competencies. We are particularly committed to building bridges between scholars, educators, and librarians. When professional development learning experiences are developed collaboratively, spanning the disciplines of literacy education, communication, and media studies, they have relevance to a wider audience of educators in both formal and informal education settings like libraries, museums, and nonprofit organizations.

But despite a deep commitment to engage in lifelong learning, almost every one of the nearly 800 participants we've taught at the Summer Institute in Digital Literacy could be described as overworked and underpaid. They go above and beyond the call of duty because they choose to be professionals, and they don't always get appropriate levels of support from their institutions in their efforts to continue their learning. That feeling can lead to some dark humor. We appreciate the tweet in Figure 8.3 which circulated widely because it gently captures the occasional frustration that comes from within the professional community as we navigate professional relationships with colleagues and supervisors.

Fake Library Statistics @FakeLibStats · Jan 24
Three in four librarians always agree that the fourth one needs to do it

 4   84   357

Figure 8.3 Overworked and underpaid: Library humor on Twitter.

IT'S ALL ABOUT YOUR MOTIVATION

When we first started using the term *digital literacy* to refer to our collaborative work in professional development with librarians, K–12 teachers and college educators, we began by asking participants to define the term for themselves, asking, "What does digital literacy mean to you?" We understood that digital literacy was an umbrella concept and, as a result, that people define and articulate digital literacy in different ways, depending on their disciplinary background, identity, and experience. Rather than define digital literacy in terms of media formats, skills, processes, or habits of mind, we recognized that the motivations for embracing the term *digital literacy* may be a more important metric for appreciating how educators understood the value of the term.

The concept of motivation situates human action in relation to lived experience and social context.[12] Teachers' motivations for digital learning have a strong influence on their actual use of digital media and technology because teachers decide whether, what, and how technology gets used in classrooms.[13] Research has shown that when teachers are motivated, they make greater use of digital tools and technologies in their classrooms.[14]

But this work, valuable as it is, omits consideration of the complex love-hate relationship that educators have in responding to digital media and culture. As we learned in Chapter 4, some elementary teachers and school librarians may see movies, media, YouTube, and popular culture as interfering with early childhood development. Some high school teachers may see cell phones as a significant distraction from learning; these teachers are concerned about the negative consequences of digital media and technology, and they may be well justified in having a protectionist orientation. Some elementary teachers see digital media as advantageous to student cognitive and emotional development, and some high school teachers embrace the use of remix practices that allow students to use popular culture alongside academic content. Such teachers use evidence from their own experience that justifies an empowerment perspective on digital media for learning.

Teacher motivations for digital literacy can be measured. Renee and her colleagues developed a survey instrument to assess teacher motivations for digital learning and identified 12 motivations that were developed from theories of empowerment and protection in relation to six key theoretical frames, including attitudes toward technology tools; genres and formats; message content and quality; community connectedness; texts and audiences; media systems; and learner-centered focus.[15]

Each of the authors of this book has a slightly different set of motivations for her interest in digital media literacy. Among the 12 motivations for digital literacy, Liz might be identified as a Spirit Guide because her interest in digital learning is rooted in a focus on student learning with sensitivity to the socio-emotional dimensions of student engagement. Renee might be identified as a Demystifier because, when it comes to digital learning, she focuses on helping learners generate and address "how" and "why" questions that examine the constructed nature of media messages. Pam might be identified as an Activist because of her enduring passion for fostering democratic participation through social action and interest in student voice as a catalyst for improving their communities and the wider world.

By respecting the differing motivations of librarians and teachers, we can approach professional development in a more open-hearted way. When professional development learning experiences in digital literacy invite participants to reflect on their motivations, it becomes easier to build learning experiences that expand upon the strengths of teachers' beliefs and the conceptual themes of most importance to them. Respect for diverse teacher motivations is key.

Digital Tools for Graduate Students

We think every graduate student should be familiar with these key resources for digital learning:

Mendeley. Owned by Elsevier, this free reference manager and academic social network can help you organize your research, collaborate with others online, and discover the latest research.

Screencast-o-Matic. Although they are ideal for creating short tutorials, screencasts also enable learners to demonstrate critical thinking skills and showcase creative expression.

Padlet. Easy-to-use online platform enables the creation of a customizable digital bulletin board where users can post and share images, video, text, and more.

Kami for Chrome. View and annotate PDF documents, see the annotations of your class peers, and store documents on your Google Drive.

Twitter. Use a course hashtag to participate in a knowledge community and discover the power of peer-to-world learning.

Graduate Education

In Film and Media Literacy Education

This book has been about the theory and practice of film and media education with particular attention to its application in school, academic, and public libraries. The book developed from an opportunity that Renee had to teach a special topics class called Library/Film/Education in Libraries (LSC 597) at the University of Rhode

Island's Graduate School of Library and Information Studies. Working with graduate students, she designed the class as a fully online learning experience with an optional weekly synchronous video conference meeting at a time convenient for most participants.

The course explored the potential of film and moving image media in the context of school, public, and academic libraries, with a special focus on the needs of children and teens. When Hobbs served as the founding director for the Harrington School of Communication and Media, she had imagined the creation of a school-wide learning community that would transcend disciplinary boundaries. Interdisciplinary graduate courses and academic programs were one part of that vision.

Of course, Renee wanted to provide graduate students with opportunities to develop digital skills for expression and communication, including creating infographics using tools like Infogr.am, using screencasting tools like Screencast-o-Matic, video annotation tools like Video ANT, asynchronous video dialogue tools like Flipgrid, digital bulletin boards like Padlet, and PDF annotation tools like Kami. She knew that most of her students were seeking careers in school librarianship, children's librarianship, or young adult services. Having a portfolio of work that demonstrates digital skills could be useful to them on the job market.

Through regular use of the course hashtag, #libraryfilmed, students were encouraged to continue the dialogue during the semester by sharing information resources they found independently, engaging in interactions with others interested in film and media education in libraries, and exploring the educational value and marketing potential of Twitter.

With a service-learning component baked into the design, the course was designed to advance the capacities of library and information professionals to develop innovative programs, services, materials, and collections to meet the needs of children, young people, and families. The course used a form of experiential learning involving an intense 12-week partnership with the Providence Children's Film Festival. The festival takes place in February at several venues within walking distance of downtown Providence, with 8 full days of screenings, filmmaking workshops, and free activities, along with postfilm conversations that help deepen the film-watching experience and foster critical thinking skills.

Course assignments included activities that required future librarians to reflect on the role of film and media in their lives; observe and review a film screening or media education program hosted by a local film festival; and plan, implement, and assess an original film program working collaboratively with a school and library partner.[16]

MOVIES AND MEMORIES

In one assignment entitled "Movies That Made a Difference in My Life," students composed a short memoir that takes readers back to consider some movies, videos, or television shows that shaped their childhood or young adult years. By using an authentic personal voice along with rich descriptive writing, students considered why a particular work was meaningful and how it may have affected personal and social identity. One student described *Airplane*, the 1980 comedy parody film directed by David Zucker, as a particular favorite, noticing that its cynical, irreverent take on life and its dry humor reflect an aspect of his personal identity. Another student described her love for *The Princess Bride*, the 1987 romantic comedy directed by Rob Reiner, which appealed to her for its combination of traditional fairy tale elements with surprises like "rodents of unusual size." But it wasn't just the film that made a difference in her life—it was the viewing context that is intimately associated with family and loved ones that made it so memorable. Watching it with her family members, eating popcorn in bed, and eventually being able to quote the lines verbatim as a form of social play made it all the more special.

Sometimes reflection on memories of media in childhood offers special insight on the nature of childhood. Jordanna Packtor wrote about *Labyrinth*, the 1986 adventure musical directed by Jim Henson and starring David Bowie, describing the intense feelings of identification with the main character where she recognized the self she wanted to be. She captures a sense of the wonder and mystery of how movies affect childhood when she writes:

Memory reproduces even the most mundane experiences on a mythic scale. Except they weren't mundane. Like the rain, those films transformed our bright, loud world into something duskier. Something magic. When those movies were on, anything seemed possible. We were more than kids, we were wizards. Lost boys. Heroes. And we knew we could be those things, because the hero was never who you expected. Sometimes it was a hobbit or a businessman or a Nelwyn. Sometimes, it was four siblings. Why couldn't it be us?

That was the feeling that pervaded my house at movie time and that's what made it so special. Most of the day, we were just us—sweaty-limbed and living on top of each other, going to school, playing games, getting yelled at, riding our bikes, fighting, laughing, crying. Nothing special. Just a girl and three boys.

But with the right movie in the right season at the right moment— anything seemed possible. Why couldn't we fall through a wardrobe and end up in Narnia? Why couldn't it be summer and raining? Why couldn't it be the four of us, always the four of us, still sitting in that small room somewhere, breathing in that soil smell? Why couldn't there be magic? Why couldn't the heroes be us?

By tapping into these memories, Packtor's writing reminds us of the sense of possibility that is embedded in childhood and how it can be activated through exposure to all forms of media—books, movies, TV shows, and more. For librarians of all ages, reflection and memoir can provide a valuable means to enlarge our empathy with patrons across the lifespan.

OBSERVE AND ANALYZE A FILM PROGRAM

The opportunity to observe and analyze a film program was another vital component of the graduate course. Students were required to attend one event hosted by the Providence Children's Film Festival and write a report about the program that describes and analyzes it, including a film review and a description of the program elements, including the setting, the marketing, format and structure of the program, and the behavior and reactions of the participants. This assignment asked students to apply concepts from the course readings and demonstrate the ability to handle data or evidence of program effectiveness, including head count, informal interviews, and observations.

Observations are powerful learning experiences when they include writing or other forms of reflection. Pam observed a film screening of *Let's Get the Rhythm*, a documentary by Irene Chagall that explores the universality of girls' hand-clapping games. The event was held at the Wanskuck Library, a branch of the Providence Community Library system in the North End of the city. There were 45 participants, most being children of color, along with the film festival staff, librarians, and volunteers. The film was screened in the downstairs activity room with folding chairs set up horseshoe-style in front of the screen, with popcorn in brown paper bags available at the back of the room. Children watched the film, but there was also quite of bit of horsing around. Being surrounded by friends and peers after a day at school *plus* popcorn could disrupt the expectation to sit quietly through a documentary film. Pam observed that the children were, for the most part, engaged during the first half of the film, but 53 minutes of a documentary is a mighty long slog for children aged 8–13. Eventually, some started getting up and going in search of more popcorn or leaving the room to go to the bathroom, or perhaps they moved to another part of the library. Most returned, but movement and activity for about a quarter of the children participants was common in the second half of the screening.

In her analysis of the event, Pam wished that the program would have acknowledged children's short attention spans and incorporated play with some of the hand-clapping games depicted in the film at the film's halfway point. Did the whole film need to be screened? she wondered. Could there be additional resources available at a resource table on the topic of "games from around the world"?

CREATE, IMPLEMENT, AND ASSESS A LIBRARY PROGRAM

People learn best when they create. The opportunity to create a library film/media program in a local community or school library was another vital component of the graduate course. During the semester, students developed a working relationship with both a class partner and a library partner from a local school or public library. They created a library film program that meets the needs of a particular target audience, using an online project management platform to develop all aspects of the planning, execution, and assessment of the project. In their final project, learners documented their completed library film programs and produced a final report that describes, analyzes, and reflects upon the program and the experiential learning experience. Learners produced both a print report and a 5-minute PechaKucha-style screencast.

There's no substitute for learning by doing. Bill Lancellota, a librarian at Westerly Public Library, participated in a webinar offered by the Media Education Lab on film distribution and exhibition in public libraries, where librarians were encouraged to go directly to the filmmakers themselves as they plan their programs. In reflecting on his learning experience, he described how film programs bring people together so that they can engage in new ideas, think critically about what makes an interesting film, and get the kids to stop just "hanging out" and begin to "mess around" with filmmaking. "Filmmakers can be very cooperative as they may look favorably on a chance to get their film shown," Bill wrote. "I actually did this when I contacted the makers of one of the films for my program, *Much Better Now* (a short animation directed by Philipp Comarella and Simon Griesser) and they not only provided us with a high resolution copy of their film, but sent us a bunch of promotional material as well." He explained, "We want the kids who come to the event to discover something new; a new idea, a new talent, or a new way of looking at things."

Film study guides and other types of resources can provide a valuable support for librarians and educators as they engage in innovative practices in schools and libraries. In reflecting upon the learning experience, Emily Ziemba, who works in a school library, noted that she has a newfound appreciation for the value of practical film guides that help promote active discussion. She realized how much students value the opportunity to find and select video resources in the same way they select from print sources. In her reflection essay, she wrote, "It doesn't just have to just be books! My school has a subscription to Discovery Education where I taught them how to find videos that would help them learn about their topic." Emily was thrilled when a student who wrote about Eva Peron used a clip from *Evita*, the 1996 musical created by Tim Rice and Andrew Lloyd Webber. She explained that another student did a report about Latin American music and included snippets of Jennifer Lopez portraying Tejano music star Selena in the musical drama directed by Gregory Nava. "It kills me to think she could have done this project and written a research paper without ever actually listening to the music! These theatrical elements added so much to their projects."

Five Things I Learned This Week in LSC 597—A (Not Too) Statistical Listicle

by Bill Lancellotta

Assignment: Provide a summary of the course readings in the format of a listicle.

1. **One year or more of work could be required in order to launch your shiny new program.** The American Library Association's article on planning a community-wide read provides a timetable that starts over a year before the new program is initiated. Setting goals and a timeline, building a budget, developing partnerships, developing the program, and figuring out the marketing are all tasks that need to be accomplished before the event even starts.
2. **Two out of two legendary filmmakers recommend *The Story of Movies* for students who watch film.** Listen to Clint Eastwood and Martin Scorsese. They kind of know what they are talking about. The program they are supporting, *The Story of Movies*, is a curriculum that is free for middle schools. It provides in-depth lesson plans on three classic films, all three of which have child characters that the target audiences can relate to.
3. **Three modes of participation reveal the different ways kids interact with and learn from media.** It is better to get kids actively engaged in activities. Getting kids to "mess around" instead of "hang out" is the goal of the programs detailed in Shoemaker, Martin, and Joseph's article (2010). This confirmed something I have long suspected—that teens learn better when they are actively involved in doing, instead of just observing. If we can only find a way to get teens to the third stage and get them to "geek out" over education.
4. **Four films that are thematically linked can be a powerful learning experience.** *The Film in the Classroom: A Guide for Teachers* resource contains a great deal of information about film and relates it back to specific *Masterpiece Theatre* productions. It covers various topics like film basics, adaptations, screenwriting, and literary elements.
5. **Five minutes on *Pinterest* is all it takes to find a ton of great marketing ideas.** There is no shortage of ideas when it comes to marketing for libraries. I especially loved the prescription chocolate bars with the RX label affixed and containing the message "Take 1 and call a librarian," followed by the St. Francis College Library contact information. Genius.

The Evolution of Information Literacy

Information literacy competencies are compatible with the use of film and media for learning purposes. We are thrilled to see how information literacy is now broadening in scope to include ideas about visual and mass media as well as digital culture.

A brief review of the history of the term can elucidate and help illustrate its potential future in this regard. In the 1970s, the term *information literacy* was first used to emphasize the need to expand access to information tools to the entire population. At that time, a person who is information literate can "find what is known or knowable on any subject" to solve a problem within the vast amount of information available.

With the rise of relational databases, new competencies were needed to search and find information using these technologies. Back in the 1980s, for example, Renee fondly remembers the academic librarian at Babson College, where she was a young assistant professor, who showed her the power of searching databases to retrieve scholarly articles and other information. This was unlike anything she had experienced in graduate school at Harvard University and, to her, it was simply magical! Today, many senior scholars can barely remember the browsing, consultation of bibliographic lists, and other research processes we used to use when searching an academic library before computerized tools were invented.

When the concept of information literacy was first introduced to the world of education, it caused quite a stir. It was developed by the American Association of School Librarians (AASL) and the Association for Educational Communications and Technology (AECT) and called *Information Power: Guidelines for School Library Media Programs* in 1988, and it was like a thunderbolt in the world of education. Renee remembers meeting with librarians in Washington, DC, during this time as we explored the intersections between information literacy and media literacy. It was an exciting time to be considering how the concept of literacy was expanding to include new forms of communication and expression, even at a time when traditional conceptualizations of print literacy, rooted in a focus on literature, were normative. There were many parallels between media literacy and information literacy in their active approach to promoting the competencies needed for contemporary life.

When computers were first introduced into schools, the computer labs were located in the library and school librarians maintained them. Renee's mother, Rosemarie Shilcusky, a teacher and librarian, was one of these pioneers. Working in a parochial school in suburban Detroit in the 1980s, she learned how to program in Basic and constructed simple educational games for children to learn computer skills. During the 1990s, school librarians were expected to work cooperatively with teachers and administrators to ensure that these information skills were integrated into the school curriculum. When *Information Power* was revised in the 1990s, it shifted the focus to emphasize students as lifelong learners.[17]

Sadly, by the early 2000s, the pace of change had ramped up and school librarians in many communities were simply not able to bring the appropriate knowledge and skills to the practice of integrating technology into the curriculum. Gradually, a new specialist role emerged in the K–12 and university worlds—that of the instructional technology specialist. This was not a technical manager of the school's computing and Internet services but a person who worked directly with educators and students to use digital media for learning purposes.

When these new jobs were created, it resulted in some turf wars. Librarians and technology specialists experienced role confusion. For example, in one study of school librarians' role in technology integration in their schools, some librarians were found to have a competitive relationship with the instructional technology specialist. This tension was most often mentioned as a barrier preventing the school librarian from participating in a leadership role in instructional technology integration.[18] Renee participated in many professional development programs in Pennsylvania that brought together librarians and educational technology support professionals during the 2000s to promote mutual respect and develop skills of knowledge sharing and collaboration. Gradually, the tension between librarians and educational technology staff subsided, and in many communities, a genuine spirit of collaboration eventually emerged.

Today, the vision for the library as the heart of the school is still alive. In the AASL National School Library Standards, released in 2017, school librarians acknowledge an "environment in which learners and educators have unprecedented access to teaching and learning opportunities," and value the provision of resources and instruction to all learners through "an inquiry-based research model that supports questioning and the creation of new knowledge focused on learners' interests and real-world problems." To accomplish this, school librarians need to "embrace, lead, and model progressive pedagogies, including co-teaching, personalized learning, and face-to-face and virtual active learning environments." They need to build "virtual collections, encourage active collaborative learning, and create spaces and learning structures within flexible library spaces."[19]

Some Challenges

LIBRARIANS AND THEIR LIBGUIDES

As outsiders to the field, there are still many peculiarities in library land that mystify us. However you look at it, librarians love their LibGuides. These were developed in 2007 as a digital version of the Pathfinder, which was an innovative approach to library research in the 1970s where students learned to "find a path" using the resources of their academic library and the conventions of scholarly communication. Designed for the earliest phases of the research process, Pathfinders were uniform in arrangement and content and limited to a single sheet. In the 1990s, librarians placed their Pathfinder documents online, but librarians' lack of web skills was an impediment to the cultivation of effective, focused, up-to-date guides, especially in ensuring that hyperlinks were continually updated.

LibGuides, which is a fee-based subscription platform, enable librarians to produce guides quickly for specific audiences, courses, and assignments, thus potentially better targeting the needs of users. But some scholars have suggested that LibGuides are in fact now too easy to create.[20] Renee has observed that some librarians use LibGuides to publish online content (say, for example, to announce a conference or promote an event) even when the most appropriate format for these particular communication goals would be a website, a social media post, or even a digital flyer or newsletter. Why would librarians use a LibGuide for promoting a conference? It's possible that the LibGuide platform may be the only online publishing platform that some librarians are familiar with.

Although many librarians are enthusiastic about them, even after 10 years, there is scant empirical evidence on the value of LibGuides for learners. We have seen some LibGuides demonstrate how experts struggle with the "curse of knowledge," as their content shows a lack of sensitivity to how beginners in a discipline gain entry to a knowledge community. In analyzing the behavior of LibGuide creators, researchers found most librarians were unaware of how (or whether) the guides they created were being used. Some scholars have found that nonuniversity users are the most frequent patrons of LibGuides, not members of the university community. To better understand how university users of LibGuides found the resources, researchers analyzed the search terms entered into the search interface that resulted in accessing university LibGuide. Most users find LibGuides through Google by searching for the course number along with the university name. One third of all searches also referenced the name of a particular librarian, suggesting that students had previously learned about the LibGuide.[21] To support student use of film and media resources, the search process for finding such resources could be easier.

Of course, sometimes LibGuides is the perfect tool for the job. We have seen LibGuides used quite well. At Georgetown University Library, Melissa Jones has created a LibGuide with undergraduate students in mind. The homepage reads: "Help me to:

- Find scholarly books and articles
- Find background information
- Find industry data and ratings
- Watch streaming video
- Find films and media
- Use citation tools

These are indeed the core needs of most undergraduate students who are studying film and media. When you click on "find films and media," you access a search bar to search for streaming media, DVD, CD, or other media formats. You can also browse by genre and language. We have every expectation that libraries will continue to invent web-based tools and resources—including and moving beyond the LibGuide—to help people gain competencies in finding and curating meaningful audiovisual content.

The Past Is Prologue

Through learning and experience, people can come to love the artifacts of the past. We hope your curiosity was engaged when reading Chapter 7 about the history of film and media education in libraries. Learning about the past is a lifelong process, and Pam and Renee have found that it seems to grow in importance as you get older.

Young people also need exposure to historical artifacts as part of their education in order to appreciate the value of learning from the past. For example, when 5-year-old Lewis was visiting Rhode Island with his mother, Hongyan Lu, who was a visiting scholar from Ningxia, China, they attended a public screening of *Singing in the Rain*, the 1952 musical starring and directed by Gene Kelly. The film captivated the imagination of young Lewis. For weeks after the screening, he could be found dancing and singing around the house, copying some of the dance moves performed in that great film. It's likely to be a happy part of his childhood memories as he grows up.

Renee remembers that, when her children were small, she consciously exposed them to films from previous generations. They even went to movie screenings where silent films were screened with a soundtrack performed by a professional organist. With her children, she discussed why these films were in black and white, and why they seemed different than modern films. Regular screening of old movies helped her children appreciate these gems as they were growing up. Renee's daughter Rachel was perhaps the only child of her time who loved *A Funny Thing Happened on the Way to the Forum* and her son Roger was enamored of Orson Welles's classic *Citizen Kane*. We are delighted that Common Sense Media has developed a list of "50 Movies All Kids Should Watch Before They are 12" that includes the 1936 film *Modern Times* by Charlie Chaplin and the 1946 classics *It's a Wonderful Life* and *Miracle on 34th Street*.[22] Librarians can support this type of intergenerational learning through the design and implementation of creative film screening programs.

Even those of us who dislike or shy away from older films respect the idea that film and media are a key part of cultural heritage that needs to be preserved and protected. Film and media preservation doesn't often get much media attention, but the rise of the Internet and digital culture has increased people's awareness of the potential recovery and/or loss of history that is underway with the transition to digital culture. In our present-focused society, with the baby boomers now in their golden years, there's a potential audience for old films and television programs. But it's far from clear yet whether media corporations will make old movies available to consumers on digital streaming platforms. Only two years after its launch, both FilmStruck and Warner Instant Movies were canceled by WarnerMedia, which was officially acquired by AT&T in 2018. These digital streaming services made old films available to consumers.[23]

To understand the challenges of film and media preservation today, it's important to distinguish between archives that preserve original films, and libraries, which make digital copies available for distribution and use. Film and media companies recognize the financial value of protecting their film archives for future audiences. For example, in the 1980s, Paramount spent over $35 million in preserving film materials. In 1990, it opened a new $11 million archives building, with environmentally controlled vaults for preprint and color materials.

Attention to the viewing, archiving, and preservation of digital and visual media resources in LIS education is not a new thing. For librarians and information professionals who are interested in film and media, a focus on preservation management, conservation, and archiving is an important specialization. It's an inherently multidisciplinary field, which includes a focus on the history of moving images, along with concepts from science and engineering to understand the technical processes of how media are created, deteriorate, and can be restored. At New York University's graduate program in Moving Image Archiving and Preservation, librarians learn to cope with both the transition of older materials to digital formats, and to ensure that materials being created today can be retrieved 100 years from now. At UCLA, a specialization in Media Archival Studies enables students to develop competencies in collection development, appraisal, preservation, and restoration of media collections and materials. Since only 20% of the films made in the 1920s and 50% of all feature films made before 1950 have been preserved, media archivists have significant work ahead of them.

It's an open question: Will commercially available streaming services help or hinder the process of preservation? Back in the VHS era, film studios found it profitable to make available their backlist of films from the past. With them, they could stock the shelves of Blockbuster stores with all sorts of titles from previous decades. But today, in the streaming era, audiences are not provided with the same level of access to works from the past. For example, Netflix offers more than 4,700 titles available for streaming, but only 19 were released before 1950.[24] Some film scholars believe that mass-market streaming, with its focus on present-day fare, is contributing to declining interest in classic films. This is an issue for concern. Without an audience for older works, there will be little motivation to invest in preservation. On the other hand, it's possible that digital storage and streaming will increase the likelihood of old films finding their loyal audiences.

Here's where film and media education in libraries may come in. When school, public, and academic libraries include old films and television shows as part of film screening and discussion events, they raise the visibility and the value of film and television as part of cultural heritage. As streaming makes home viewing the norm for most people, public events that tap into people's specialized interests can help to build a sense of community within and across communities. For these reasons, we think more attention to archival and classic films should be part of every film program in school, public and academic libraries.

Film screenings of old films and programs that showcase film history can increase public awareness of the value of preservation efforts like the Section 108 Due Diligence Project. So can new forms of media education that are designed to reach adult learners outside of a formal educational context. When film professor Peter DeCherney created a self-paced massive open online course (MOOC), "Hollywood: History, Institution, Art," he wanted adult learners to understand the upheaval and redefinition that are part and parcel of the history of Hollywood, as Figure 8.4 shows. He wanted to reach adult learners with interests in film and create a dialogue between the history of film and the contemporary issues facing the industry today. In the MOOC, he features the Lansdowne Theater, a historic cinema in Delaware County, Pennsylvania built in 1927 with a 1,400 seat auditorium, as the location where some of the videos shot for his course were filmed.

DeCherney's MOOC course would not have been possible if not for his active leadership role in helping clarify and expand copyright exemptions, which enables people to quote from classic films and to use the copyrighted material that he transforms and repurposes in his online course for adult learners. DeCherney's copyright activism embodies his innovative work as both a historian and as a media literacy educator.

We can make better sense of the present and future of film and media if we understand its past. The Internet has challenged the one-to-many broadcast model that has defined film spectatorship over the past 100 years by enabling anyone to create media. But when film first began, it was particular and local, building upon the tradition of community theater and vaudeville. For example, Siegmund Lubin invented motion picture cameras and processing equipment, 15 years before D. W.

Hollywood: History, Industry, Art

Explore the history of Hollywood, from Edison and the birth of film to the rise of the internet.

Figure 8.4 A free, film history MOOC (massive open online course) by Peter DeCherney.

Griffith shot a movie in Hollywood. Lubin began to shoot movies in Philadelphia in 1898, opening movie theaters in 20 cities and shipping his films to exhibitors around the world. He even built a 350-acre campus for making films, complete with a western village that served as a set. Betzwood employed 700 people, including costume makers, film developers, technical staff, publicity staff, shippers, kitchen workers, and dining room help.[25] Thanks to Lawrence Greene and the film archivists of Montgomery County Community College, the rich history of Betzwood has been preserved. The Free Library of Philadelphia Rare Book Department archives the business records for the company. Over the decades, however, the film industry became centralized in Hollywood, and East Coast filmmaking was pushed to the margins. Local media makers simply couldn't compete with the big players.

With the rise of the Internet, local historical culture is again making a re-emergence. Libraries are supporting that work of getting local people's stories and media into the library. The Northern Onondaga (New York) Public Library offers the Preservation Studio at Brewerton, where patrons can convert their older analog media into newer formats. Patrons can digitize old photos, convert VHS to DVD, scan slides, and convert film negatives. As more and more viewers create media and post work to YouTube, libraries can offer screenings and public events to give more visibility to local media makers who are producing valuable forms of cultural expression right in our own neighborhoods.

Public awareness of film cultural heritage is important. When asked about his one wish for the future of film and media education in the context of higher education, James Steffen, a film librarian at Emory University wishes that both the public and librarians could fully appreciate the fragility of our film heritage and our need for ongoing efforts at restoration and the need to keep abreast of new restorations. Stefen was a consultant on the digital restoration on the film *The Color of Pomegranates*, a magnificent surrealist film-poem created in 1969 by Soviet film director Sergei Parajanov. Experimental films, home movies, and films from other countries can shake us out of our comfort zone in a way that promotes insight. Renee's own film awakening and her commitment to media literacy first began when she viewed the classic 1929 film *Man with a Movie Camera* by Russian filmmaker Dziga Vertov. Pam was so moved by the US-China coproduction *Shadow Magic* directed by Ann Hu, about the introduction of film to China in early 20th century, she made her entire media literacy graduate class in New York City watch it with her one night. Sometimes films from around the world can awaken your senses and transform your life.

So when we really understand film history, it helps us think more deeply and reflect critically upon the technology of the present time. For all these reasons, preservation of film, media, and digital arts is important and exploration of film and media history is equally important. Librarians bring these two major issues together through programs and services in school, public, and academic libraries.

In *Re-collection: Art, New Media, and Social Memory* by Richard Rinehart and Jon Ippolito, the authors point out that many aspects of the present-day culture will be lost to history without a drastic change in the technologies, institutions, laws, and social norms that now govern cultural preservation. They note, "preservation is a future-oriented and not a past-oriented activity; that preservation is inseparable from presentation; that the heavy lifting may be done by amateurs rather than experts; and that storage as a dominant strategy will give way to migration, emulation, and reinterpretation."[26] This book, with its invitation to librarians, parents, educators, and community leaders, is a small part of that hoped-for transformation.

9

Future

Librarians are going to have to develop a new relationship with film and
media in order to serve patrons' information and knowledge needs.
—Amy Garmer, *Aspen Institute Dialogue on Public Libraries*

Questions Answered in This Chapter

- What role should film and media literacy education play in the future of libraries?
- What benefits are to be expected as librarianship becomes more truly interdisciplinary?
- Are libraries prepared to transform into community media centers to enable film and media education to thrive in their communities?
- How are library spaces transforming to support new ways of viewing and creating media?
- How can YouTube become a more useful resource within school, public, and academic libraries?
- How do librarians come to see patrons as information resources?
- What is the role of design thinking in advancing the future of film and media literacy education in libraries?

Librarians can help youth and adults alike to become critical consumers of the media worlds in which they travel, using film and media resources for both lifelong learning and creative expression. At this point in reading this book, we hope you agree that we have more than proved this point.

Videos, film, and media are too beautiful, too important, and too powerful to be conceptualized as subordinate to the printed word. We wrote this book because we wanted to imagine a future where people actively gather, both face to face and online, to talk about audiovisual media, including the movies, TV shows, apps, videogames, and social media that are now part of our everyday leisure, work, and citizenship. We imagine neighborhoods and cities where, using the power of communication and information, people identify social problems; document them using language, image, sound, and multimedia; and share, discuss, and ultimately collaborate to invent and implement practical, civic solutions. We see both analyzing and creating media as important parts of the process of civic agency and social change. And we see libraries in all venues as an integral part of that picture.

As we experience the challenge of increasing political polarization in our communities, we want to rediscover the joys of our diverse communities by talking about news and TV shows and movies together. Despite our differences, we can laugh, cry, and enjoy media together. There has never been a more important time to step back from the isolated consumer model of viewing and media consumption to discover the power that comes from community-based viewing, dialogue, and discussion. After all, movies and media offer up ideas about what we aspire to, what we value, and what (and who) we fear.

In this book we have shared more than 170 examples from all across the United States to demonstrate the value of harnessing the power of the moving image for learning in the context of school, public, and academic libraries. Film and media education must grow and evolve in order to become a more important part of the future of librarianship. We've demonstrated how dialogue about film and media can help bring a community together and even heal some of the rifts that are developing in an increasingly polarized world. We have offered numerous examples of how school, public, and academic libraries help people find and participate in discourse communities to discover and reflect on issues that matter to them both personally and professionally. As media literacy educators, we respect and celebrate differences in interpretation and meaning-making. We hope that children and young people all around the United States and around the world will someday grow up with routine and regular opportunities using dialogue with and about media to ask critical questions about what we watch, see, and read.

Why does the future matter? The time is now to consider how libraries can better support people's lifelong learning needs with audiovisual media. In considering the future of school, public, and academic libraries, we believe that film and media literacy education programs can strengthen and support the key features that make libraries so important to our culture. Throughout this book, we have shown that as people, platforms, and places, libraries transform communities and provide opportunities for personal growth and civic engagement, using the emotional power of moving image media to connect heads, hearts, and hands.

In this chapter, we conclude by wondering about the future: 10 years from now, will one third of library circulations still consist of movies and media? Will film and media still be treated as a second-class resource? Will film and media literacy education be a bigger part of the library's future or not? In the pages that follow, we discuss these questions with library leaders who offer insight on the issues raised in this book. Then we offer some recommendations that rise to the top of our wish list for the years ahead.

Change Is a Constant

Imagine a future where you can:

> ➤ Contribute to a virtual film discussion group, sharing comments about a film you've just viewed using an app where you can listen to and respond to people from your neighborhood (and all over the world) as they react to and reflect on the film you have both just viewed.
> ➤ Visit the library to offer an opinion about an upcoming public issue or city council meeting, using a simple "Story Corps" style media production booth to make sure that your point of view is shared with local leaders and people in the community.
> ➤ Find creative collaborators to develop a community YouTube channel that features the work of people from all walks of life who are creating videos in your community.

To elevate the place of movies, videos, and media use in the library, we must appreciate the many flavors of film and media literacy pedagogy that prepare people for a lifetime of learning. After the 2014 Digital Youth Think Tank, University of Washington i-School professor Michael Eisenberg explained that too many adults still have a knee-jerk negative reaction to adolescents' use of handheld digital media. This predominant mentality needs to change.[1]

Providing access to audiovisual entertainment and information to all is an idea that matters. It's also an idea that has been around for a long time. But it's not just about access. Opportunities for discussion, dialogue, and evaluation of the quality of audiovisual media have long been understood as valuable, too.

History offers insights here. Back in the 1930s, groups of Midwestern women gathered to evaluate and discuss the quality of radio programming available to children, teens, and adults. The Wisconsin Association for Better Radio Listening compiled lists of radio programs and created booklets on "good listening" dating back to 1935. Jean Pierre Golay, who experienced Nazi propaganda in Switzerland in the 1930s, later became determined to help his students learn "to look around, listen, question, discuss, take time to think." He helped them "experience production" with tape recorders, printers, and various media production tools.[2] The National Telemedia Council in Madison, Wisconsin, led by media literacy educator and leader Marieli Rowe, is an outgrowth of these efforts.[3] In postwar Italy and other European countries, cinema clubs popped up all over, in big cities and tiny villages alike. Italian education professor and media literacy historian Damiano Felini has documented how these clubs encouraged people to talk about relationships, social issues, and community values in relation to the challenges and community pressures of rebuilding Italian society.[4]

The active process of dialogue about movies forces us to make transparent our own values and priorities. When we talk together about film, we inevitably show others how we see the world around us as we react to the film's careful construction of reality and relationships. When we talk about movies and media, we end up talking about ourselves.

In the 1960s, Kit Laybourne and other artists in New York City started the original makerspaces, working in public schools using super 8mm film with children and teens, helping them to create stop-motion animation, narrative storytelling, and documentary films. *The Animation Book*, published originally in 1979, offers ideas about how media-making experiences help to support personal creative development and create community-engaged learners. When we create media, we present our ideas and ourselves in a very public way to others. Both practices—analyzing and creating media—take sensitivity, openness, and courage.

Today, new technologies continue to provide people with access to movies, television shows, and videos. In some public libraries, the GoChip Beam is enabling people to access movies and television shows anytime, anywhere, and on any device—even without Internet connectivity. In 2017, the Fayetteville Public Library pilot-tested a lending program where users could access five movies of a similar genre or a whole season of a television series. Heather Robideaux, manager of adult services at Fayetteville Public Library explained, "Allowing cardholders access to content in new and convenient ways is part of our overall mission."[5] Libraries are also exploring the potential of virtual reality devices, hoping that its potential for learning is not eclipsed by its potential for thrill seeking and escape.[6]

Today, some future librarians are learning to create video as part of their graduate education. To address the complex role of gentrification in Seattle, Matthew Jackson, Domonique Meeks, and Freddy Mora created *Soul of Seattle*, a six-part mini-documentary as part of their Capstone project at the University of Washington. By exploring issues concerning technology, information needs, and cultural preservation, the project enabled students to synthesize ideas from their coursework in the master's program in science in information management. "We wanted to have a medium where people would actually take time to watch," Jackson said. "Nobody would read a 25-page paper, but maybe they will sit down and watch a six-minute video."[7] We would like future librarians at every library school to have such creative opportunities engaging with people in their communities.

Envisioning the Future
BEYOND ACCESS TO ENGAGEMENT

What role can film and media literacy education play in the future of libraries? Amy Garmer, director of the Aspen Institute Dialogue on Public Libraries, has been thinking about the future of libraries as she identified networks of pioneering, outward-facing librarians. That's why we asked for her insight on the role of film and media education in relation to the changing world of public, school, and academic libraries. At the Aspen Institute, Amy spearheaded a multiyear initiative to explore, develop, and champion new ways of thinking about US public libraries and also led the development, publication, and outreach of a white paper series inspired by the Knight Commission on the Information Needs of Communities. In that work, she examined policy designed to foster universal broadband access and adoption, digital and media literacy, local journalism and information hubs, public service media, civic engagement, and government transparency.

Libraries are becoming places where content gets created, not just consumed. Garmer expects that more and more content will be created in and through the library as a platform. She explains, "Much of that created content will be media as we think about that category broadly—video, photos and other forms of images and art, gaming and gamification, digital audio, and hybrids."[8] She notes that it may also include software, apps, and content that is integrated into virtual and augmented reality technologies (especially related to lifelong learning and training), which will be breaking onto the scene over the next 10 years in big ways.

Garmer is aware of how traditional organizations and institutions—long the providers of content and knowledge that are circulated through libraries—have become open to video and other mediated and blended forms of information and have expanded their capacity to create such content. She explains, "It's exciting to observe how new generations of video content producers are exploring the power and potential of video content, new technologies, new techniques, new forms of storytelling, and new curricula for learning—including just-in-time training and learning opportunities." As libraries become places of creation and develop their capacity for curating what is created there, Garmer anticipates there will be more video and media content available to circulate.

Garmer understands that the concept of circulation is changing today. As more content is created, consumed, and shared in digital formats, the concept of circulation is nearly synonymous with sharing and use. She asks, "Does circulation mean only the library's holdings, or does it include digital media accessed through shared databases, networks, and cloud computing that the library subscribes to, such as the Digital Public Library of America?" Garmer believes that the concept of circulation will evolve to become less dependent on "pull"—that is, the users or patrons determining what they need or want to access and use. She sees much potential for "push" aspects to circulation, where the library itself serves up information, materials, or content and initiates the circulation. Film and media can be very good at this because of the way that moving-image media engages the emotions and inspires action.

When we asked Amy Garmer, "Ten years from now, will librarians still treat film and media as a second-class resource, with print books getting the lion's share of attention?" she admitted that 10 years is not a very long time for the kind of cultural shift that will be required for film and media to rise to equal status among all librarians and libraries. After all, she noted, placing a premium value on the written word has been in place for a long time, given its foundational role in literacy and knowledge.

The value of the written word exists in relation to librarians' more ambivalent anxieties and concerns about the potential limitations, liabilities, risks, and harms of mass media, popular culture, and digital media. Changes in digital media and technology are not likely to disrupt the dialectic of empowerment and protection. In fact, they are likely to perpetuate it. However, with generational change both within the profession *and* among patrons, attitudes about the value of film and media relative to books as a resource are coming closer to parity, she believes.

In order for film and media education to become a more important part of the library's future, Amy Garmer sees the need for librarians to be willing to go beyond merely providing access to film and media content and resources. As John Szabo, city librarian of the Los Angeles Public Library put it, "We are a learning institution, not just an access institution." There, they offer many film and media education programs, like the 2017 lecture featuring Mindy Johnson, about the often-overlooked women animators at the Walt Disney Studios, which was sponsored by the library's Photo Collection. These events, videotaped by Russell Pyle, are part of a series called *LA in Focus*. Pyle uses the Vimeo platform so that people all over the world can benefit from the learning experience hosted at the public library.[9]

If film and media education became more important and more valued to school, public, and academic librarians, Garmer sees that it could lead to an even more integrated and interdisciplinary approach to learning, knowledge, and literacy. She explains, "Media is a thread connecting so many different areas that film and media literacy education could cultivate more thinking outside of silos. Film and media are a natural playground for people from many diverse subgroups to be able to tell and share their stories. I think if film and media education were more valued in these library settings, it would lead to greater engagement of libraries and librarians with subgroups they may not engage with or know as much about—people of color, immigrants, LGBTQ, youth, disabled, and many other populations and people, as groups and individuals."

Imagine that: The inclusion of film and media literacy education practices in libraries could make libraries and librarianship seem more relevant to people's lives, thus attracting more diverse people into the profession!

But Garmer also recognizes some potential risks, especially in the hyperpartisan society that we're living in now. "Because film and media can involve very passionate and emotional appeals and messaging," she explained, "this would undoubtedly increase the number of difficult conversations librarians would be involved in." When people's emotions are stoked by manipulative propaganda, for example, they may not listen well to opinions that contradict their existing beliefs. Still, Amy Garmer is optimistic, noting that there is a learning curve to address, particularly in and around educational institutions that are dealing with pitched battles from left and right and all around, so this could be turned into an opportunity for educating and engaging stakeholders.

BUILDING BRIDGES BETWEEN LIBRARY, MEDIA, AND COMMUNITY

Are libraries prepared to transform into community media centers to enable film and media education to thrive in their communities? Colin Rhinesmith is an assistant professor in the School of Library and Information Science at Simmons College and a faculty associate with the Berkman Klein Center for Internet & Society at Harvard University. Colin studies policy aspects of information and communication technology, particularly in areas related to digital equity and community technology. His deep understanding of local access television, which has been under attack in the transition from cable to broadband access, has given him a unique perspective on localism and self-determination in relation to community media centers.

As Rhinesmith sees it, "The shift from collections to people opens up possibilities for media education in libraries. As libraries shift to become community media centers, some people will rely on communicating the value of these new services in relation to workforce development and the economic opportunities that are provided through the development of digital literacy competencies. Others will value the importance of providing services that support creativity and self-expression or civic engagement."

Now Colin Rhinesmith is teaching the next generation of librarians and information professionals, helping them deepen their awareness of the habits of mind and competencies of people in community-building roles. He sees the shift toward librarians providing more services as a community media center as a way to foster digital inclusion and promote sustainable broadband adoption community-wide, helping connect civic organizations and local residents. There's tremendous power in the work of outward-facing librarians who support film and media education through partnerships and collaborations that take advantage of easy access to digital media texts, tools, and technologies.

STRATEGIC RENEWAL INCLUDES FOCUS ON LIBRARIANS AS LEARNERS

How will librarians advance their own skills and knowledge to embrace the opportunity to bring film and media education to their patrons? Jason Kucsma is among the most progressive library leaders we know. As the deputy director of the Toledo Lucas County Public Library system, Kucsma is now leading this metropolitan library system through a process of strategic renewal. As the former executive director of the Metropolitan New York Library Council (METRO), he managed a team of informational professionals in the service of more than 250 libraries and helped start Empire State Digital Network, the state's conduit to the Digital Public Library of America. And Kucsma knows a lot about the power of media to enhance community development. As one of the founders of the Allied Media Conference, Jason advanced the concept of do-it-yourself media as a means to bring together people with interests in using participatory media as a strategy for social justice organizing.

Jason Kucsma appreciates the value of professional development for his staff. He supported children's librarians participation in the digital media literacy training offered at five Ohio locations in 2018. The program helps librarians assist parents and caregivers as they navigate the digital world and guide families toward digital media experiences that promote positive and productive lifelong learning skills. Developed in response to the Association for Library Service to Children (ALSC) white paper titled "Media Mentorship in Libraries Serving Youth," librarians learn how to use technology effectively during storytime and gain knowledge about a number of trusted sources used for making technology and interactive media recommendations.[10]

Although librarians are under no contractual obligation to receive professional development, the community embraces information sharing and learning. Kucsma explains, "Lifelong learning for librarians is a choice; it's not something they are obligated to do. But we have a cultural expectation that staff continue to actively learn throughout their careers." Jason describes how they worked with Mozilla to roll out web literacy training to all library staff, not just the librarians. They've ensured that all 20 Toledo branch libraries offer book scan stations to convert photo prints to digital copies that enable people to create digital collages or slideshows. Some branches provide patrons with access to VHS to DVD conversion equipment and even access to convert film negatives and slides to digital files. As they renovate the historic Toledo main library, they'll use 35,000 square feet of space to increase access to technology and audiovisual resources. Jason Kucsma explains, "As we move to increasing access to streaming media, we are blurring the line between makerspace, teen center, and media center."

Of course, there's risk in the vision we've outlined in this book, and Jason recognizes it. Engaging with film and media education more deeply requires getting out of one's comfort zone. When describing the increased need for librarian skill sets to evolve to meet changing needs, Kucsma notes, "We need to think carefully about where are we leveraging community expertise versus what do we need to learn ourselves." As a learning organization, it's all about getting fluency and not expecting people to be experts all at once. The librarians entering the field today who expect to spend a lifetime learning have inspired him. When it comes to digital and media technologies, "they're confident that they can learn—and that's the spirit we need," Kucsma said.

Forward to Innovation

We thus imagine the future by briefly considering three ideas that are ripe for expansion and that help advance our vision of film and media education in libraries:

- Supporting spaces for experiential learning, including viewing, discussion, and media making, in school, public, and academic libraries
- Welcoming YouTubers into the library to support the lifelong learning needs of patrons, including librarians, who must themselves become effective critics and media makers as they develop skill sets to meet the needs of patrons
- Promoting reflection and vision in library leadership in advancing film and media education in school, public, and academic libraries

SUPPORTING SPACES FOR EXPERIENTIAL LEARNING

Libraries that cultivate community and film viewing and media making embody the practice of community building. Programs and happenings and events, held in school, public, and academic libraries, help bring people together for shared learning experiences. They reshape people's expectations about what a library can be. Programs, events, and services, when they are continually experimental and experiential, enable librarians to continually respond to the changing needs of patrons and users.

One way librarians are preparing to become places of convening is in the design of flexible library spaces that can support a range of programs and experiences. As they experiment with supporting viewing and discussion through both face-to-face and online discussion experiences, librarians better understand how spaces can support this practice.

As they develop programs that empower patrons as media makers, the development of community media arts center spaces can be a natural extension of the services provided. We are delighted to find that community spaces for gatherings and discussions are increasingly recognized as key features for libraries. For example, when The New York Public Library closed the historic Donnell Library on West 53rd Street in 2008, people lost their neighborhood library. The new space would be only one third the size of the former, occupying the lower three floors of a new high-rise hotel. Originally slated for completion in 2013, but pushed off repeatedly due to a bad economy and deals that fell through, the "new Donnell" did not open its doors until 2016.

Community spaces and gathering areas factored heavily into the new library design, while some collections would be redistributed to be housed at other branches.[11] A prominent feature of the new library is an open area between levels with wide bleacher steps that double as the seating of an amphitheater. In a 2013 article, architect Enrique Norten commented on the library space, saying, "It has become more like a cultural space, which is about gathering people, giving people the opportunity to encounter each other. It's not really about just being a repository of books."[12]

Academic librarians are also reconfiguring their space to showcase the audio-visual works of students and faculty. For example, digital media librarian Jason Evans Groth describes an initiative that enables students to create multimedia installations for the iPearl Immersion Theater and other spaces at the North Carolina State University (NCSU) Hunt Library. There, students and faculty have access to tools to grow their digital media literacy competencies and share their work with larger audiences. For example, Groth guided students as they created "Shooting Wars: Documentary Images of American Military Conflicts," a provocative multiscreen, multimedia, and interactive exhibition presented on a gigantic display in the Hunt Library's GameLab.

Developed in collaboration with Professor Marsha Gordon and students enrolled in a course entitled War Documentaries, the multimedia exhibit explores select American conflicts through the eyes and camera lenses of documentary filmmakers. Students produced short video projects on topics including the Vietnam War, the Korean conflict, the Cold War, and the War on Terror. Working collaboratively with Groth, this project led the professor to rethink how she taught film studies. She now appreciates the importance of having a more nuanced appreciation of the complex relationship between media analysis and production as pedagogical strategies that support student learning. Says Groth, "What happened as a result of this project was five graduate students and a professor—instead of writing five papers that one professor would potentially only ever be the audience for—created an ambitious multimedia interactive project that was shown publicly for almost a week to over 150 viewers."[13]

But space is not a requirement for such powerful learning to take place. Today, it's easy for students to share what they are learning using online video tools. At the Bay Shore Middle School, school librarian Kristina Holzweiss used Flipgrid to help children describe their independent learning during Genius Hour. It's a term sometimes used to describe efforts that allow students to explore their own passions and intellectual curiosity in the classroom. Students have choice to determine what they learn during a set period of time during school. They document their learning by creating some form of media using print or digital tools available from home and school. Getting a chance to pursue one's intellectual curiosity turns out to be the best way to ignite the engines of a lifelong learner.

PLAY AND LEARNING WITH YOUTUBE

"Learning how to learn" is the heart of true empowerment, and yet there are vast differences between those who are self-motivated, trial-and-error explorers and those who don't have well-developed habits of mind to support a lifetime of learning. YouTube offers a wealth of practical knowledge, shared by ordinary people who offer step-by-step procedural instructions that may affect learning, transfer, and performance. You can learn to frost a cake or chop garlic by watching a YouTube video, and you can also learn complicated coding and programming skills this way, too. You can gain knowledge of sophisticated engineering concepts or get an orientation to learning to read classical Greek. As researchers have explained, "The popularity of YouTube hinges on its ability to create a social and digital community of individuals interested in a specialized topic and expertise."[14] Sadly, many librarians and patrons may not recognize the educational value of YouTube, since it is conventionally understood as a medium for entertainment, rather than an educational tool.

Librarians could help fix that misunderstanding. If librarians used YouTube for learning purposes, they might be able to create a robust learning community where patrons, librarians, and staff describe how they share ideas, discover content, and achieve specific learning goals. Videos that document the intellectual curiosity of others might turn out to be inspiring! As the second largest search engine in the world, people already perceive YouTube as highly useful but libraries and librarians must become a bigger and more influential part of this vital learning community.

Think about it: One third of all Internet users use YouTube to watch videos. It's a free source of information and entertainment. There are 1.5 billion YouTube users and an additional 3 billion users are expected by 2020. YouTube is gaining value as a source of prime-time entertainment, as more 18- to 49-year-olds use YouTube between 8 p.m. and 11 p.m. than any TV network. People's attention is shifting to YouTube, and it's a truly global distribution platform. And supporting patrons' strategic use of YouTube doesn't require any special technology apart from access to a smartphone and the Internet. Even more than talent, people share ideas by offering authenticity. In a world full of fake, YouTubers seem real and that makes them compelling sources of information and entertainment. YouTubers can inspire others because there is pleasure in hearing what other people have to say and the voices of authentic, ordinary people can actually be more relevant and meaningful than mass-marketed celebrity culture.

But too many people simply watch YouTube videos instead of creating them. Many people are unaware that, if they have a Google Gmail account, they have a YouTube channel. It takes practice to use YouTube well: Subscribing to channels, commenting, creating playlists, and participating as a media maker are practices that help people develop an appreciation for its utility. Active YouTube users will find others whose messages resonate with their own experience. YouTubers come from small towns and big cities, from the United States and Canada, India, the Philippines, Europe, Latin America, and all over the world. Amateur media makers are transforming learning by enabling everyone to learn from everyone. And sharing is not always about information. There is plenty of entertainment and persuasion out there, too.

Plenty of library patrons are amateur musicians, comedians, makeup artists, filmmakers, business entrepreneurs or storytellers. Because librarians value the interplay of entertainment and information, they are well-poised to support people's appreciation of the richness and depth of YouTube culture. When we value all these forms of creative expression, we open up new relationships and connections between people and media. For librarians to advance the capacity of patrons to be content creators on YouTube, they will need to have experience as media creators themselves, and they will have to value the expertise of both YouTubers and the people in their communities.

REINVENTING LIBRARY LEADERSHIP THROUGH REFLECTION AND SERVICE

Great libraries have great leadership, says Karen Hyman, a strategic thinker and library leader who encourages librarians to continue to reinvent themselves to meet the needs of their patrons. As a leadership development expert in library land, she once served as Executive Director of the South Jersey Regional Library Cooperative, developing services for 600 member libraries. Hyman believes that librarians can improve their services by simply trying something different and noticing what works. That's why passionate, enthusiastic staff, people who have ideas and inspiration to try new things, are critical to the success and possibly the longevity of any library.

Such people engage in strategic reflection and thrive on a sense of shared mission. At the Rangeview Library District in Colorado, the librarians have written a manifesto. It represents their goals for providing extraordinary service to the 441,000 people of Adams County. The Anythink Libraries—all seven of them plus a bookmobile—have been able to expand services dramatically because they helped the voters of the community crave opportunities "to learn about anything under the sun" in engaging, beautiful places. In their manifesto, Anythink librarians defined their vision for exemplary service. As they put it, "You are not just an employee, volunteer, or board member. You do not merely catalog books, organize periodicals, or manage resources. Members guide with wise suggestions, helping transfer knowledge, and connecting people with possibility."[15]

Anythink Director Pam Sandlian Smith (a past president of the Public Library Association) notes that her organization is growing into a place of learning, experimentation, and discovery. She writes, "The idea of a library is morphing from a place of books to a place where the community connects with information and creates content" because "success in today's society requires information literacy, a spirit of self-reliance, and a strong ability to collaborate, communicate effectively, and solve problems."[16] Under Pam Sandlian Smith's leadership, Anythink has embraced the idea that anyone can be a media creator, not just a consumer. For example, At The Studio at Anythink Wright Farms, teens can explore the digital learning lab, a place to socialize, use digital technologies for self-expression, and build relationships with community artists in workshops that emphasize creativity. They can use graphic design software and photo-editing equipment. Teens have access to HD cameras with tripods and lighting kits and use video editing software to make short films. There's a complete audio recording studio with a MIDI keyboard and microphones. The library hires photographers and media makers to provide support for patrons through structured weekly programs and informal drop-in learning experiences.

In 2015, the Anythink York Street Teen Horror Club made a short film entitled *Attack of the Library Werewolf*, a 1-minute scene where camera angles, music, and sound effects build toward suspenseful conflict between teen and werewolf. Inspired by students who share their passion for all things horror, teens viewed, discussed, and made a short horror film to explore their developing understanding of cinematography, makeup techniques, and the key features of the genre. The team of librarians and media professionals who support this form of learning have to be "part wizard, part genius, and part explorer" as they take risks to try new things— like a teen horror film club at the library—that engage, entertain, inform, and educate young library patrons.

Today, access to technologies (including tablets, smartphones, GoPro-type cameras, Bluetooth speakers, Smartboards, etc.) are making both screening and creating visual media easier and more affordable for people of all ages. For example, when the tiny Auburn Public Library in Maine established its Create! Media Lab, they understood that users wanted to design and create digital media, including photography, filmmaking, and making music. Resources and programs that support patrons as media makers, not just as media consumers, are a vital part of the future of public libraries. Film and media education activities provide many opportunities for partnering with the community.

Academic librarians are also increasing their support for local, homegrown digital media production activities in the context of both academic and informal work. Debra Mandel heads the Digital Media Commons Studio at Northeastern University, where students, faculty, and staff use specialized workspaces to create projects. She collaborates with faculty across the curriculum to help plan and implement media-based assignments and teach skills. Northeastern students showcase their work on the library portal. One great project was developed by students enrolled in Professor Moya Bailey's class, entitled Gender, Race, and Medicine. Students created a podcast about race and sexual health among Black and Japanese women, exploring the role of media representations in shaping sexual attitudes and behaviors.

There's no doubt about it: Librarians are at the forefront of digital learning. When Anu Vendantham headed the David B. Weigle Information Commons at the University of Pennsylvania Library, she sponsored Lightning Round sessions, where faculty, students, and librarians shared their teaching and learning experiences using digital media in 5-minute Ignite-style presentations. For example, at one session, participants learned about creating digital polls and annotation tools. In another session, Professor Louise Krasniewicz described her work asking students to analyze and compare two films using concepts from anthropology, including theories of symbolism, metaphor, ritual, narrative, and culture. Instead of a traditional academic paper, students presented the material in a visual format. The concept behind the assignment was to help students understand the organization of ideas and images required to present information visually. According to the professor, this approach gets students to slow down and consider the films they were analyzing more carefully. It also helps students think about how to translate ideas into images. She notes, "Since more and more daily communication takes this form, this effort to advance the students' visual literacy has both academic and practical implications."[17] Under Vedantham's leadership, the library created a variety of student contests and funded internships that helped increase the visibility of digital literacy across the campus.

At the heart of such library innovation and leadership is the practice of design thinking, a mindset that helps librarians see problems as opportunities. With this approach, libraries have developed new spaces that promote play in the context of children's library services and created new programs that facilitate users to teach one another about digital media resources. Design thinking involves identifying challenges, imagining solutions, and using rapid prototyping to test ideas in the field. Brian Bannon, director of the Chicago Public Library, says that a design thinking approach has enabled librarians to provide new and revitalized services. "A benefit we hadn't fully anticipated has been the positive impact on our staff and organizational culture," he notes. "Providing staff the encouragement, tools, and responsibility to explore new services has ignited a culture shift. Their successes and failures, from which we've also learned, have built confidence in our collective ability to lead."[18]

Conclusion

Throughout human history, people have used storytelling to reduce feelings of isolation and loneliness and help people develop shared social values that enable their community to be resilient. Film and digital media provide meaningful feelings of emotional engagement and social connectedness while providing a particular worldview, replete with biases and limitations of perspective. As people move from being readers only to becoming writers who read, using print but also images and multimedia to share meaning, they become highly aware of the constructed nature of authorship. Awareness of the limitations of expression deepens sensitivity and informs the reading process. Figure 9.1 shows a creative tweet from a library conference showing an idea about the power of "creating to learn" in libraries. We think that both "making" and "taking" are intertwined processes that are central to full participation in culture today.

Merely banging a drum about the importance of libraries will not make them important. Jonathan Hunt is one of many educators who fears the possibility that school libraries will be increasingly seen as peripheral, not central, to teaching and learning. In his work at the San Diego County Office of Education, he has observed that the promotional messages that school librarians send do not always resonate with educational and civic leaders. He recognizes that skillful resource curation could save school districts a lot of money. Imagine shifting money from the textbook budget to the library budget by getting librarians and teachers to collaborate on the skillful curation of information resources.[19] And he imagines the impact on student attendance when every high school library has a vibrant media arts center where student creativity can flourish and extend authentic and meaningful learning. Thanks to leadership from school library leaders like Glen Warren of Encinitas Union School District, progress is happening all around us. Warren is determined to connect the dots between the practices of information literacy, media literacy and digital learning. Under his leadership, the California Department of Education sponsored its first Media and Information Literacy Summit in 2018, attracting more than a hundred school administrators and teachers from across the state.

We think that school, public and academic librarians who embrace film and digital media are essential to this important vision. In this book, we have chronicled what we have learned so far about how academic, public, and school librarians are advancing film and media education. But we see your work as central to the future of librarianship. You can add your work to this book by visiting the companion website (www.libraryscreenscene.com) to show how you bring film and media literacy education into school, public and academic libraries.

Figure 9.1 Tweet from the Designing Libraries Conference, 2017.

It all comes down to lifelong learning. As Florida State University professor Lisa Tripp explained:

> If libraries are to fully capitalize on the potential of new media to engage young people in learning and if librarians are to become more central figures in training young people in new media literacies, then the education of librarians must be addressed. It appears increasingly critical that youth services and school media librarians become adept with digital media and new media literacies. Although this clearly includes a variety of technical skills, it also includes social skills and cultural competencies related to appropriating and remixing media, contributing to distributed and collaborative productions, circulating and promoting media, and much more. In other words, it includes the full gamut of socio-technical competencies needed to participate actively and appropriately in new media cultures.[20]

Today, school, public, and academic libraries are becoming community hubs for digital and media literacy education. Despite her current concerns about the possibility that media literacy could exacerbate levels of public cynicism, research scholar and activist danah boyd once pointed out, "The library is a natural site of media literacy."[21]

In his profile of a Massachusetts high school library turned learning commons that promotes interactivity and collaboration through the incorporation of activities such as open mic sessions, poetry readings, poetry slams, and music sessions, Paul Mihailidis of Emerson College argues that school libraries need to shift into "dynamic media literacy learning hub[s], anchoring entire schools around knowledge, expression, collaboration, and creation in both virtual and physical spaces. As libraries transition into places of collective activity, "media literacy education has the ability to ground the library in more active and collaborative learning approaches for the entire school, and to help recast its image as a creative and collaborative space."[22]

That's the future we want to see. Because no matter how digital media technologies continue to change, we know that moving image media will always be part of the way humans express and share our deepest hopes, dreams, fears, and wishes for the future.

Acknowledgments

It has been a labor of love. This book would not have been possible without the vision of Anisa Raoof, the executive director of the Providence Children's Film Festival, who helped us conceptualize this project as we imagined the ways in which children, parents, families, and communities grow and learn through shared film viewing and discussion experiences. For 8 years now, we have been deepening our love of independent children's film as a result of Anisa's leadership and dedication to showcasing films for young viewers. Families and film lovers are lucky to have her talent, hard work, and creative imagination as a significant community resource.

Thanks also goes to Mary Moen at the University of Rhode Island's Harrington School of Communication and Media's graduate program in Library and Information Studies. As a talented school librarian, Mary led the Media Smart Libraries IMLS-funded statewide initiative immediately after completing her PhD in Education where she researched teachers' use of media and technology in 1:1 schools. Mary's growing leadership as a school library professor is inspiring!

We are also grateful for the Rhode Island librarians and educators who sat in Renee's living room one winter day as we first gathered to imagine possibilities about the role of film and media literacy education in libraries. Renee also thanks coauthors Pam Steager and Liz Deslauriers along with University of Rhode Island GSLIS graduate students who enrolled in LSC597, Libraries and Film Education, the course where some of the ideas presented in this book were first explored. We are also grateful to the librarians and archivists at the Providence Public Library, the Cleveland Public Library, and the Philadelphia Free Library who helped us find resources about the history of film screenings in public libraries. We gratefully acknowledge the entire Oxford University Press editorial and production teams, including Norman Hirschy, Lauralee Yeary, and Raj Suthan, all of whom provided valuable talent, service and support in bringing this book to life.

Pam offers much gratitude to all those librarians and educators who shared their time and stories to help make this book come alive, and to those unnamed, underpaid, and overworked ones who may read it and find information and inspiration that enable them to continue informing and inspiring others.

Pam also thanks her coauthors for their genial companionship on this adventure, and especially for the steadfast, encouraging guidance of lead author, Renee Hobbs, whose genius and passion continue to elevate, challenge, and exhaust, nearly 20 years after our first close encounter in the Felton Media Literacy Scholars Program. Pam is grateful to friends and family who endured a reduced relationship throughout the writing process, especially beloved daughters and grandchildren, who have indulged or shared a devotion to books and films that transport and transform, providing cherished moments together. And lastly, she acknowledges her parents, Edward Steager and Florence Hutson Steager, who sparked and fueled the flame of love and appreciation for great storytelling in all forms.

Additionally, Liz thanks her coauthors for the privilege of writing this book together. Renee and Pam's inspiring careers in media literacy are guideposts to her as she ventures into this critically important field. To Liz's family and friends who supported her during the work of this book, especially her husband, Glen, thank you. Finally, unending thanks to all the wonderful librarians who make their communities better.

Copyright, Fair Use, and Licensing Issues

The Purpose of Copyright

According to the US Constitution, the purpose of copyright law is to promote innovation and the spread of knowledge. This is accomplished through the careful balancing of the rights of owners and users. Owners may choose to control access to their works through permissions and licensing. But copyright law includes many provisions that protect users. Section 107 is the broadest of these exemptions. Users are exempt from payment and permission if their particular use of a copyrighted work qualifies as a fair use. Section 108 protects the rights of librarians to be able to copy copyrighted works as part of the services they provide. Section 110 protects the rights of educators to use copyrighted content in the classroom and for distance learning purposes.

Section 107: The Doctrine of Fair Use

The fair use doctrine is the part of copyright law that protects the rights of users. It has a useful flexibility that allows the law to adjust to evolving circumstances as needs and practices differ as a result of changing technologies and changing social norms across different user communities. Rather than following a prescriptive formula, lawyers and judges decide whether a particular use of copyrighted material is "fair" according to an "equitable rule of reason." They are required to take all the facts and circumstances into account to decide whether an unlicensed use of copyrighted material generates social or cultural benefits that are greater than the costs it imposes on the copyright owner.[1] The Supreme Court has pointed out that it is fair use that keeps copyright from violating the First Amendment; without fair use and related exceptions, copyright would create an unconstitutional constraint on free expression. Different knowledge communities (including those in academic libraries, media literacy educators, and documentary filmmakers) have identified the most common ways in which the doctrine of fair use affects their work and created useful statements that help inform people of the scope and limitations of their rights under the law.

Section 108

Section 108 of the Copyright Act lays out a series of specific protections for reproduction and distribution of copyrighted works by libraries and archives. The law strikes a balance between the needs of libraries and the market prerogatives of copyright holders, especially publishers. It allows libraries to make reproductions for library users, for preservation and replacement, and for other purposes. The law allows librarians to make copies of content that is lost damaged, stolen, deteriorating, or in an obsolete format. VHS video is a deteriorating format. But before making copies, Section 108 requires librarians to make a reasonable search to determine that an unused copy of the title is not available at a fair price. They must document evidence of their search efforts. The Due Diligence Project enables librarians to coordinate this work. When it comes to digital copies, Section 108 prohibits sharing of unpublished works to anyone outside the library or archives for any reason. Fortunately, Section 108 includes a provision stating that libraries and archives can rely upon fair use to the same extent that any other user of a copyrighted work may. Although publishers want this part of the law revised, librarians and legal experts are concerned that changes to the law might contribute to the further erosion of librarians' and users' rights.[2]

Section 110A: Classroom Use of Film and Video

Section 110(a) of the Copyright Act of 1976 enables the performance or display of a work by instructors or pupils in the course of face-to-face teaching activities of a nonprofit educational institution, in a classroom or similar place devoted to instruction.

All that is required for these teaching uses is a lawfully made copy of the work. A DVD purchased at Walmart is considered a lawfully acquired copy and so is the purchase of a DVD for $2 at a garage sale. Educators may use the entire work or a short portion and are free to determine the appropriate use of film and video materials in class to meet the learning needs of their students.

Section 110B: Copyright Materials in Distance Learning

Section 110(B), also called the Technology, Education, and Copyright Harmonization (TEACH) Act, was meant to address the use of copyrighted materials and the performance of audio and video works in distance learning to create equivalence between face-to-face teaching and online learning. However, this law was passed in 2002 when there was tremendous angst about online file sharing. The law is highly detailed about the conditions under which digital media can be used in distance learning. As a result, many institutions don't even try to take advantage of TEACH Act, preferring to rely on the flexibility of Section 107, the doctrine of fair use.

Licensing

Licensing processes are commercial contracts that authorize the publication, performance, or display of copyrighted work. If a film screening is open to the public, a public performance license must be obtained, whether or not an admission fee is charged, whether the institution or organization is commercial or nonprofit, or whether a federal or state agency is involved. Willful infringement is a federal crime carrying a maximum sentence of up to 5 years in jail and/or a $250,000 fine. Even inadvertent infringement is subject to substantial civil damages. Because licenses are contractual agreements, they supersede and replace the flexible user rights established by fair use.

Copyfraud

Some publishers, distributors, and vendors intentionally exploit the ignorance of educators and librarians by claiming the licenses are required for classroom teaching or by offering a dizzying variety of tiered pricing schemes, charging different prices to different users for the same content.[3]

Learn More

American Library Association (2019). Copyright Advocacy. Retrieved from http://www.ala.org/advocacy/copyright

Russell, C. (2012). *Complete copyright for K-12 librarians and educators.* Office of Information Technology Policy. Chicago: American Library Association.

Notes

Chapter 1

1. Ito, M., Baumer, S., Bittanti, M., Cody, R., Stephenson, B. H., Horst, H. A., . . . Perkel, D. (2009). *Hanging out, messing around, and geeking out: Kids living and learning with new media.* Cambridge, MA: MIT Press.

2. Jenkins, H., Ford, S., & Green, J. (2013). *Spreadable media: Creating value and meaning in a networked culture* New York, NY: New York University Press.

3. Wee, V. (2017). Youth audiences and the media in the digital era: The intensification of multimedia engagement and interaction. *Cinema Journal, 57*(1), 133–139.

4. Koblin, J. (2017, February 19). NBC takes shot at counting streaming views. *New York Times.*

5. TV viewership sees double-digit decline, according to Accenture (2016, November 26). *Screen Media Daily.* Retrieved from http://screenmediadaily.com/tv-viewership-sees-double-digit-decline-according-to-accenture/.

6. Wee, V. (2017). Youth audiences and the media in the digital era: The intensification of multimedia engagement and interaction. *Cinema Journal, 57*(1), 133–139.

7. Hobbs, R. (2016). Literacy. In K. B. Jensen, E. Rothenbuhler, & R. Craig (Eds.), *International encyclopedia of communication theory and philosophy* (pp. 1–11). New York, NY: Wiley Blackwell.

8. Angus Digital Media and Scottish Screen. (2009). *Moving image education in Scotland.* Retrieved from http://www.scottishscreen.com/images/documents/moving%20image_2009.pdf

9. Hobbs, R. (2010). *Digital and media literacy: A plan of action.* Washington, DC: John S. and James L. Knight Foundation and Aspen Institute.

10. Hofferton, B. (2017). Under the surface. Materials survey 2017. *Library Journal.* Retrieved from http://reviews.libraryjournal.com/2017/02/collection-development/under-the-surface-materials-survey-2017

11. Nielsen Company. (2017). *Mobile kids: The parent, the child and the smartphone.* Retrieved from http://www.nielsen.com/us/en/insights/news/2017/mobile-kids--the-parent-the-child-and-the-smartphone.html

12. Shellenbarger, S. (2016, November 21). Most students don't know when news is fake, Stanford study finds. *Wall Street Journal.*

13. LeMay, E. (2017, May 2). Fake news invasion: Teaching media literacy skills to teens. Retrieved from https://emilygracelemay.wordpress.com/2017/03/02/fake-news-invasion-teaching-media-literacy-skills-to-teens/#more-2445

14. Alvarez, B. (2017, January 1). Public libraries in the age of fake news. *Public Library Association Magazine.* Retrieved from http://publiclibrariesonline.org/2017/01/feature-public-libraries-in-the-age-of-fake-news/

15. Bambino, D. (2002). Critical friends. *Educational Leadership, 59*(6), 25–27.

16. Lankes, R., Newman, W., Kowalski, S., Tench, B., Gould, C., Silk, K., & Britton, L. (2016). *The new librarianship field guide*. Cambridge, MA: MIT Press.

17. Blake, V. (1989). The role of reviews and reviewing media in the selection process. *Collection Management, 11*(1–2), 1–40. https://doi.org/10.1300/J105v11n01_01

18. Valenza, J., & Hobbs, R. (2016). School librarians as stakeholders in the children and media community: A dialogue. *Journal of Children and Media, 10*(2), 147–155. doi:10.1080/17482798.2015.1127841

19. Irons, K. (2014). *Film programs for public libraries*. Chicago, IL: Public Library Association.

20. Plantinga, C. (2009). *Moving viewers: American film and the spectator's experience*. Berkeley: University of California Press.

21. Hobbs, R., Stauffer, J., Frost, R., & Davis, A. (1988). How first time viewers comprehend editing. *Journal of Communication, 38*(4), 50–60.

22. Platinga, C. (2016, November 21). Moving pictures. Retrieved from http://eprints.lse.ac.uk/71429/1/30%20The%20Forum%20%E2%80%93%20Moving%20Pictures.pdf

23. Mason, M. (ND). Librarians and their use of television and radio to answer reference questions. Retrieved from http://www.moyak.com/papers/reference-questions-tv-radio.html

24. Grant, M. (2017). How *Stranger Things* influenced my reading life. *Book Riot*. Retrieved from https://bookriot.com/2017/11/21/stranger-things-influenced-my-reading-life/

25. Mikkelson, D. (2017). Did *Happy Days* promote a 500% increase in library card applications? *Snopes*. Retrieved from https://www.snopes.com/fact-check/getting-carded/

26. American Library Association. (2010). FAQ. Retrieved from http://www.ala.org/Template.cfm?Section=alafaq&template=/cfapps/faq/faq.cfm

27. Mikkelson, D. (2017). Did *Happy Days* produce a 500% increase in library card applications? *Snopes*. Retrieved from https://www.snopes.com/radiotv/tv/librarycards.asp

28. Telephone interview with Susan Conlon, October 4, 2017.

29. Glassman, J., Lee, S., Salomon, D., & Worsham, D. (2017). Community collections: Nurturing student curators. In S. Arnold-Garza & C. Tomlinson (Eds.), *Students lead the library: The importance of student contributions to the academic library* (pp. 77–92). Chicago, IL: American Library Association.

30. Miller, K. E. (2014). Imagine! On the future of teaching and learning and the academic research library. *Portal: Libraries and the Academy, 14*(3), 329–351.

31. Palfrey, J. (2015). *BiblioTech: Why libraries matter more than ever in the age of Google*. New York, NY: Basic Books.

Chapter 2

1. Stark, S., Kramer, S., Metni, J., & Carr, V. (2016). Can texting save lives [Video]. *New York Times*. Retrieved from https://www.nytimes.com/video/opinion/100000005178504/can-texting-save-lives.html

2. Into Film. (2016). Retrieved from https://www.intofilm.org/about

3. Cep, C. (2014, March 12). The last picture show. *Pacific Standard*. Retrieved from https://psmag.com/social-justice/last-picture-show-movies-television-computer-screens-76291

4. Flowers, M. (2011). The movie is (sometimes) better than the book: Adaptations as literary analysis. *Young Adult Library Services, 9*(4), 21–24.

5. Parrott, K. (2011). Circulating iPads in the library. ALSC Blog. Retrieved from https://www.alsc.ala.org/blog/2011/11/circulating-ipads-in-the-childrens-library/

6. O'Neil, K. E. (2011). Reading pictures: Developing visual literacy for greater comprehension. *Read Teach, 65*, 214–223. doi:10.1002/TRTR.01026

7. Considine, D. M. (1986). Visual literacy and children's books: An integrated approach. *School Library Journal, 33*(1), 38–42.

8. Nikolajeva, M., & Scott, C. 2000. The dynamics of picturebook communication. *Children's Literature in Education, 31*(4), 225–239.

9. Deggens, E. (2016, February 22). Hollywood has a major diversity problem, USC study finds. The Two Way. NPR. Retrieved from http://www.npr.org/sections/thetwo-way/2016/02/22/467665890/hollywood-has-a-major-diversity-problem-usc-study-finds

10. Brooks, D. E., & Hébert, L. P. (2006). Gender, race, and media representation. *Handbook of Gender and Communication, 16*, 297–317.

11. Irons, K. (2014). *Film programming for public libraries.* Chicago, IL: American Library Association.

12. Albion College. (2017). Student life. Movie viewing. Retrieved from https://www.albion.edu/student-life/campus-programs-and-organizations/event-scheduling-and-program-policies/movie-viewing

13. Burns, K. (2016). Teaching the Vietnam War. PBS Learning Media. Retrieved from https://ri.pbslearningmedia.org/collection/ken-burns-the-vietnam-war/#.Wph1TRPwaRs

14. Programming Librarian. (2017, July 10). Film programs with *The Vietnam War* [Webinar]. Retrieved from http://www.programminglibrarian.org/learn/film-programs-vietnam-war-film-ken-burns-and-lynn-novick

15. Ibid.

16. RaVision Productions. (2008). *Santa Claus in Baghdad* [Film]. Written and directed by Raouf Zaki. Retrieved from http://www.ravision.net/santa-claus-in-baghdad.html

17. Hobbs, R., Cabral, N., Ebrahimi, A., Yoon, J., & Al-Humaidan, R. (2011). Field-based teacher education in elementary media literacy as a means to promote global understanding. *Action in Teacher Education, 33*(2), 144–156.

18. Ibid.

19. Hobbs, R., & Moore, D. C. (2013). *Discovering media literacy: Digital media and popular culture in elementary school.* Thousand Oaks, CA: Corwin/Sage.

20. Jenkins, B. (2011). Barry Loves da Kids [Video]. Retrieved from https://vimeo.com/29845569

21. Haines, C., & Campbell, C. (2016). *Becoming a media mentor: A guide for working with children and families.* Chicago, IL: American Library Association.

22. Ibid.

23. Spiewak, T. (2017, July 26). Judging a book by more than its cover: Exploring features of traditional and e-book reading experiences that support children's learning. Joan Ganz Cooney Center. Retrieved from http://joanganzcooneycenter.org/2017/07/26/judging-a-book-by-more-than-its-cover-exploring-features-of-traditional-and-e-book-reading-experiences-that-support-childrens-learning/

24. Guernsey, L., & Levine, M. (2017). *How to bring early learning and family engagement into the digital age.* New America Foundation. Retrieved from http://joanganzcooneycenter.org/wp-content/uploads/2017/04/digital_age.pdf

25. Ellis, E. (2017, July 5). Filtering your world is understandable—But it's not helpful. *Wired.* Retrieved from https://www.wired.com/story/vidangel-movie-filtering/

26. Watkins, A. R. (2006). Surgical safe harbors: The Family Movie Act and the future of fair use legislation. *Berkeley Technical Library Journal, 21*, 241.

27. Hobbs, R. (2011). *Copyright clarity: How fair use supports digital learning.* Thousand Oaks, CA: Corwin/Sage.

28. Hobbs, R. (2016). Lessons in Copyright activism: K-12 education and the DMCA 1201 exemption rulemaking process. *International Journal of Information and Communication Technology Education (IJICTE), 12*(1), 50–63

29. Common Sense Media. (2015). Digital bytes [Multimedia]. Retrieved from http://digitalbytes.commonsensemedia.org/

30. Ribble, M. (2011). *Digital citizenship in schools.* International Society for Technology in Education.

31. Jones, M. (2017, February 7). What teenagers are learning from online porn. *New York Times Magazine*. Retrieved from https://www.nytimes.com/2018/02/07/magazine/teenagers-learning-online-porn-literacy-sex-education.html

32. Bickford, J. (2010). Consumerism: How it impacts play and its presence in library collections. *Children & Libraries, 8*(3), 53–56.

33. Hamblin, J. (2015, September 15). The money spent selling sugar to Americans is staggering. *The Atlantic.* Retrieved from https://www.theatlantic.com/health/archive/2015/09/the-money-spent-selling-sugar-to-americans-is-staggering/407350/

34. McLean, S. A., Paxton, S. J., & Wertheim, E. H. (2016). The role of media literacy in body dissatisfaction and disordered eating: A systematic review. *Body Image, 19,* 9–23. http://doi.org/10.1016/j.bodyim.2016.08.002

35. Girl Scout Research Institute. (2011). Real to me: Girls and reality TV. Retrieved from http://www.girlscouts.org/ research/pdf/real_to_me_factsheet.pdf

36. Peek, H. S., & Beresin, E. (2016). Reality check: How reality television can affect youth and how a media literacy curriculum can help. *Academic Psychiatry, 40*(1), 177–181. http://doi.org/10.1007/s40596-015-0382-1

37. Vickery, J. R., & Watkins, S. C. (2017). *Worried about the wrong things.* Cambridge, MA: MIT Press.

38. McLean, S. A., Paxton, S. J., & Wertheim, E. H. (2016). Does media literacy mitigate risk for reduced body satisfaction following exposure to thin-ideal media? *Journal of Youth and Adolescence, 45*(8), 1678–1695. http://doi.org/10.1007/s10964-016-0440-3

39. Department of Education, Kentucky. (2018). Kentucky education facts. Retrieved from https://education.ky.gov/comm/edfacts/Pages/default.aspx

40. Broadband Now Kentucky. (2017). Broadband Internet in Kentucky. Retrieved from https://broadbandnow.com/Kentucky

41. Cook, J. (2013). Wake me up before you go-go: Using unlikely examples to engage students in information literacy. *LOEX Quarterly, 39*(4), 9–11.

42. Petersen, A. (2012). What we talk about when we talk about Brangelina. In the Library with the Lead Pipe. Retrieved from http://www.inthelibrarywiththeleadpipe.org/2012/what-we-talk-about-when-we-talk-about-brangelina/

43. Stone, B. (2011). The power of story. TED Ex Sheffield. Retrieved from https://www.youtube.com/watch?v=wqlShMeTZHE

44. Kammen, M. (1996). *The lively arts: Gilbert Seldes and the transformation of cultural criticism in the United States.* New York, NY: Oxford University Press.

Chapter 3

1. Valenza, J. (2016). Social media curation. Retrieved from https://www.youtube.com/watch?v=nMnaecWgykE

2. Hatch, M. (2014). *The maker movement manifesto.* New York, NY: McGraw-Hill.

3. Ibid..

4. Waters, J. (2016, October 20). What makes a great makerspace? *THE Journal.* Retrieved from https://thejournal.com/articles/2016/10/20/what-makes-a-great-makerspace.aspx?admgarea=Features1

5. Alliance for Excellent Education. (2017). Future ready librarians. Empowering students as creators [Webinar]. https://all4ed.org/webinar-event/jun-13-2017/

6. Bolley, C. (2016). Young filmmakers' sandbox. *Children & Libraries, 14*(4), 6–7.

7. Wolske, M., Rhinesmith, C., & Kumar, B. (2014). Community informatics studio: Designing experiential learning to support teaching, research, and practice. *Journal of Education for Library and Information Science, 55*(2), 166–177.

8. Mihailidis, P. (2018). Civic media literacies: Re-imagining engagement for civic intentionality. *Learning, Media and Technology, 43*(2), 1–13.

9. Levin, S., & Levin, S. (2010). Student created videos. *Knowledge Quest, 38*(4), 52–55. http://doi.org/Article

10. Hobbs, R. (2017). *Create to learn: Introduction to digital literacy.* New York, NY: Wiley.

11. Association of College and Research Libraries. (2016). *Framework for information literacy for higher education.* Retrieved from http://www.ala.org/acrl/standards/ilframework#authority

12. Hobbs, R. (2017). *Create to learn: Introduction to digital literacy.* New York, NY: Wiley.

13. Ibid.

14. Bennett, S. (2008). The information or the learning commons: Which will we have? *Journal of Academic Librarianship, 34* (3), 183–187.

15. Vedantham, A. (2011). Making YouTube and Facebook videos: Gender differences in online video creation among first-year undergraduate students attending a highly selective research university. PhD dissertation, University of Pennsylvania.

16. Vendantham, A. (2017). Re-imagining libraries—Two models from Massachusetts. North Carolina State University. https://vimeo.com/234533347

17. Personal communication with Anu Vedantham, October 16, 2017.

18. Lee, M. (2013, February 20). Library as filmmaker: The creation of a California town's gay prom. *Library Journal.* Retrieved from https://lj.libraryjournal.com/2013/02/library-services/library-as-filmmaker-documenting-the-creation-of-a-california-towns-gay-prom/#_

19. Cannell Library at Clark College. (2015). The A.S.P.E.C.T Checklist for Evaluating Information. Retrieved from http://libraryguides.library.clark.edu/ld.php?content_id=22123050

20. Gamble, A. (2016, December 12). Multimedia creation in the small campus library. *Against the Grain, 28*(5). http://bit.ly/2gER9D1

21. Hobbs, R. (2017). *Create to learn: Introduction to digital literacy.* New York, NY: Wiley Blackwell.

22. Ellis, E. (2010). Book trailers: Available at a library near you. *Indiana Libraries, 29*(2), 24–26.

23. Community builders. (2012). *Library Journal, 137*(5), 25.

24. Voigt, K. (2013). Becoming trivial: The book trailer. *Culture Unbound: Journal of Current Cultural Research, 5*(4), 671–689.

25. Gunter, G., & Kenny, R. (2008). Digital booktalk: Digital media for reluctant readers. *Contemporary Issues in Technology and Teacher Education, 8*(1), 84–99.

26. Dalton, B., & Grisham, D. L. (2013). Love that book. *The Reading Teacher, 67*(3), 220–225.

27. Phillips, N. C., & Smith, B. E. (2012). Multimodality and aurality: Sound spaces in student digital book trailers. In P. J. Dunston, S. K. Fullerton, C. C. Bates, K. Headley, & P. M. Stecker (Eds.), *61st yearbook of the literacy research association* (pp. 84–99). Oak Creek, WI: Literacy Research Association.

28. Semingson, P., Mora, R. A., & Chiquito, T. (2017). BookTubing: Reader response meets 21st century literacies. *ALAN Review, 44*(1), 61–68.

29. Desmet, C. (2009). Teaching Shakespeare with YouTube. *English Journal, 99*(1), 65–70.

30. Leitch, T. (2008). Adaptation studies at a crossroads. *Adaptation, 1*(1), 63–77. https://doi-org.uri.idm.oclc.org/10.1093/adaptation/apm005

31. Leitch, T. M. (2003). Twelve fallacies in contemporary adaptation theory. *Criticism, 45*(2), 149–171. http://doi.org/10.1353/crt.2004.0001

32. Leitch, G. (2009). *Film adaptation and its discontents.* Baltimore, MD: Johns Hopkins University Press.

33. Beach, R., Appleman, D., Fecho, B., & Simon, R. (2016). *Teaching literature to adolescents* (3rd ed.). New York, NY: Routledge.

34. Zerne, L. H. (2013). Ideology in the *Lizzie Bennet Diaries.* Persuasions Online. *Jane Austen Society of North America, 34*(1). Retrieved from http://www.jasna.org/persuasions/on-line/vol34no1/zerne.html

35. University of Arkansas. (2018). Remaking monsters and heroines. Retrieved from https://monstersandheroines.uark.edu/

36. Lissette Lopez Szwydky, personal communication, September 30, 2018.
37. Flynn, S. (2015, May 19). She is the school's go-to person. *Newport Daily News*. Retrieved from http://www.newportri.com/newportdailynews/news/page_one/she-is-school-s-go-to-person/article_a62f7cfb-2a31-5a00-bf60-d1a02cb75082.html
38. Robinson, J. (2018, February 9). Personal communication with Renee Hobbs.
39. Urban Libraries Council. All about the books. Retrieved from https://www.urbanlibraries.org/-all-about-the-books--music-video-innovation-1184.php?page_id=428

Chapter 4

1. Byeon, H., & Hong, S. (2015). Relationship between television viewing and language delay in toddlers: Evidence from a Korea national cross-sectional survey. *PLoS ONE*, *10*(3), e0120663. http://doi.org/10.1371/journal.pone.0120663
2. Hirsh-Pasek, K., Zosh, J. M., Golinkoff, R. M., Gray, J. H., Robb, M. B., & Kaufman, J. (2015). Putting education in "educational" apps: Lessons from the science of learning. *Psychology and Science in the Public Interest*, *16*, 3–34. doi:10.1177/1529100615569721
3. Zimmerman, F. J., & Christakis, D. A. (2005). Children's television viewing and cognitive outcomes: A longitudinal analysis of national data. *Archives of Pediatric Adolescent Medicine*, *159*, 619–625. doi:10.1001/archpedi.159.7.619
4. Vandewater, E. A., Bickham, D. S., Lee, J. H., Cummings, H. M., Wartella, E. A., & Rideout, V. J. (2005). When the television is always on. *American Behavioral Scientist*, *48*(5), 562–577. http://doi.org/10.1177/0002764204271496
5. Tomopoulos, S., Brockmeyer Cates, C., Dreyer, B. P., Fierman, A. H., Berkule, S. B., & Mendelsohn, A. L. (2014). Children under the age of two are more likely to watch inappropriate background media than older children. *Acta Paediatrica (Oslo, Norway: 1992)*, *103*(5), 546–552.
6. Fashina, A., & Nathanson, A. I. (2016). What preschoolers bring to the show: The relation between viewer characteristics and children's learning from educational television. *Media Psychology*, *19*(3), 406–430.
7. Linebarger, D. L., & Piotrowski, J. T. (2009). TV as storyteller: How exposure to television narratives impacts at-risk preschoolers' story knowledge and narrative skills. *British Journal of Developmental Psychology*, *27*(1), 47–69. http://doi.org/10.1348/026151008X400445
8. Huesmann, L. R., & Eron, L. D. (Eds.). (2013). *Television and the aggressive child: A cross-national comparison*. New York: Routledge.
9. Huesmann, L. R. (2007). The impact of electronic media violence: Scientific theory and research. *Journal of Adolescent Health*, *41*(6), S6–S13.
10. American Academy of Pediatrics. (2016). Media and young minds. Council on Comunications and Media. Policy statement. Retrieved from http://pediatrics.aappublications.org/content/138/5/e20162591..info
11. Lareau, A. (2011). *Unequal childhoods: Class, race, and family life*. Berkeley: University of California Press..
12. Gee, J. P. (2007). *Good video games+ good learning: Collected essays on video games, learning, and literacy*. New York, NY: Peter Lang.
13. Jenkins, H. (2007). A few thoughts on media violence. Confessions of an ACA Fan. Retrieved from http://henryjenkins.org/blog/2007/04/a_few_thoughts_on_media_violen.html
14. Gerbner, G., Gross, L., Morgan, M., Signorielli, N., & Shanahan, J. (2002). Growing up with television: Cultivation processes. In B. Jennings & D. Zillmann (Eds.), *Media effects: Advances in theory and research* (2nd ed., pp. 43–67). Mahwah, NJ: Lawrence Elbaum Associates.
15. National Research Council and Institute of Medicine. (2006). *Media consumption as a public health issue*. Studying Media Effects on Children and Youth: Improving Methods and Measures. Workshop Summary. Washington, DC: The National Academies Press. doi:10.17226/11706.

16. Jenkins, H., Purushotma, R., Weigel, M., Clinton, K., & Robison, A. J. (2009). *Confronting the challenges of participatory culture: Media education for the 21st century*. Cambridge, MA: MIT Press.
17. Personal communication with Bonnie Nishihara, October 20, 2016.
18. Hobbs, R., & RobbGrieco, M. (2012). African-American children's active reasoning about media texts as a precursor to media literacy. *Journal of Children and Media, 6*(4), 502–519.
19. Diergarten, A. K., Möckel, T., Nieding, G., & Ohler, P. (2017). The impact of media literacy on children's learning from films and hypermedia. *Journal of Applied Developmental Psychology, 48*, 33–41. http://doi.org/10.1016/j.appdev.2016.11.007
20. Rasmussen, E. (2017). Children and media man. How to maximize kids' learning from educational media. Retrieved from https://childrenandmediaman.com/2017/08/24/how-to-maximize-kids-learning-from-educational-media/
21. Miller, A. (2016, January 17). Questions: What if they don't come up with the right ones? *The Contrarian Librarian*. Retrieved from https://thecontrarianlibrarian.com/2016/01/17/questions-what-if-they-dont-come-up-with-the-right-ones/
22. Hains, R. (2014). *The princess problem: Guiding our girls through the princess obsessed years*. New York, NY: Sourcebooks.
23. Common Sense Media. (2016). *Watching gender: How stereotypes in movies and TV impact kids' development*. Retrieved from https://www.commonsensemedia.org/research/watching-gender
24. Common Sense Media. (2016). *Watching gender: How stereotypes in movies and TV impact kids' development*. Retrieved from https://www.commonsensemedia.org/research/watching-gender
25. Boske, C., & McCormack, S. (2011). Building an understanding of the role of media literacy for Latino/a high school students. *The High School Journal, 94*(4), 167–186.
26. Dargis, M. (2006, November 17). Bring on Da Hoofers on Ice. *New York Times*. https://www.nytimes.com/2006/11/17/movies/17feet.html
27. Hobbs, R., & Jensen, A. (2009). The past, present and future of media literacy education. *Journal of Media Literacy Education 1*(1), 1–11.
28. Fisher, D., & Frey, N. (2012). Close reading in elementary schools. *Reading Teacher, 66*(3), 179–188. http://doi.org/10.1002/TRTR.01117
29. Stoddard, J. D., & Marcus, A. S. (2010). More than "showing what happened": Exploring the potential of teaching history with film. *The High School Journal, 93*(2), 83–90.
30. Media Education Lab. (2015). Media and information literacy at the Mark Day School. Retrieved from https://mediaeducationlab.com/sites/default/files/Mark%2520Day%2520School%2520Final%2520Report_0.pdf
31. Kist, W. (2013). New literacies and the Common Core. *Educational Leadership*. Retrieved from http://www.ascd.org/publications/educational-leadership/mar13/vol70/num06/New-Literacies-and-the-Common-Core.aspx
32. Lehman, C., & Roberts, K. (2014). *Falling in love with close reading*. Portsmouth, NH: Heinemann.
33. Cox-Stanton, T. (2017). Nearing the heart of a film: Toward a cinephilic pedagogy. In R. W. Richards & D. T. Johnson (Eds.), *For the love of cinema*. Indianapolis: Indiana University Press.
34. Ibid.
35. Into Film. (2017). About. Retrieved from https://www.intofilm.org/about
36. Into Film. (2017). Teaching literacy through film. Retrieved from https://www.futurelearn.com/courses/teaching-literacy-through-film
37. The Film Space. (2017). Teaching trailers. Retrieved from http://thefilmspace.org/teachingtrailers/2017/
38. The Film Space. (2017). Teaching trailers teacher's guide. Retrieved from http://thefilmspace.org/teachingtrailers/2017/
39. Ibid.

40. Gentile, D. A., Reimer, R. A., Nathanson, A. I., Walsh, D. A., & Eisenmann, J. C. (2014). Protective effects of parental monitoring of children's media use a prospective study. *JAMA Pediatrics, 168*(5), 479–484. http://doi.org/10.1001/jamapediatrics.2014.146

41. Bluth, D., & Goldman, G. (1997). *Anastasia* [Motion picture]. USA: 20th Century Fox..

42. Caro, N. (2003). *Whale Rider* [Motion picture]. USA: Walt Disney Studios.

43. Hobbs, R. (2006). Non-optimal uses of video in the classroom. *Learning, Media and Technology, 31*(1), 45–50.

44. KIPP Colorado Northeast Elementary (2017). School Handbook 2017–2018. Retrieved from https://kippcolorado.org/wp-content/uploads/2018/05/KNE-English-Handbook-Final-Version-17_18-as-of-7.7.17.pdf

45. Gross, D., Pietri, E. S., Anderson, G., Moyano-Camihort, K., & Graham, M. J. (2015). Increased preclass preparation underlies student outcome improvement in the flipped classroom. *CBE Life Sciences Education, 14*(4), 1–8. http://doi.org/10.1187/cbe.15-02-0040

46. Wineburg, S., & McGrew, S. (2016). Why students can't Google their way to the truth. *Education Week, 36*(11), 22–28.

47. Graber, D. A. (1990). Seeing is remembering: How visuals contribute to learning from television news. *Journal of Communication, 40*(3), 134–156.

48. Flanagin, A. J., & Metzger, M. J. (2007). The role of site features, user attributes, and information verification behaviors on the perceived credibility of web-based information. *New Media & Society, 9*(2), 319–342.

49. Stanford History Education Group, Wineburg, S., McGrew, S., Breakstone, J., & Ortega, T. (2016). Evaluating information: The cornerstone of civic online reasoning. *Stanford Digital Repository, 29*. Retrieved from http://purl.stanford.edu/fv751yt5934

50. Tewell, E. C. (2014). Tying television comedies to information literacy: A mixed-methods investigation. *Journal of Academic Librarianship, 40*, 134–141.

51. Estevez, E. (2018). Emilio Estevez. *American Libraries, 49*(3/4), 28–32.

52. Radford, G., & Radford, M. (2001). Libraries, librarians, and the discourse of fear. *The Library Quarterly, 71*(3), 299–329.

53. Radford, M., & Radford, G. (2003). Librarians and party girls: Cultural studies and the meaning of the librarian. *The Library Quarterly, 73*(1), 54–69.

54. Waller, M. (2017). Grey literature, experimental works, and shifting roles: Case studies, opportunities, and legal challenges around students as producers. *Against the Grain, 29*(4). Retrieved from http://bit.ly/2gEPxJk

55. Dixon, J. (2017, September 7). The academic mainstream [Streaming video]. *Library Journal*. Retrieved from http://bit.ly/2icRLTW

56. Ibid. http://bit.ly/2icRLTW

57. Ibid.

Chapter 5

1. Otto, J. J. (2014). University educators describe their use of moving images in teaching and learning and their perceptions of the library's role in that use. *College & Research Libraries, 75*(2), 115–144. http://doi.org/10.5860/crl12-399

2. Kelly, M. (2015). Collection development policies in public libraries in Australia: A qualitative content analysis. *Public Library Quarterly, 34*(1), 44–62.

3. Weller, S. (2017, March 29). Without school librarians, we're on a dystopian path. *Chicago Tribune*. Retrieved from http://www.chicagotribune.com/news/opinion/commentary/ct-school-librarians-cuts-dystopia-perspec-0330-jm-20170329-story.html

4. Fernandez, L (2017, December 18). 30 percent of Oakland school libraries closed. KTVU. Retrieved from http://www.ktvu.com/news/thirty-percent-of-oakland-school-libraries-closed-district-lays-off-head-librarian

5. Johnson, D. (2017, December 15). Librarians and the scarcity mentality. Blue Skunk Blog. Retrieved from http://doug-johnson.squarespace.com/blue-skunk-blog/2017/12/15/librarians-and-the-scarcity-mentality.html

6. Waite, M. J. (2010). Room with a view. *Knowledge Quest, 38*(4), 59–61.

7. Mihailidis, P., & Diggs, V. (2010). From information reserve to media literacy learning commons: Revisiting the 21st century library as the home for media literacy education. *Public Library Quarterly, 29*(4), 279–292.

8. Motley Fool. (2017). YouTube has over one billion users. Retrieved from https://fxn.ws/2pCZI5P

9. Snelson, C. (2011). YouTube across the disciplines: A review of the literature. *MERLOT Journal of Online Learning and Teaching, 7*(1), 159–69.

10. YouTube Creator Academy. (2017, August 28). The algorithm: How YouTube search and discovery works. YouTube. Retrieved from https://youtu.be/hPxnIix5ExI

11. Wakabayashi, D. (2018 January 25). YouTube moves to make conspiracy theory videos harder to find. The New York Times. Retrieved from https://www.nytimes.com/2019/01/25/technology/youtube-conspiracy-theory-videos.html

12. Anderson, C. (July 2010). How web video powers global innovation. TED. Retrieved from https://www.ted.com/talks/chris_anderson_how_web_video_powers_global_innovation

13. Alexander, B., Becker, S. A., Cummins, M., & Giesinger, C. H. (2017). *Digital literacy in higher education, Part II: An NMC Horizon project strategic brief* (pp. 1–37). Washington, D.C.: The New Media Consortium.

14. Mihailidis, P. (2015). Digital curation and digital literacy: Evaluating the role of curation in developing critical literacies for participation in digital culture. *E-learning and Digital Media, 12*(5–6), 443–458.

15. Mihailidis, P., & Cohen, J. (2013). Exploring curation as a core competency in digital and media literacy education. *Journal of Interactive Media in Education, 2013*(1).

16. Valenza, J. (2017). Curation situations: Let us count the ways. *School Library Journal.* Retrieved from http://blogs.slj.com/neverendingsearch/2017/07/05/curation-situations-let-us-count-the-ways/

17. Gibson (2007) as quoted in Mackey, T. P., & Jacobson, T. E. (2011). Reframing information literacy as a metaliteracy. *College & Research Libraries, 72*(1), 62–78, p. 68.

18. Ibid.

19. Luhtala, M. (2012, June 14). Just an average day at New Canaan school library. YouTube. https://youtu.be/Sww4M8f7UfU

20. Luhtala, M. (2012, August 28). We trust you 2012. YouTube. Retrieved from https://youtu.be/yIZ48MQIp48

21. Luhtala M. (2013, February 14). 6 concerning trends in digital collection. Bibliotech. Retrieved from http://mluhtala.blogspot.com/2013/02/six-concerns-about-digital-collection.html

22. Saunders, T. (2002). *Celluloid saints.* Macon, GA: Mercer University Press.

23. Scott, A. O. (2016). Better living through criticism. New York, NY: Penguin.

24. Stuckmann, C. (2018). Chris Stuckmann. YouTube. Retrieved from https://www.youtube.com/user/ChrisStuckmann

25. Stuckmann, C. (2016). About. Chris Stuckmann. Retrieved from http://www.chrisstuckmann.com/

26. Coggan, D. (2016, June 23). Male film critics greatly outnumber female critics, study finds. *Entertainment Weekly.* Retrieved from http://ew.com/article/2016/06/23/film-criticism-gender-study/

27. Haney, W. (2016). Ghostbusters is a perfect example of how internet movie ratings are broken. FiveThirtyEight. Retrieved from https://fivethirtyeight.com/features/ghostbusters-is-a-perfect-example-of-how-internet-ratings-are-broken/

28. Chen, S. (2017). Wonderstruck movie review. Common Sense Media. Retrieved from https://www.commonsensemedia.org/movie-reviews/wonderstruck

29. Chen, S. (2017). My Life as a Zucchini movie review. Common Sense Media. Retrieved from https://www.commonsensemedia.org/movie-reviews/my-life-as-a-zucchini

30. Singer, N. (2015, April 25). Turning a children's rating system into an advocacy army. *New York Times*. Retrieved from https://www.nytimes.com/2015/04/27/technology/turning-a-childrens-rating-system-into-an-advocacy-army.html?_r=2

31. American Library Association. (2015). Ratings. An interpretation of the Library Bill of Rights. Retrieved from http://www.ala.org/advocacy/intfreedom/librarybill/interpretations/rating-systems

32. Price, V. (2013). *The V-Chip: Content filtering from television to the internet.* New York, NY: Routledge.

33. Gentile, D. A., Humphrey, J., & Walsh, D. A. (2005). Media ratings for movies, music, video games, and television: A review of the research and recommendations for improvements. *Adolescent Medicine Clinics, 16*(2), 427.

34. LeRoy, D., LeRoy, J., & Reed, C. (2016, February 29). Study reveals surprising diversity among public TV viewership. *Current.* Retrieved from http://bit.ly/2skisL2

35. Chattoo, C., & Jenkins, W. (2017). When movies go to Washington: Documentary films and public policy in the United States. Volume 1. Retrieved from http://cmsimpact.org/wp-content/uploads/2017/04/CMSI_Washington.pdf

36. Merry, L. (2004). The devil in the details. *Library Collections, Acquisitions, and Technical Services, 28*(3), 298–311. doi:10.1080/14649055.2004.10765998

37. Spicer, S. (2018). Perspectives on the role of instructional video in higher education: Evolving pedagogy, copyright challenges and support models. In R. Hobbs (Ed.), *The Routledge companion on media education, copyright and fair use* (pp. 236–257). New York, NY: Routledge.

38. Handman, G. (2010). License to look: Evolving models for library video acquisition and access. *Library Trends, 58*(3), 324–334.

39. Bergman, B., Peters, V., & Schomberg, J. (2007). Video collecting for the sometimes media librarian: Tips and tricks for selecting, purchasing, and cataloging videos for an academic library. *College & Undergraduate Libraries, 14*(1), 57–77.

40. King, R. (2016). Access to circulating videos in academic libraries: From policy review to action plan. *Collection Management, 41*(4), 209–220.

41. Dimmock, N. (2007). A popular DVD collection in an academic library. *New Library World* 108 (3–4), 141–150, p. 141. doi:10.1108/03074800710735348

42. Handman, G. (2010). License to look: Evolving models for library video acquisition and access. *Library Trends, 58*(3), 324–334.

43. Otto, J. J. (2014). University educators describe their use of moving images in teaching and learning and their perceptions of the library's role in that use. *College & Research Libraries, 75*(2), 115–144. http://doi.org/10.5860/crl12-399

44. Otto, J. J. (2014). University educators describe their use of moving images in teaching and learning and their perceptions of the library's role in that use. *College & Research Libraries, 75*(2), 115–144. http://doi.org/10.5860/crl12-399

45. Barry, D. S., Marzouk, F., Chulak-Oglu, K., Bennett, D., Tierney, P., & O'Keeffe, G. W. (2016). Anatomy education for the YouTube generation. *Anatomical Sciences Education, 9*(1), 90–96.

46. O'Callaghan, F. V., Neumann, D. L., Jones, L., & Creed, P. (2017). The use of lecture recordings in higher education: A review of institutional, student, and lecturer issues. *Education and Information Technologies, 22*(1), 399–415.

47. Kraus, M. (2017). Why academic librarians hate Netflix: Digital copyright and the challenge of acquiring and providing on-demand streaming media for classroom use. MA thesis, Moving Image Archiving and Preservation Program Department of Cinema Studies, New York University.

48. American Library Association. (2012). Performance of or showing films in the classroom. Retrieved from http://libguides.ala.org/copyright/video

49. Fitzgerald, R. (2010). Using Netflix at an academic library. Tame the Web. Library Innovators. Retrieved from http://tametheweb.com/2010/09/09/using-netflix-at-anacademic-library-a-ttw-guest-post-by-rebecca-fitzgerald/.

50. Russell, C. (2010). The best of copyright and VideoLib. *Library Trends, 58*(3), 349–357. http://doi.org/10.1353/lib.0.009

51. Steffen, J. (2018). Personal communication, January 4.

52. Jambon, M., & Smetana, J. (2012). College students' moral evaluations of illegal music downloading. *Journal of Applied Developmental Psychology, 33*, 31–39. doi:10.1016/j.appdev.2011.09.001.

53. Irdeto. (2017). Irdeto Global Consumer Piracy Report. Retrieved from https://resources.irdeto.com/piracy-cybercrime/irdeto-global-cusumer-piracy-survey-report

54. Benally, M., Campbell, C., Mendez, A., & Saito, A. (2017). *Digital piracy: Legal consumption vs illegal media downloading selling and sharing.* Utah Valley University, Department of Criminal Justice. Retrieved from https://www.uvu.edu/criminaljustice/docs/student-research/digitalpiracy.pdf

55. BBC Newsbeat. (2017, May 19). Student banned from university for downloading *Chicken Run.* Retrieved from http://www.bbc.co.uk/newsbeat/article/39961502/student-banned-from-university-wi-fi-for-downloading-chicken-run

56. Rodgers, W. (2017). Buy, borrow, or steal? Film access for film studies students. *College and Research Libraries.* Retrieved from http://crl.acrl.org/index.php/crl/article/download/16730/18237

57. Otto, J. J. (2014). University educators describe their use of moving images in teaching and learning and their perceptions of the library's role in that use. *College & Research Libraries, 75*(2), 115–144. http://doi.org/10.5860/crl12-399

58. Lohmann, S., & Frederiksen, L. (2017). Educators' awareness and perception of streaming video for teaching. *Collection Management.* doi:10.1080/01462679.2017.1382411

59. Leffler, J., Hayden, J., & Enoch, T. (2017). Juggling a new format with existing tools: Incorporating streaming video into technical services workflows. *The Serials Librarian, 72*(1–2), 102–104. doi:10.1080/0361526X.2017.1284498

60. Ibid.

61. King, R. (2014). House of cards: The academic library media center in the era of streaming. *The Serials Librarian, 67*(3), 289–306.. doi:10.1080/0361526X.2014.948699

62. Ibid., p. 303.

63. Spicer, S. (2018). Perspectives on the role of instructional video in higher education: Evolving pedagogy, copyright challenges and support models. In R. Hobbs (Ed.), *The Routledge companion on media education, copyright and fair use* (pp. 236–257). New York, NY: Routledge, p. 254.

Chapter 6

1. Dennis, M. (2012). Outreach initiatives in academic libraries, 2009–2011. *Reference Services Review, 40*(3), 368–383. doi:10.1108/00907321211254643

2. StoryCorps. (2016). The Bookmobile [Video]. Retrieved from https://youtu.be/11OvHcgh-E4

3. Rudin, P. (2008). No fixed address: The evolution of outreach library services on university campuses. *The Reference Librarian, 49*(1), 55–75.

4. Dowd, N. (2013, August 5). If you don't have time for partnerships, chances are your community won't have time for you. *Library Journal.* Retrieved from http://lj.libraryjournal.com/2013/08/marketing/if-you-dont-have-time-for-partnerships-chances-are-your-community-wont-have-time-for-you/#_

5. Sagor, R. (2000). *Guiding school improvement with action research.* Alexandria, VA: Association for Supervision and Curriculum Development. http://www.ascd.org/publications/books/100047/chapters/What-Is-Action-Research%C2%A2.aspx

6. Arc of the Ozarks. (2027). About. Retrieved from http://www.thearcoftheozarks.org/

7. O'Dell, K. (2015, November 15). Creating a level of comfort. *Library Journal.* Retrieved from http://lj.libraryjournal.com/2015/11/opinion/programs-that-pop/creating-a-level-of-comfort-programs-that-pop/

8. American Library Association. (2014). *National Impact of Library Public Programs Assessment.* Retrieved from http://www.ala.org/aboutala/offices/ppo/resources/benefitspublic

9. Stephens, W. (2017, July 27). Parsing the new ALA school librarian competencies framework. *School Library Journal.* Retrieved from https://www.slj.com/2017/07/industry-news/parsing-the-new-ala-school-librarian-competencies-framework/#_

10. Remiesiewicz, N. (2014, April 19). Alec Baldwin to host fundraiser for CF Library. WPRI. com. Retrieved from http://wpri.com/2014/04/19/alec-baldwin-to-host-fundraiser-for-cf-library

11. Smylie, M. A., & Wenzel, S. A. (2003). *The Chicago Annenberg Challenge: Successes, failures, and lessons for the future.* Final Technical Report of the Chicago Annenberg Research Project. Retrieved from https://consortium.uchicago.edu/downloads/p62.pdf.

12. Yowell, C., & Rhoten, D. (2008). Digital media and learning. Forum futures, p. 15. Retrieved from http://retawprojects.com/uploads/digital_media_and_learning.pdf

13. Digital Media and Learning. (2013). Project: Connect. Retrieved from https://dml5.dmlcompetition.net/

14. MacArthur Foundation. (2013, May 9). Grant competition to provide $150,000 for summer youth programs [Press release]. Retrieved from https://www.macfound.org/press/press-releases/grant-competition-provide-150000-summer-youth-programs/

15. Charlotte Mecklenburg Library. (2017). Celebrate Hispanic heritage month. Retrieved from https://www.cmlibrary.org/blog/celebrate-hispanic-heritage-month

16. Aspen Institute. (2014). *Dialogue on public libraries.* Retrieved from http://csreports.aspeninstitute.org/Dialogue-on-Public-Libraries/2014/report

17. Rhode Island College. (2018, February 6). Extravaganza de Espanol. Retrieved from http://henrybarnardschool.org/extravaganza-de-espanol/

18. Nooksack Valley Heritage. (2015). Washington Rural Heritage. Washington State Library. Retrieved from http://www.washingtonruralheritage.org/cdm/about/collection/nooksack

19. Friends of Everson MacBeith Library. (2015, June 24). Facebook. Retrieved from https://www.facebook.com/Everson.Friends/posts/1086138578069901

20. New York Film Academy. (2018). The most comprehensive list of film festivals on the Internet. Retrieved from https://www.nyfa.edu/student-resources/film-festivals/

21. Ibid.

22. Media Education Lab. (2015, October 28). Webinar in film distribution and exhibition in public libraries. Retrieved from https://www.youtube.com/watch?v=gsiR-c4hA6g#t=60

23. Dancoff, J. (2012). Getting your film ready for school. Retrieved from https://www.documentary.org/magazine/getting-your-film-ready-school-it%E2%80%99s-academic-diy

24. Mobile Film Classroom. (2017). Programs. Retrieved from https://www.mobilefilmclassroom.org/programs/

25. American Association of School Librarians. (2018, February 22). Connecting competencies: Learner, school librarian and school library. Retrieved from http://www.ala.org/aasl/ecollab/competencies

26. Irons, K. (2014). *Film programming for public libraries.* Chicago, IL: American Library Association, Public Library Association..

27. Kelly, K. (2016, February 18). Film Screenings 101. *Programming Librarian.* Retrieved from http://www.programminglibrarian.org/blog/film-screenings-101

28. American Library Association. (2003). One book, one community. Public Programs Office. Retrieved from http://www.ala.org/tools/sites/ala.org.tools/files/content/onebook/files/onebookguide.pdf

29. Personal interview with Susan Conlon, Princeton Public Library, August 23, 2017.

30. Haidt, L. (2016, June 27). Storymakers 2016 winners. Retrieved from http://forums.techsoup.org/cs/community/b/tsblog/archive/2016/06/27/storymakers-2016-winners.aspx

31. Nashvillle Public Library. (2016). All about the books. Retrieved from https://youtu.be/Pduszh4ADTU

32. Personal interview with Andrea Fanta, Nashville Public Library, March 16, 2018.

33. Aspen Institute. (2015). Rising to the challenge: Re-envisioning public libraries. Retrieved from http:// https://csreports.aspeninstitute.org/documents/AspenLibrariesReport.pdf

34. WebJunction and TechSoup for Libraries. (2017). Social media and libraries webinar series. Learner Guide. Retrieved from https://www.webjunction.org/content/dam/WebJunction/Documents/webJunction/2017-10/guide-libraries-social-media-webinar-series.pdf

35. Genett, J. (2014). Measuring outcomes for teen technology programs. *Young Adult Library Services, 13*(1), 25–28.

36. Marquez, J., & Downey, A. (2015). Service design: An introduction to a holistic assessment methodology of library services. *Weave, 1*(2). Retrieved from http://dx.doi.org/10.3998/weave.12535642.0001.201

37. Cooksey, A. (2017, April 13). Celebrate #SLM17 with Flipgrid. *Knowledge Quest*. Retrieved from http://knowledgequest.aasl.org/celebrate-slm17-flipgrid/

38. Harmon, A. (2017, October 4). Make reflections, discussions and assessments easier with Flipgrid. The Art of Education. Retrieved from https://www.theartofed.com/2017/10/04/3-ways-use-flipgrid-art-room/

39. Miller, S. M. (2013, December 13). Flipgrid allows for students to find their voice giving book talks. *The Library Voice*. Retrieved from http://vanmeterlibraryvoice.blogspot.com/2013/12/flipgrid-allows-for-students-to-find.html

40. American Library Association. (2017). Policy manual crosswalk. Retrieved from http://www.ala.org/aboutala/governance/policymanual/updatedpolicymanual/section1/1mission

Chapter 7

1. Providence Public Library. (1949). Annual Report, p. 6.

2. Providence Public Library. (1950). Annual Report, p. 4.

3. Stauffer, S. (2017). Utilizing this new medium of mass communication: The regional film distribution programme at the Cleveland Public Library, 1948–1951. *Library and Information History, 33*(4), 258–274, p. 258.

4. Rossi-Snook, E. (2005). Persistence of vision: Public library 16mm film collections in America. *The Moving Image, 5*(1), 1–26.

5. Davis, M. (1978). Tune in at the library. *Wisconsin Library Bulletin, 73*, 173–174.

6. Sigler, R. F. (1978). A rationale for the film as a public library resource and service. *Library Trends, 26*, 9–26.

7. Horne, J. (2011). A history long overdue: The public library and motion pictures. In C. Acland & H. Wasson (Eds.), *Useful cinema* (pp. 149–177). Durham, NC: Duke University Press, p. 172.

8. Ibid.

9. Ibid., p. 154.

10. Providence Public Library. (1923). Annual Report, p. 12.

11. Rossi-Snook, E. (2005). Persistence of vision: Public library 16mm film collections in America. *The Moving Image, 5*(1), 1–26, p. 7.

12. Ibid., p. 8.
13. Luckerson, V. (2016, January 19). This is how much Netflix we're all watching every day. *Time*. Retrieved from http://time.com/4186137/netflix-hours-per-day/
14. Grieveson, L., & Wasson, H. (2008). *Inventing film studies*. Durham, NC: Duke University Press.
15. Horne, J. (2011). A history long overdue: The public library and motion pictures. In C. Acland & H. Wasson (Eds.), *Useful cinema* (pp. 149–177). Durham, NC: Duke University Press, p. 152.
16. Stevens, J. D. (1983). Sex as education: A note on pre-1930 social hygiene films. *Film & History: An Interdisciplinary Journal of Film and Television Studies, 13*(4), 84–87.
17. Hoyt, E. (2012). *Hollywood vault: The business of film libraries, 1915–1960*. Doctoral dissertation, University of Southern California.
18. Hale, B. (2014, November 12). The history of the Hollywood movie industry. History Cooperative. Retrieved from http://historycooperative.org/the-history-of-the-hollywood-movie-industry/
19. Most Films Lurid, Says Censor Board. *Philadelphia Inquirer*, February 19, 1916.
20. Lorentz, P., & Ernst, M. (1930). *Censored: The private life of the movie*. New York, NY: Corwall Press.
21. Charters, W. W. (1933). Motion pictures and youth: A summary. Bureau of Educational Research, Ohio State University. Retrieved from http://bit.ly/2vUvgFz
22. Holaday, P. W., & Stoddard, G. D. (1933). *Getting ideas from the movies*. New York, NY: Macmillan.
23. Brown, N. (2013). "A new movie-going public": 1930s Hollywood and the emergence of the "family" film. *Historical Journal of Film, Radio and Television, 33*(1), 1–23.
24. Why this bulletin? (1934, October 15). *Motion Picture and the Family*, p. 1.
25. Fuchs, E., Bruch, A., & Annegarn-Gläß, M. (2016). Educational films: A historical review of media innovation in schools. *Journal of Educational Media, Memory and Society, 8*(1), 1–13.
26. Gracy, K. (2017). See the movie, read the book! Cleveland Public Library's bookmarks programme, 1923–1972. *Library & Information History, 33*(4), 236–257.
27. Telephone bureau grows at the Los Angeles Public Library. (1934, November 15). *The Motion Picture and the Family*, p. 8.
28. Sigler, R. F. (1978). A rationale for the film as a public library resource and service. *Library Trends, 26*, 9–26.
29. Horne, J. (2011). A history long overdue: the public library and motion pictures. In C. Acland & H. Wasson (Eds.), *Useful cinema* (pp. 149–177). Durham, NC: Duke University Press, p. 173.
30. Rossi-Snook, E. (2005). Persistence of vision: Public library 16mm film collections in America. *The Moving Image, 5*(1), 1–26, pp. 8–9.
31. Ibid., p. 11.
32. Sigler, R. F. (1978). A rationale for the film as a public library resource and service. *Library Trends, 26*, 12.
33. Martin, M. (1939, August 22). Films aid public library. *Philadelphia Inquirer*, p. 21.
34. Rossi-Snook, E. (2012). Continuing ed: Educational film collections in libraries and archives. In D. Orgeron, M. Orgeron, & D. Streible (Eds.), *Learning with the lights off* (pp. 457–477). New York, NY: Oxford University Press.
35. Ibid.
36. Ibid., p. 466.
37. Stauffer, S. (2017). Utilizing this new medium of mass communication: The regional film distribution programme at the Cleveland Public Library, 1948–1951. *Library & Information History, 33*(4), 258–274. doi:10.1080/17583489.2017.1372915
38. Grierson, J. (1946). The library in an international world. *ALA Bulletin, 40*(10), 293–303.
39. Finch, H. (1940). Motion picture activities in the high school. *The English Journal, 29*(4), 465–470, p. 466.

40. Chalk, P. (2017). Edgar Dale's film appreciation programme: An early education in adaptation. *Historical Journal of Film, Radio and Television 18*(2), 1 – 14.. doi:10.1080/01439685.2017.1413040

41. McDonald, G. (1942). *Educational motion pictures and libraries.* Chicago, IL: American Library Association.

42. Stauffer, S. (2017). Utilizing this new medium of mass communication: The regional film distribution programme at the Cleveland Public Library, 1948–1951. *Library & Information History, 33*(4), 258–274, p. 264.

43. Rossi-Snook, E (2005). Persistence of vision: Public library 16mm film collections in America. *The Moving Image, 5*(1), 1–26, p. 14.

44. Stauffer, S. (2017). Utilizing this new medium of mass communication: The regional film distribution programme at the Cleveland Public Library, 1948–1951. *Library & Information History, 33*(4), 258–274, p. 265. doi:10.1080/17583489.2017.1372915

45. Larson, L. C. (1942). *A proposed plan for an Educational Film Library Association.* Retrieved from https://collections.libraries.indiana.edu/IULMIA/files/original/e6d2bb00d5a01a824c14623001913d19.pdf

46. Hazelton, H. J. (1994). Film libraries and librarianship. In W. A. Wiegand & D. G. Davis (Eds.), *Encyclopedia of library history* (pp. 196–198). New York, NY: Routledge.

47. Lincoln Center Live. (2016). Elena Rossi-Snook from NYPL for the Performing Arts Reserve Library. Retrieved from https://web.facebook.com/LincolnCenterNYC/videos/elena-rossi-snook-from-new-york-public-library-for-the-performing-arts-reserve-f/10154539765758187/

48. Spain, F. C., & Scoggin, M.C. (1962). They still read books. In R. L. Shayton (Ed.), *The eighth art: Twenty-three views of television today* (pp. 176–197). New York, NY: Holt Rinehart Winston;

49. Parker, E. (1963). The effects of television on public library circulation. *The public Opinion Quarterly Image, 27*(4), 578–589.

50. Rossi-Snook, E. (2005). Persistence of vision: Public library 16mm film collections in America. *The Moving Image, 5*(1), 1–26, p. 18.

51. Ibid.

52. Grieveson, L., & Wasson, L. (2008). *Inventing film studies.* Durham, NC: Duke University Press.

53. Rossi-Snook, E (2005). Persistence of vision: Public library 16mm film collections in America. *The Moving Image, 5*(1), 1–26, p. 18.

54. Rossi-Snook, E. (2012). Continuing ed: Educational film collections in libraries and archives. In D. Orgeron, M. Orgeron, & D. Streible (Eds.), *Learning with the lights off* (pp. 457–477). New York, NY: Oxford University Press.

55. Symons, A. K., & Stoffle, C. J. (1998). When values conflict. *American Libraries, 29*, 56–59.

56. American Library Association. (1977). *The Speaker:* Film discussion guide. Retrieved from http://ala14.ala.org/files/ala14/Speaker_Discussion_Guide_1977.pdf

57. Berry, J. (1977, June 1). A whimper for freedom. *Library Journal, 102*, 1227.

58. 8mm Forum. (2018, March 5). Disney on 16mm. Retrieved from http://8mmforum.filmtech.com/cgi-bin/ubb/ultimatebb.cgi?ubb=get_topic;f=5;t=001774

59. Providence Public Library. (1972). Annual Report, no page number.

60. Reddy, I. (1972). *Programmes for children.* Hamilton, ON: South Central Regional Library System..

61. Gracy, K. (2013). The evolution and integration of moving image preservation work into cultural heritage institutions. *Information & Culture, 48*(3), 368–389.

62. Ibid.

63. Quoted in Ibid., p. 380.

64. Brandt, K. (1977). Audiovisuals in public libraries? A Wisconsin survey shows the trend. *Wisconsin Library Bulletin, 73*, 175.

65. Eagen, D. (2011). Celebrating Home Movie Day. Retrieved from https://www.smithsonianmag.com/arts-culture/celebrating-home-movie-day-10317482

66. Minnesota library to lend video players and tapes. (1978, February). *School Library Journal, 24,* 16.

67. Vollmar-Grone, M. (2002). Public library video collections. In G. Handman (Ed.), *Video collection development in multi-type libraries.* Westport, CT: Greenwood Press.

68. Ho, J. (2013). Cataloging practices and access methods for videos at ARL and public libraries in the United States. *Library Resources & Technical Services, 48*(2), 107–121.

69. Capital Area District Libraries. The last VCR: The library's history with VHS, DVD and Beyond. Retrieved from http://www.cadl.org/news/2016/08/03/the-last-vcr-the-librarys-history-with-film-vhs-dvd-and-beyond/

70. Ibid.

71. Walters, W. H. (2003). Video media acquisitions in a college library. *Library Resources & Technical Services, 47*(4), 160.

72. RobbGrieco, M. (in press). *Making media literacy.* Lanham, MD: Lexington Books.

73. Ibid.

74. Otto, J. J. (2014). University faculty describe their use of moving images in teaching and learning and their perceptions of the library's role in that use. *College & Research Libraries, 75*(2), 115–44. doi:10.5860/crl12-399.

75. Bergman, B. J. (2010). Making the most of your video collection: Trends in patron access and resource sharing. *Library Trends, 58*(3), 335–348.

76. Albitz, R. S., & Bolger, D. F. (2000). Video interlibrary loan: Challenges facing the small college library. *Journal of Interlibrary Loan, Document Delivery & Information Supply, 11*(2), 77–87, p. 75.

77. Bergman, B. J. (2010). Making the most of your video collection: Trends in patron access and resource sharing. *Library Trends, 58*(3), 335–348.

78. Snelson, C., & Perkins, R. (2009). From silent film to YouTube TM: Tracing the historical roots of motion picture technologies in education. *Journal of Visual Literacy, 28*(1), 1–27.

79. Edmondon, R. (2016). *Audiovisual archiving philosophy and principles* (3rd ed.). Bangkok: UNESCO.

80. Patti, L. (2017). Cinephilia and paratexts DVD pedagogy in the era of instant streaming. In R. W. Richards & D. T. Johnson (Eds.), *For the love of cinema* (pp. 179–194). Bloomington: Indiana University Press.

81. Spicer, S., & Horbal, A. (2017). The future of video playback capability in college and university classrooms. *College & Research Libraries, 78*(5), 706–722. http://doi.org/10.5860/crl.78.5.706

82. Gracy, K. (2013). The evolution and integration of moving image preservation work into cultural heritage institutions. *Information & Culture, 48*(3), 368–389, p. 382.

83. Enis, M. (2016, June 9). Please rewind. *Library Journal.* Retrieved from https://lj.libraryjournal.com/2016/06/technology/please-rewind-preservation/#_

84. Academic Libraries Video Trust. (2017). About us. Retrieved from http://videotrust.org/about/faq

85. Spicer, S., & Horbal, A. (2017). The future of video playback capability in college and university classrooms. *College & Research Libraries, 78*(5), 706–722. http://doi.org/10.5860/crl.78.5.706

86. Adademic Libraries Video Trust. (2018). Update. Retrieved from https://www.nmm.net/academic-libraries-video-trust/

87. Casey, M. (2015). Why media preservation can't wait: The gathering storm. Presentation slides. Retrieved from https://www.avpreserve.com/wp-content/uploads/2017/07/casey_amia2013.pdf

88. Matthew, K. (2017). About the Institute of Museum and Library Services. Retrieved from https://www.imls.gov/sites/default/files/publications/documents/plsfy2014.pdf.

89. Bibbs, R. (2016, October 10). North Madison libraries consider their future as circulation declines. *The Herald Bulletin*. Retrieved from http://www.heraldbulletin.com/news/local_news/north-madison-libraries-consider-their-future-as-circulation-declines/article_b5bc29a2-8f4f-11e6-851f-a395937ff954.html

Chapter 8

1. Dale, E. (1970). *The literature of cinema.* New York, NY: Arno Press and the New York Times.
2. Heartland Film. (2012). Teaching with movies: A guide for parents and educators. Retrieved from http://www.heartlandfilm.org/wp-content/uploads/TeachingwithMoviesguide.pdf
3. Ridley, J. (2012, February 27). Five cool movies hidden on a shelf Nashville Public Library. Retrieved from https://www.nashvillescene.com/arts-culture/article/13042007/five-cool-movies-hidden-on-the-shelf-at-nashville-public-library
4. Cocciolo, A. (2013). Public libraries and PBS partnering to enhance civic engagement: A study of a nationwide initiative. *Public Library Quarterly*, 32(1), 1–20.,
5. Colburn, S., & Haines, L. (2012). Measuring libraries' use of YouTube as a promotional tool: An exploratory study and proposed best practices. *Journal of Web Librarianship*, 6(1), 5–31.
6. Gingerich, W. J., Abel, E. M., D'Aprix, A., Nordquist, G., & Riebschleger, J. (1999). Using a listserv to extend classroom learning: A content analysis. *Journal of Technology in Human Services*, 16(4), 1–16.
7. Aufderheide, P. (1993). *Media literacy. A report of the National Leadership Conference on Media Literacy.* Washington, DC: Aspen Institute, Communications and Society Program.
8. European Union. (2016). Background on media literacy. Retrieved from https://ec.europa.eu/digital-single-market/en/news/media-literacy-background-documents
9. International Federation of Library Associations. (2012). Moscow Declaration on Media and Information Literacy. Retrieved from https://www.ifla.org/publications/moscow-declaration-on-media-and-information-literacy
10. Huysmans, F. (2016). Promoting media and information literacy in libraries. European Parliament Committees. Retrieved from http://www.europarl.europa.eu/supporting-analyses
11. Ito, M., Gutiérrez, K., Livingstone, S., Penuel, B., Rhodes, J., Salen, K., Schor, J., Sefton-Green, J., & Watkins, S. C. (2013). *Connected learning: An agenda for research and design.* Chicago, IL: John D. and Catherine T. MacArthur Foundation, Digital Media and Learning Research Hub. .
12. Ryan, R., & Stiller, K. (1991). The social context of internalization: Parent and teacher influence on autonomy, motivation and learning In R. Pintrich & M. Maehr (Eds.), *Advances in motivation and achievement.* Volume 7. Goals and Self Regulatory Processes (pp. 115–149). Greenwich, CT: Jai Press.
13. Conway, P., & Zhao, Y. (2001). From luddites to designers: Portraits of teachers and technology in political documents. Paper presented at the American Educational Research Association (AERA) annual meeting, Seattle, WA, April 10–14.
14. Karsenti, T., Villeneuve, S., & Goyer, S. (2006, March). The impact of motivation on prospective teachers' use of Information and Communication Technologies (ICTs). Paper presented at the International de la Society of Information Technology in Teacher Education, Orlando, Florida.
15. Hobbs, R., & Tuzel, S. (2017). Teacher motivations for digital and media literacy: An examination of Turkish educators. *British Journal of Educational Technology*, 48(1), 7–22. doi:10.1111/bjet.12326
16. Hobbs, R. (2016). Syllabus, LSC 597 Library/Film Education. University of Rhode Island Graduate School of Library and Information Studies. Retrieved from https://libraryfilmed.files.wordpress.com/2015/09/lsc597-film-education-in-lis-syllabus-spring-20161.pdf

17. American Association of School Librarians & Association for Educational Communications and Technology. (1998). *Information power: Building partnerships for learning*. Chicago, IL: American Library Association.

18. Wine, L. (2016). School librarians as technology leaders: An evolution in practice. *Journal of Education for Library and Information Science Online, 57*(2), 207–220. http://doi.org/10.12783/issn.2328-2967/57/2/12

19. Keeling, M., & Standards, A. (2017). Supporting you, Supporting the standards: AASL's implementation plan. *Knowledge Quest, 46*(2), 80–85

20. Leibiger, C. A., & Aldrich, A. W. (2013). The mother of all LibGuides: Applying principles of communication and network theory in LibGuide design. In *Imagine, Innovate, Inspire: Proceedings of the ACRL 2013 Conference* (pp. 429–441), Indianapolis, IN.

21. Gessner, G. C., Chandler, A., & Wilcox, W. (2015). Are you reaching your audience? The intersection between LibGuide authors and LibGuide users. *International Journal of Operations and Production Manage, 43*(3), 491–508. http://doi.org/10.1108/EL-01-2014-002

22. Common Sense Media. (2018). 50 movies kids should watch before they're 12. Retrieved from https://www.commonsensemedia.org/lists/50-movies-all-kids-should-watch-before-theyre-12

23. Sims, D. (2018, October 31). The demise of FilmStruck is part of a bigger problem. *The Atlantic.* Retrieved from https://www.theatlantic.com/entertainment/archive/2018/10/filmstruck-warnermedia-att-criterion-collection-demise/574435/

24. Warner Instant Movies. (2017). Warner Archives. Retrieved from https://www.warnerarchive.com/

25. Montgomery County Community College Library. (2013). Betzwood. Retrieved from https://mc3.libguides.com/betzwood/home

26. Rinehart, R., & Ippolito, J. (2014). *Re-collection: Art, new media, and social memory.* Cambridge, MA: MIT Press.

Chapter 9

1. University of Washington i-School. (2015, November 2). DYSTI: Mike Eisenberg [Video]. Retrieved from https://youtu.be/aYb1s7-0sIA

2. Jolls, T., & Wilson, C. (2010). The core concepts: Fundamental to media literacy yesterday, today and tomorrow. Center for Media Literacy. Retrieved from http://www.medialit.org/reading-room/core-concepts-fundamental-media-literacy-yesterday-today-and-tomorrow

3. Morgenthaler, D., & Jolls, T. (2011). Interview with Marieli Rowe. Center for Media Literacy. Retrieved from http://www.medialit.org/sites/default/files/Voices_of_ML_Marieli_Rowe_1.pdf

4. Felini, D. (2016). *Educare al cinema: le origini.* Rome, Italy: Guerini Scientifica.

5. Fayettville Public Library. (2017, November 17). Fayettville Public Library Launches GoChip Beam. Retrieved from https://www.faylib.org/news/fayetteville-public-library-launches-gochip-beam

6. Figueroa, M. (2018, March). In a virtual world. *American Libraries, 49*(3/4), 28–32.

7. University of Washington I-School. (2016). Capstone film project captures entrepreneurial Soul of Seattle. Retrieved from https://ischool.uw.edu/news/2016/11/capstone-film-project-captures-entrepreneurial-soul-seattle

8. Garmer, A. (2018). Personal communication, February 22.

9. Pyle, R. (2017, October 17). LA in focus: Paint, pencils & pixels: How women transformed Walt Disney's animation—Mindy Johnson. Retrieved from https://vimeo.com/242092665

10. Campbell, C., Haines, C., Koester, A., & Stoltz, D. (2015). *Media mentorship in libraries: Serving youth.* Chicago, IL: American Library Association, Association for Library Service to Children.

11. Pogrebin, R. (2016, May 6). A place to hang out (read, too). *New York Times*. Retrieved from http://www.nytimes.com/2013/05/07/books/design-for-new-donnell-library-by-enrique-norten.html

12. Dunlap, D. (2016, June 20). An amphitheater. A laptop bar. It's a New York library like no other. Retrieved from https://www.nytimes.com/2016/06/21/nyregion/an-amphitheater-a-laptop-bar-its-a-new-york-library-like-no-other.html?_r=0

13. Library Journal. (2016). Movers and shakers. Retrieved from https://lj.libraryjournal.com/2016/03/people/movers-shakers-2016/jason-evans-groth-movers-shakers-2016-tech-leaders/

14. Lee, D. Y., & Lehto, M. R. (2013). User acceptance of YouTube for procedural learning: An extension of the Technology Acceptance Model. *Computers & Education, 61*, 193–208.

15. Anythink. (2008). Staff manifesto. Retrieved from https://www.anythinklibraries.org/sites/default/files/imce_uploads/Anythink_Staff_Manifesto.pdf

16. Anythink. (2017). Annual budget and strategic plan. Retrieved from https://www.anythinklibraries.org/sites/default/files/pages/2017_budget_document_final.pdf

17. Krasniewicz: Video Showcase. (2008). David B. Weigle Information Commons. University of Pennsylvania Libraries. Retrieved from http://commons.library.upenn.edu/showcase-krasniewicz-anth-courses-2008-videos

18. IDEO. (2015). Design thinking for libraries: A toolkit. Retrieved from http://designthinkingforlibraries.com/, p. 19.

19. Hunt, J. (2018, January 2). Advocate this, not that. *School Library Journal*. Retrieved from http://www.slj.com/2018/01/opinion/advocate-this-not-that/

20. Tripp, L. (2011). Digital youth, libraries, and new media literacy. *The Reference Librarian, 52*(4), 329–341.

21. Gahran, A. (2010, February 16). Partnering with libraries, "natural sites of media literacy." Knight Digital Media Center. Retrieved from http://archive.knightdigitalmediacenter.org/leadership_blog/   comments/20100215_partnering_with_libraries_natural_sites_of_media_literacy

22. Mihailidis, P. (2012). Media literacy and learning commons in the digital age: Toward a knowledge model for successful integration into the 21st century school library. *The Journal of Research on Libraries and Young Adults*. Retrieved from http://www.yalsa.ala.org/ jrlya/2012/04/media-literacy-and-learning-commons-in-the-digital-age-toward-a-knowledge-model-for-successful-integration-into-the-21st-century-school-library/

Appendix

1. Association of Research Libraries. (2012). Code of Best Practices in Fair Use for Academic and Research Libraries, January, 29. Retrieved from http://www.arl.org/bm~doc/code-of-best-practices-fair-use.pdf

2. Butler, B., & Russell, C. (2017). Section 108 Revision: Nothing new under the sun. *Journal of Copyright in Education and Librarianship, 2*(1), 1–37. http://doi.org/10.1148/radiol.11111690

3. Butler, B. (2011). Copyfraud and classroom performance rights: Two common bogus copyright claims. *Research Library Issues, 276*(20), 20 – 28. .

Bibliography

8mm Forum. (2018, March 5). Disney on 16mm. Retrieved from http://8mmforum.film-tech. com/cgi-bin/ubb/ultimatebb.cgi?ubb=get_topic;f=5;t=001774

Academic Libraries Video Trust. (2017). About us. Retrieved from http://videotrust.org/about/ faq

Adademic Libraries Video Trust. (2018). Update. Retrieved from https://www.nmm.net/ academic-libraries-video-trust/

Albion College. (2017). Student life. Movie viewing. Retrieved from https://www.albion.edu/ student-life/campus-programs-and-organizations/event-scheduling-and-program-policies/ movie-viewing

Albitz, R. S., & Bolger, D. F. (2000). Video interlibrary loan: Challenges facing the small college library. *Journal of Interlibrary Loan, Document Delivery & Information Supply,11*(2), 77–87.

Alexander, B., Becker, S. A., Cummins, M., & Giesinger, C. H. (2017). *Digital literacy in higher education, Part II: An NMC Horizon project strategic brief* (pp. 1–37). Washington, DC: The New Media Consortium.

Alliance for Excellent Education. (2017). Future ready librarians. Empowering students as creators. Webinar. Retrieved from https://all4ed.org/webinar-event/jun-13-2017/

Alvarez, B. (2017, January 1). Public libraries in the age of fake news. Public Library Association Magazine. Retrieved from http://publiclibrariesonline.org/2017/01/feature-public-libraries-in-the-age-of-fake-news/

American Academy of Pediatrics. (2016). Media and young minds. Council on Communications and Media. Policy Statement. Retrieved from http://pediatrics.aappublications.org/content/ 138/5/e20162591

American Association of School Librarians. (2018, February 22). Connecting competencies: Learner, school librarian and school library. Webinar. Retrieved from https://standards.aasl.org/event/ connecting-dots-look-national-school-library-standards-policymakers-2/

American Association of School Librarians & Association for Educational Communications and Technology. (1998). *Information power: Building partnerships for learning.* Chicago, IL: American Library Association.

American Library Association. (1977). *The Speaker:* Film discussion guide. Retrieved from http:// ala14.ala.org/files/ala14/Speaker_Discussion_Guide_1977.pdf

American Library Association. (2003). One book, one community. Public Programs Office. Retrieved from http://www.ala.org/tools/sites/ala.org.tools/files/content/onebook/files/ onebookguide.pdf

American Library Association. (2010). FAQ. Retrieved from http://www.ala.org/Template. cfm?Section=alafaq&template=/cfapps/faq/faq.cfm

American Library Association. (2012). Performance of or showing films in the classroom. Retrieved from http://libguides.ala.org/copyright/video

American Library Association. (2014). *National impact of library public programs assessment.* Retrieved from http://www.ala.org/aboutala/offices/ppo/resources/benefitspublic

American Library Association. (2015). Ratings. An interpretation of the Library Bill of Rights. Retrieved from http://www.ala.org/advocacy/intfreedom/librarybill/interpretations/rating-systems

Anderson, C. (July 2010). How web video powers global innovation. Retrieved from https://www.ted.com/talks/chris_anderson_how_web_video_powers_global_innovation

Angus Digital Media and Scottish Screen. (2009). *Moving image education in Scotland.* Retrieved from www.scottishscreen.com/images/documents/moving%20image_2009.pdf

Anythink. (2008). Staff manifesto. Retrieved from https://www.anythinklibraries.org/sites/default/files/imce_uploads/Anythink_Staff_Manifesto.pdf

Anythink. (2017). Annual budget and strategic plan. Retrieved from https://www.anythinklibraries.org/sites/default/files/pages/2017_budget_document_final.pdf

Arc of the Ozarks. (2017). About. Retrieved from http://www.thearcoftheozarks.org/

Aspen Institute. (2014). *Dialogue on public libraries.* Retrieved from http://csreports.aspeninstitute.org/Dialogue-on-Public-Libraries/2014/report

Aspen Institute. (2015). Rising to the challenge: Re-envisioning public libraries. Retrieved from https://csreports.aspeninstitute.org/documents/AspenLibrariesReport.pdf

Association of College and Research Libraries. (2016). *Framework for information literacy for higher education.* Retrieved from http://www.ala.org/acrl/standards/ilframework#authority

Aufderheide, P. (1993). *Media literacy. A report of the National Leadership Conference on Media Literacy.* Washington, DC: Aspen Institute, Communications and Society Program.

Bambino, D. (2002). Critical friends. *Educational Leadership, 59*(6), 25–27.

Barry, D. S., Marzouk, F., Chulak-Oglu, K., Bennett, D., Tierney, P., & O'Keeffe, G. W. (2016). Anatomy education for the YouTube generation. *Anatomical Sciences Education, 9*(1), 90–96.

BBC Newsbeat. (2017, May 19). Student banned from university for downloading *Chicken Run.* Retrieved from http://www.bbc.co.uk/newsbeat/article/39961502/student-banned-from-university-wi-fi-for-downloading-chicken-run

Beach, R., Appleman, D., Fecho, B., & Simon, R. (2016). *Teaching literature to adolescents* (3rd ed.). New York, NY: Routledge.

Benally, M., Campbell, C., Mendez, A., & Saito, A. (2017). Digital piracy: Legal consumption vs illegal media downloading selling and sharing. Department of Criminal Justice, Utah Valley University. Retrieved from https://www.uvu.edu/criminaljustice/docs/student-research/digitalpiracy.pdf

Bennett, S. (2008). The information or the learning commons: Which will we have? *Journal of Academic Librarianship, 34*(3), 183–187.

Bergman, B. J. (2010). Making the most of your video collection: Trends in patron access and resource sharing. *Library Trends, 58*(3), 335–348.

Bergman, B., Peters, V., & Schomberg, J. (2007). Video collecting for the sometimes media librarian: Tips and tricks for selecting, purchasing, and cataloging videos for an academic library. *College & Undergraduate Libraries, 14*(1), 57–77.

Berry, J. (1977, June 1). A whimper for freedom. *Library Journal, 102,* 1227–1230.

Bibbs, R. (2016, October 10). North Madison libraries consider their future as circulation declines. *The Herald Bulletin.* Retrieved from http://www.heraldbulletin.com/news/local_news/north-madison-libraries-consider-their-future-as-circulation-declines/article_b5bc29a2-8f4f-11e6-851f-a395937ff954.html

Bickford, J. (2010). Consumerism: How it impacts play and its presence in library collections. *Children & Libraries, 8*(3), 53–56.

Blake, V. (1989). The role of reviews and reviewing media in the selection process. *Collection Management, 11*(1–2), 1–40. http://doi.org/10.1300/J105v11n01

Bluth, D. (Producer/Director), & Goldman, G. (Producer/Director) (1997). *Anastasia* [Motion picture]. United States: 20th Century Fox.

Bolley, C. (2016). Young filmmakers' sandbox. *Children & Libraries 14*(4), 6–7.

Boske, C., & McCormack, S. (2011). Building an understanding of the role of media literacy for Latino/a high school students. *The High School Journal, 94*(4), 167–186.

Brandt, K. (1977). Audiovisuals in public libraries? A Wisconsin survey shows the trend. *Wisconsin Library Bulletin, 73,* 175.

Broadband Now Kentucky. (2017). Broadband Internet in Kentucky. Retrieved from https://broadbandnow.com/Kentucky

Brooks, D. E., & Hébert, L. P. (2006). Gender, race, and media representation. *Handbook of Gender and Communication, 16,* 297–317.

Brown, N. (2013). "A new movie-going public": 1930s Hollywood and the emergence of the "family" film. *Historical Journal of Film, Radio and Television, 33*(1), 1–23.

Burns, K. (2016). Teaching the Vietnam War. PBS Learning Media. Retrieved from https://ri.pbslearningmedia.org/collection/ken-burns-the-vietnam-war/#.Wph1TRPwaRs

Byeon, H., & Hong, S. (2015). Relationship between television viewing and language delay in toddlers: Evidence from a Korea national cross-sectional survey. *PLoS ONE, 10*(3), e0120663. http://doi.org/10.1371/journal.pone.0120663

Campbell, C., Haines, C., Koester, A., & Stoltz, D. (2015). *Media mentorship in libraries: Serving youth.* Chicago, IL: American Library Association, Association for Library Service to Children.

The Campus Guide to Copyright Compliance. (2008). Copyright Basics: The TEACH Act. Retrieved from http://wwwdem1.copyright.com/Services/copyrightoncampus/basics/teach.html

Cannell Library at Clark College. (2015). The A.S.P.E.C.T. Checklist for Evaluating Information. Retrieved from http://libraryguides.library.clark.edu/ld.php?content_id=22123050

Capital Area District Libraries. The last VCR: The library's history with VHS, DVD and Beyond. Retrieved from http://www.cadl.org/news/2016/08/03/the-last-vcr-the-librarys-history-with-film-vhs-dvd-and-beyond/

Caro, N. (Director) (2003). *Whale Rider* [Motion picture]. USA: Walt Disney Studios.

Casey, M. (2015). Why media preservation can't wait: The gathering storm [Presentation slides.] Retrieved from https://www.avpreserve.com/wp-content/uploads/2017/07/casey_amia2013.pdf

Cep, C. (2014, March 12). The last picture show. *Pacific Standard.* Retrieved from https://psmag.com/social-justice/last-picture-show-movies-television-computer-screens-76291

Chalk, P. (2017). Edgar Dale's film appreciation programme: An early education in adaptation. *Historical Journal of Film, Radio and Television, 18*(2), 1–14. doi:10.1080/01439685.2017.1413040

Charlotte Mecklenburg Library. (2017). Celebrate Hispanic Heritage Month. Retrieved from https://www.cmlibrary.org/blog/celebrate-hispanic-heritage-month

Charters, W. W. (1933). Motion pictures and youth: A summary. Columbus, OH: Bureau of Educational Research, Ohio State University. Retrieved from http://bit.ly/2vUvgFz

Chattoo, C., & Jenkins. W. (2017). When movies go to Washington: Documentary films and public policy in the United States. Volume 1. Retrieved from http://cmsimpact.org/wp-content/uploads/2017/04/CMSI_Washington.pdf

Chen, S. (2017). My Life as a Zucchini movie review. Common Sense Media. Retrieved from https://www.commonsensemedia.org/movie-reviews/my-life-as-a-zucchini

Chen, S. (2017). Wonderstruck movie review. Common Sense Media. Retrieved from https://www.commonsensemedia.org/movie-reviews/wonderstruck

Cocciolo, A. (2013). Public libraries and PBS partnering to enhance civic engagement: A study of a nationwide initiative. *Public Library Quarterly, 32*(1), 1–20.

Coggan, D. (2016, June 23). Male film critics greatly outnumber female critics, study finds. *Entertainment Weekly.* Retrieved from http://ew.com/article/2016/06/23/film-criticism-gender-study/

Colburn, S., & Haines, L. (2012). Measuring libraries' use of YouTube as a promotional tool: An exploratory study and proposed best practices. *Journal of Web Librarianship, 6*(1), 5–31.

Common Sense Media. (2015). Digital bytes [Multimedia]. Retrieved from http://digitalbytes. commonsensemedia.org/

Common Sense Media. (2016). *Watching gender: How stereotypes in movies and TV impact kids' development.* Retrieved from https://www.commonsensemedia.org/research/watching-gender

Common Sense Media. (2018). 50 movies kids should watch before they're 12. Retrieved from https://www.commonsensemedia.org/lists/50-movies-all-kids-should-watch-before-theyre-12

Community builders. (2012). *Library Journal, 137*(5), 25.

Considine, D. M. (1986). Visual literacy and children's books: An integrated approach. *School Library Journal, 33*(1), 38–42.

Conway, P., & Zhao, Y. (2001). From luddites to designers: Portraits of teachers and technology in political documents. Paper presented at the American Educational Research Association (AERA) annual meeting. Seattle, WA, April 10–14.

Cook, J. (2013). Wake me up before you go-go: Using unlikely examples to engage students in information literacy. *LOEX Quarterly, 39*(4), 9–11.

Cooksey, A. (2017, April 13). Celebrate #SLM17 with Flipgrid. Knowledge Quest. Retrieved from http://knowledgequest.aasl.org/celebrate-slm17-flipgrid/

Cox-Stanton, T. (2017). Nearing the heart of a film: Toward a cinephilic pedagogy. In R. W. Richards & D. T. Johnson (Eds.), *For the love of cinema* (pp. 79–93). Indianapolis: Indiana University Press.

Dale, E. (1970). *The literature of cinema.* New York, NY: Arno Press and the New York Times.

Dalton, B., & Grisham, D. L. (2013). Love that book. *The Reading Teacher, 67*(3), 220–225.

Dancoff, J. (2012). Getting your film ready for school. Retrieved from https://www.documentary. org/magazine/getting-your-film-ready-school-it%E2%80%99s-academic-diy

Dargis, M. (2006, November 17). Bring on Da Hoofers on Ice. *New York Times.* Retrieved from https://www.nytimes.com/2006/11/17/movies/17feet.html

Davis, M. (1978). Tune in at the library. *Wisconsin Library Bulletin, 73*, 173–174.

Deggens, E. (2016, February 22). Hollywood has a major diversity problem, USC study finds. The Two Way. NPR. Retrieved from http://www.npr.org/sections/thetwo-way/2016/02/22/ 467665890/hollywood-has-a-major-diversity-problem-usc-study-finds

Dennis, M. (2012). Outreach initiatives in academic libraries, 2009–2011. *Reference Services Review, 40*(3), 368–383. doi:10.1108/00907321211254643

Department of Education, Kentucky. (2018). Kentucky Education Facts. Retrieved from https:// education.ky.gov/comm/edfacts/Pages/default.aspx

Desmet, C. (2009). Teaching Shakespeare with YouTube. *English Journal, 99*(1), 65–70.

Diergarten, A. K., Möckel, T., Nieding, G., & Ohler, P. (2017). The impact of media literacy on children's learning from films and hypermedia. *Journal of Applied Developmental Psychology, 48*, 33–41. http://doi.org/10.1016/j.appdev.2016.11.007

Digital Media and Learning. (2013). Project: Connect. Retrieved from https://dml5.dml-competition.net/

Dimmock, N. (2007). A popular DVD collection in an academic library. *New Library World, 108*(3–4), 141–150. doi:10.1108/03074800710735348

Dixon, J. (2017, September 7). The academic mainstream | streaming video. *Library Journal.* Retrieved from http://bit.ly/2icRLTW

Dowd, N. (2013, August 5). If you don't have time for partnerships, chances are your community won't have time for you. *Library Journal.* Retrieved from http://lj.libraryjournal.com/2013/ 08/marketing/if-you-dont-have-time-for-partnerships-chances-are-your-community-wont-have-time-for-you/#_

Dunlap, D. (2016, June 20). An amphitheater. A laptop bar. It's a New York library like no other. Retrieved from https://www.nytimes.com/2016/06/21/nyregion/an-amphitheater-a-laptop-bar-its-a-new-york-library-like-no-other.html?_r=0

Eagen, D. (2011). Celebrating home movie day. Retrieved from https://www.smithsonianmag. com/arts-culture/celebrating-home-movie-day-10317482

Edmondon, R. (2016). *Audiovisual archiving philosophy and principles* (3rd ed.). Bangkok, Thailand: UNESCO Bangkok.

Ellis, E. (2010). Book trailers: Available at a library near you. *Indiana Libraries, 29*(2), 24–26.

Ellis, E. (2017, July 5). Filtering your world is understandable—But it's not helpful. *Wired.* Retrieved from https://www.wired.com/story/vidangel-movie-filtering/

Enis, M. (2016, June 9). Please rewind. *Library Journal.* Retrieved from https://lj.libraryjournal. com/2016/06/technology/please-rewind-preservation/#_

Estevez, E. (2018). Emilio Estevez. *American Libraries, 49*(3/4), 28–32.

European Union. (2016). Background on media literacy. Retrieved from https://ec.europa.eu/ digital-single-market/en/news/media-literacy-background-documents

Fashina, A., & Nathanson, A. I. (2016). What preschoolers bring to the show: The relation between viewer characteristics and children's learning from educational television. *Media Psychology. 19*(3), 406–430.

Fayetteville Public Library. (2017, November 17). Fayettville Public Library Launches GoChip Beam. Retrieved from https://www.faylib.org/news/fayetteville-public-library-launches-gochip-beam

Felini, D.(2016). *Educare al cinema: Le origini.* Rome, Italy: Guerini Scientifica.

Fernandez, L (2017, December 18). 30% of Oakland school libraries closed. KTVU. Retrieved from http://www.ktvu.com/news/thirty-percent-of-oakland-school-libraries-closed-district-lays-off-head-librarian

Figueroa, M. (2018, March). In a virtual world. *American Libraries, 49*(3/4), 28–32.

The Film Space. (2017). *Teaching trailers teacher's guide.* Retrieved from http://thefilmspace.org/ teachingtrailers/2017/

Finch, H. (1940). Motion picture activities in the high school. *The English Journal, 29*(4), 465–470.

Fisher, D., & Frey, N. (2012). Close reading in elementary schools. *Reading Teacher, 66*(3), 179–188. http://doi.org/10.1002/TRTR.01117

Fitzgerald, R. (2010). Using Netflix at an academic library. Tame the Web. Library Innovators. Retrieved from http://tametheweb.com/2010/09/09/using-netflix-at-anacademic-library-a-ttw-guest-post-by-rebecca-fitzgerald/.

Flanagin, A. J., & Metzger, M. J. (2007). The role of site features, user attributes, and information verification behaviors on the perceived credibility of web-based information. *New Media & Society, 9*(2), 319–342.

Flowers, M. (2011). The movie is (sometimes) better than the book: Adaptations as literary analysis. *Young Adult Library Services, 9*(4), 21–24.

Flynn, S. (2015, May 19). She is the school's go-to person. *Newport Daily News.* Retrieved from http://www.newportri.com/newportdailynews/news/page_one/she-is-school-s-go-to-person/article_a62f7cfb-2a31-5a00-bf60-d1a02cb75082.html

Friends of Everson MacBeith Library. (2015, June 24). Facebook. Retrieved from https://www. facebook.com/Everson.Friends/posts/1086138578069901

Fuchs, E., Bruch, A., and Annegarn-Gläß, M. (2016). Educational films: A historical review of media innovation in schools. *Journal of Educational Media, Memory and Society, 8*(1), 1–13.

Gahran, A. (2010, February 16). Partnering with libraries, "natural sites of media literacy." Knight Digital Media Center. Retrieved from http://archive.knightdigitalmediacenter.org/ leadership_ blog/ comments/20100215_partnering_with_libraries_natural_sites_of_ media_literacy

Gamble, A. (2016, December 12). Multimedia creation in the small campus library. *Against the Grain, 28*(5). Retrieved from http://bit.ly/2gER9D1

Gee, J. P. (2007). *Good video games+ good learning: Collected essays on video games, learning, and literacy.* New York, NY: Peter Lang.

Genett, J. (2014). Measuring outcomes for teen technology programs. *Young Adult Library Services, 13*(1), 25–28.

Gentile, D. A., Humphrey, J., & Walsh, D. A. (2005). Media ratings for movies, music, video games, and television: A review of the research and recommendations for improvements. *Adolescent Medicine Clinics, 16*(2), 427.

Gentile, D. A., Reimer, R. A., Nathanson, A. I., Walsh, D. A., & Eisenmann, J. C. (2014). Protective effects of parental monitoring of children's media use a prospective study. *JAMA Pediatrics, 168*(5), 479–484. http://doi.org/10.1001/jamapediatrics.2014.146

Gerbner, G., Gross, L., Morgan, M., Signorielli, N., & Shanahan, J. (2002). Growing up with television: Cultivation processes. In B. Jennings & D. Zillmann (Eds.), *Media effects: advances in theory and research* (2nd ed., pp. 43–67). Mahwah, NJ: Lawrence Erlbaum Associates.

Gessner, G. C., Chandler, A., & Wilcox, W. (2015). Are you reaching your audience? The intersection between LibGuide authors and LibGuide users. *International Journal of Operations and Production Manage, 43*(3), 491–508. http://doi.org/10.1108/EL-01-2014-002

Gingerich, W. J., Abel, E. M., D'Aprix, A., Nordquist, G., & Riebschleger, J. (1999). Using a listserv to extend classroom learning: A content analysis. *Journal of Technology in Human Services, 16*(4), 1–16.

Girl Scout Research Institute. (2011). Real to me: Girls and reality TV. Retrieved from http://www.girlscouts.org/ research/pdf/real_to_me_factsheet.pdf

Glassman, J., Lee, S., Salomon, D., & Worsham, D. (2017). Community collections: Nurturing student curators. In S. Arnold-Garza & C. Tomlinson (Eds.), *Students lead the library: The importance of student contributions to the academic library* (pp. 77–92). Chicago, IL: American Library Association.

Graber, D. A. (1990). Seeing is remembering: How visuals contribute to learning from television news. *Journal of Communication, 40*(3), 134–156.

Gracy, K. (2013). The evolution and integration of moving image preservation work into cultural heritage institutions. *Information & Culture, 48*(3), 368–389.

Gracy, K. (2017). See the movie, read the book! Cleveland Public Library's bookmarks programme, 1923–1972. *Library & Information History, 33*(4), 236–257.

Grant, M. (2017). How *Stranger Things* influenced my reading life. Book Riot. Retrieved from https://bookriot.com/2017/11/21/stranger-things-influenced-my-reading-life/

Grierson, J. (1946). The library in an international world. *ALA Bulletin, 40*(10), 293–303.

Grieveson, L., & Wasson, H. (2008). *Inventing film studies*. Durham, NC: Duke University Press.

Gross, D., Pietri, E. S., Anderson, G., Moyano-Camihort, K., & Graham, M. J. (2015). Increased preclass preparation underlies student outcome improvement in the flipped classroom. *CBE Life Sciences Education, 14*(4), 1–8. http://doi.org/10.1187/cbe.15-02-0040

Guernsey, L., & Levine, M. (2017). *How to bring early learning and family engagement into the digital age*. New America Foundation. Retrieved from http://joanganzcooneycenter.org/wp-content/uploads/2017/04/digital_age.pdf

Gunter, G., & Kenny, R. (2008). Digital booktalk: Digital media for reluctant readers. *Contemporary Issues in Technology and Teacher Education, 8*(1), 84–99.

Haidt, L. (2016, June 27). Storymakers 2016 winners. Retrieved from http://forums.techsoup.org/cs/community/b/tsblog/archive/2016/06/27/storymakers-2016-winners.aspx

Haines, C., & Campbell, C. (2016). *Becoming a media mentor: A guide for working with children and families*. Association for Library Service to Children. Chicago, IL: American Library Association.

Hains, R. (2014). *The princess problem: Guiding our girls through the princess obsessed years*. New York, NY: Sourcebooks.

Hale, B. (2014, November 12). The history of the Hollywood movie industry. History Cooperative. Retrieved from http://historycooperative.org/the-history-of-the-hollywood-movie-industry/

Hamblin, J. (2015, September 15). The money spent selling sugar to Americans is staggering. *The Atlantic*. Retrieved from https://www.theatlantic.com/health/archive/2015/09/the-money-spent-selling-sugar-to-americans-is-staggering/407350/

Handman, G. (2010). License to look: Evolving models for library video acquisition and access. *Library Trends, 58*(3), 324–334.

Haney, W. (2016). Ghostbusters is a perfect example of how internet movie ratings are broken. FiveThirtyEight. Retrieved from https://fivethirtyeight.com/features/ghostbusters-is-a-perfect-example-of-how-internet-ratings-are-broken/

Harmon, A. (2017, October 4). Make reflections, discussions and assessments easier with Flipgrid. The Art of Education. Retrieved from https://www.theartofed.com/2017/10/04/3-ways-use-flipgrid-art-room/

Hatch, M. (2014). *The maker movement manifesto.* New York, NY: McGraw Hill.

Hazelton, H. J. (1994). Film libraries and librarianship. In W. A. Wiegand & D. G. Davis (Eds.), *Encyclopedia of library history.* New York, NY: Routledge.

Heartland Film. (2012). Teaching with movies: A guide for parents and educators. Retrieved from http://www.heartlandfilm.org/wp-content/uploads/TeachingwithMoviesguide.pdf

Hirsh-Pasek, K., Zosh, J. M., Golinkoff, R. M., Gray, J. H., Robb, M. B., & Kaufman, J. (2015). Putting education in "educational" apps: Lessons from the science of learning. *Psychology and Science in the Public Interest, 16,* 3–34. doi:10.1177/1529100615569721

Ho, J. (2013). Cataloging practices and access methods for videos at ARL and public libraries in the United States. *Library Resources & Technical Services, 48*(2), 107–121.

Hobbs, R. (2006). Non-optimal uses of video in the classroom. *Learning, Media and Technology, 31*(1), 45–50.

Hobbs, R. (2010). *Digital and media literacy: A plan of action.* Washington, DC: John S. and James L. Knight Foundation and Aspen Institute.

Hobbs, R. (2011). *Copyright clarity: How fair use supports digital learning.* Thousand Oaks, CA: Corwin/Sage.

Hobbs, R. (2016a). Lessons in copyright activism: K-12 education and the DMCA 1201 exemption rulemaking process. *International Journal of Information and Communication Technology Education (IJICTE), 12*(1), 50–63.

Hobbs, R. (2016b). Literacy. In K. B. Jensen, E. Rothenbuhler, & R. Craig (Eds.), *International encyclopedia of communication theory and philosophy* (pp. 1–11). Hoboken, NJ: Wiley Blackwell.

Hobbs, R. (2016c). Syllabus, LSC 597 Library/Film Education. University of Rhode Island Graduate School of Library and Information Studies. https://libraryfilmed.files.wordpress.com/2015/09/lsc597-film-education-in-lis-syllabus-spring-20161.pdf

Hobbs, R. (2017). *Create to learn: Introduction to digital literacy.* Hoboken, NJ: Wiley Blackwell.

Hobbs, R., Cabral, N., Ebrahimi, A., Yoon, J., & Al-Humaidan, R. (2011). Field-based teacher education in elementary media literacy as a means to promote global understanding. *Action in Teacher Education, 33,* 144–156.

Hobbs, R., & Jensen, A. (2009). The past, present and future of media literacy education. *Journal of Media Literacy Education, 1*(1), 1–11.

Hobbs, R., & Moore, D. C. (2013). *Discovering media literacy: Digital media and popular culture in elementary school.* Thousand Oaks, CA: Corwin/Sage.

Hobbs, R., & RobbGrieco, M. (2012). African-American children's active reasoning about media texts as a precursor to media literacy. *Journal of Children and Media, 6*(4), 502–519.

Hobbs, R., Stauffer, J., Frost, R., & Davis, A. (1988). How first time viewers comprehend editing. *Journal of Communication, 38*(4), 50–60.

Hobbs, R., & Tuzel, S. (2017). Teacher motivations for digital and media literacy: An examination of Turkish educators. *British Journal of Educational Technology, 48*(1), 7–22. doi:10.1111/bjet.12326

Hofferton, B. (2017). Under the surface. Materials survey 2017. *Library Journal.* Retrieved from http://reviews.libraryjournal.com/2017/02/collection-development/under-the-surface-materials-survey-2017

Holaday, P. W., & Stoddard, G. D. (1933). *Getting ideas from the movies.* New York, NY: Macmillan.

Horne, J. (2011). A history long overdue: The public library and motion pictures. In C. Acland & H. Wasson (Eds.), *Useful cinema* (pp. 149–177). Durham, NC: Duke University Press.

Hoyt, E. (2012). *Hollywood vault: The business of film libraries, 1915–1960.* PhD dissertation, University of Southern California.

Huesmann, L. R. (2007). The impact of electronic media violence: Scientific theory and research. *Journal of Adolescent Health, 41*(6), S6–S13.

Hunt, J. (2018, January 2). Advocate this, not that. *School Library Journal.* Retrieved from http://www.slj.com/2018/01/opinion/advocate-this-not-that/

Huysmans, F. (2016). Promoting media and information literacy in libraries. European Parliament Committees. Retrieved from http://www.europarl.europa.eu/supporting-analyses

IDEO. (2015). Design Thinking for Libraries: A Toolkit. Retrieved from http://designthinkingforlibraries.com/, p. 19.

International Federation of Library Associations. (2012). Moscow Declaration on Media and Information Literacy. Retrieved from https://www.ifla.org/publications/moscow-declaration-on-media-and-information-literacy

Into Film. (2017a). Teaching Literacy through Film. Retrieved from https://www.futurelearn.com/courses/teaching-literacy-through-film

Into Film. (2017b). About. Retrieved from https://www.intofilm.org/about

Irdeto. (2017). Irdeto Global Consumer Piracy Report. Retrieved from https://resources.irdeto.com/piracy-cybercrime/irdeto-global-cusumer-piracy-survey-report

Irons, K. (2014). *Film programs for public libraries.* Chicago. IL: Public Library Association.

Ito, M., Baumer, S., Bittanti, M., Cody, R., Stephenson, B. H., Horst, H. A., . . . Perkel, D. (2009). *Hanging out, messing around, and geeking out: Kids living and learning with new media.* Cambridge, MA: MIT Press.

Ito, M., Gutiérrez, K., Livingstone, S., Penuel, B., Rhodes, J., Salen, K., . . . Watkins, S. C. (2013). *Connected learning: An agenda for research and design.* Chicago, IL: John D. and Catherine T. MacArthur Foundation: Digital Media and Learning Research Hub.

Jambon, M., & Smetana, J. (2012). College students' moral evaluations of illegal music downloading. *Journal of Applied Developmental Psychology, 33,* 31–39. doi:10.1016/j.appdev.2011.09.001.

Jenkins, B. (2011). Barry Loves da Kids [Video]. Retrieved from https://vimeo.com/29845569

Jenkins, H. (2007). A few thoughts on media violence. Confessions of an ACA fan. Retrieved from http://henryjenkins.org/blog/2007/04/a_few_thoughts_on_media_violen.html

Jenkins, H., Ford, S., & Green, J. (2013). *Spreadable media: Creating value and meaning in a networked culture.* New York, NY: New York University Press.

Jenkins, H., Purushotma, R., Weigel, M., Clinton, K., & Robison, A. J. (2009). *Confronting the challenges of participatory culture: Media education for the 21st century.* Cambridge, MA: MIT Press.

Johnson, D. (2017, December 15). Librarians and the scarcity mentality. Blue Skunk Blog. Retrieved from http://doug-johnson.squarespace.com/blue-skunk-blog/2017/12/15/librarians-and-the-scarcity-mentality.html

Jolls, T., & Wilson, C. (2010). The core concepts: Fundamental to media literacy yesterday, today and tomorrow. Center for Media Literacy. Retrieved from http://www.medialit.org/reading-room/core-concepts-fundamental-media-literacy-yesterday-today-and-tomorrow

Jones, M. (2017, February 7). What teenagers are learning from online porn. *New York Times Magazine.* Retrieved from https://www.nytimes.com/2018/02/07/magazine/teenagers-learning-online-porn-literacy-sex-education.html

Kammen, M. (1996). *The lively arts: Gilbert Seldes and the transformation of cultural criticism in the United States.* New York, NY: Oxford University Press.

Karsenti, T., Villeneuve, S., & Goyer, S. (2006, March). The impact of motivation on prospective teachers' use of Information and Communication Technologies (ICTs). Paper presented at the International de la Society of Information Technology in Teacher Education, Orlando, Florida.

Keeling, M., & Standards, A. (2017). Supporting you, Supporting the standards: AASL's implementation plan. *Knowledge Quest, 46*(2), 80–85.

Kelly, K. (2016, February 18). Film Screenings 101. *Programming Librarian.* http://www.programminglibrarian.org/blog/film-screenings-101

Kelly, M. (2015). Collection development policies in public libraries in Australia: A qualitative content analysis. *Public Library Quarterly, 34*(1), 44–62.

King, R. (2016). Access to circulating videos in academic libraries: From policy review to action plan. *Collection Management, 41*(4), 209–220.

King, R. (2014). House of cards: The academic library media center in the era of streaming. *The Serials Librarian,* 289–306. doi:10.1080/0361526X.2014.948699

Kist, W. (2013). New literacies and the Common Core. *Educational Leadership.* http://www.ascd.org/publications/educational-leadership/mar13/vol70/num06/New-Literacies-and-the-Common-Core.aspx

Koblin, J. (2017, February 19). NBC takes shot at counting streaming views. *New York Times.*

Krasniewicz: Video Showcase. (2008). David B. Weigle Information Commons. University of Pennsylvania Libraries. Retrieved from http://commons.library.upenn.edu/showcase-krasniewicz-anth-courses-2008-videos

Kraus, M. (2017). Why academic librarians hate Netflix: Digital copyright and the challenge of acquiring and providing on-demand streaming media for classroom use. MA thesis, Moving Image Archiving and Preservation Program, Department of Cinema Studies, New York University.

Lankes, R., Newman, W., Kowalski, S., Tench, B., Gould, C., Silk, K., & Britton, L. (2016). *The new librarianship field guide.* Cambridge, MA: MIT Press.

Lareau, A. (2011). *Unequal childhoods: Class, race, and family life.* Berkeley: University of California Press.

Larson, L. C. (1942). *A proposed plan for an Educational Film Library Association.* Retrieved from https://collections.libraries.indiana.edu/IULMIA/files/original/e6d2bb00d5a01a824c14623001913d19.pdf

Lee, D. Y., & Lehto, M. R. (2013). User acceptance of YouTube for procedural learning: An extension of the Technology Acceptance Model. *Computers & Education, 61,* 193–208.

Lee, M. (2013, February 20). Library as filmmaker: The creation of a California town's gay prom. *Library Journal.* Retrieved from https://lj.libraryjournal.com/2013/02/library-services/library-as-filmmaker-documenting-the-creation-of-a-california-towns-gay-prom/#_

Leffler, J., Hayden. J., & Enoch, T. (2017). Juggling a new format with existing tools: Incorporating streaming video into technical services workflows, *The Serials Librarian, 72*(1–4), 102–104. doi:10.1080/0361526X.2017.1284498

Lehman, C., & Roberts, K. (2014). *Falling in love with close reading.* Portsmouth, NH: Heinemann.

Leibiger, C. A., & Aldrich, A. W. (2013). The mother of all LibGuides': Applying principles of communication and network theory in LibGuide design. In *Imagine, Innovate, Inspire: Proceedings of the ACRL 2013 Conference* (pp. 429–441). Indianapolis, IN.

Leitch, G. (2008). Adaptation studies at a crossroads. *Adaptation, 1*(1), 63–77. https://doi-org.uri.idm.oclc.org/10.1093/adaptation/apm005

Leitch, G. (2009). *Film adaptation and its discontents.* Baltimore, MD: Johns Hopkins University Press.

Leitch, T. M. (2003). Twelve fallacies in contemporary adaptation theory. *Criticism, 45*(2), 149–171. http://doi.org/10.1353/crt.2004.0001

LeMay, E. (2017, May 2). Fake news invasion: Teaching media literacy skills to teens. https://emilygracelemay.wordpress.com/2017/03/02/fake-news-invasion-teaching-media-literacy-skills-to-teens/#more-2445

LeRoy, D., LeRoy, J., & Reed, C. (2016, February 29). Study reveals surprising diversity among public TV viewership. *Current.* Retrieved from http://bit.ly/2skisL2

Levin, S., & Levin, S. (2010). Student created videos. *Knowledge Quest, 38*(4), 52–55.

Library Association. (2017). Policy manual crosswalk. Retrieved from http://www.ala.org/aboutala/governance/policymanual/updatedpolicymanual/section1/1mission

Library Journal. (2016). Movers and shakers. Retrieved from https://lj.libraryjournal.com/2016/03/people/movers-shakers-2016/jason-evans-groth-movers-shakers-2016-tech-leaders/

Lincoln Center Live. (2016). Elena Rossi-Snook from NYPL for the Performing Arts Reserve Library. Retrieved from https://web.facebook.com/LincolnCenterNYC/videos/elena-rossi-snook-from-new-york-public-library-for-the-performing-arts-reserve-f/10154539765758187/

Linebarger, D. L., & Piotrowski, J. T. (2009). TV as storyteller: How exposure to television narratives impacts at-risk preschoolers' story knowledge and narrative skills. *British Journal of Developmental Psychology, 27*(1), 47–69. http://doi.org/10.1348/026151008X400445

Lohmann, S., & Frederiksen, L. (2017). Educators' awareness and perception of streaming video for teaching. *Collection Management, 43*(2), 101–119. doi:10.1080/01462679.2017.1382411

Lorentz, P., & Ernst, M. (1930). *Censored: The private life of the movie.* New York, NY: Corwall Press.

Luckerson, V. (2016, January 19). This is how much Netflix we're all watching every day. *Time.* Retrieved from http://time.com/4186137/netflix-hours-per-day/

Luhtala, M. (2012, June 14). Just an average day at New Canaan school library. YouTube. Retrieved from https://youtu.be/Sww4M8f7UfU

Luhtala, M. (2012, August 28). We trust you 2012. YouTube. Retrieved from https://youtu.be/yIZ48MQIp48

Luhtala, M. (2013, February 14). 6 concerning trends in digital collection. Bibliotech. Retrieved from http://mluhtala.blogspot.com/2013/02/six-concerns-about-digital-collection.html

MacArthur Foundation. (2013, May 9). Grant competition to provide $150,000 for summer youth programs [Press release]. Retrieved from https://www.macfound.org/press/press-releases/grant-competition-provide-150000-summer-youth-programs/

Mackey, T. P., & Jacobson, T. E. (2011). Reframing information literacy as a metaliteracy. *College & Research Libraries, 72*(1), 62–78.

Marquez, J., & Downey, A. (2015). Service design: An introduction to a holistic assessment methodology of library services. *Weave, 1*(2). http://dx.doi.org/10.3998/weave.12535642.0001.201

Martin, M. (1939, August 22). Films aid public library. *Philadelphia Inquirer, p. 19.*

Mason, M. (n.d.). Librarians and their use of television and radio to answer reference questions. Retrieved from http://www.moyak.com/papers/reference-questions-tv-radio.html

Matthew, K. (2017). About the Institute of Museum and Library Services. Retrieved from https://www.imls.gov/sites/default/files/publications/documents/plsfy2014.pdf.

McDonald, G. (1942). *Educational motion pictures and libraries.* Chicago, IL: American Library Association.

McLean, S. A., Paxton, S. J., & Wertheim, E. H. (2016). Does media literacy mitigate risk for reduced body satisfaction following exposure to thin-ideal media? *Journal of Youth and Adolescence, 45*(8), 1678–1695. http://doi.org/10.1007/s10964-016-0440-3

Media Education Lab. (2015, October 28). Webinar in film distribution and exhibition in public libraries. Retrieved from https://www.youtube.com/watch?v=gsiR-c4hA6g#t=60

Media Education Lab. (2015). Media and information literacy at the Mark Day School. Retrieved from https://mediaeducationlab.com/sites/default/files/Mark%2520Day%2520School%2520Final%2520Report_0.pdf

Merry, L. (2004). The devil in the details. *Library Collections, Acquisitions, and Technical Services, 28*(3), 298–311. doi:10.1080/14649055.2004.10765998

Mihailidis, P. (2012). Media literacy and learning commons in the digital age: Toward a knowledge model for successful integration into the 21st century school library. *The Journal of Research on Libraries and Young Adults.* Retrieved from http://www.yalsa.ala.org/ jrlya/2012/04/media-literacy-and-learning-commons-in-the-digital-age-toward-a-knowledge-model-for-successful-integration-into-the-21st-century-school-library/

Mihailidis, P. (2015). Digital curation and digital literacy: evaluating the role of curation in developing critical literacies for participation in digital culture. *E-learning and Digital Media, 12*(5–6), 443–458.

Mihailidis, P. (2018). Civic media literacies: Re-imagining engagement for civic intentionality. *Learning, Media and Technology 43*(2), 152-164.

Mihailidis, P., & Cohen, J. (2013). Exploring curation as a core competency in digital and media literacy education. *Journal of Interactive Media in Education, 2013*(1).

Mihailidis, P., & Diggs, V. (2010). From information reserve to media literacy learning commons: Revisiting the 21st century library as the home for media literacy education. *Public Library Quarterly, 29*(4), 279–292.

Mikkelson, D. (2017). Did *Happy Days* produce a 500% increase in library card applications? *Snopes.* Retrieved from https://www.snopes.com/radiotv/tv/librarycards.asp

Miller, A. (2016, January 17). Questions: What if they don't come up with the right ones? *The Contrarian Librarian.* Retrieved from https://thecontrarianlibrarian.com/2016/01/17/questions-what-if-they-dont-come-up-with-the-right-ones/

Miller, K. E. (2014). Imagine! On the future of teaching and learning and the academic research library. *Portal: Libraries and the Academy, 14*(3), 329–351.

Miller, S. M. (2013, December 13). Flipgrid allows for students to find their voice giving book talks. *The Library Voice.* Retrieved from http://vanmeterlibraryvoice.blogspot.com/2013/12/flipgrid-allows-for-students-to-find.html

Minnesota library to lend video players and tapes. (1978, February). *School Library Journal, 24,* 16.

Mobile Film Classroom. (2017). Programs. Retrieved from https://www.mobilefilmclassroom.org/programs/

Montgomery County Community College Library. (2013). Betzwood. Retrieved from https://mc3.libguides.com/betzwood/home

Morgenthaler, D., & Jolls, T. (2011). Interview with Marieli Rowe. Center for Media Literacy. Retrieved from http://www.medialit.org/sites/default/files/Voices_of_ML_Marieli_Rowe_1.pdf

Most Films Lurid, Says Censor Board. (1916, February 19). *Philadelphia Inquirer.*

Motley Fool. (2017). YouTube has over one billion users. Retrieved from https://fxn.ws/2pCZI5P

Nashvillle Public Library. (2016). All about the books. Retrieved from https://youtu.be/Pduszh4ADTU

National Research Council and Institute of Medicine. (2006). *Media consumption as a public health issue.* Studying Media Effects on Children and Youth: Improving Methods and Measures. Workshop Summary. Washington, DC: The National Academies Press. doi:10.17226/11706.

New York Film Academy. (2018). The most comprehensive list of film festivals on the Internet. Retrieved from https://www.nyfa.edu/student-resources/film-festivals/

Nielsen Company. (2017). *Mobile kids: The parent, the child and the smartphone.* Retrieved from http://www.nielsen.com/us/en/insights/news/2017/mobile-kids--the-parent-the-child-and-the-smartphone.html

Nikolajeva, M., & Scott, C. (2000). The dynamics of picturebook communication. *Children's Literature in Education, 31*(4), 225–239.

Nooksack Valley Heritage. (2015). Washington Rural Heritage. Washington State Library. Retrieved from http://www.washingtonruralheritage.org/cdm/about/collection/nooksack

O'Callaghan, F. V., Neumann, D. L., Jones, L., & Creed, P. (2017). The use of lecture recordings in higher education: A review of institutional, student, and lecturer issues. *Education and Information Technologies, 22*(1), 399–415.

O'Dell, K. (2015, November 15). Creating a level of comfort. *Library Journal.* Retrieved from http://lj.libraryjournal.com/2015/11/opinion/programs-that-pop/creating-a-level-of-comfort-programs-that-pop/

O'Neil, K. E. (2011). Reading pictures: Developing visual literacy for greater comprehension. *Reading Teacher, 65,* 214–223. doi:10.1002/TRTR.01026

Otto, J. J. (2014). University faculty describe their use of moving images in teaching and learning and their perceptions of the library's role in that use. *College & Research Libraries, 75*(2), 115–44. doi:10.5860/crl12-399.

Palfrey, J. (2015). *BiblioTech: Why libraries matter more than ever in the age of Google.* New York, NY: Basic.

Parrott, K. (2011). Circulating iPads in the library. ALSC Blog. Retrieved from https://www.alsc.ala.org/blog/2011/11/circulating-ipads-in-the-childrens-library/

Patti, L. (2017). Cinephilia and paratexts DVD pedagogy in the era of instant streaming. In R. W. Richards & D. T. Johnson (Eds.), *For the love of cinema* (pp. 179–194). Bloomington: Indiana University Press.

Peek, H. S., & Beresin, E. (2016). Reality check: How reality television can affect youth and how a media literacy curriculum can help. *Academic Psychiatry*, 40(1), 177–181. http://doi.org/10.1007/s40596-015-0382-1

Petersen, A. (2012). What we talk about when we talk about Brangelina. In the Library with the Lead Pipe. Retrieved from http://www.inthelibrarywiththeleadpipe.org/2012/what-we-talk-about-when-we-talk-about-brangelina/

Phillips, N. C., & Smith, B. E. (2012). Multimodality and aurality: Sound spaces in student digital book trailers. In P. J. Dunston, S. K. Fullerton, C. C. Bates, K. Headley, & P. M. Stecker (Eds.), *61st Yearbook of the Literacy Research Association* (pp. 84–99). Oak Creek, WI: Literacy Research Association.

Plantinga, C. (2009). *Moving viewers: American film and the spectator's experience.* Berkeley: University of California Press.

Platinga, C. (2016, November 21). Moving pictures. Retrieved from http://blogs.lse.ac.uk/theforum/moving-pictures/

Pogrebin, R. (2016, May 6). A place to hang out (read, too). New York Times. Retrieved from http://www.nytimes.com/2013/05/07/books/design-for-new-donnell-library-by-enrique-norten.html

Price, V. (2013). *The V-Chip: Content filtering from television to the internet.* New York, NY: Routledge.

Programming Librarian. (2017, July 10). Film programs with *The Vietnam War* [Webinar]. Retrieved from http://www.programminglibrarian.org/learn/film-programs-vietnam-war-film-ken-burns-and-lynn-novick

Providence Public Library. (1923). Annual Report. Historical collection, Providence Public Library. Providence Rhode Island.

Providence Public Library. (1949). Annual Report. Historical collection, Providence Public Library. Providence Rhode Island.

Providence Public Library. (1950). Annual Report. Historical collection, Providence Public Library. Providence Rhode Island.

Providence Public Library. (1972). Annual Report. Historical collection, Providence Public Library. Providence Rhode Island.

Pyle, R. (2017, October 17). LA in focus: Paint, pencils & pixels: How women transformed Walt Disney's animation—Mindy Johnson. Retrieved from https://vimeo.com/242092665

Radford, G., & Radford, M. (2001). Libraries, librarians, and the discourse of fear. *The Library Quarterly*, 71(3), 299–329.

Radford, M., & Radford, G. (2003). Librarians and party girls: cultural studies and the meaning of the librarian. *The Library Quarterly*, 73(1), 54–69.

Rasmussen, E. (2017). Children and media man. How to maximize kids' learning from educational media. Retrieved from https://childrenandmediaman.com/2017/08/24/how-to-maximize-kids-learning-from-educational-media/

Reddy, I. (1972). *Programmes for children.* Hamilton, ON: South Central Regional Library System.

Remiesiewicz, N. (2014, April 19). Alec Baldwin to host fundraiser for CF Library. WPRI.com. Retrieved from http://wpri.com/2014/04/19/alec-baldwin-to-host-fundraiser-for-cf-library

Rhode Island College. (2018, February 6). Extravaganza de Espanol. Providence, RI. Retrieved from http://henrybarnardschool.org/extravaganza-de-espanol/

Ribble, M. (2011). *Digital citizenship in schools.* Arlington, VA: International Society for Technology in Education.

Ridley, J. (2012, February 27). Five cool movies hidden on a shelf Nashville Public Library. Retrieved from https://www.nashvillescene.com/arts-culture/article/13042007/five-cool-movies-hidden-on-the-shelf-at-nashville-public-library

Rinehart, R., & Ippolito, J. (2014). *Re-collection: Art, new media, and social memory.* Cambridge, MA: MIT Press.

RobbGrieco, M. (2018). *Making media literacy in America.* Lanham, MD: Lexington Books.

Rodgers, W. (2017). Buy, borrow, or steal? Film access for film studies students. College and Research Libraries. Retrieved from http://crl.acrl.org/index.php/crl/article/download/16730/18237

Rossi-Snook, E. (2005). Persistence of vision: Public library 16mm film collections in America. *The Moving Image, 5*(1), 1–26.

Rossi-Snook, E. (2012). Continuing ed: Educational film collections in libraries and archives. In D. Orgeron, M. Orgeron, & D. Streible (Eds.), *Learning with the lights off* (pp. 457–477). New York, NY: Oxford University Press.

Rudin, P. (2008). No fixed address: The evolution of outreach library services on university campuses. *The Reference Librarian, 49*(1), 55–75.

Russell, C. (2010). The best of copyright and VideoLib. *Library Trends, 58*(3), 349–357. http://doi.org/10.1353/lib.0.009

Ryan, R., & Stiller, K. (1991). The social context of internalization: Parent and teacher influence on autonomy, motivation and learning. In R. Pintrich & M. Maehr (Eds.), *Advances in motivation and achievement.* Volume 7. Goals and Self Regulatory Processes (pp. 115–149). Greenwich, CT: Jai Press.

Sagor, R. (2000). *Guiding school improvement with action research.* Alexandria, VA: Association for Supervision and Curriculum Development.

Saunders, T. (2002). *Celluloid saints.* Macon, GA: Mercer University Press.

Scott, A. O. (2016). *Better living through criticism.* New York, NY: Penguin.

Semingson, P., Mora, R. A., & Chiquito, T. (2017). BookTubing: Reader response meets 21st century literacies. *ALAN Review, 44*(1), 61–68.

Shellenbarger, S. (2016, November 21). Most students don't know when news is fake, Stanford study finds. *Wall Street Journal.*

Sigler, R. F. (1978). A rationale for the film as a public library resource and service. *Library Trends, 27,* 9–26.

Singer, N. (2015, April 25). Turning a children's rating system into an advocacy army. *New York Times.* Retrieved from https://www.nytimes.com/2015/04/27/technology/turning-a-childrens-rating-system-into-an-advocacy-army.html?_r=2

Smylie, M. A., & Wenzel, S. A. (2003). *The Chicago Annenberg challenge: Successes, failures, and lessons for the future.* Final Technical Report of the Chicago Annenberg Research Project. Chicago: Annenberg Foundation.

Snelson, C. (2011). YouTube across the disciplines: A review of the literature. *MERLOT Journal of Online Learning and Teaching, 7*(1), 159–69.

Snelson, C., & Perkins, R. (2009). From silent film to YouTube TM : Tracing the historical roots of motion picture technologies in education. *Journal of Visual Literacy, 28*(1), 1–27.

Spain, F. C., & Scoggin, M. C. (1962). They still read books. In R. L. Shayton (Ed.), *The eighth art: Twenty-three views of television today* (pp. 176–197). New York, NY: Holt Rinehart Winston.

Spicer, S. (2018). Perspectives on the role of instructional video in higher education: Evolving pedagogy, copyright challenges and support models (pp. 236–257). In R. Hobbs (Ed.), *The Routledge companion on media education, copyright and fair use.* New York, NY: Routledge.

Spicer, S., & Horbal, A. (2017). The future of video playback capability in college and university classrooms. *College & Research Libraries, 78*(5), 706–722.

Spiewak, T. (2017, July 26). Judging a book by more than its cover: Exploring features of traditional and e-book reading experiences that support children's learning. Joan Ganz Cooney Center. Retrieved from http://joanganzcooneycenter.org/2017/07/26/judging-a-book-by-more-than-its-cover-exploring-features-of-traditional-and-e-book-reading-experiences-that-support-childrens-learning/

Stanford History Education Group, Wineburg, S., McGrew, S., Breakstone, J., & Ortega, T. (2016). Evaluating information: The cornerstone of civic online reasoning. *Stanford Digital Repository, 29*. Retrieved from http://purl.stanford.edu/fv751yt5934

Stark, S., Kramer, S., Metni, J., & Carr, V. (2016). Can texting save lives [Video]. *New York Times*. Retrieved from https://www.nytimes.com/video/opinion/100000005178504/can-texting-save-lives.html

Stauffer, S. (2017). Utilizing this new medium of mass communication: The regional film distribution programme at the Cleveland Public Library, 1948–1951. *Library and Information History, 33*(4), 258–274.

Stephens, W. (2017, July 27). Parsing the new ALA school librarian competencies framework. *School Library Journal*. Retrieved from https://www.slj.com/2017/07/industry-news/parsing-the-new-ala-school-librarian-competencies-framework/#_

Stevens, J. D. (1983). Sex as education: A note on pre-1930 social hygiene films. *Film & History: An Interdisciplinary Journal of Film and Television Studies, 13*(4), 84–87.

Stoddard, J. D., & Marcus, A. S. (2010). More than "showing what happened": Exploring the potential of teaching history with film. *The High School Journal, 93*(2), 83–90.

Stone, B. (2011). The power of story. TED Ex Sheffield. Retrieved from https://www.youtube.com/watch?v=wqlShMeTZHE

StoryCorps (2016). The Bookmobile [Video]. Retrieved from https://youtu.be/11OvHcgh-E4

Stuckmann, C. (2016). About. Chris Stuckmann. Retrieved from http://www.chrisstuckmann.com/

Stuckmann, C. (2018). Chris Stuckmann. YouTube. Retrieved from https://www.youtube.com/user/ChrisStuckmann

Symons, A. K., & Stoffle, C. J. (1998). When values conflict. *American Libraries, 29*, 56–59.

Telephone bureau grows at the Los Angeles Public Library (1934, November 15). *The Motion Picture and the Family*, p. 8.

Tewell, E. C. (2014). Tying television comedies to information literacy: A mixed-methods investigation. *Journal of Academic Librarianship, 40*, 134–141.

Tomopoulos, S., Brockmeyer Cates, C., Dreyer, B. P., Fierman, A. H., Berkule, S. B., & Mendelsohn, A. L. (2014). Children under the age of two are more likely to watch inappropriate background media than older children. *Acta Paediatrica (Oslo, Norway: 1992), 103*(5), 546–552.

Tripp, L. (2011). Digital youth, libraries, and new media literacy. *The Reference Librarian, 52*(4), 329–341.

TV viewership sees double-digit decline, according to Accenture (2016, November 26). *Screen Media Daily*. http://screenmediadaily.com/tv-viewership-sees-double-digit-decline-according-to-accenture/

University of Arkansas. (2018). Remaking monsters and heroines. Retrieved from https://monstersandheroines.uark.edu/

University of Washington i-School. (2015, November 2). DYSTT: Mike Eisenberg [Video]. https://youtu.be/aYb1s7-0sIA

University of Washington I-School. (2016). Capstone film project captures entrepreneurial Soul of Seattle. Retrieved from https://ischool.uw.edu/news/2016/11/capstone-film-project-captures-entrepreneurial-soul-seattle

Urban Libraries Council (2015). All about the books. Retrieved from https://www.urbanlibraries.org/-all-about-the-books--music-video-innovation-1184.php?page_id=428

Valenza, J. (2016). Social media curation. Retrieved from https://www.youtube.com/watch?v=nMnaecWgykE

Valenza, J. (2017). Curation situations: Let us count the ways. *School Library Journal*. Retrieved from http://blogs.slj.com/neverendingsearch/2017/07/05/curation-situations-let-us-count-the-ways/

Valenza, J., & Hobbs, R. (2016). School librarians as stakeholders in the children and media community: A dialogue. *Journal of Children and Media, 10*(2), 147–155. doi:10.1080/17482798.2015.1127841

Vandewater, E. A., Bickham, D. S., Lee, J. H., Cummings, H. M., Wartella, E. A., & Rideout, V. J. (2005). When the television is always on. *American Behavioral Scientist*, 48(5), 562–577. http://doi.org/10.1177/0002764204271496

Vedantham, A. (2011). Making YouTube and Facebook videos: Gender differences in online video creation among first-year undergraduate students attending a highly selective research university. PhD dissertation, University of Pennsylvania.

Vendantham, A. (2017). Re-imagining libraries—Two models from Massachusetts. North Carolina State University. Retrieved from https://vimeo.com/234533347

Vickery, J. R., & Watkins, S. C. (2017). *Worried about the wrong things*. Cambridge, MA: MIT Press.

Voigt, K. (2013). Becoming trivial: The book trailer. *Culture Unbound: Journal of Current Cultural Research*, 5(4), 671–689.

Vollmar-Grone, M. (2002). Public library video collections. In G. Handman (Ed.), *Video collection development in multi-type libraries*. Westport, CT: Greenwood Press.

Waite, M. J. (2010). Room with a view. *Knowledge Quest*, 38(4), 59–61.

Waller, M. (2017). Grey literature, experimental works, and shifting roles: Case studies, opportunities, and legal challenges around students as producers. *Against the Grain*, 29(4). http://bit.ly/2gEPxJk

Walters, W. H. (2003). Video media acquisitions in a college library. *Library Resources & Technical Services*, 47(4), 160.

Warner Instant Movies. (2017). Warner archives. Retrieved from https://www.warnerarchive.com/

Waters, J. (2016, October 20). What makes a great makerspace? *THE Journal*. Retrieved from https://thejournal.com/articles/2016/10/20/what-makes-a-great-makerspace.aspx?admgarea=Features1

Watkins, A. R. (2006). Surgical safe harbors: The Family Movie Act and the future of fair use legislation. *Berkeley Technology Law Journal*, 21, 241.

WebJunction and TechSoup for Libraries. (2017). Social media and libraries webinar series. *Learner Guide*. Retrieved from https://www.webjunction.org/content/dam/WebJunction/Documents/webJunction/2017-10/guide-libraries-social-media-webinar-series.pdf

Wee, V. (2017). Youth audiences and the media in the digital era: The intensification of multimedia engagement and interaction. *Cinema Journal*, 57(1), 133–139.

Weller, S. (2017, March 29). Without school librarians, we're on a dystopian path. *Chicago Tribune*. Retrieved from http://www.chicagotribune.com/news/opinion/commentary/ct-school-librarians-cuts-dystopia-perspec-0330-jm-20170329-story.html

Why this bulletin? (1934, October 15). *Motion picture and the family*, p. 1.

Wine, L. (2016). School librarians as technology leaders: An evolution in practice. *Journal of Education for Library and Information Science Online*, 57(2), 207–220. http://doi.org/10.12783/issn.2328-2967/57/2/12

Wineburg, S., & McGrew, S. (2016). Why students can't Google their way to the truth. *Education Week*, 36(11), 22–28.

Wolske, M., Rhinesmith, C., & Kumar, B. (2014). Community informatics studio: Designing experiential learning to support teaching, research, and practice. *Journal of Education for Library and Information Science*, 55(2), 166–177.

YouTube Creator Academy. (2017, August 28). The algorithm: How YouTube search and discovery works. YouTube. Retrieved from https://youtu.be/hPxnIix5ExI

Yowell, C., & Rhoten, D. (2008). Digital media and learning. Forum Futures, p. 15. Retrieved from http://retawprojects.com/uploads/digital_media_and_learning.pdf

Zaki, R. (Director and Writer). (2008). *Santa Claus in Baghdad* [Film]. Boston, MA: RaVision Productions. Retrieved from http://www.ravision.net/santa-claus-in-baghdad.html

Zerne, L. H. (2013). Ideology in the *Lizzie Bennet Diaries*. Persuasions Online. *Jane Austen Society of North America*, 34(1). http://www.jasna.org/persuasions/on-line/vol34no1/zerne.html

Zimmerman, F. J., &Christakis, D. A. (2005). Children's television viewing and cognitive outcomes: A longitudinal analysis of national data. *Archives of Pediatric Adolescent Medicine*, 159, 619–625. doi:10.1001/archpedi.159.7.619

Index

#ALATT Facebook page, 46, 159
1:1 laptop programs, 75, 156
13th (film), 176
16 mm film
  access to film projectors, 238
  collapse of market, 255
  collection of 16mm films, 232

3D scanning, 137–38
50/50 (film), 213*b*
50 Movies Kids Should Watch Before They are
  12, 285
60–Second Shakespeare, 202
90–Second Newbery, 202

Aardman Animations, 177
A Better Life (film), 40–41
Abrams, Floyd, 245
abuse of video in schools, 127–28
academic libraries, 24, 63–64, 136, 167–80, 269
Academic Libraries Video Trust, 256–57
academic testing, 97–98
Academy Awards, 263
acceptable use policies, 58
access to digital devices for children, 54
ACRL Information Literacy Frameworks, 75
Adam, T.R., 232
Adams Memorial Library (RI), 185
adaptation, 91, 93–95
Addams, Jane, 226
Adobe Creative Cloud, 72
African Americans, 36, 51, 90, 164, 189*b*, 221–22
  depictions of, 245
A Funny Thing Happened on the Way to the Forum
  (film), 285
Agee, James, 51
AIDS, 40–41

Airplane (film), 277–78
ALA Black Caucus, 245
Alachua County Library, 38
Alan B. Shepard Middle School (IL) 67, 213
Albion College, 45–46
Alexander Street, 142, 172, 173
algorithms, 90, 151
Allen, Paul G., 187
Alliance for a Media Literate America, 252*b*
Allied Media Conference, 297–98
Alvarez, Daylily, 159
amateur film, 144, 249
Amazon, 13, 172
American Academy of Pediatrics, 109*b*, 109
American Association of School Libraries (AASL),
  202, 282, 283
American Association of University Women, 233
American Film and Video Association, 246*b*
American labor movement, 241–42
American Library Association, 46, 48–49, 162*b*,
  175, 184–85, 217, 231, 235, 237–38, 240,
  244–45, 281
American University, 256
Americorps volunteers, 88
Anastasia (film), 124–25
Anderson, Chris, 152–53
Anderson Monarchs (film), 200
animation, 76*b*, 80–81, 83
animation workshop, 86–87
anime club, 222
Annenberg Challenge Grant, 186–87
Anne of Green Gables (film), 146–47
Anoka County Library (MN), 250
Antarctic Edge 70° South (film), 193
anti–immigration videos, 151
Anythink Libraries, 302
Anythink York Street Teen Horror Club, 303
Apollo 11 mission, 246–47
Appalachian State University, 34

Apple IIe computers, 148
app reviews, 53
apps and e–books in storytime, 34, 52, 53
Arbuckle, Fatty, 226
archetypes, 22
archives, film and media, 252*b*, 254, 286
Arc of the Ozarks, 184
Arizona State University, 256
Armstrong, Annie, 76–77
A Separation (film), 40–41
Asher, Jay, 37
Asheville Community Theater, 202
Asheville Public Library (NC), 202
Aspen Institute Dialogue on Public Libraries, 196,
    207, 291, 294–95
Association for Educational Communications and
    Technology, 282
Association for Library Services to Children,
    35, 302
Association of Moving Image Archivists, 254, 258
Association of Research Libraries, 251
asynchronous video, for learning, 262
Athenaeum (Providence, Rhode Island),
    22, 198–99
Attack of the Library Werewolf (video), 303
Attenborough, Richard, 66
attitudes of librarians, towards film, 222
Auburn (ME) Public Library, 303
audiovisual era, 246–47
Aufderheide, Patricia, 165
Aurora Public Library (IL), 202
Austen, Jane, 93–94
authentic audience, 96
authenticity, 201
authority, 130–31
authors, 35, 49
Avi, 202
AV support professionals, 257
awards, 48–49

Babson College, 282
Baby Einstein, 104
Bacon, David, 41
Bailey, Moya, 303
Baker, Frank, 120–21
Baldwin, Alec, 185
Ballard, Susan, 185, 202–3
ballroom dancing, 66
Band, Jonathan, 175
banned books, 99–100
Bannon, Brian, 304
Barrington Public Library (RI), 181, 197
Basic Black (television series), 164
Baum, L. Frank, 232–33
Bauman, Jeff, 42*b*

Bay Shore Middle School, 300
Baz Luhrmann, 66
BBC, 165*b*
Beach, Richard, 93
Beargrass Media, 86
Beaver County Pioneer Library (OK), 146–47
Bechdel, Alison, 158
Bechdel–Wallace Test, 158
Beirne, Heather, 64
Benson, Raymond, 42*b*
Berg, Jim, 195
Berkman Klein Center for Internet and Society, 297
Berman, Barbara, 253
Berry, John, 245
Betzwood, 287–88
bias, 7
Bickford, Jill, 59–60
Bieber, Justin, 99–100
Billings Public Library (MT) 147
Billou, Guy, 35
Bilodeau, Eric, 197–98
Birdy (film), 47
BitTorrent, 176, 177
Black, Jennifer, 40–41, 42–43, 46
Black Panther (film), 36
Blair, Patricia, 238–39
Blockbuster, 286
Bluestone, George: Novels into Film, 91
Bluth, Don, 125
Bobker, Lee, 244–45
Bonzell, Beth, 124
book baiting, 224, 248–49
book is always better, 92
book making, 112
Book–of–the–Month Club, 233
book promotion, 90
book trailers, 85, 88–90
BookTubers, 89–90
Born on the Fourth of July (film), 47
Bornschlegel, Coleen, 85
Bowie, David, 278
Boxford (MA) Public Library, 151
boyd, danah, 306
Boyle, T.C., 41
Boy Scouts, 224
Boys and Girls Club, 208
BrainPop, 119–20, 156
Braverman, Chuck, 255–56
breaking the rules, 78
Brenner, Robin, 37–38
Brigham Young University, 127
Bristol University, England, 177
Britain, 111*b*
British Film Institute, 121–22
broadband access, 297
Broadbent, Sabrina, 30–31

Brookline (MA) Public Library, 37–38
Brownell, Tina, 95–96, 97–98
Brown University, 170
Burnett, Charles, 222
Burns, Ken, 46

cable television, 105–6
Cabot Science Library, 78
Caldecott Medal, 35
Cal Humanities, 80
California Department of Education, 305
call and response video project, 51
Cambridge Analytica, 151
Campbell, Cen, 52
Camp Lejeune, 165
Campbell, Alison, 81–82
Canada, 248
Can I Stream It? 173
Capra, Frank, 233–34
Capstone Press, 74–75
captioning, 114*b*
Carnegie Corporation, 234, 237–38, 239
Caro, Niki, 125
Carol Stream Public Library (IL), 221–22
Carrico, Mandy, 47
Cars 3 (film), 122
Catholic, 158, 252*b*
cell phone videos, 29–31, 81, 83
censorship, film, 225, 227
Center for Media and Social Impact, 165
Center for Media and Values, 252*b*
Center for Media Literacy, 252*b*
Center Grove High School, 85–86
Central Falls, Rhode Island, 185
Certificate in Instructional Technologies and
    Online Learning, 77
Chagall, Irene, 279
Chalfant, Henry, 204
Chalk, Penny, 236
challenges of sustaining media production
    programs, 95
Chamberlain, William, 265
Chan, Priscilla, 156
Chandler, Curtis, 127
Chaplin, Charlie, 285
Chapman University, 207
Character Day, 213*b*
Charlie Chaplin, 66
Charlotte Mecklenburg Library (NC), 189
Charters, W.W., 227–28
Chasnoff, Debra, 80
Chazelle, Damien, 201
Chbosky, Stephen, 212
Chelmsford (MA) High School library, 149
Chicago, Illinois, 39–40

Chicago Film Archives, 247–48
Chicago Public High School for Metropolitan
    Studies, 247–48
Chicago Public Library, 304
Chicago Public Schools, 148
Chicken Run (film), 177
children
    and depictions of sexuality, 61–62
    and identity, 69–70
    and language development, 103
    and media, 53, 103–4, 111*b*, 161–62
    and media impact, 103–4, 111*b*, 228–30
    and media policy issues, 161–62
    and the digital media marketplace, 53
    and war, 172
children's librarians, 32–33, 52–53, 297–98
Children's Media Review, 53
Choice, 13
Christ, Judith, 158
Chun, Traci, 71–72
circulation, library
    decrease from impact of movies and TV, 240–42
    of film, 239, 249, 295
citizen action groups, 252*b*
Citizen Kane (film), 285
civic engagement, 267, 294–95
Clearinghouse of Information on Children's Radio
    and Television, 252*b*
Clear Play, 54
Cleary, Beverly, 68–69
Clement, Ina, 224
Clements, Ron, 67
Cleveland, Ohio, 8
Cleveland Public Library, 230, 238, 242, 307
clips, film and video, 166
    for adult education, 238
    for teaching, 126, 166
closed captioning, 43
closed stacks, 169–70, 253
close reading, 118–20
cloud filmmaking, 213*b*
CNN, 7
Cocciolo, Anthony, 266, 267–68
Cochran, Chris, 74–75
Coiro, Julie, 273–74
Colburn, Selene, 268
collaboration, 184, 185
collections
    film in higher education, 144–45, 169, 251
    by ordinary people, 153
College of Charleston, 178
colonialism, 46
Columbia College Chicago, 86*b*
Comarella, Philipp, 280
commercially-sponsored films, in libraries, 239
Common Core State Standards, 120

Common Sense Media, 24, 53, 57*b*, 74–75, 106,
     111*b*, 123–24, 143, 160–61, 285
Common Sense Seal, 160
community, 193
community engagement, 266
community media centers, 291
Comport, Susan, 194
compressed narrative, 202
concerns about film influence on children, 226, 227
conflict, documentary images of military, 300
Congress, 165
Conlon, Susan, 23, 193, 206
connected learning, 187–88
Connolly, Robert, 204
Connors, Sean, 94
Considine, David, 34, 35
Consortium of University Film Centers, 248
conspiracy theory videos, 151
consumerism, impact on children, 59–60
content delivery, 128
controversial content in film, 246
Coogler, Ryan, 36
Cooksey, Ashley, 216–17
copyfraud, 311
copying VHS tapes, 171*b*
copy–paste culture, 57
copyright, 55, 309
     confusion, 176
     and fair use, 136
     industry perspective on copyright, 55
     and Section 107, 309–10
     and Section 108, 171*b*, 256, 287, 309, 310
     Section 110, 55, 171–41*b*, 175, 309, 310–11
corporate support for makerspaces, 72
Corporation for Public Broadcasting, 164–65
counterprogramming strategy, 251
County of Los Angeles Public Library, 201*b*
Crash Course, 151
Cravan, Arthur, 152
create to learn in libraries, 69–70, 82, 166,
     171*b*, 305
creative collaboration, 293
creative freedom and control, 75
credibility, 129–30
Crichton, Michael, 17
Criterion Collection, 82, 271
critical analysis of media, 74, 157
critical consumers of media, 291
Critical Race and Sociocultural Media Literacy
     Collection, 166–67
critical thinking, 273*f*
critical viewing, 126
Cukor, George, 236
cultivation effects, 59–62
cult of celebrity, 226
cultural participation, 273*f*

cultural screening events, 189–90
curation, 53, 136, 145–46, 153–54
     curation as pedagogy, 157
     curriculum as, 145–46
current events, 157
curriculum for film analysis, 281
curse of knowledge, 284
cyberbullying, 58, 186

DaCosta, Morton, 232*b*
Dahlstrom, Sue, 51
Daily Herald (newspaper), 42*b*
Dale, Edgar, 236, 264
Dallas Public Library, 83
Dalton, Bridget, 89
Damiani, Catherine, 210
Dancoff, Judith, 200
Dandurand, Karen, 74–75
Darien Public Library, 146
dark side of the web, 186
databases, 282
Daviess County Public Library (KY), 206–7
Davis, Margaret, 223
Davy Crockett (television series), 240
day in the life video, 88
Dayton, Lyman, 125
deaccessioning films, 239–40
deadline pressure, 79, 86*b*
Dead Man (film), 178–79
Dear Mom (film), 181–82
DeCherney, Peter, 55, 287
Deerfield Public Library (IL), 69
Defiance (OH) Public Library, 72
Demy, Jacques, 265
Denver Public Library, 233–34
depictions of children's sexuality, 61–62
design thinking, 304
Despicable Me (film), 122–23
Destiny Quest, 155–56
DeVoe, Erica, 116
Dewey, Melvil, 231
dialogue, the power of, 217
Diary of a City Priest (film), 200
Dick, Kirby, 163
Dickens, Charles, 148
differences in interpretation, 292
Diggs, Valerie, 110
digital
     authorship, 49, 166
     citizenship, 57–58
     content collection development
          policies, 156
     identity, 113
     learning, 270
     media and learning, 186, 187–88

picture books, 53
piracy, 176–77
platforms, 156, 270
presentations in English and History classes, 72
  tools, 276–81b
Digital Booktalks, 89
Digital Bytes, 57b
Digital Media Commons Studio, 303
Digital Public Library of America, 295, 297–98
Digital–Storytime.com, 53
digital media literacy, 4, 5, 114, 134–35, 154, 274,
  275–76, 297
digitization, in libraries, 298
  at small colleges, 257
  for preservation, 256
  of faculty collections, 257
  services, 195, 250
dimensions of active reasoning, 115
Dimmock, Nora, 170
disabling YouTube in schools, 150
disciplinary boundaries, transcending, 277
Discovery Education, 280–81
discussing film characters, 44–45
Disney, 22, 247, 296
  film club, 184
Disneyworld, 42b
disparity between print and nonprint media in
  libraries, 13
distance learning, 175
distribution of video and film, 259
DiVenere, Dayna, 212
diversity
  libraries and, 201, 296
  of views, in film collections, 246
DMCA Act, 55, 138, 166, 171b
documentaries, 29, 80, 83–84, 142, 166–67, 173–74,
  251, 294
  as propaganda, 165b
  impact on public policy, 165
  filmmakers, 165
  movement, 234–35
  production, 76–77
  student–produced, 75
Do It Your Damn Self Film Festival, 83
Dolan, Christopher, 123
Donnell Library, 242–43, 299–300
Donors Choose, 71–72
Dore, Mary, 166–67
Doros, Dennis, 271–72
Doroshow, Shelby, 83
Dove, Rita, 210
Dowd, Nancy, 183–84
Downey, Annie, 214–15
downloading YouTube videos, 150
Due Diligence Project, 256, 287
Duffer, Matt, 18

Dunbar, Lisa, 93
Dunkirk (film), 123
Dust Bowl, 234
DVDs, 33, 54, 55, 221
  ancillary materials, 271
  bonus features, 82, 124, 177
  collections, 147, 265
  declines in circulation, 259
  obsolescence, 255
  rentals, 177
  ripping, 179

Eastern Kentucky University, 63
Eastman, Linda Anne, 231
economics of YouTube, 151
education, 273–74
educational film, 144, 246–47
Educational Film Lending Library, 233–34
Educational Film Library Association,
  239, 246b
educational technology, 243
Eisenberg, Michael, 293
Elbow, Peter, 121
elementary school, 49, 194
E–Link, 154b
Elliott, Debbie, 66
Ellis, Emily, 85
Elorza, Jorge, 191
email skills, 270–71
Emerson College, 306
Emmy Awards, 93–94
Emory University, 174, 176
emoticons, 57
emotional power of film, 16, 39, 65–66, 79
Empire State Digital Network, 297–98
empowerment, 227, 275
Encinitas Union School District, 305
engagement, student, 155–56
Enoch Pratt Free Library, 255–56
Environmental Film Festival, 206
ER (television show), 17
Eraser Button Bill, 161–62
Erin Brokovich (film), 251
Estevez, Emilio, 134b
European Commission, 272
European Educational Film Congress, 230
evaluation, 273
Everson Branch Library (WA), 195
Every Child Ready to Read, 52
Evita (film), 280–81
experiential learning, 279
experimental film, 84, 144
experiments in filmmaking by teachers and
  students, 247–48
Explore Movie Club, 184

exposure to quality film, impact of, 234
external speakers, 44

Fab Lab, 72
Facebook, 156
Facebook Groups, 136–37
fact checking, 130
faculty
    awareness of library film and video resources,
        168, 177–78
    fellowships for creating media resources, 166
    questions about classroom media use, 171*b*
    use of film and media in higher education, 167
fair use, 287. *Also see* copyright
fake news, 6–8, 129–30, 165*b*, 175
Family Entertainment and Copyright Act, 54
family life, media in, 277–78
family media plan, 109
Fandango, 159
fantasy/reality judgment, 107–8
Farhadi, Asghar, 40–41
Farrelly, Deg, 256
Farrokhzad, Forough, 265
Fassbinder, R.W., 265
Fayetteville Public Library, 294
Fee, Brian, 122
feedback
    approaches to gathering, 216
    from patrons, academic libraries, 214–16
    use of Flipgrid for, 216–17
Feerrar, Julia, 134–35
Feig, Paul, 159
Felini, Damiano, 293
Felton Media Literacy Scholars, 308
Ferris Bueller's Day Off (film), 42*b*
fidelity in adaptation, 92
Fields, W.C., 242–43
film
    aesthetics, 31–32, 236
    character development in, 261–62
    collections, 238, 239–40
    cooperatives, history of, 239
    cultural heritage, 233, 285–86
    discussion groups, 41, 233, 245
    distribution, 200
    editing, 17
    education, 3, 4, 14–16, 235
    emotional power of, 261–62, 294, 296–97
    festivals, 192, 196–99
    history of, 287–88
    language use in, 261–62
    love of, 159
    and media partnerships, 199
    media studies programs, higher education,
        169
    preservation, 258, 286–89

programs in libraries, 31–32, 38–39, 225,
    239–40, 242–43, 279–81
projectors, access to, 255–56
purpose of, 264–65
quality, renewed interest in, 241–42
ratings, 128
resources, history of, 248–49, 252–53
review aggregation websites, 159
reviews, 227, 238
screenings in libraries, 43, 183–84, 230,
    233–34, 267
study guides, 47, 236, 265, 280–81
viewing clubs, in high schools, 236
films displace reading, 226
Films on Demand, 173
filmstrip, 243
Film Forum Project, 234
Film Forward, 188
film industry public relations, 229–30
Film Library Quarterly, 242–43
filmmaker–librarian relationships, 182–83
filmmakers, independent, 200
filmmaker visit to schools, 48–50
film narratives about immigrants, 191
Film Platform, 172, 173
First Amendment, 245
First Man (film) 201
Flanagin, Andrew, 130
Flipgrid, 216–17, 262, 281*b*, 300
flipped classroom, 128, 136–37
Florida Gulf Coast University, 89
Florida State University, 306
Flotsam (book) 35
Flowers, Mark, 32
flyers, 38
Follett, 155–56
Fonsi, Luis, 99–100
Fonzie's library card, 20–21
Food for the Ancestors (film), 189
Forbidden Films (film), 141–42, 143
foreign language books in libraries, 38
format obsolescence, 256
Foucault, Michel, 134*b*
four P's of reading picture books, 35
FOX, 61–62
Fox Point Library, Providence (RI),
    36–37, 208
Franklin (MA) High School, 148–49
freedom of speech, 244–45
Freedom to View, 246*b*
fresh eyes, 184–85
Frieden, James, 66
Friesem, Yonty, 86*b*
Fristoe, Travis, 38
From Mambo to Hip Hop (film), 204
Fukushima Daiichi Nuclear Power Plant, 133
Fuller, Samuel, 265

funding for film and media programs in libraries, 162, 185–86
Future Ready Librarians, 71

Gainesville, Florida, 38
Gandhi (film), 66
Garfield County Public Library District (Colorado), 53
Garmer, Amy, 291
Gast, Leon, 65
gathering space in libraries, 299–300
gay prom, 80
Gee, Jim, 110
gender and media, 36–37, 57, 303
gender differences in online media production, 77–78
gender stereotypes, 117–18, 125, 158, 159
Genius Hour, 300
genres, film, 83
George Mason University, 45–46
Georgetown University, 284
Georgia Public Broadcasting, 164
Georgia Traveler (television series), 164
Ghostbusters 3 (film), 159
Gire, Dann, 42b
girls: and beauty culture, 61
Girl Scouts of America, 61
Give Me 5, 86b
Glassman, Julia, 24
Glatzer, Richard, 189–90
GlenViewings, 39–41, 42b
Glenview Public Library, 39–40
Global Action Project, 187
globalization, 40–41, 110
glossary of film terms, 281
Gmail, 150–51
GoChip Beam, 294
Golay Jean Pierre, 293
Google, 150–51, 155–56, 284
    Home, 106
    Scholar, 155–56
    Search, 270
    Trends, 4
Gordimer, Nadine, 41
Gordon, Marsha, 300
Gosling, Ryan, 201
Graceffa, Joey, 161
Gracy, Karen, 248, 255
graduate education, 261, 276–77
Graney, Brian, 250
Grant, Matt, 18
Great Depression, 234
Great Recession of 2007, 148–49
Great Train Robbery, The (film), 225–26
Great War, 41, 226
Green, Hank, 93–94, 151
Green, John, 151

Greene, Lawrence, 287–88
Greene, Sean, 37
Greene County Public Library (OH), 76b
Greenwood (IN) Public Library, 85
Grierson, John, 235
Griesser, Simon, 280
Griffith, D.W., 227, 287
Grisham, John, 251
Groth, Jason Evans, 300
Guernsey, Lisa, 54

Haines, Laura, 268
Hains, Rebecca, 117
Haley, Gail, 34
Handbrake, 166
Handman, Gary, 169, 170
Haney, Walt, 159
hanging out, messing around, geeking out, 186, 280, 281
Hansen, James R. 201
Happy Days (television series), 20
Happy Feet (film), 118
Hardmon, Tony, 165
Hardwick Chris, 64
Harkness, Rachael, 191–92
Harmon, Wynita, 216–17
Harris County Public Libraries, 47–48
Harvard University, 17, 78, 282, 297
Harvey, Joe, 111–12
Hasbro, 87
hashtag, 277
Hatch, Mark, 69–70
hater and trolls, 57
Hawthorne Public Library (WI), 222
Haynes, Claudia, 52–53
Haynes, Todd, 160–61
Hays, Will, 228–29
Hayward Public Library (CA), 80
Heartland Film, 265
Hennepin County Library, 214
Henry Barnard Laboratory School, 194
Henson, Jim, 278
Herbes–Sommers, Christine, 166–67
Hero Steps (film), 191
High Plains (CO) Library, 179
Hispanic Heritage Month, 38, 189
historical artifacts, in education, 285–87
history
    local 195
    of film in libraries, 222, 224,
    research, 113
Hive Digital Media Learning Fund, 187
Hobart and Smith Colleges, 82
Hohimer, Frank, 265
Hollywood, 65, 144, 226
    films, librarian attitudes towards, 242–43

Hollywood: History, Institution, Art, 287
Holzweiss, Kristina, 300
homelessness, 134b
home movies, 250
Hoopla, 147, 173
horror movies, 255–56
Horval, Andrew, 255, 257
Hour of Code, 67
Housedon, Roger, 41
House Un–American Activities Committee, 235
Houston, Texas, 47–48
how and why questions, 122–23
Howard, Ron, 20
how–to videos, 73–74, 77, 80, 149–50,
    155, 300–1
Hoyt, Eric, 226
HPV, 17–18
Hu, Ann, 288
Hugo, Victor, 227
Hulu, 172
Hunt, Jonathan, 305
Hyman, Karen, 302

I am Cuba (film), 271–72
identification with characters, 278
identity, 36, 136
iffy stuff, 160–61
illegal downloading of film and video, 176
Illegal People (book), 41
illustrators, 35
image collections, 157
imagination, 31
Imhoff, Harriet, 224
imitation, children's tendency towards, 226
iMotion, 72
impact of screen media on reading, 107
inappropriate language, 129
incidental viewing, impact of, 107
independent film, 14, 144
Independent Movie Database, 159
Indiana University, 239, 258
Indieflix, 184
inequality of access to streaming media, 176
inferences, 34, 115
influence marketing, 90
influence of television on patron choices, 240
informatics, 72–73
information literacy, 4, 81–82, 261, 282–83
information literacy, and media literacy,
    definitions, 273
information overload, 13
Information Power, 282
informed consumers, and choice, 227
inquiry learning, 105–6, 116–17, 273–74
Institute for Museum and Library Services, 188

instructional technology services in education,
    167, 283–84
  tensions with librarians, 283
Insua, Glenda, 76–77
integrity of literary adaptation, 91, 92
intellectual curiosity, 69, 152–53, 300
interdisciplinarity, 263, 291
intergenerational learning, 285
International Dada Archive, 152
International Federation of Library Associations, 273
International Society for Technology in Education
    (ISTE), 58
internships, undergraduate, 304
Into Film, 121–22
introducing a film, 44
Iowa, 47
iPearl Immersion Theater, 300
Iran, 41
Irons, Kati, 203–4
It (film) 18
Ito, Mimi, 186
iTunes, 142
It's a Wonderful Life (film), 285

Jackson, Helen Hunt, 230
Jackson, Matthew, 294
Jaffe, Karen, 252b
Jaszi, Peter, 175
Jaye, Cassie, 172
Jeffrey (film), 191
Jenemann, Laura, 45–46
Jenkins, Barry, 50–51
Jenkins, Henry, 110
Jennings, Brien, 73
Jennings, Garth, 43
Jim Jarmusch, 178–79
Johnson County Public Library, 85
Johnson, Doug, 148
Johnson, Mindy, 296
Jones, Maggie, 59
Jones, Melissa, 284–85
JotheGreat, 90
journalism, 7
Judge, Maureen, 172
just hit play and walk away, 43–44
just in time vs just in case, 169

Kael, Pauline, 158
Kaiser Family Foundation, 17, 106
Kalatozov, Mikhail, 271–72
Kami for Chrome, 276b, 281b
Kanopy, 172, 173, 179
Kanopy Story Time collection, 172
Kansas Department of Education, 148

Kartemquin Films, 43
Katz, Linda, 150
Keene State University, 167
Kellogg Foundation, 214
Kelly, Gene, 285
Kelly, Katy, 204
Kennedy, James, 202
Kenney, Robert, 89
Kent County (MI) Library, 83
Kent State University, 120–21
Kentucky Youth Film Festival, 86
Khan Academy videos, 128, 156
KIDSNET archive, 252*b*
Kiesling, Barrett, 236
Kindle, 147
King, Rachel, 169–70, 179
KIPP, 127–28
Kirkus, 13
Kist, Bill, 120–21
Klose, Stephanie, 22–23
Kluver, Carisa, 53
Knappenberger, Brian, 8
Knight, Travis, 222
Knight Commission on the Information Needs of
    Communities, 294–95
Krasniewicz, Louise, 304
Kraus, Michelle, 174
Kubo and the Two Strings (film), 222
Kucsma, Jason, 297–98

Labyrinth (film), 278
lack of documentation of film screenings in
    libraries, 222–23
LA in Focus (video series), 296
LaMantia, Katie, 22–23
LaMotte, Jason, 261
Lancellota, Bill, 280, 281–62*b*
Landfill Harmonic (film), 194
Lane, Anthony, 158
Lanning, Scott, 150
Lansdowne Theater, 287
Lansing (MI) Public Library, 250–51
Lareau, Annette, 110
Larson, L.C., 239
Latina Women's League, 38
Latino films for children, 191
Lavall, Giancarlo, 37
Laybourne, Kit, 294
lazy research, listservs as, 270
learning
    commons, 68–69, 77
    from entertainment television, 17–18
    how to learn, 300–1
    management systems, 173, 179
    radio and television as tools for, 223

Lee, Susanna, 137–38
Leer Despacito, 99–100
Leitch, George, 92
LeMay, Emily, 6–8
lending policies for VHS in academic libraries, 253
Let It Ripple, 213*b*
Let's Get the Rhythm (film), 279
Levin, Sarah, 75
Levine, Michael, 54
Libert, Rachel, 165
LibGuide, 96, 153, 261, 283–84
    how students find them, 284
librarian partnerships, 179
librarian–filmmaker relationship, 200–1
librarians, 14, 191
    attitudes about media, 18, 80–82, 224, 249, 250–
        51, 259, 263–64, 267, 277, 295–96
    competition with exhibitors, 224
    as content creators, 73, 302
    job frustrations, 274
    as risk–averse, 257
    training in discussion facilitation, 267–68
    use of YouTube for marketing, 268
librarianship, social responsibilities of, 217
libraries
    antidote to testing culture of schools, 69
    and community building, 181–83, 191–95, 299
    as community media centers, 297
    displays about film production process, 230
    future of, 292, 297
    as leaders in media literacy, 306
    as learning institutions, 296, 298
    as places and platforms, 183, 295–96
    as places of creation, 295
    public attitudes towards, 8–9
Libraries Transform Teaser (video), 206–7
library
    leadership, risk taking in, 298, 299
    makerspace, 298
    manifesto, 302
    marketing, 183–84
    media center, 298
    mission, 16
    partnerships, 189*b*
    programs, 191–92
    promotional videos, 207
    reform movement, 224–25
    renovation, 298
    teen center, 298
    websites, design of, 146–47
Library and Information Science, discipline,
    150, 273
library–film collaboration, history of, 231–35
Library Journal, 13, 22–23, 158, 177, 238, 245
Library of Congress, 166, 239
Library Trends, 169–70

licensing, 200, 311
Life, Above All (film) 40–41
Life, Animated (film), 184
lifelong learning for librarians, 298
likes and shares, 57
LinkedIn, 76b
List.ly, 154b
listicle, 281b
listservs, for lifelong learning, 270–71
    inaccuracies in, 270
    librarians' use of, 261
    as online networks, 270–72
literacy, 4, 34, 35
Literary Guild, 233
Little E–Lit, 52
Litwin, Roy, 269
Livingstone, Sonia, 58, 186
Lizzy Bennet Diaries, 93–94
local, 227
    access television, 297
    filmmaking traditions, 287–88
    journalism, 294–95
Loevy, Netta, 172
logic models, for assessment, 214
Lorentz, Pare, 233, 234
Los Angeles, 41
Los Angeles Public Library, 201b, 224, 231, 296
Los Angeles Zine Fest, 24
loss of film history, 285–86
Louisiana State University, 222–23
Louisville Free Library, 86
Louisville International Festival of Films, 86
Louisville Public Library, 179
love–hate relationship with media, 31, 105
Lu, Hongyan, 285
Lubin, Siegmund, 287
Luhtala, Michelle, 155–56
lunchtime film screenings in public libraries, 238
lurking on listservs, 270–71
Lynch, David, 31
Lynda.com, 76b
Lyons, Norm, 123–24
L'Engle, Madeleine, 202

MacArthur Foundation, 186–88
Macquarie University, 82
makerspaces, 71, 299. See media centers
making film clips for classroom use, 55
malware, 186
Mandel, Debra, 303
Mann, Michael, 265
Man on the Flying Trapeze (film), 242–43
Man with a Movie Camera (film), 287–88
Maori, 125
Marian the Librarian, 232–46b

Marines, 165
Mark Day School, 111–12, 123–24
marketing library programs, 281
    to youth, 57
Marquez, Joe, 214–15
Marshall, Garry, 20
Marshall, James, 172
Marston, Elsa, 49
Martin, Eugene, 200
Martin, Jack, 185–86
Martin, Joseph, 128
Mary Pickford Institute for Film Education, 201b
Mashup Contest, 136
Maslin, Janet, 158
Massachusetts School Library Association, 149
Masterpiece Theater, 281
matinee screening, 39–40
McAuliffe, Christa, 246–47
McClessky, Sarah, 257–58
McDonald, Gerald, 234, 237–38
McRobbie, Michael, 258
meaning, 36
Media&Values (magazine), 252b
Media Action Research Center, 252b
media, 275, 297–98
    centers, 70–73, 303 (see media production)
    education, 4
    and information literacy, 262–63, 272, 305
    librarians, 141, 168–69, 257–58
    media preservation, 254
    mentors, 52–53, 298
    production, 98, 192, 302–3
    regulation, 163
    reviews, 13
    and social justice, 297–98
    studies, 82
    violence, 110–25
Media Archival Studies, 286
Media Digitization and Preservation Initiative, 258
Media Education Lab, 86b, 137
media literacy, 4, 49, 62, 115–16, 118, 119,
        120–21, 252b
    competencies, 114–15
    definition, 89, 272
    education, history of, 236
    Europe, 272
    future of, 292
    Italy, 293
    law, 57–58
    as media reform, 252b
Media Literacy Now, 162
Media Resource Center, University of California,
        Berkeley, 166, 169
Media SmART! 88, 188–89
Media Smart Libraries, 188, 210, 307
Meeks, Domonique, 294

memories, of movies, 277–78
Mendeley, 276b
men's rights movement, 172
merchandising, 22
Mercury Theater of the Air, 258
metacognition, 153
Metacritic, 159
metaliteracy, 154
Metcalf, Clarence, 238
Metropolitan New York Library Council, 297–98
Metzger, Miriam, 130
Mihailidis, Paul, 149, 306
Milestone Film & Video, 271–72
millennials, 172
Miller, Angie, 116
Miller, Erin DeWitt, 271
Miller, George, 118
Miller, Kelly, 23
Miller, Shannon McClintock, 216–17
minorities in films, 36
Miracle on 34th Street (film), 285
Moana (film), 67, 222
Mobile Film Classroom, 201b
mobile media carts, 78
Modern Times (film), 285
Moeller, Felix, 141–42
Moen, Mary, 307
MOOC, 287
Mora, Freddy, 294
morality, concerns about, 228
Morgan, Stella, 233
Morse, David, 200
Mota, Bethany, 161
Mother Goose on the Loose, 52
Motion Picture Association of America (MPAA),
    163, 228–29
movies
    and books, 262–63
    and childhood wonder, 278–79
    and memories, 277–78
    in American society, history of, 225
Moving Image Archiving and Preservation
    program, 286
moving image media, 5, 277
Mozilla, 298
MPAA ratings, 143
MTV Cribs (television series), 269
Much Better Now (film), 280
Mueller, Karen, 1
multimedia installations in libraries, 300
Multimedia Teaching and Learning Initiative, 166
multitasking during movie screenings, 46
Munn, Russell, 238
Munsterberg, Hugo, 17
Murphy, Amanda, 116
Muschietti, Andy, 18

music
    and critical thinking, 194
    Latin American, 280–81
    video, 84, 99, 207
My Life as a Zucchini (film), 161
My Millennial Life (film), 172

Nagib, Holly, 194
Nahas, Albert, 47
Napoleon Dynamite (film) 127
Narnia, 278
Narragansett Elementary School, 73
narrative, 157, 261
Nashville, Tennessee, 207
Nashville Public Library, 99, 207, 265
National Association for Media Literacy Education,
    162, 189b, 252b
National Board of Review of Motion Pictures, 227
National Catholic Reporter, 158
National Committee for Better Films, 227, 230
National Council of Jewish Women, 233
National Council of Teachers of English, 230
National Day Calendar, 189b
National Endowment for the Arts, 188–89
National Foundation for the Improvement of
    Education, 252b
National Home Movie Day, 249–50
National Impact of Library Public
    Programs, 184–85
National Leadership Conference on Media
    Literacy, 272
National Leadership Grant, 188
National Library Week, 207
National Media Literacy Week, 189b
National Media Market and Conference, 256–57
National Public Radio, 164
National Telemedia Council, 293
Netflix, 13, 37, 54, 141, 167–68, 172, 174, 176,
    225, 286
    bias against institutional use, 174–75
    history of, 258–59
New Canaan High School (CT), 155
New Haven Public Schools, 236
Newport Documentary Project, 92
Newport Public Schools, 95–97
New York City, 294
New York Public Library, 76b, 151, 222–23, 230,
    237–38, 239–40, 242–43, 299
New York Times, 13
New York Times Film Club, 29–31
New York University, 286
Nielsen ratings, 145
Niffennegger, Emily, 262
Nishihara, Bonnie, 112
Nobody Speak (film) 8

noncirculating collections, 170
nonoptimal use of video in education, 126–28
non–users of public libraries, 182
Nooksack Valley Heritage Center, 195
Nordberg, Ron, 247–48
Norten, Enrique, 299–300
North Carolina Museum of History, 137–38
North Carolina State University, 80–81, 82, 300
Northeastern University, 303
Northeast Historical Film, 250
Northern Onondaga (NY) Public Library, 288
North Madison County Public Libraries, 259
Northwestern University, 233
note–taking from video, 126
Novack, Lynn, 46

Oak Lane Branch Library, Philadelphia, 222
Oakland (CA) Unified School District, 148
Oakley, Tyler, 161
Obama, Barack, 7, 165
objectionable content, editing out, 54–55
observation, the power of, 279
obsolescence of media formats, 254–55
Ocean County (NJ) Library, 83
Ocean State Libraries, 198
O'Dell, Kathleen, 184
Office of Communication (OFCOM), 106
Ohio State University, 236
Ohler, Jason, 58
Olaynack, Lisa, 93, 97–98
One Book, One Community, 205–6
One–Button Studio, 80
online
    civic reasoning, 131
    learning, 276–77
    project management platform, 279
    repositories, 138–39
    syllabus exchange, 168
    video conferencing, 141
open and closed questions, 117
open–ended questions, 39
Opiekun, Brendan, 88b
Orange County School Media Specialists, 89
Orange Public Library, 207
    origins of, 160
Ortiz, Pam, 191
Oscar Awards, 41, 42b
Otto, Jane Johnson, 167, 177
outreach librarianship, 183

Pacatte, Rose, 158
Packtor, Jordanna, 278
Padlet, 276b, 281b
Paik, Nam June, 247
pair–share, 39
Palfrey, John, 25

panel discussion, post–viewing, 181–82
Paper Planes, 204
Parajanov, Sergei, 288
Paramount, 286
parental control of media in the home, 56
parent–child communication, 53
parent media literacy, 116
parents, 13
parents, making media choices for children, 160
Parker, Alan, 47
Parker, Edwin, 240–41
parody, 99
Parrott, Kiera, 33
Partnership for Media Education, 252b
partnerships, 69, 94, 184, 204–5
passive viewing, 31–32
Pathfinders, 283–84
patrons
    as film critics, 159
    as information resources, 291
    knowledge and attitude change, 268
    in library promotion competitions, 91, 269
    media use tastes, 242
    queries, 18, 150
Patti, Lisa, 82
Pauline Center for Media Studies, 158
Pawcatuck Middle School, 204
Payne Foundation, 227–29
Payne Fund, 236
PBS, 18, 37, 164, 206, 266, 268
    documentaries, 165b
    library partnerships, 46
PBS Video Collection, 189
PCFF, 204–5
Pearlman, Karen, 82
pecha–kucha, 279, 304
Penn Language Center, 77
Pennsylvania State Board of Censors, 227
people with disabilities, 184
People's Institute, 233
Perez, Yanillys, 191
personalized learning, 156
Petersen, Anne Helen, 65
PewDiePie, 161
Philadelphia, 50, 200
    in film history, 287–88
Philadelphia Free Library, 172, 187–88, 222,
    287–88, 307
philanthropies, funding strategies of, 187–88
philanthropy, film education, 228, 237–38
Photoshop, 7
picture books, 34
Pillsbury, Sam, 125
Pink Matter (film), 181–82
Pinterest, 281
Pirate Bay, 176, 177

Pitman, Randy, 271
planning process, developing shared goals, 205–6
planning tools, 79
Platinga, Carl, 17
play and learning, in making videos, 85–86
playlists, 153, 156
podcast, on film, 265
Polan, Dana, 3
polarization, political, 292, 296–97
policies, for film and video, 169–70
political economy, 155
Pop Culture Advisory, 22–23
pop culture coaching, 117
pop music, 43
popular culture
    in the library, 43, 63–64, 65, 133
    risks of ignoring, 66
pornography, 58, 61–62, 186
Porter, Edwin, 225–26
Portland Public Library (ME), 191
POV (television series), 206, 266
Powerful Voices for Kids, 50
PowerPoint, 72
preaching to the choir, 137
predictions, 34
preschool children, 111b
Prescott Valley (AZ) Public Library, 85
preservation, film, 257
Preservation Studio, 288
preservice teachers, 120–21
Prime Time Family Reading Time, 52
princess stereotypes, 22
Princeton (NJ) Public Library, 193
Princeton Environmental Film Festival, 23, 193
Princeton Public Library, 23, 206
Princeton Student Film Festival, 23
procedural knowledge, 300–1
Production Code, 228–29
production roles, 93
professional development, 273–74
    for librarians, 88–89, 94–95, 112, 134–35, 137,
        261, 284, 302
programming
    assessing library film, 213–15
    finding contributors, 209
    for non–native speakers, lack of, 54
    planning process in, 203–4, 208–10, 281
    role of failure in, 204
    role of local experts in, 204
Project: Connect Summer Youth Programming
    Competition, 187–88
promotional materials, used in libraries as
    educational material, 230
promotional video for libraries, 84
propaganda, 46, 141–42, 165–71b, 225,
    235–36, 245

in film, 226
in WWII, 233–34
Nazi, 235
on Facebook and YouTube, 165b
protectionist approaches to digital and media
    literacy, 227, 275, 293
Providence, Rhode Island, 36–37, 191
Providence Children's Film Festival, 86–87, 88b,
    188, 191, 192, 194, 198, 277, 279, 307
Providence Community Library, 7, 147, 181, 279
Providence Elementary Schools, 88
Providence Public Library, 185–86, 222, 247,
    254, 307
PTSD, 47
public broadcasting
    audiences, 164–65
    economics, 164–65
    origins, 164
public health research on sexual risk, 62
Public Library Survey, 259
public officials, 191
public performance license 174, 311
public service media, 294–95
Publisher's Weekly, 13
publishing industry, 90
push and pull marketing, 295
Pyle, Russell, 296

questioning a filmmaker, 50–1
questions, 123
Quinceañera (film), 189–90

Race: The Power of an Illusion (film), 166–67
racial inequity, criminal justice system, 176
racism, 245
Radford, Gary, 134b
Radford, Marie, 134b
Radnor, Pennsylvania, 51
Ramona (film), 230
Rangeview Library District, 302
rank ordered collections, 157
Raoof, Anisa, 307
rapid prototyping, 184
Rappe, Virginia, 226
Rasmussen, Eric, 116
ratings systems, 141
ratings systems controversies, 162b, 251
Rawls, Wilson, 125
readers' advisory, 53
read the book, watch the movie, 232–33
reciprocal relationship between books and
    movies, 92
recontextualization, 92
Recycled Orchestra, 194

Reddick Library (IL), 224
Reddit, 270
Reed College, 214–15
Reel Connections, 191
reference
    desk, 52
    librarians, 150
    services, 183
Rehrauer, George, 248–49
Reiner, Rob, 277–78
relationship between books and film, 35, 235
remix, 171–42b
removal of print collections, 78
Rendina, Diana, 71–72
repeated viewing, 123
representation, 36, 50–51
    of librarians in film, 134b, 232
    of the Middle East, 49–50
research on library community engagement
        through film, 266–67
resentment towards DVD rental, 33
restricted access to VHS tapes, 251, 253
restrictive school policies for the use of video,
        129b, 129
reviewers, 13, 157–58
Reynolds, Aaron, 172
Rhinesmith, Colin, 297–98
Rhode Island College, 194–95
Rhode Island Council for the Arts, 185–86
Rhode Island Council for the Humanities, 198
Rhode Island Library Film Cooperative, 247
Rhode Island Office of Library and Information
        Services, 188
Rhode Island State Council on the Arts Education
        Program, 86b
Ribble, Mike, 58
Rice, Tim, 280–81
Rideout, Vicky, 106
Ridgefield (CT) Library, 62
Riefenstahl, Leni, 235
right question technique, 116–17
Rincon, Henry, 191
Rinehart, Richard, 289
ripping DVDs, 138
risk and harm typology, 186
risks and harms of media use, 58, 104, 186
Robb, Michael, 123–24
RobbGrieco, Michael, 252b
Robideaux, Heather, 294
Robinson, Jen, 96, 98
Rockefeller Foundation, 237–38
role of pictures in learning to read, 34
Romeo and Juliet (film), 236
room setup for film screenings, 38
Rossi, Snook, Elena, 222–23, 233, 239–40, 242
Rotten Tomatoes, 159

Rowe, Marieli, 293
Royce City High School, 83
Russell, Carrie, 175
Russia Today, 165b
Ruston, Delaney, 56
Rutgers Media Collections Research Guide, 168
Rutgers University, 167

Sachem Public Library (NY), 146–47
Saettler, Paul, 246–47
Salem witch trials, 113
Sanchez, Frank, 194–95
Sanders, Theresa, 158
Sanders, Tim, 125
San Diego County Office of Education, 305
San Mateo (CA) Library, 83
Santa Claus in Baghdad (film), 49–50
Saved by Beauty (book), 41
scarcity mentality, 141, 148
Schaumburg Township District Library, 22–23
scheduling film programs, 45
Schmitz, Oliver, 40–41
school libraries, 194–95, 202–3
    budget cuts, 148–49, 305
    fundraising, 71
    unintentional messages, 305
School Library Journal, 13, 34
School Library Month, 216–17
school videos, 85
school wide media use survey, 124
Scorsese, Martin, 281
Scott, A.O., 158
Screenagers (film), 56, 123–24
screen capture, 171b
Screencast–o–Matic, 276b, 281b
screening and discussion, 37, 267–68
screening spaces, 43
search–and–find videos, 152–53
Seattle Public Library, 224
Seay, Jared, 178
Seidel, Dena, 193
Seldes, Gilbert, 66
Selena (celebrity), 280–81
self–censorship of film, 227
self–expression, 72–73
selfies, 62
self–paced learning, 76b
self–service scheduling, 78
Selma Lord Selma (film), 222
Selznick, Brian, 35, 160–61
Semper Fi: Always Faithful (film), 165
sensationalism, 151
service learning, 277
setting limits on children's viewing, 109
sexting, 62

Shadow Magic (film), 288
sharing interpretations, 45
Shaw, Eileen, 195
Shawnee Public Schools, 148
Shea, Casey, 71
Sherman, Shawna, 80
She's Beautiful When She's Angry (film) 166–67
Shilcusky, Rosemarie, 282
Shinego, Lisa, 93
Shlain, Tiffany, 213*b*
short form media, 82
showing short portions of a film, 55
silent film, 85
Silicon Valley, 146
    investment in makerspaces, 71
Simon and Schuster Children's
        Publishing, 48–49
Sing (film), 43
Singing in the Rain (film), 82–83, 285
Sixteen Candles (film), 42*b*
skateboarders, 37
Skloot, Rebecca, 221–22
Skyview High School, 71
Slate, 132
Sloan, Bill, 242–43
Smash His Camera (film), 65
Smith, Pam Sandlian, 302–3
social hygiene films, 226
social media, 154
    curation, 153
    marketing, 38, 209–10
    use in the home, 56
social networking, 155
social science research on film and
        children, 228
social work, 226
Society of Cinema and Media Studies, 242
Soechtig, Stephanie, 172
Something's Not Quite Right (book), 35
Sonoma County Office of Education, 71
Soul of Seattle (film), 294
sound, 34
Soundings (book), 152
sound quality, 44
South Africa, 41
Southern Illinois University Carbondale, Morris
        Library, 169
South Jersey Regional Library Cooperative, 302
South Side Library, Milwaukee (WI), 224
space, design issues in libraries, 299
Spanish language, 75, 99–100, 194
special collections librarian, 152–53
Spicer, Scott, 169, 180, 227, 257
Spielberg, Steven, 41
Spiller, Kate, 50
sponsored content, 131–32

Springfield–Greene County Library District
        (MO), 184
SquibblesRead, 89–90
staffing film programs, 45–46
standards, AASL, 202–3, 205*b*, 283
Stanford University, 240–41
Stanton, Tracy Cox, 121
State of Rhode Island, 57–58
Stauffer, Suzanne, 222–23, 234
Steele, Danielle, 251
Steffen, James, 176, 271–72, 288
Stephen King, 18
stereotypes, 22, 36, 114
Steyer, Jim, 160
Stone, Brendan, 65–66
Stone, Oliver, 47
Stonehill College Library, 257
storyboard, 87–88, 88*b*
Story Corps, 293
Story Corps, 183
storytelling, 65–66, 201, 304–5
Stranger Things, 18
streaming, 170, 178–79
    economic future of, 179
    faculty perceptions of, 178
    film and video services, 141, 142
    for online learning, 173–74
    impact on interest in historic film, 286
    legal and financial barriers, 176
    licenses, 178
    limitations for patrons, 172
    media, use in online education, 171*b*
    patron discovery of, 173–74
    platforms, filmmaker revenue from, 172
    questions about the future of, 180
Strictly Ballroom (film), 66
Stronger (film), 42*b*
Stuckmann, Chris, 158–59
student contests and juries, 236, 304
student media creation, 79
Su, Bernie, 93–94
subtitling films, 190–91
suicide, 37–38
Sullivan, Kevin, 146–47
Summer Institute in Digital Literacy, 210,
        273–74
Summit Public Schools, 156
Sundance Film Festival, 188, 189–90
super 8mm film, 294
survey research, 143, 266–67
Suskind, Owen, 184
sustainability programs in libraries, 192
Swank Motion Pictures, 40, 173, 178–79
Symons, Ann, 244–45
Szabo, Jon, 296
Szwydky, Lissette Lopez, 94

Tacoma Public Library, 187
Tampa Preparatory School, 71
Teach Act, 175
Teacher Librarian (magazine), 149
teacher librarians, 202–3. *See also* librarians
teacher motivation, 261
teaching
  about advertising, 113
  film trailers, 121–22
  with and about film, history of, 230
  with film, challenges of, 236
Teach with Movies, 66
technology, 33
TechSoup, 206–7, 209–10
Tecipio, 176
Teen Advisory Board, 42*b*
teen film festival, 83, 85–86
Tel Aviv, 172
Telecommunications Act of 1998, 163
telephone service for film recommendations, 231
television influence on library circulation, 240
television shows for information literacy, 133
television viewing, 145
Temple University, 252*b*
Temple University Libraries Special
    Collections, 252*b*
Tennessee Valley Authority, 234–35
terms of use, 150, 175
TES Blendspace, 154*b*
Tewell, Eamon, 133
texting, 57
The Adaptable Mind (film), 213*b*
The Animation Book, 294
The Bitter Tears of Petra von Kant (film), 265
the book is always better, 32–33
The Bookmobile (film), 183
The Breakfast Club (film) 134*b*
The Color of Pomegranates (film), 288
The Film in the Classroom: A Guide for
    Teachers, 281
The Film is Not Yet Rated (film), 163
The Florida Project (film), 42*b*
The Green Man (book), 34
The House is Black (film), 265
The Immortal Life of Henrietta Lacks, 221–22
The Invention of Hugo Cabret (film), 35
Theisen, Colleen, 151–53
The Library (film), 261
The Life of a Retired Kid (book), 51
The Man Who Invented Christmas (film), 160
The Mick (television series), 61–62
The Motion Picture and the Family
    (magazine), 229
The Music Man (film), 232–46*b*
The New Yorker, 13, 158
theology as story, 158

theories of human development, 110
The Other Side of the Wall (film), 191
The Photoplay: A Psychological Study (book), 17
The Plow That Broke the Plains (film), 234
Polar Express (film), The, 146–47
power of two, 79
Princess Bride, The, 277–78
The Public (film) 134*b*
The Red Pill (film), 172
The Rise of Fake News (film) 8
The River (film), 233
The River (film), 234
The Science of Character (film), 213*b*
The Seven Lively Arts (book), 66
The Speaker (film), 244–45
The Story of Movies, 281
The Studio at Anythink Wright Farms, 302–3
The Vietnam War (film), 46
The Walking Dead (television series), 64, 176
The Whale Rider (film), 125
The Wizard of Oz (film), 43
The Wizard of Oz (film), 232–33
The Young Girls of Rochefort (film), 265
Thief (film), 265
thin–ideal internalization, 62
Thirteen Reasons Why, 37
Thoman, Elizabeth, 252*b*
Thomas, Sally, 80
Thompson, Ian, 189
time management, 205–6
Toca Boca, 53
To Kill a Mockingbird, 93
Toledo Lucas County (OH) Public Library, 297–98
Torrance (CA) Public Library, 91
Tortilla Curtain (book), 41
toxic chemicals, exposure to, 165
trailers, 123–8
Trainor, Meaghan, 99, 207
transmedia storytelling, 93–94
Treasures of New York (television series), 164
Tripp, Lisa, 306
Trudeau, Andrea, 68–69
Truly Moving Picture Award, 265
Trump, Donald, 151
Tumblr, 270
Turner Classic Movies, 285–86
TV ratings, 143, 163–64
Twitter, 210, 270, 276*b*, 277, 285–86
  as research discovery tool, 209–10
  best practices in, 210–14
  librarians' use of, 68–69, 210–14
Tyrell Public Library (TX), 232

U.S. Copyright Office, 55
U.S. Department of Education, 188–89

U.S. embargo on Iran, 49
UCLA, 286
undergraduate students, 248, 300
understanding genre, 107–8
Under the Gun (film), 172
Underworld, U.S.A (film), 265
United Kingdom, 121–22
United States Film Service, 234–35
universality of film, 17
University of Alabama, 151
University of Arkansas, 94–5
University of California, Berkeley, 166
University of California, Los Angeles, 24
University of California, Santa Barbara, 167
University of Dayton, 204
University of Illinois, Chicago, 76–77, 186
University of Illinois Champaign–Urbana, 244–45
University of Indiana, Bloomington, 258
University of Iowa, 152
University of Maryland, Baltimore County, 254
University of Michigan, 91, 248
University of Minnesota, 169, 180, 269
University of Nebraska, Lincoln, 169
University of North Carolina, 179
University of North Texas, 200
University of Pennsylvania, 77, 304
University of Rhode Island., 86b, 137, 188, 210,
    273–74, 276–77, 307
University of Sheffield, 65–66
University of South Florida, 81–82
University of Washington, 293, 294
unrealistic beauty standards, 62
Urban High School, 75
URLs in Twitter posts, 212
user demand for film, 145
user working group, for academic libraries, 214–15
Utah Valley University, 176

Valenza, Joyce, 69, 153
V–chip, 163
Vedantham, Anu, 77–78, 136–37, 304
Vertov, Dziga, 288
veterans, 69
VHS, 253, 286
    history of, 250
    library rental of, 250–51
    players in university classrooms, access to, 254
    preservation, 256–58
Victoria and Abdul (film), 42b
Vid Angel, 54
Video Ant, 281b
video, 176, 177–78, 253
    annotations, 114b
    collection policies, higher education, 169
    collections, 167, 170

content producers, 295
    editing, 96
    oral histories, 195
    rental store donations, 191
    viewing as engagement, 119
video games and learning, 110
VideoLAN, 166
VideoLib, 178–79, 271
Video Librarian, 13, 158
Vietnam, 46, 47
    immigrants in Houston, 48
viewer discretion advised, 163
viewing media on a cell phone, 56
ViewPure, 114b
Vimeo, 176
Vinci, Emily, 22–23
Vinke, Dana, 91
Virginia Tech, 134–36
virtual film discussion group, 293
visual literacy, 4, 304
Vitale Digital Media Lab, 77
VLC, 166
vlog, 149
VUDU, 178–79

Waite, Mary Jane, 148–49
Walters, William, 251
Wanskuck Library (RI), 279
War Horse (film), 41
Warren, Glen, 305
Warriors Remembered (book), 47
Washington State University, 178
Wayne Elementary School, 51
Weaver Library (RI) 210
Webber, Andrew Lloyd, 280–81
WebJunction, 209–10
Weigle information Commons, 77, 304
Weil, Marion, 224
Weisman, Lynda, 76b
Weisner, David, 35
Weitz, Chris, 40–41
Welles, Orson, 258, 285
Wesleyan University, 158
Westerly High School (RI), 116, 280
Westmoreland, Wash, 189–90
WETA, 46
WGBH Boston, 164
Whatcom County Library System, 195
Where the Red Fern Grows (film), 125
whole school integration of media literacy, 111–12
Why We Fight, 233–34
wifi blocking, in higher education, 177
Wiley, Luke, 85–86
William Paterson University, 256
Williams, Roger Ross, 184

Willis Laurie, 80
Wilson, Meredith, 232*b*
Wineburg, Sam, 130
Winkler, Henry, 20
Wisconsin Association for Better Radio Listening, 293
Wichita Public Schools, 148
WNET New York, 164
Wolfe, George, 221–22
Wonder (film), 212
Wonderstruck (film), 160–61
Wood, Susan, 194
wordless books, 35
word–of–mouth marketing, 192
workshops, history of, 248
World Class Kids (film), 172
World War II, 123, 235
Woven (film), 37
Wright, Amy, 53
write it down and stick it up, 210
writing teachers, 24–2

Yale University Library, 255–56
You Can't Cheat an Honest Man (film), 242–43
Young, Neil, 178–79
young adults, 277–78

youth media, 23, 37, 72–73, 86*b*, 303
  history of, 247–48, 294
  and informal learning, 187–88
  screening events, 181–82
YouTube, 36, 90, 93–94, 104, 127, 141, 149–50, 155, 202, 261, 291, 300–2
  as a resource in education, 167–68, 174
  celebrities, 32–33
  Creator Academy, 150–51
  for library promotion, 268
  labels, 165*b*
YouTubers, 158, 161
  in the library, 299
YouTube Search, 150
Yowell, Connie, 186–87

Zaki, Raouf, 50
Zeitgeist (distribution company), 142
Zemekis, Robert, 146–47
Zerne, Lori Halvorsen, 93–94
Ziemba, Emily, 280–81
zines, 24
Zoom, 141
Zucker, David, 277–78
Zuckerberg, Mark, 156